Though historically essays were the province of revered writers such as Samuel Johnson, Ralph Waldo Emerson, W. B. Yeats, William Hazlitt, D. H. Lawrence, and Virginia Woolf, the word *essay* has come to be a general rather than specific term for any type of prose writing other than fiction. Formally slighted, excluded from literary study, and relegated to a lesser status behind fiction and poetry, the essay nonetheless maintains an uncelebrated popularity through contemporary writers such as Annie Dillard, Joan Didion, Paul Theroux, and James Baldwin.

In *Essays on the Essay*, Alexander Butrym has assembled twenty-one essayists who explore the limits of this "abandoned" genre—through history, criticism, and appreciation. Scott Russell Sanders claims that while "most language served up in public these days is textureless, tasteless mush," the essay allows a first-person narrator to explore writing in ways not possible in other, more strictly defined genres. Barbara Mellix channels into her essay a mastery of and appreciation for language learned through speaking "black" English at home and writing "proper" English at school. O. B. Hardison, Jr., insists that the essay is the predominant form of modern writing and, in fact, is one of two forms of writing read by everyone, "the other being the memo." Other essays look specifically at the work of T. S. Eliot, Loren Eiseley, and Aldo Leopold, as well as the writings of historically celebrated essayists who expanded the boundaries of acceptability in essay writing and added their own interpretations of the genre. The collection also includes specific pieces about teaching the form, defining the genre, and analyzing the structures of essays.

Arguing for the vitality and popularity of an often underrated genre, Butrym presents an assortment of essays reflecting in themselves how varied the form can be.

Essays on the Essay

Essays on the Essay

Redefining the Genre

EDITED BY
Alexander J. Butrym

90-1945

The University of Georgia Press
ATHENS AND LONDON

© 1989 by the University of Georgia Press
Athens, Georgia 30602
"'Ecstasy & Eloquence': The Method of Emerson's Essays"
© 1989 by Robert Atwan
"Itinerant Passages: Recent American Essays" © 1989 by William Howarth
All rights reserved

Set in 10/12 Linotron 202 Sabon
Typeset by The Composing Room
Printed and bound by Thomson-Shore

The paper in this book meets the guidelines for
permanence and durability of the Committee on
Production Guidelines for Book Longevity of the
Council on Library Resources.

Printed in the United States of America

93 92 91 90 89   5 4 3 2 1

Library of Congress Cataloging in Publication Data

Essays on the essay : redefining the genre / edited by Alexander J.
   Butrym.
       p.   cm.
     Papers from a symposium held at Seton Hall University in the
   spring of 1987.
     Bibliography: p.
     ISBN 0-8203-1160-X (alk. paper). — ISBN 0-8203-1168-5 (pbk. :
   alk. paper)
     1. Essays—Authorship.   I. Butrym, Alexander J.
   PN4500.E73   1989
   809.4—dc20   89-4912
                                                              CIP

British Library Cataloging in Publication Data available

Contents

Contents

Part Four
Theory and Definition

Contents

Acknowledgments

Early versions of some of these essays appeared in various periodicals.

"Binding Proteus: An Essay on the Essay" by O. B. Hardison, Jr.; "The Singular First Person" by Scott Russell Sanders; and "Itinerant Passages: Recent American Essays" by William Howarth, all appeared in the fall 1988 issue of the *Sewanee Review*.

"From Outside, In," by Barbara Mellix, appeared in the *Georgia Review* (Summer 1957) special issue on the autobiographical essay.

"Autobiographical Memory and Sense of Place," by Rockwell Gray, appeared in *North Dakota Quarterly*, vol. 56, no. 1 (Winter 1988).

"The Modernist Essay: The Case of T. S. Eliot—Poet as Critic," by J. P. Riquelme, first appeared in the *Southern Review*, October 1985.

"The Literary Achievement of Loren Eiseley," by E. Fred Carlisle, is reprinted from *Prairie Schooner*, by permission of the University of Nebraska Press. Copyright 1987 University of Nebraska Press.

"The Husbandry of the Wild," by Sherman Paul, was first published in 1987 in the *Iowa Review*.

"A Common Ground: The Essay in the Academy," by Kurt Spellmeyer, appeared in *College English* (March 1989).

"A Dialogic Approach to the Essay," by Thomas Recchio, appeared in *Issues in Composition* (April 1989).

"The Skewed Path: Essaying as Unmethodical Method," by R. Lane Kauffmann, was awarded a prize at its presentation during the Seton Hall Conference. It was published in translation as "La voie diagonale de l'essai: Une méthode sans méthode," in *Diogène*, 143 (July-September 1988), 68–93.

Introduction

Alexander J. Butrym

The essay's ability to draw us by indirection out of ourselves makes it a popular genre. Through it we speak to each other across the boundaries of our narrower lives. Ordinary writing often seems done by formula: newspaper reporters hew to their five w's and an h; technical and scientific documents are organized on the time-honored pattern of introduction, materials and methods, results, discussion, and conclusions. But the unprogrammed form of the essay speaks to everyone; there is more to medicine than doctoring. To discover this fullness, doctor must speak not to doctor but to pianist, rancher, monk, and even professor of English. The essay is the lingua franca of the overly specialized. It raises questions about culture, and its "essayistic" conclusions are local and subject to revision.

But such popularity itself signals misunderstanding of the essay's nature. The entries under the subject and title headings "Essay" or "Essays" in most card catalogues, for instance, fill two or more drawers. In the on-line catalogue of the Firestone Library at Princeton University, there are about 30,000 entries under "Essays" between the years 1980 and 1988. The large count in itself is not very helpful to the reader searching for collections of essays or for critical commentary on the genre. It does, however, invite inferences about the essay as a form, as a way of shaping experience, in a culture fragmented by many narrow voices.

Even more telling, *Library of Congress Subject Headings* notes that collections of essays will be found under "Essays." A search for them confronts the reader with the dreary task of flipping through drawers full of cards listing collections that may have such titles as *Essays in Microdynamic Economics, Essays in Medieval History Presented to Bertie Wilkinson, Essays on Biosynthesis and Microbial Development,* and *The Essays Throwing Light on the Gandharvas, the Apsarases, the Yakshas, and the Kinnaras.* Other titles and topics are much duller, and relentlessly

I

so, except to small coteries of scholars. The system jumbles learned treatises of all sorts with the works of classical essay writers such as Montaigne, Lamb, and Bacon. As Richard Kostelanetz commented in another context, were it not silly to do so, we might equally well call all these pieces "writing" rather than essays (ix). In many of these pieces, the genre's freedom to range has been restricted, and the essay has been forced into narrow servitude. The term has almost become a word that connotes without denoting: it suggests a piece of writing that tends toward or away from respectably, formally, and intellectually presenting a more or less subjective view of a more or less objective phenomenon. Such an "essay" may or may not need to be as thoroughly documented as a scholarly article ought to be.

The genre itself is possibly to blame for its own subversion: essays are as comfortable with microbes and microdynamics as with France in the seventeenth century and California in the twentieth. Consequently, they willingly accommodate scientific, theoretical, and analytical discussions which aspire to a level of philosophical generalization similar to that of *An Essay Concerning Human Understanding.* But such pieces are certainly not formed on the model of the essays in, for instance, the *Georgia Review,* which favors "essays that appeal simultaneously to two rather different audiences: the educated general reader interested in confronting new ideas and areas of knowledge, and a range of professionals and academic specialists looking for refinements of, and challenges to, their already extensive studies" (Lindberg, 247).

But the essay undercuts its own status in another way. Its formlessness, which allows us to speak beyond ourselves—or beyond persons much like ourselves—scatters the essay so broadly that it sometimes seems marginally effective as literature. The heading "collections of essays" in the *Library of Congress Subject Headings* omits much; one does not find the work of contemporary literary essayists. Although every card catalogue lists Pope's *Essay on Man,* Lamb's *Essays of Elia,* and editions of Emerson and Thoreau, other collections, by such writers as Richard Selzer, Joan Didion, and Annie Dillard—let alone Alice Walker, Tillie Olson, Gore Vidal, Theodore Weiss, Gretel Erlich, and Lewis Thomas—are typically scattered across the alphabet. The Library of Congress's subject heading for Annie Dillard's *Encounters with Chinese Writers* is "Chinese Literature—20th century—anecdotes, facetiae, satires, etc." For *Teaching a Stone to Talk,* the subject headings are "1. Nature" and "2. Life." Readers of drama, or poetry, or short fiction—forms read far less often than essays—know where to look for collections of such pieces. But essays, like the insights they disclose, must be sought at random and discovered by accident.

Obviously, the literary essay itself does not receive the respect accorded its literary and nonliterary counterparts. When E. B. White spoke of essayists as second-class citizens, he was voicing the opinion not of fellow essayists but of everyone else. Nowadays, though, even Joseph Epstein seems to grant the essay a diminished status in relation to other genres and in relation to the position that the essay itself once held in the minds of Victorian and early twentieth-century readers. Among many "professional writers," as among professional readers within the academy, the essay has the low status that it is given in *Leaven of Malice,* the second novel of Robertson Davies's "Salterton Trilogy." In this work, Swithin Shillito is a seventy-eight-year-old newspaper reporter who hopes to drop in harness, almost as though he is afraid of boredom in retirement, which would leave him alone with his own mind.

Shillito's journalistic forte (his stint, as he calls it) is the personal piece—the short, whimsical essay on such topics as the fate of the toothpick, the vanishing of walking sticks, and "the importance of snuff and birdseed." His work is described: "The mantle of the eighteenth-century essayist—old, frowsy, tattered, greasy and patched with Addison's gout rags and the seat of the gentle Elia's pants—had fallen upon Swithin Shillito, and he strutted and postured in it every day" (263). Gloster Ridley, his editor, is realistic about the world and his work; a vigorous, intellectually demanding editor, he dismisses Shillito's trivia and his pretensions. Serious pieces are editorials about government plans for seaway projects. Robertson Davies has himself been a college teacher as well as a novelist and dramatist, and he by no means champions the newspaper editorial or the practical journalistic article over any literary work. But he does portray essay and essay writer as denizens of the past, long past their primes and long overdue for retirement.

The academic world did not conspire to devalue the essay as a literary form, nor did it displace the form suddenly or melodramatically. Instead, little jolts led to major dislocation. One of these jolts dropped distinctions between the essay and popular journalistic feature writing, and the essay lost its cachet as a belletristic form. Another jolt related to the general inclination in modern popular culture for immediate satisfaction and instant entertainment, and this also tended to devalue the essay's appeal, which depends on pleasures experienced by a meditative mind free to meander leisurely in quiet moments. The essay was buffeted again when professors insisted that students use it to learn "writing skills." English

3

teachers found the essay a new place in the curriculum: further obscuring the distinction between the literary and the practical, composition teachers turned the essay into a source of exemplary materials. An early example of this phenomenon, Burgess Johnson's 1927 textbook *Essaying the Essay*, describes itself as "not so much about essays as about essay writing. Selection from the work of past masters has been made with training in view, and not with any idea of furnishing a textbook for those interested solely in the place the Essay occupies in literature" (vii).

This devaluation of the essay seems to have gone so far that, when essays were taught, the tendency was to overlook elements which made them unsuitable as examples of effective exposition and to see and teach only those aspects of them which fit preconceived notions of what good, straightforward prose ought to be. The upshot is that, when literary values are discussed in the first year of the college English course, essays are seldom considered. Only a fairly limited canon of poems, plays, and fiction comes in for attention.

In relegating essays to the role of models for students to imitate in freshman composition, in other words, English departments over the years have gradually and quietly excluded the essay from serious literary study and have in effect "abandoned" the genre. This academic dissociation has also reinforced the idea among educated readers that the essay is somehow isolated from other allegedly more important types of literature. It has led to skewed notions that imagination and creativity are divorced from fact and that style and flair in writing are restricted to fiction, poetry, and drama as well as to odd notions of just what distinguishes objective viewpoints from subjective and personal styles from impersonal.

If the essay's first problem is lack of clear definition, its second is such lack of status. The essay is associated with the facetious, the trivial, and the anecdotal on the one hand and with the learned treatise and useful, effective expository writing on the other. Neither of these is the concern of the traditional, liberal-arts-oriented literature department.

But the status of the essay affects more than the English curriculum. It affects all of the humanities, because the essay concerns itself with all of humanistic education—biography, literature, philosophy (with its special concern for ethical, moral, and aesthetic relations), history, and theology. With Montaigne, the personal essay was grounded in humanistic thought. One of Montaigne's inspirations came from the Latin poet Terence: "Homo sum, humani nil a me alienum puto." The essay is based, according to Montaigne's practice, on the investigation of the self in its manifold relations. An understanding of the art of the essay in its tech-

4

nical variety and its sensitivity to broadly human concerns prepares students for a lifelong process of personal discovery and education in the humanities.

If the definition and status of the genre are unclear, perhaps the cause is that academic criticism of the genre has also languished. Returning to the library card catalogue, under the heading "Essay" one should find works on the essay as a literary form—but there are not many of them, and most of these are not written in English. A cursory analysis of the nineteen-page polyglot bibliography in one monograph (*Teoria del Ensayo*, 147–165) illustrates the point more concretely. Most of the works on the essay written between 1950 and 1980 were in Spanish, and the majority were articles. German writers made a showing during the 1950s and 1960s; again articles outnumbered monographs by nearly 3 to 1. In English most of the work was done in the 1920s and 1930s, with a flurry occurring from the 1950s to 1970s. These latter works were frequently introductions to essay anthologies, many of which are composition textbooks that restrict their scope to the "college" essay. Or they are reprints in the Essay Index Reprint series. The past decade has seen very few additions to this list. Writing on the essay as a genre has been done from a nonacademic viewpoint: it is the response of the practitioner rather than that of the professor.

And yet essays continue to be written and read with interest. Although they may not be in collections clearly labeled for the cataloguers' convenience, they can be found in many literary quarterlies, which include them in addition to the usual freight of "critical" literary essays. They are found not only in the *Georgia Review* but also in such periodicals as the *Sewanee Review*, the *Kenyon Review, Antaeus, Hudson Review, Antioch Review, TriQuarterly, Prairie Schooner*, the *Southern Review, Yale Review*, and *North American Review*. They also appear in several leading popular magazines for general readers, including *Harper's*, the *Atlantic Monthly*, and *Esquire*. In addition, many news magazines with general circulation highlight pieces of special interest by labeling them essays.

The problem, then, is threefold. In the first place, it is a matter of definition. Just what is an essay? Are essays truly to be classed as literature? Is it still possible to point to a work and say this or that in it aids the taxonomy?

Second, and a consequence of the difficulty with nomenclature, is the problem of status. Why are essayists considered second-class citizens? Was E. B. White's remark to be taken at face value? Or is such self-deprecation a convention of the form? Does the essay have a place as a major literary form, as poems, plays, and novels do?

Third, what part should the essay play in the modern curriculum? Is it more than a tool for use in composition courses? If, in the first year of college English, the essay were taught with a better understanding of the nature of the personal commitment involved in writing it, might the course entail less mechanical drudgery and more of the traditional liberal arts which English faculties pride themselves on professing?

The essays in the present volume originated in "The Essay: Redefining a Genre for the Humanities," a two-part symposium held at Seton Hall University in the spring of 1987. A few papers reprinted here from literary quarterlies first appeared shortly after the collection was conceived and have been included here for their contribution to an understanding of the genre and its importance. Our hope is to renew academic interest in the literary essay. We are concerned less with defending the essay form than with stimulating a discussion of it.

The essay by O. B. Hardison, Jr., "Binding Proteus: An Essay on the Essay," should be regarded as sounding the keynote for this discussion. As a survey of historical practice, it introduces the genre and provides a context for many of the pieces that follow it.

The writers in the next group, described as "Essayists on Their Work," have all written as essayists, not as professors. Scott Russell Sanders, Barbara Mellix, and Rockwell Gray explore the personal nature of the essayist's point of view, language, location, and commitment to the genre.

Various moments in the history of the essay are described by the third group of writers, those concerned with history, criticism, and appreciation. These essays include investigations and evaluations of changes that have been rung upon the form, of various conceptions classical essayists have had of it, and of the practice of some contemporary essayists. Paul Korshin discusses changes in literary reputation resulting from changes in the audiences of Sam Johnson's *The Rambler*. Robert Atwan provides a transition from theoretical to practical criticism; in describing Emerson's method as an essayist, Atwan introduces considerations of the status of the essay as a literary form. Also in this section, Michael Hall suggests ways in which literary essays reflected cultural assumptions of their times and the varying needs for information and meditation. Hall describes the essay as a philosophical, psychological, and literary metaphor in the history of the idea of exploration.

Nancy Enright examines William Hazlitt's ideas about the "familiar style" in order to suggest a new understanding of the place of the literary essay in the writing teacher's scheme of things.

J. P. Riquelme, Duane Edwards, Georgia Johnston, and Charles O'Neill describe the ways in which T. S. Eliot, D. H. Lawrence, Virginia Woolf, and W. B. Yeats—all better known for their work in other gen-

6

res—extended the essay and affected its literary reputation by their practice.

In the fourth group, "Critical Theory and Definition," writers define the essay's structure, function, and relation to both literature and humane learning in general. George Core charts the changing interests and practices of E. B. White, A. J. Leibling, and Joseph Mitchell, all of whom wrote for the *New Yorker* and moved the American essay in a new direction. William Howarth writes about contemporary essayists responding to their times and places. R. Lane Kauffmann surveys the theoretical underpinnings provided for a certain kind of essay by contemporary Continental philosopher-critics.

The final group of writers deals with questions of pedagogy, including broad issues relating to the place of the essay in the modern humanities curriculum. Kurt Spellmeyer's "A Common Ground: The Essay in the Academy" offers a deeper, less mechanical, and more humane understanding of what is entailed in the process of learning to write than is frequently provided in college English departments. Thomas Recchio and Douglas Hesse relate teaching to current critical textual and communication research and theory.

A book of this nature is plainly not the product of one person's initiative, effort, or imagination. I acknowledge with gratitude support received from the New Jersey Department of Higher Education. Without a grant from the department's Humanities Program, the symposium—and the meeting of critical minds that it made possible—would not have taken place. On a more personal note, special thanks go to Robert Atwan, whose many ideas and suggestions have been both seminal and practical in fashioning this book and the symposium from which it grew. I also thank Stanley Lindberg for helpful suggestions regarding the manuscript and George Core for encouragement. To Beth Harrison and William Howarth in the Department of English at Princeton University, I am grateful for making available working space while my own college removed asbestos. In his evaluation of the conference, Emory Elliott, also of Princeton University, made many comments which helped me decide the book's contents. I thank Jane Jubilee for typing and Marcia Brubeck for her outstanding copyediting of the manuscript. And finally, to the provost of Seton Hall University and to the dean of the College of Arts and Sciences I owe thanks for the sabbatical year which gave me the time to edit this volume.

Works Cited

Davies, Robertson. *Leaven of Malice*. The Salterton Trilogy. New York: Viking-Penguin, 1986.

Gómez-Martínez, José Luis. "Teoría del ensayo." Univ. de Salamanca, 1981.

Johnson, Burgess. *Essaying the Essay*. Essay Index Reprint Series. Freeport, N.Y., 1927, 1970.

Kostelanetz, Richard, ed. *Essaying Essays: Alternative Forms of Exposition*. New York: Out of London Press, 1975.

Lindberg, Stanley, and Edward Corey. "Focus on Autobiographical Essays." *Georgia Review*, vol. 41, no. 2 (Summer 1987), 247–248.

Part One

Keynote

Binding Proteus:
An Essay on the Essay

O. B. Hardison, Jr.

Sed quanto ille magis formas se vertet in omnis
tam tu, nate, magis contende tenacia vincla. . . .
—*Georgics*, IV, 411–12

The ancient god Proteus knew the secrets of the past and the future. Those who would learn them were required to bind him with chains before asking their questions. When bound, Proteus would change into all manner of shapes to escape. Menelaus visited Proteus when becalmed at Pharos and forced him to reveal the fates of Agamemnon and Odysseus (*Odyssey*, IV, 355ff.). Aristaeus, a shepherd of Tempe, was told by his mother Cyrene to visit Proteus when his bees were dying. As Vergil announces in the *Georgics*, she advised: "The more he turns himself into different shapes, the more you, my son, must hold onto those strong chains."

Writing an essay on the essay is doubtless appropriate in an age that delights in strange loops and Gödelian recursions and that has announced, more often perhaps than it really needs to, that every art form is first and foremost a comment on itself. Of all literary forms the essay most successfully resists the effort to pin it down, which is like trying to bind Proteus.

Let me put one card on the table immediately. There is a rumor going about that the essay is an endangered species. There have even been calls to "save the essay," as there are calls to save whales and condors. Nothing could be more absurd. The essay is not a sensitive species on the point of extinction. It is tough, infinitely adaptable, and ubiquitous. It has more in common with the German cockroach than the Tennessee snail darter. The analogy has hidden relevance. The cockroach is a primitive creature. It

11

appears very early on the evolutionary chain. The essay is also primitive. Roland Barthes suggests that, in the evolution of projections of the imagination, it may precede the formation of all concepts of genre.

I recall the newspapers of my childhood. In addition to printing letters to the editor, they regularly paid homage to "literature" by including uplifting poems. The poems were often lugubrious and sometimes egregious, but they were recognizably poems.

Today, how many poems do you find in the newspaper? Unless you read a paper that comes out once a week in a remote rural county and has a name something like the *Culpeper Eagle,* you do not find a single one. Instead, in any up-to-date newspaper you find essays. They are called op-ed pieces, and their authors are nationally syndicated. These authors do not need support from Foundations. They earn more in an hour than most Americans do in six months. People read their essays. Today, the essay is one of only two literary genres of which this can be said, the other being the memo.

To return, now, to the myth I have invoked. The basic characteristic of Proteus is elusiveness. If there is no genre more widespread in modern letters than the essay, there is also no genre that takes so many shapes and that refuses so successfully to resolve itself, finally, into its own shape.

Francis Bacon concludes in *The Wisdom of the Ancients* that Proteus symbolizes matter. He adds, "If any skillful servant of Nature shall bring force to bear on matter, and shall vex it and drive it to extremities as if with the purpose of reducing it to nothing," it will assume all shapes but return "at last to itself."

I take heart from Bacon's *Wisdom.* In spite of the danger that the essay may fight back, I propose in the following pages to vex it and drive it to extremities in the hope that by the end it will return to itself and reveal something of its true nature.

The word "essay" comes from Old French *essai,* defined by Partridge as "a trial, an attempt." From this meaning comes English "to essay" in the sense of "to make a trial or an attempt," as in Emerson's statement, "I also will essay to be." The word also comes into English via the Norman French *assaier,* "to assay," meaning to try or test, as in testing the quality of a mineral ore.

German has two words for essay, *Abhandlung,* a "dealing with" something, and *Aufsatz,* a "setting forth." Herder's "Essay on the Origin of Speech" is an Abhandlung; Martin Heidegger's essay on thingliness—*Das Ding*—is an Aufsatz. Abhandlungen tend to be ponderous and, you might say, Germanic. Aufsätze have an altogether lighter touch—a touch, one imagines, like that of Goethe tapping out the rhythms of the hexameter on the back of his Roman mistress:

Oftmals hab' ich auch schon in ihren Armen gedichtet
  Und des hexameters Maas leise mit fingernder Hand
Ihr auf dem Rücken bezählt.

As far as I have been able to learn, the first use of "Essay" to mean a literary composition occurred in the title of the most famous collection of such compositions ever published—Montaigne's *Essais*. If you look for the first English use of the term in this sense in the *Oxford English Dictionary*, you may be surprised at what you find. Instead of a majestic series of entries marching forward from the Middle Ages, you encounter the following bald statement: "Essay. A composition of moderate length on any particular subject, or branch of a subject; originally implying want of finish . . . but now said of a composition more or less elaborate in style though limited in range. The use in this sense is apparently taken from Montaigne, whose *essais* were first published in 1580."

In other words, Montaigne invented the term, and the English took it directly from him. Another surprise. In English the term was first used on the title page of the *Essayes* that Francis Bacon published in 1597. It made its second appearance on the title page of John Florio's translation of — you guessed it—Montaigne's *Essayes; or, Morall, Politike, and Militarie Discourses*, published in 1603. Thereafter, the term was applied more and more broadly to any composition that did not fall obviously into some other, better defined category. It plays the same role in literary criticism that the term "miscellaneous" does in budgeting.

Three historical facts supplement these lexicographical observations. First, the essay did not appear ab ovo. Montaigne's principal guide and mentor in the art of the essay was Plutarch, whose *Moralia* consists of short compositions on topics of general interest, such as the cessation of oracles, whether fish or land animals are more crafty, whether water or fire is more useful, the reasons for not running into debt, and the man in the moon. According to Montaigne, "of all the authors I know, [Plutarch] most successfully commingled art with nature and insight with knowledge" (III, 6). Another writer much admired by Montaigne and more so by Bacon is Seneca, whose unfailingly uplifting letters often come close to being essays.

Second, in spite of these and other precedents, the essay *is* something new. In the sixteenth century, the standard prose form was the oration. Orations are utilitarian; they seek to accomplish something. As the rhetoric books say, their object is to persuade. Montaigne calls this characteristic the *Hoc age*—the "Do this!"—impulse. To persuade efficiently, orators developed a standard kind of organization called *dispositio*. Dispositio is the literary equivalent of the foregone conclusion.

Dispositio remains familiar today. All rhetoricians, from Aristotle to Hughes and Duhamel, agree that a proper oration should begin with an *exordium* stating the main point and largest divisions of the argument. The body of the oration consists of arguments in favor (*confirmatio*), plus a demolition of arguments against (*refutatio*). The work should end with a *peroratio* that summarizes the argument and restates the main point.

Montaigne carefully disavows all such advance planning. In the essay "On Education" (I, 26), he quotes with obvious relish the comment of the king of Sparta on a long speech by the ambassadors from Samos: "As for your beginning and exordium, I no longer remember it; nor consequently, the middle; as for the conclusion, I do not desire to do anything about it." In "On the Resemblance of Children" (II, 37), he asserts, "I do not correct my first ideas by later ones. . . . I wish to represent the progress of my moods, and that each part shall be seen at its birth." In another context he adds: "I have no other drill-master than chance to arrange my writings. As my thoughts present themselves to my mind, I bring them together" (II, 9). So much for dispositio.

As Sir Philip Sidney's *Defence of Poesie* shows, orations can be impressive and informative. They can even, on occasion, be persuasive. There is little room in them, however, for spontaneity. They move ahead with the elephantine thump of the Abhandlung rather than the butterfly tango of the Aufsatz. The point of orations is not to reveal private feelings but to make things happen.

In fact, the essay is the opposite of an oration. It is a literary trial balloon, an informal stringing together of ideas to see what happens. Let's be frank. From the standpoint of the oration, the essay is feckless. It does not seek to *do* anything, and it has no standard method even for doing nothing. Montaigne calls essay writing "that stupid enterprise" ("cette sotte entrepris," II, 8), and when Roland Barthes delivered an oration indicating his acceptance of a chair at the Collège de France, he apologized for his literary philandering. "I must admit," he said, ". . . that I have produced only essays."

Third fact. Even in its infancy, the essay shows its Protean heritage. Montaigne's essays are associative, discursive, informal, meandering, and slovenly. Being the first of their kind, they ought at least to have become models for what followed, in the same way that even disreputable people—muggers, prostitutes, con men, and so forth—will become models if they are really good at what they do. They did not. Bacon's essays were inspired by Montaigne's, but are, if anything, anti-Montaignian. Especially in their 1597 form, they are aphoristic, staccato, assertive, hortatory, abrasive.

This brings us to style.

Morris Croll wrote the classic study of sixteenth-century prose style. He calls Montaigne's style "libertine" and Bacon's "Tacitean." Libertine sentences slither along from phrase to phrase with no proper ending. They are just what you would expect from writing that uses quotations promiscuously and refuses to organize itself. "Tacitean" comes from the name of the Roman historian Tacitus. Tacitus was curt to the point of obscurity, and his name has the same root as English "taciturn." That too is appropriate. In their first edition, Bacon's *Essayes* are curt and businesslike. Not a word wasted. Time is money.

In fact both Montaigne and Bacon were reacting not only against the oration, with its preordained *dispositio*, but also against the rhetorical exhibitionism of the periodic sentence, a sentence as unspontaneous as *dispositio* itself. In the earlier Renaissance, Cicero was the preeminent model for such writing. His sentences make language into a kind of sound sculpture with its closest English equivalent in the elegantly figured prose of John Milton's *Areopagitica*.

Montaigne and Bacon, however, were anti-Ciceronian. In "Of the Education of Children" (I, 26), Montaigne recalls, "At the height of Cicero's eloquence many were moved to admiration; but Cato merely laughed at it. . . . I would have the *subject* predominate, and so fill the imagination of him who listens that he shall have no remembrance of the words." And again, in "Of Books" (II, 9): "To confess the truth boldly . . . [Cicero's] manner of writing seems to me irksome. . . . If I spend an hour reading him . . . , I find oftenest only wind."

Bacon put the same idea in terms of *res* and *verba*—in terms, that is, of meaning and hot air. In the *Advancement of Learning* he observes that the Ciceronian humanists searched "more after wordes than matter, and more after the choisenesse of the Phrase, and the round and cleane composition of the sentence, and the sweet falling of the clauses . . . then after the weight of matter, worth of subject, soundnesse of argument, life of invention, or depth of judgement."

His style enacts this rejection of humanism. Its harshness is a way of announcing his contempt for Ciceronian flatulence—his commitment to weight of matter rather than to choiceness of phrase.

Does this mean that the early essay abandons rhetoric? Absolutely not. It means, first, that the early essay substitutes one kind of rhetoric for another. Since the new kind of rhetoric is unconventional and thus unfamiliar, it means, second, that the early essay seeks to give the impression of novelty. And since the impression of novelty depends on the use of formulas that are unfamiliar and therefore not obvious to the reader, it means, third, that the early essay seems to create the illusion of being unstudied and spontaneous. It pretends to spring either from the freely associating imagination of the author or from the Draconian grammar of the world of things.

There is a formula for such a style: "ars celare artem," art that conceals art. Montaigne announces: "The way of speaking that I like is a simple and natural speech, the same on paper as on the lips . . . , far removed from affectation, free, loose, and bold" (I, 26). The statement is charming, but it is demonstrably false. Both Montaigne and Bacon revised their essays over and over again. The lack of artifice is an illusion created by years of effort.

I think we have some chains around Proteus. Now let us begin to vex him.

The first edition of Montaigne's *Essais* appeared in 1580. It lacked the present Book III. Another, moderately augmented edition appeared in 1582. A third version, with a new book (incorrectly labeled "Book V") and with major revisions and additions, appeared in 1588. Finally, Montaigne's famous "fille d'alliance" Marie de Gournay issued a posthumous edition in 1595 with further major changes which was the basis of standard editions of the *Essais* until the twentieth century.

The record shows that Montaigne was a familiar type, the literary neurotic who can never let his works alone, even after they are published. In general, as he revised, the self-revelation of the essays became more overt. That is, the more clothes he put on, the more naked he became. And as his nakedness increased, the more he—and his readers—became aware that he was not a single, consistent identity but a boiling pot of conflicts and changes.

The first edition of Bacon's essays (1597) offers ten essays. They may be said to initiate literary minimalism. They seem to consist chiefly of sayings from Bacon's commonplace book. The Renaissance would have called the sayings "flowers" or "sentences." Bacon's strategy may owe something to the hugely successful collection of aphorisms made by Erasmus—the *Adagia*—but Erasmus could never resist the temptation to gild every aphorism with a commentary, whether it was a lily or a dandelion. In the first edition of the *Essayes*, Bacon offers his flowers plain.

Like Montaigne, Bacon revised compulsively. By 1625, the ten original essays had grown to fifty-eight plus an incomplete fifty-ninth. The essays also grew obese over the years. "Of Studies," for example, roughly doubled in size between 1597 and 1625.

As Montaigne revised, his essays became richer. Bacon's revisions seem to me to have been less happy. As his essays enlarge, they lose the taciturnity—the aggressive minimalism—that is a principal source of their power. The sentences become more sequential, more official, more pontifical, more—shall I say it?—like sentences in an oration.

In addition to making the essays more official, Bacon tried to give them philosophical status by suggesting that they are part of the grand philosophical scheme outlined in the *Novum Organum*. In the Renaissance classification of the sciences, ethics, economics, and politics occupy an area equivalent to the domain of today's "social sciences." By calling his essays "civil and moral," Bacon was proposing them as contributions to the social sciences—specifically, to politics and ethics. In my own opinion, which conflicts with official wisdom in this case, the connection of the essays to the program of the *Novum Organum* was an afterthought intended to enhance their dignity.

Whatever the case, philosophy is directly relevant to the early history of the essay. In *Representative Men* Emerson properly calls Montaigne "the skeptic." The first of the *Essais* to be composed is also the longest, most ponderous essay of the lot—Montaigne's *Apology for Raimond Sebond,* which is essay 12 in Book II. Sebond was a late medieval theologian who wrote a *Theologia Naturalis* showing how design in Nature will convince even the most depraved agnostic of the truth of the Christian religion. At his father's request, Montaigne translated it from Latin into French.

The work is the culmination of a long tradition of pious fatuity about the Book of Nature. Once his father was safely in the ground, Montaigne deconstructed it. The deconstruction became so devastating that by the end, very little basis remained for believing in God or design in Nature or in anything else. Hamlet seems to have read the *Apology,* since he quotes from it when he observes that the earth is a pestilent congregation of vapors and man a quintessence of dust.

When you think about them, Hamlet's quotations are appropriate. Long before Hamlet began questioning the state of Denmark, Montaigne's world had been made problematic by the religious controversies of the Reformation and the collapse of traditional verities. This is what the *Apology for Raimond Sebond* is all about. The St. Bartholomew Day Massacre, which occurred just eight years before the first edition of the *Essais,* magnified the shock. If Christians who proclaim themselves models of piety can establish their position only by slaughtering those Christians who disagree with them, what evidence is there that reason has any place at all in religion? In short, a world that had once seemed solid, reasonable, and self-evident had shown itself to be none of the above. There were times when it seemed to Montaigne like a pestilent contagion of vapors. John Donne makes the same point in familiar lines from his first *Anniversary* on the death of Elizabeth Drury that almost everyone knows by heart:

> The new philosophy calls all in doubt,
> The element of fire is quite put out;
> 'Tis all in pieces, all coherence gone,
> All just supply and all relation.

Historians argue about whether Montaigne was a fideist or a skeptic. The terms are so close that we need not quibble. The fideist believes that God and His ways are utterly beyond human comprehension. Therefore we must accept whatever law or custom or the local tyrant tells us to believe. The skeptic, as far as Montaigne and his contemporaries are concerned, is a follower of the ancient philosopher Pyrrho of Elis (fl. 300 B.C.) and of his disciple Sextus Empiricus, whose works were published with a Latin translation by Henri Estienne in about 1560. The skeptics developed a systematic demonstration that man is deceived both by sense-evidence and by reason.

If so, the proper stance for the philosopher is to doubt everything. This is not nihilism but a reserving of judgment, a determination to be a detached observer rather than a partisan. The Greek term for such detachment is *ataraxia,* which means "calmness" and, by extension, a refusal to become involved. Montaigne explains in the *Apology:* "This attitude of [the skeptics] . . . , accepting all objects without inclination and consent, leads them to their Ataraxy, which is a placid, settled condition of life, exempt from the emotions that we experience. . . . They are even exempted thereby from zeal about their own doctrine" (I, 12). At its coolest, ataraxy produces the spectator who views life ironically and refuses to become involved—the spectator. However, spectators are also outsiders, and for outsiders, detachment sometimes becomes a perverse form of engagement. Hamlet's detachment is announced by his black suit and his refusal to be drawn into the *Gemütlichkeit* of the Danish court. It is closer to despair than freedom from passion, and its result is not a series of essays enacting the process of self-realization but soliloquies in which the speaker alternates between murder and suicide.

This takes us to the dark outer edge of the early essay. It is a darkness that was acknowledged by Montaigne but one that lies, for the most part, beyond the emotional boundaries he set for himself.

Having been led by his own analysis to doubt the world as he had conceived it, Montaigne turned inward in the quest for certainty. The basic question of the *Essais* is "What do I know"—"Que sçais-je?" This is Montaigne's official motto, and as we learn in the *Apology*, he inscribed it under a picture of a pair of scales symbolizing ataraxy—the balancing of alternatives.

Montaigne's innumerable quotations are intended as part of the answer to the question of what we know. André Gide remarks in an often-quoted essay that they are there "to show that man is always and everywhere the same"—that is, there *is* a stable, universal something that can be called "human nature." Unfortunately, the quotations do not show this. As Michael Hall observes, the quotations are inconsistent. Evidently, when you collect several centuries' worth of wisdom on a topic, you do not get a philosophy, you get a chain of contradictory platitudes reminiscent of Polonius's advice to Laertes.

Turning inward was no more helpful than consulting the sages. When he turned inward, Montaigne discovered not universality but infinite variety. He was forced to conclude that the self is as various, as elusive, and as many-shaped as the world.

Without fully understanding what he was doing, Montaigne was searching for a central "I"—what Descartes would later call the *cogito*, and as a matter of fact, Montaigne powerfully influenced the Cartesian project. But he was more radical than Descartes. Descartes admitted that we may be dreaming the world, but he insisted that the cogito is beyond doubt—so solid, in fact, as to be the rock on which everything else can be built.

Montaigne concluded from his inquiry that there is no rock. There is only an endless series of illusions. Early in the *Essais,* he announces, "We must remove the mask from things as from persons" (I, 21). He adds that "being truthful is the beginning of virtue" (II, 18); but his great discovery is that man is as Protean as the world: "Every man has within himself the entire human condition" (III, 2). Later still, Montaigne uses metaphors of the arational to describe his discovery of himself: "I have seen no monster or miracle on earth more evident than myself. . . . the better I know myself, the more my misshapenness astonishes me, and the less do I comprehend myself" (III, 11).

In the famous introduction to "Of Repenting," the second essay in Book III, we read:

> Others shape the man; I narrate him, and offer to view a special one, very ill-made, and whom, could I fashion him over, I should certainly make very different from what he is; but there is no doing that. The world is but

perpetual motion; all things in it move incessantly. . . . I can not anchor my subject; he is always restless and staggering with an unsteadiness natural to him. I catch him in the state that he is in at the moment when I turn my attention to him. I do not paint his being, I paint his passing—not the passing from one age to another . . . but from day to day, from moment to moment. . . . Writers commune with the world with some special and peculiar badge; I am the first to do this with my general being, as Michel de Montaigne.

Here, I think, we have the authentic note of the *Essais* and of the essay as a genre. The essay is the enactment of a process by which the soul realizes itself even as it is passing from day to day and from moment to moment. It is the literary response to a world that has become problematic. In its complexity Montaigne's text works to disguise this fact but it has always been an open secret.

And Montaigne perseveres. Each essay is the prelude to the next. In view of Cyrene's advice on binding Proteus, it is significant that one of the mottos of the skeptics was "Hang on." Montaigne explains in the *Apology:* "Their symbolic word is *epécho*—that is to say, 'I hold on, I do not budge' " (I, 12).

Now let us return to Bacon. If Montaigne's essays suggest how the mind feels as it seeks by constant adjustments to find a path through a labyrinth, Bacon's method is to assert the existence of a path whether one is there or not. In the *De Argumentis Scientiarum* Bacon calls his method "initiative" in contrast to "magisterial." The magisterial method is used for teaching. It has a well-defined shape, namely that of an oration. The initiative method is, by contrast, suggestive. As Bacon explains: "The initiative intimates. The magisterial requires that what is told should be believed; the initiative that it should be examined." Like Montaigne, Bacon was strongly attracted to skepticism. He admitted: "The doctrine of those who have denied that certainty could be attained at all has some agreement with my way of proceeding." Although he argued that empiricism offers an escape from uncertainty, he believed that most of the received knowledge of his age was false—the result of "errors and vanities," which he categorized using the metaphor of Idols: Idols of the tribe, Idols of the cave, Idols of the marketplace, Idols of the theater.

Bacon did not spend much time on religion; perhaps he found it beyond—or beneath—the reach of reason. He never attacked it, but his heavyhanded condescension resembles thinly disguised contempt. Conversely, the collapse during the sixteenth century of scientific doctrines accepted as verities for thousands of years fascinated him. The prime example was the toppling of Ptolemaic astronomy by Copernican, but astronomy was only one of many areas in which received knowledge crumbled when it was put to the test. Each failure of a traditional theory was a demonstration of the validity of the theory of Idols.

This kind of skepticism looks forward to a fully developed scientific method. It underlies Sir Thomas Browne's *Pseudodoxia Epidemica,* better known as *Vulgar Errors,* which systematically exposes many superstitions of the sort deconstructed in Montaigne's *Apology.* The *Pseudodoxia* went through six editions in Browne's lifetime. In matters of religion, Browne was a fideist. Montaigne ends the *Apology* with the remark that man "will be lifted up if God by special favor lends him his hand; he will be lifted up, when abandoning and renouncing his own means, he lets himself be upheld by purely heavenly means" (II, 12). Browne writes in *Religio Medici:* "Me thinkes there be not impossibilities enough in Religion for an active faith. . . . I love to lose myself in a mystery, to pursue my reason to an *Oh Altitudo.* . . . I learned of *Tertullian, Certum est quia impossible est.*"

Bacon's dedication of the ten essays of 1597 claims only that they are "medicinable." The dominant meaning is simply that they are useful— they expose various errors and vanities and provide compass bearings for a world in flux. But the term "medicinable" is a metaphor, and its implications invite comment. According to the metaphor, the reader needs to be cured. In other words, there is some kind of metaphysical plague going around. It is a plague of doubt. Jimmy Carter felt the same thing about twentieth-century America and, in one of his more disastrous orations, called it a malaise. If Bacon had been around, he would have called it a failure of nerve and would have voted for Ronald Reagan. Bacon's essays are intended to be a cure for social malaise. They are medicinable because they distill wisdom gained from life in what Bacon's heirs have insisted ever since on calling "the real world."

For the same reason, they often have the quality of a pep talk by the coach of a losing team. The strategy is to create what might be called a "rhetoric of assurance." Accordingly, in the first edition, the sentences are chiefly commands and assertions. Omission of understood words (zeugma) gives the sentences a telegraphic quality reinforced by the paring away of modifiers, modifying phrases, and subordinate clauses. Further economy is achieved by parallelism and balance. The word order is standard. The speaker knows what he wants to say and says it directly. The main units are set off by paragraph marks—which Bacon uses as we would use "bullets" today. The modern term is appropriate. Bacon wants each sentence to have the force of a pistol shot: "• Reade not to contradict, not to believe, but to waigh and consider. • Some books are to bee

tasted, others to bee swallowed, and some few to bee chewed and digested. . . . • Reading maketh a full man, conference a readye man, and
writing an exacte man. . . . • Histories make men wise, Poets wittie: the
Mathematickes subtle, naturall Phylosophie deepe: Morall grave, Log-
icke and Rhetoricke able to contend."

The sentences often have an edge of cynicism, of *Realpolitik,* reminding
us that Bacon had read his Machiavelli: ambition is a winding stair; those
who marry give hostages to fortune; the stage is more beholden to Love
than the life of man; wounds cannot be cured without searching; a mixture of lie doth ever add pleasure.

You can hear a subtext under the words: "Son, I know things are rotten
in Denmark. There is some sort of malaise going around. But look here.
Life never was a bed of roses. You might even say it is an unweeded garden. That's no reason to whine. Remember, son, you can't weed a garden
without getting dirt on your boots." If you probe the *Essayes* a little further, you begin to hear the voice of King Lear on the heath: "Robes and
furr'd gowns hide all; plate sin with gold and the strong lance of justice
hurtless breaks; a dog's obeyed in office."

Is this *Realpolitik* or despair? Whatever it is, the message of the *Essayes*
is, "So be it." That's how things are in the real world, and that's how they
always will be.

Let us recall one other legacy from Montaigne and Bacon. Both men were
authors. Therefore, it follows that, having invented a form, both pro-
ceeded to muck it up. As we have seen, neither could let an essay alone
once it had been written. This habit is arguably a virtue in Montaigne
and not fatal in Bacon, but its implications are ominous. The constant
revision implies a change in the concept of the essay from the enactment of
a process to something that suspiciously resembles literature—perhaps
an oration propped up like a scarecrow on the scaffolding of its *dispositio.*

To turn the essay into literature is to domesticate it—to make it not
very different from a letter by Seneca or one of Plutarch's *moralia.* Recall
Florio's use of the word "discourse" as a rough synonym for "essay." The
usage is pregnant with future confusion. John Locke's *Essay concerning
Human Understanding* is splendid philosophy. It might even be called
an "essay" on the basis of being an exploration of its subject, but if so,
any work of philosophy short of Nietzsche's *Thus Spake Zarathustra*
can be called an essay. Its proper title is obviously "discourse," maybe
Abhandlung.

To turn the essay into literature is also to encourage authors to display
beautiful—or delicately anguished, or nostalgic, or ironic, or outraged,

or extroverted, or misanthropic—souls or, alternatively, to create prose confections, oxymorons of languid rhythms and fevered images.

I admit this sometimes happens to the essay, but I think the really surprising thing is that in spite of all temptations, the essay has tended to remain true to its heritage. I mean not that essays are products of what you might call "troubled times" but that the essay was born from a moment of profound, even terrifying, doubt and that its rhetoric has often been adopted by authors who have sensed the power of the forces of dissolution. Matthew Arnold entitled his most famous collection of essays *Culture and Anarchy,* and Joan Didion named her first collection from the apocalyptic image in Yeats's poem "Second Coming": *Slouching towards Bethlehem.*

Essays are written on an infinite variety of subjects from infinitely various points of view. However, time and time again, the essay reverts to its original forms—on the one hand to the Montaignian enactment of the process of self-realization in a world without order: "I do not paint [my subject's] being, I paint his passing . . . from day to day, from moment to moment." And on the other hand, to Baconian assertiveness in a world that threatens to reduce assertions to black comedy: "I will do such things . . . . what they are, I know not, but they shall be the terrors of the earth."

The eighteenth century approved the idea of cool detachment from the malaise of things. Addison and Steele are officially "men of sentiment" in *The Tatler.* Under the surface, however, lies the old motif of the search for the self. Steele concludes *The Tatler* with the image of the world as labyrinth: "I must confess, it has been a most exquisite pleasure to me . . . to enquire into the Seeds of Vanity and Affectation, to lay before my Readers the Emptiness of Ambition: In a Word, to trace Humane Life through all its Mazes and Recesses." The *Spectator* has even more obvious relations to its ancestry. A spectator is someone who withholds assent—a skeptic, an observer, an outsider. This is exactly the point made by Addison in the introduction to the new journal: "I live in the World rather as a Spectator of Mankind, than as one of the species. . . . I have acted in all the Parts of my Life as a looker-on, which is the Character I intend to preserve in this Paper."

For the most part, the *Spectator* preserves its detachment, but occasionally there is a powerful updraft of emotion. The terror—or the malaise—of the world makes people want to be spectators, but as Werner Heisenberg has shown, spectators are always tangled up in the things they are observing. The following comment, from *Spectator* number 420, is directly traceable to the tangling of human motive with the world that science has revealed. It is all the more striking because it is not what you would expect from an eighteenth-century spectator:

> If . . . we contemplate those wide Fields of *Ether,* that reach in height as far from *Saturn* as to the fixt stars, and run abroad almost to an infinitude, our Imagination finds its Capacity filled with so immense a Prospect . . . [it] puts it self upon the Stretch to comprehend it. But if we yet rise higher, and consider the fixt Stars as so many Oceans of Flame . . . and still discover new Firmaments and new Lights, that are sunk further in those unfathomable Depths of *Ether,* so as not to be seen by the strongest of our Telescopes, we are lost in . . . a Labyrinth of Suns and Worlds, and confounded with the Immensity and magnificence of Nature. . . . Let a Man try to conceive the different bulk of an Animal, which is twenty, from another which is a hundred times less than a Mite, or to compare, in his Thoughts, a length of a thousand Diameters of the Earth, with that of a Million, and he will quickly discover that he has no . . . Measure in his Mind, adjusted to such extraordinary Degrees of Grandeur or Minuteness. The Understanding, indeed, opens an infinite Space on every side of us, but the Imagination, after a few faint efforts, is immediately at a stand, and finds her self swallowed up in the immensity of the Void that surrounds it.

At the beginning of the nineteenth century, the spectator becomes a refugee. Charles Lamb's Elias solves his problems by infantile regression. He is no more ashamed of this habit than Montaigne was of revealing inner monstrosities. Regression is the secret of his modest success. Lamb explains: "The impressions of infancy had burnt into him, and he resented the impertinence of manhood. These were weaknesses; but such as they were, they are a key to explicate some of his writings."

The addiction of Elias to medicinable fantasies undoubtedly objectifies feelings of his creator. Charles Lamb went through a bout of madness himself and lived with a sister who had murdered their mother in a fit of insanity. But the fantasies don't quite work. Reality is always breaking in. In "Dream Children," Elias recalls an interview with two imaginary children named Alice and John. The children ask about their dead mother, also named Alice and also imaginary:

> Suddenly, turning to Alice, the soul of the first Alice looked out at her eyes with such a reality of re-presentment, that I became in doubt which of them stood there before me, or whose that bright hair was; and while I stood gazing, both of the children gradually grew fainter to my view, receding, and still receding till nothing at last but two mournful features were seen in the uttermost distance, which, without speech, strangely impressed upon me the effects of speech; "We are not of Alice, nor of thee, nor are we children at all. . . . We are only what might have been."

24

"Dream Children" is affecting, but it is almost literature. Emerson comes closer, I think, than Lamb to the scope and brilliance—and the breezy solipsism—of Montaigne. Speaking of the achievements of Plato, Shakespeare, and Milton, Emerson creates one of the great literary puns: "I dare; I also will essay to be." Writing an essay is an exercise in self-fashioning.

The sentiment is pure Montaigne. In *Nature,* Emerson expands the image: "Every man's condition is a solution in hieroglyphic to those enquiries he would put on. He acts it as life, before he apprehends it as truth." "Experience" recreates the terror of a problematic world: "Where do we find ourselves? In a series of which we do not know the extremes, and believe that it has none. We wake and find ourselves on a stair; there are stairs below us, which we seem to have ascended; there are stairs above us, many a one, which go upward and out of sight. . . . All things swim and glitter. Our life is not so much threatened as our perception. Ghostlike, we glide through nature, and should not know our place again."

Emerson's title—"Experience"—invokes Baconian empiricism only to reject it. The metaphor of the infinite stair recalls Addison's image of the self "swallowed up in the immensity of the void that surrounds it." It also anticipates the infinite library of Babel imagined in the twentieth century by Jorge Louis Borges.

In the later nineteenth century, the essay underwent a mutation. The prose poem can be defined as literature's revenge on the essay—an essay in which style has become substance. You can see the beginning of the prose poem as early as Sir Thomas Browne's *Urn Burial.* The body of the animal begins to push through the chrysalis with De Quincey's *Confessions,* and it unfurls its iridescent wings and flaps them in Walter Pater's *Renaissance.* But the prose poem appears first in full lepidopteran glory in France: in Baudelaire's *Le spleen de Paris* and Rimbaud's *Les illuminations.* From there it migrates back to the English-speaking world. We are reminded by William Gass's *On Being Blue* of its flight across the vastness of the Atlantic Ocean to the New World.

One other modern development of the genre must be recognized. It is the topical essay, brief, pointed, often amusing, and closely related to a theme, or an event or personality, of current interest. Bacon's essay "Of Friendship" is a prototype for the form. It did not begin by being topical, but in its final, much-augmented form, it commemorates his lifelong attachment to Sir Tobie Matthew. "Of Plantations" is explicitly topical, being a consideration of issues raised by the Virginia colony. The topical essay also owes much to Addison and Steele. That is not surprising, because its native habitat is the newspaper. The Homeric catalogue of its modern practitioners includes Art Buchwald, Mary McGrory, Ralph Kilpatrick, David Broder, Russell Baker, Carl Rowan, James Reston, William Raspberry, Ellen Goodman, and George Will. This catalogue moves us to the present, which is, after all, the main interest of any essay, including an essay on the essay. I suppose most modern essays are Baconian and Addisonian, but the Montaignian essay is still impressively alive.

Much scholarship appears in the form of—you are correct—the critical essay. This, of course, raises the question of what the word "article" refers to. William Gass has solved the problem: "The essay," he writes, "is obviously the opposite of that awful object, 'the article' . . . , [whose] appearance is proof of the presence, nearby, of the Professor, the way one might, perceiving a certain sort of speckled egg, infer that its mother was a certain sort of speckled bird."

Speckled birds aside, many of the classic works of our age are essays. I am thinking, for example, of Wallace Stevens's "The Noble Rider and the Sound of Words," Leslie Fiedler's "Come Back to the Raft Again, Huck, Honey," Roland Barthes's "Eiffel Tower," Tom Wolfe's "Kandy-Color, Tangerine-Flake, Streamline Baby," Martin Heidegger's "The Thing," R. Buckminster Fuller's "Grunch of Giants," Werner Heisenberg's "Abstraction in Modern Science," and Robert Nozick's "Fiction," which is a nonfictional essay written by a fictional character who is still asking the Emersonian question: "Must there be a top floor somewhere, a world that is itself, not created in someone else's fiction? Or can the hierarchy go on infinitely?"

Nozick's question seems to me to capture the fascination of the essay for our time. An essay is not an oration or an Abhandlung or a prose poem. It is "essaying to be," in Emerson's conceit, and "thought thinking about itself"—*andenkende Denken*—in Heidegger's. It is the enactment of the process of accommodation between the world and the "I," and thus it is consciousness real-izing itself.

A few years ago I wrote a book of essays called *Entering the Maze: Identity and Change in Modern Culture*. The title and subtitle did not take much thought; they seemed inevitable. I might have written a novel. I was never even tempted to do so. To choose fiction is to assert that you know the difference between fiction and fact, when, in fact, I wanted to dramatize the constant redrawing of the line between the two that is taking place in modern culture. Maybe fiction is possible in societies that change slowly. Maybe that is why the novel was popular in the eighteenth and nineteenth centuries. But who, today, knows the difference between the real, and what was real, and what is not—or not yet—real?

If you think about the novel, you will see that it has taken paths in the twentieth century that lead in the direction of the essay. One kind of novel moves toward becoming a record of hallucinations—I think of Joyce's *Finnegans Wake,* Gaddis's *The Recognitions,* Barth's *Giles Goat Boy.* Another type of novel records a special type of hallucination—a vision of a future presumed to be real—*Erehwon, Brave New World, 1984.* Yet another type aspires to the condition of news, for example, *In Cold Blood.* There is also the tendency, apparently irresistible since *Portrait of the Artist,* for novelists to pack their work with essays spoken by characters or by a figure whom, in deference to the fondness of the present age for critical terms, I will label "the intrusive author." Some novels, in fact, seem to consist of almost nothing but essays. Given these tendencies in the novel, why not write essays from the beginning?

But I would like to end with some more challenging notion. I do not think we live in a solid, empirical world of the sort Bacon dangled tantalizingly in front of readers of *The Advancement of Learning* even as he demonstrated that it was an illusion. We live in a world of changes and shadows, a world where the real dissolves as we reach for it and meets us as we turn away. It is a world of mazes and illusions and metaphors and idols and stairways that proceed upward and downward to infinity.

We live at a time much like the sixteenth century. It is a time of immense destructive and constructive change, and there is no way of knowing whether the destructive or the constructive forces are more powerful. It is a time when the world looks like an unweeded garden and doubt is a condition of consciousness. The essay is as uniquely suited to expressing this contemporary mode of being-in-culture as it was when Montaigne began writing the *Apology for Raimond Sebond.*

But what *is* the essay? If there is such a thing as an essential essay—a *real* Proteus—it changes into so many shapes so unlike the real one that it requires an act of faith to believe the shapes merely variations on a single underlying identity. For this reason, of course, Proteus adopted the strategy of change in the first place. People who lack faith will turn away convinced that nothing is there. *We,* however, will remember the advice of Cyrene: "The more he turns himself into all shapes, the more, my son, you must hold onto the chains."

Holding on may be important. If the essay is an enactment of the creation of the self—if we must essay to be—and the essay does not exist, then you might legitimately ask whether that which the essay enacts can be said to exist. The epigraph of the last *Spectator* is from Persius: "Respue quod non es," "Throw away what you are not." It is good advice, but it assumes that, after you throw everything superfluous away, something is left.

If you have bound Proteus and all the changes have occurred, and if he returns to his own shape, he will have already answered your first question: something is there. But is it? Maybe you are seeing only another counterfeit, another Idol.

That's the way things are, and the essay is the most expressive literary form of our age because it comes closest to being what all literature is supposed to be—an imitation of the real. You can vex the essay and drive it to extremities. Maybe the result will be nothing. Your action will be doubtful, but in the real world, to get a piece of the action, you, however doubtful, must follow advice: "Hold on, son."

Part Two

Essayists on Their Work

The Singular First Person

Scott Russell Sanders

The first soapbox orator I ever saw was haranguing a crowd beside the Greyhound station in Providence about the evils of fluoridated water. What the man stood on was actually an upturned milk crate, all the genuine soapboxes presumably having been snapped up by antique dealers. He wore an orange plaid sports coat and a matching bow tie and held aloft a bottle filled with mossy green liquid. I have forgotten the details of his spiel except his warning that fluoride was an invention of the Communists designed to weaken our bones and thereby make us pushovers for a Red invasion. What amazed me, as a tongue-tied kid of seventeen newly arrived in the city from the boondocks, was not his message but his courage in delivering it to a mob of strangers. It would have been easier for me to jump straight over the Greyhound station than to stand there on that milk crate and utter my thoughts.

To this day, when I read or when I compose one of those curious monologues we call the personal essay, I often recall that soapbox orator. Nobody had asked him for his two cents' worth, but there he was, declaring it with all the eloquence he could muster. The essay, although enacted in private, is no less arrogant a performance. Unlike novelists and playwrights, who lurk behind the scenes while distracting our attention with the puppet show of imaginary characters—and unlike scholars and journalists, who quote the opinions of others and take cover behind the hedges of neutrality—the essayist has nowhere to hide. While the poet can lean back on a several-thousand-year-old legacy of ecstatic speech, the essayist inherits a much briefer and skimpier tradition. The poet is allowed to quit in less than a page, but the essayist must generally hold forth over several thousand words. It is an arrogant and foolhardy form, this one-man or one-woman circus, which relies on the tricks of anecdote, memory, conjecture, and wit to hold our attention.

It seems all the more brazen or preposterous to address a monologue to the world when you consider what a tiny fraction of the human chorus any single voice is. At the Boston Museum of Science an electronic meter records with flashing lights the population of the United States. Figuring in the rate of births, deaths, emigrants leaving the country, and immigrants arriving, the meter calculates that we add one fellow citizen every twenty-one seconds. When I looked at it recently, the count stood at 242,958,483. As I wrote the figure in my notebook, the final number jumped from 3 to 4. Another mouth, another set of ears and eyes, another brain. A counter for the earth's population would stand somewhere past 5 billion at the moment and would be rising in a blur of digits. Amid this avalanche of selves, it is a wonder that anyone finds the gumption to sit down and write one of those naked, lonely, quixotic letters to the world.

A surprising number do find the gumption. In fact, I have the impression that there are more essayists at work in America today, and more gifted ones, than at any other time in recent decades. Whom do I have in mind? Here is a sampler: Edward Abbey, James Baldwin, Wendell Berry, Carol Bly, Joan Didion, Annie Dillard, Stephen Jay Gould, Elizabeth Hardwick, Edward Hoagland, Barry Lopez, Peter Matthiessen, John McPhee, Cynthia Ozick, Paul Theroux, Lewis Thomas, and Tom Wolfe. No doubt you could make up a list of your own—with a greater ethnic range, say, or fewer nature enthusiasts—and one that would provide even more convincing support for my view that we are blessed right now with an abundance of essayists. We have no one to rival Emerson or Thoreau, but in sheer quantity of first-rate work our time stands comparison with any period since the heyday of the form in the mid-nineteenth century.

In the manner of a soapbox orator, I now turn my hunch into a fact and state boldly that in America these days the personal essay is flourishing. Why are so many writers taking up this risky form, and why are so many readers—to judge by the statistics of book and magazine publication—seeking it out?

In this era of prepackaged thought, the essay is the closest thing we have, on paper, to a record of the individual mind at work and at play. It is an amateur's raid in a world of specialists. Feeling overwhelmed by data, random information, and the flotsam and jetsam of mass culture, we relish the spectacle of a single consciousness making sense of a portion of the chaos. We are grateful to Lewis Thomas for shining his light into the dark corners of biology, to John McPhee for laying bare the geology beneath our landscape, to Annie Dillard for showing us the universal fire blazing in the branches of a cedar, to Peter Matthiessen for chasing after snow leopards and mystical insights in the Himalayas. No matter if they are sketchy, these maps of meaning are still welcome. As Joan Didion observes in her own collection of essays, *The White Album,* "We live entirely, especially if we are writers, by the imposition of a narrative line upon disparate images, by the 'ideas' with which we have learned to freeze the shifting phantasmagoria which is our actual experience" (Didion, 11). Dizzy from a dance that seems to accelerate hour by hour, we cling to the narrative line, even though it may be as pure an invention as the shapes drawn by Greeks to identify the constellations.

The essay is a haven for the private, idiosyncratic voice in an era of anonymous babble. Like the blandburgers served in their millions along our highways, most language served up in public these days is textureless, tasteless mush. On television, over the phone, in the newspaper, wherever humans bandy words about, we encounter more and more abstractions, more empty formulas. Think of the pablum ladled out by politicians. Think of the fluffy white bread of advertising. Think, Lord help us, of committee reports. In contrast, the essay remains stubbornly concrete and particular: it confronts you with an oil-smeared toilet at the Sunoco station, a red vinyl purse shaped like a valentine heart, a bow-legged dentist hunting deer with an elephant gun. As Orwell forcefully argued, and as dictators seem to agree, such a bypassing of abstractions, such an insistence on the concrete, is a politically subversive act. Clinging to this door, that child, this grief, following the zigzag motions of an inquisitive mind, the essay renews language and clears trash from the springs of thought. A century and a half ago, Emerson called on a new generation of writers to cast off the hand-me-down rhetoric of the day, to "pierce this rotten diction and fasten words again to visible things" (Emerson, 30). The essayist aspires to do just that.

As if all these virtues were not enough to account for a renaissance of this protean genre, the essay has also taken over some of the territory abdicated by contemporary fiction. Pared down to the brittle bones of plot, camouflaged with irony, muttering in brief sentences and grade-school vocabulary, today's fashionable fiction avoids disclosing where the author stands on anything. Most of the trends in the novel and short story over the past twenty years have led away from candor—toward satire, artsy jokes, close-lipped coyness, metafictional hocus-pocus, anything but a direct statement of what the author thinks and feels. If you hide behind enough screens, no one will ever hold you to an opinion or demand from you a coherent vision or take you for a charlatan.

The essay is not fenced round by these literary inhibitions. You may

33

speak without disguise of what moves and worries and excites you. In fact, you had better speak from a region pretty close to the heart, or the reader will detect the wind of phoniness whistling through your hollow phrases. In the essay you may be caught with your pants down, your ignorance and sentimentality showing, while you trot recklessly about on one of your hobbyhorses. You cannot stand back from the action, as Joyce instructed us to do, and pare your fingernails. You cannot palm off your cockamamie notions on some hapless character. If the words you put down are foolish, everyone knows precisely who the fool is.

To our list of the essay's contemporary attractions we should add the perennial ones of verbal play, mental adventure, and sheer anarchic high spirits. The writing of an essay is like finding one's way through a forest without being quite sure what game you are chasing, what landmark you are seeking. You sniff down one path until some heady smell tugs you in a new direction, and then off you go, dodging and circling, lured on by the songs of unfamiliar birds, puzzled by the tracks of strange beasts, leaping from stone to stone across rivers, barking up one tree after another. Much of the pleasure in writing an essay—and, when the writing is any good, the pleasure in reading it—comes from this dodging and leaping, this movement of the mind. It must not be idle movement, however, if the essay is to hold up; it must be driven by deep concerns. The surface of a river is alive with lights and reflections, the breaking of foam over rocks, but beneath that dazzle it is going somewhere. We should expect as much from an essay: the shimmer and play of mind on the surface and in the depths a strong current.

To see how the capricious mind can be led astray, consider the foregoing paragraph, in which the making of essays is likened first to the romping of a dog and then to the surge of a river. That is bad enough, but it could have been worse. For example, I began to draft a sentence in that paragraph with the following words: "More than once, in sitting down to beaver away at a narrative, felling trees of memory and dragging brush to build a dam that might slow down the waters of time . . ." I had set out to make some innocent remark, and here I was gnawing down trees and building dams, all because I had let that "beaver" slip in. On this occasion I had the good sense to throw out the unruly word.

I might as well drag in another metaphor—and another unoffending animal—by saying that each doggy sentence, as it noses forward into the underbrush of thought, scatters a bunch of rabbits that rush off in all directions. The essayist can afford to chase more of those rabbits than the fiction writer can but fewer than the poet. If you refuse to chase any of them, and keep plodding along in a straight line, you and your reader will have a dull outing. If you chase too many, you will soon wind up lost in a thicket of confusion with your tongue hanging out.

The pursuit of mental rabbits was strictly forbidden by the teachers who instructed me in English composition. For that matter, nearly all the qualities of the personal essay, as I have been sketching them, violate the rules that many of us were taught in school. You recall that we were supposed to begin with an outline and stick by it faithfully, like a train riding its rails, avoiding sidetracks. Each paragraph was to have a topic sentence pasted near the front, and these orderly paragraphs were to be coupled end to end like so many boxcars. Every item in those boxcars was to bear the stamp of some external authority, preferably a footnote referring to a thick book, although appeals to magazines and newspapers would do in a pinch. Our diction was to be formal and dignified, shunning the vernacular. Polysyllabic words derived from Latin were preferable to the blunt lingo of the streets. Metaphors were to be used only in emergencies, and no two of them were to be mixed. And even in emergencies we could not speak in the first person singular.

Already as a schoolboy, I chafed against those rules. Now I break them shamelessly, in particular the taboo against using the lonely capital *I*. My speculations about the state of the essay arise from my own practice as reader and writer, and they reflect my own tastes, no matter how I may pretend to gaze dispassionately down on the question from a hot-air balloon. As Thoreau declares in his brash manner on the opening page of *Walden:* "In most books the *I*, or first person, is omitted; in this it will be retained; that, in respect to egotism, is the main difference. We commonly do not remember that it is, after all, always the first person that is speaking. I should not talk so much about myself if there were anybody else whom I knew as well" (Thoreau, 3). True for the personal essay, it is doubly true for an essay about the essay: one speaks always and inescapably in the first person singular.

We could sort out essays along a spectrum, according to the degree to which the writer's ego is on display—with John McPhee, perhaps, at the extreme of self-effacement and Norman Mailer at the opposite extreme of self-dramatization. Brassy or shy, stage center or hanging back in the wings, the author's persona commands our attention. For the length of an essay, or a book of essays, we respond to that persona as we would to a friend caught up in a rapturous monologue. When the monologue is finished, we may not be able to say precisely what it was about, any more than we can draw conclusions from a piece of music. "Essays don't usually boil down to a summary, as articles do," notes Edward Hoagland, one of the least summarizable of companions, "and the style of the writer has a 'nap' to it, a combination of personality and originality and energetic loose ends that stand up like the nap of a piece of wool and can't be brushed flat" (Hoagland, 25–26). We make assumptions about that speaking voice, assumptions that we cannot validly make about the narrators in fiction. Only a sophomore is permitted to ask how many children had Huckleberry Finn. But even literary sophisticates wonder in print about Thoreau's love life, Montaigne's domestic arrangements, De Quincey's opium habit, Virginia Woolf's depression.

Montaigne, who not only invented the form but perfected it as well, announced from the start that his true subject was himself. In his note "To the Reader," he slyly proclaimed: "I want to be seen here in my simple, natural, ordinary fashion, without straining or artifice; for it is myself that I portray. My defects will here be read to the life, and also my natural form, as far as respect for the public has allowed. Had I been placed among those nations which are said to live still in the sweet freedom of nature's first laws, I assure you I should very gladly have portrayed myself here entire and wholly naked" (Montaigne, 6). A few pages after this disarming introduction, we are told of the Emperor Maximilien, who was so prudish about displaying his private parts that he would not let a servant dress him or see him in the bath. The emperor went so far as to give orders that he be buried in his underdrawers. Having let us in on this intimacy about Maximilien, Montaigne then confessed that he himself, although "bold-mouthed," was equally prudish, and that "except under great stress of necessity or voluptuousness," he never allowed anyone to see him naked (11). Such modesty, he feared, was unbecoming in a soldier. But such honesty is quite becoming in an essayist. The very confession of his prudery is a far more revealing gesture than any doffing of clothes.

Every English major knows that the word "essay," as adapted by Montaigne, means a trial or attempt. The Latin root carries the more vivid sense of a weighing out. In the days when that root was alive and green, merchants discovered the value of goods and alchemists discovered the composition of unknown metals by the use of scales. Just so the essay, as Montaigne was the first to show, is a weighing out, an inquiry into the value, meaning, and true nature of experience; it is a private experiment carried out in public. In each of three successive editions, Montaigne inserted new material into his essays without revising the old material. Often the new statements contradicted the original ones, but Montaigne let them stand, since he believed that the only consistent fact about human beings is their inconsistency. Lewis Thomas has remarked of him that "he [was] fond of his mind, and affectionately entertained by everything in his head" (Thomas, 148). Whatever Montaigne wrote about, and he wrote about everything under the sun—fears, smells, growing old, the pleasures of scratching—he weighed on the scales of his own character.

It is the *singularity* of the first person—its warts and crotchets and turn of voice—that lures many of us into reading essays and that lingers with us after we finish. Consider the lonely, melancholy persona of Loren Eiseley, forever wandering, forever brooding on our dim and bestial past, his lips frosty with the chill of the Ice Age. Consider the volatile, Dionysian persona of D. H. Lawrence, with his incandescent gaze, his habit of turning peasants into gods and trees into flames, his quick hatred and quicker love. Consider that philosophical farmer, Wendell Berry, who speaks with a countryman's knowledge and a deacon's severity. Consider E. B. White, with his cheery affection for brown eggs and dachshunds and his unflappable way of herding geese while the radio warns of an approaching hurricane.

E. B. White, that engaging master of the genre, a champion of idiosyncrasy, introduced one of his own collections by admitting the danger of narcissism:

> I think some people find the essay the last resort of the egoist, a much too self-conscious and self-serving form for their taste; they feel that it is presumptuous of a writer to assume that his little excursions or his small observations will interest the reader. There is some justice in their complaint. I have always been aware that I am by nature self-absorbed and egoistical; to write of myself to the extent I have done indicates a too great attention to my own life, not enough to the lives of others. [White, viii]

Yet the self-absorbed Mr. White was in fact a delighted observer of the world and shared his delight with us. Thus, after describing memorably how a circus girl practiced her bareback riding in the leisure moments between shows ("The Ring of Time"), he confessed: "As a writing man, or secretary, I have always felt charged with the safekeeping of all unexpected items of worldly or unworldly enchantment, as though I might be held personally responsible if even a small one were to be lost" (White, 153). That statement may still be presumptuous, but the presumption is turned outward on the world.

Such looking outward on the world helps distinguish the essay from pure autobiography, which dwells more complacently on the self. Mass murderers, movie stars, sports heroes, Wall Street crooks, and defrocked politicians may blather on about whatever high jinks or low jinks made them temporarily famous and may chronicle their exploits, their diets, and their hobbies in perfect confidence that the public is eager to gobble up every least gossipy scrap. And the public, according to sales figures, generally is. On the other hand, I assume that the public does not give a hoot about my private life (an assumption also borne out by sales figures). If I write of hiking up a mountain, with my one-year-old boy riding like a papoose on my back, and of what he babbled to me while we gazed down from the summit onto the scudding clouds, I do so not because I am deluded into believing that my baby, like the offspring of Prince Charles, matters to the great world. I do so because I know that the great world produces babies of its own and watches them change cloud-fast before its doting eyes. To make that climb up the mountain vividly present for readers is harder work than the climb itself. I choose to write about my experience not because it is mine but because it seems to me a door through which others might pass.

On that cocky first page of *Walden,* Thoreau justified his own seeming self-absorption by saying that he wrote the book for the sake of his fellow citizens, who kept asking him to account for his peculiar experiment by the pond. There is at least a sliver of truth to this, since Thoreau, a town character, had been invited more than once to speak his mind at the public lectern. Most of us, however, cannot honestly say that the townspeople have been clamoring for our words. I suspect that all writers of the essay, even Norman Mailer and Gore Vidal, must occasionally wonder whether they are egomaniacs. For the essayist, in other words, the problem of authority is inescapable. By what right does one speak? Why should anyone listen? The traditional sources of authority no longer serve. You cannot justify your words by appealing to the Bible or some other holy text; you cannot merely stitch together a patchwork of quotations from classical authors; you cannot lean on a podium at the Atheneum and deliver your wisdom to a rapt audience.

In searching for your own soapbox, a sturdy platform from which to deliver your opinionated monologues, it helps if you have already distinguished yourself at some other, less fishy form. When Yeats describes his longing for Maud Gonne or muses on Ireland's misty lore, his words are charged with the prior strength of his poetry. When Virginia Woolf, in *A Room of One's Own,* reflects on the status of women and the conditions necessary for making art, she speaks as the author of *Mrs. Dalloway* and *To the Lighthouse.* The essayist may also lay claim to our attention by having lived through events or traveled through terrains that already bear a richness of meaning. When James Baldwin writes his *Notes of a Native Son,* he does not have to convince us that racism is a troubling reality. When Barry Lopez takes us on a meditative tour of the far north in *Arctic Dreams,* he can rely on our curiosity about that fabled and forbidding place. When Paul Theroux climbs aboard a train and invites us on a journey to some exotic destination, he can count on the romance of railroads and the allure of remote cities to bear us along.

Most essayists, however, cannot draw on any source of authority from beyond the page to lend force to the page itself. They can only use language to put themselves on display and to gesture at the world. When Annie Dillard tells us in the opening lines of *Pilgrim at Tinker Creek* about the tomcat with bloody paws who jumps through the window onto her chest, why should we listen? Well, because of the voice that goes on to say: "And some mornings I'd wake in daylight to find my body covered with paw prints in blood; I looked as though I'd been painted with roses" (Dillard, 1). Listen to her explaining a few pages later what she is about in this book, this broody, zestful record of her stay in the Roanoke Valley: "I propose to keep here what Thoreau called 'a meteorological journal of the mind,' telling some tales and describing some of the sights of this rather tamed valley, and exploring, in fear and trembling, some of the unmapped dim reaches and unholy fastnesses to which those tales and sights so dizzyingly lead" (Dillard, 11). The sentence not only describes the method of her literary search but also displays the breathless, often giddy, always eloquent and spiritually hungry soul who will do the searching. If you enjoy her company, you will relish Annie Dillard's essays; otherwise you will not.

Listen to another voice which readers tend to find either captivating or insufferable:

> That summer I began to see, however dimly, that one of my ambitions,
> perhaps my governing ambition, was to belong fully to this place, to belong
> as the thrushes and the herons and the muskrats belonged, to be altogether at
> home here. That is still my ambition. But now I have come to see that it
> proposes an enormous labor. It is a spiritual ambition, like goodness. The
> wild creatures belong to the place by nature, but as a man I can belong to it
> only by understanding and by virtue. It is an ambition I cannot hope to
> succeed in wholly, but I have come to believe that it is the most worthy of all.
> [Berry, 52]

The speaker is Wendell Berry writing about his patch of Kentucky. Once you have heard that stately, moralizing, cherishing voice, laced with references to the land, you will not mistake it for anyone else's. Berry's themes are profound and arresting ones. But it is his voice, more than anything he speaks about, that either seizes us or drives us away.

Even so distinct a persona as Wendell Berry's or Annie Dillard's is still only a literary fabrication, of course. The first person singular is too narrow a gate for the whole writer to pass through. What we meet on the page is not the flesh-and-blood author but a simulacrum, a character who wears the label *I*. Introducing the lectures that became *A Room of One's Own*, Virginia Woolf reminded her listeners that "'I' is only a convenient term for somebody who has no real being. Lies will flow from my lips, but there may perhaps be some truth mixed up with them; it is for you to seek out this truth and to decide whether any part of it is worth keeping" (Woolf, 4). Here is a part I consider worth keeping: "Women have served all these centuries as looking-glasses possessing the magic and delicious power of reflecting the figure of man at twice its natural size" (Woolf, 35). It is from such elegant, revelatory sentences that we build up our notion of the "I" who speaks to us under the name of Virginia Woolf.

What the essay tells us may not be true in any sense that would satisfy a court of law. As an example, think of Orwell's brief narrative, "A Hanging," which describes an execution in Burma. Anyone who has read it remembers how the condemned man as he walked to the gallows stepped aside to avoid a puddle. Only an eyewitness should be able to report such a haunting detail. Alas, biographers, those zealous debunkers, have recently claimed that Orwell never saw such a hanging; that he reconstructed it from hearsay. What then do we make of his essay? Or has it become the sort of barefaced lie that we prefer to call a story?

Frankly, I do not much care what label we put on "A Hanging"—fiction or nonfiction, it is a powerful statement either way—but Orwell might have cared a great deal. I say so because not long ago I found one of my own essays treated in a scholarly article as a work of fiction. When I recovered from the shock of finding any reference to my work at all, I was outraged. Here was my earnest report about growing up on a military base, my heartfelt rendering of indelible memories, being confused with the airy figments of novelists! To be sure, in writing the piece I had used dialogue, scenes, settings, character descriptions, the whole fictional bag of tricks; I had picked and chosen among a thousand beckoning details; and I had downplayed some facts and highlighted others. But I was writing about the actual, not the invented. I shaped the matter, but I did not make it up.

To explain my outrage, I must break another taboo, which is to speak of the author's intention. My teachers warned me strenuously to avoid the intentional fallacy. They told me to regard poems and plays and stories as objects washed up on the page from some unknown and unknowable shores. Now that I am on the other side of the page, so to speak, I think quite recklessly of intention all the time. I believe that, if we allow the question of intent in the case of murder, we should allow it in literature.

The essay is distinguished from the short story, not by the presence or absence of literary devices, not by tone or theme or subject, but by the writer's stance toward the material. In composing an essay about what it was like to grow up on that military base, I *meant* something quite different from what I mean when I concoct a story. I meant to preserve and record and help give voice to a reality that existed independently of me. I meant to pay my respects to a minor passage of history in an out-of-the-way place. I felt responsible to the truth as known by other people. I wanted to speak directly out of my own life into the lives of others.

You can see I am teetering on the brink of metaphysics. One step farther and I will plunge into the void, wondering as I fall how to prove there is any external truth for the essayist to pay homage to. I draw back from the brink and simply declare that I believe one writes, in essays, with a regard for the actual world, with a respect for the shared substance of history, the autonomy of other lives, the being of nature, and the mystery and majesty of a creation we have not made.

When it comes to speculating about the creation, I feel more at ease with physics than with metaphysics. According to certain bold and lyrical cosmologists, there is at the center of black holes a geometrical point, the tiniest conceivable speck, where all the matter of a collapsed star has been concentrated and where everyday notions of time, space, and force break down. That point is called a singularity. The boldest and most poetic theories suggest that anything sucked into a singularity might be flung back out again, utterly changed, somewhere else in the universe. The lonely first person, the essayist's microcosmic "I," may be thought of as a verbal singularity at the center of the mind's black hole. The raw matter of experience, torn away from the axes of time and space, falls in constantly from all sides, undergoes the mind's inscrutable alchemy, and reemerges in the quirky, unprecedented shape of an essay.

Now it is time for me to step down, before another metaphor seizes hold of me, before you notice that I am standing, not on a soapbox, but on the purest air.

Works Cited

Berry, Wendell. *Recollected Essays, 1965–1980.* San Francisco: North Point, 1981.
Didion, Joan. *The White Album.* New York: Simon and Schuster, 1979.
Dillard, Annie. *Pilgrim at Tinker Creek.* New York: Harper's Magazine Press, 1974.

Emerson, Ralph Waldo. *Nature*. Vol. 1 of *The Complete Works of Ralph Waldo Emerson*. Boston: Houghton Mifflin, 1903.

Hoagland, Edward. *The Tugman's Passage*. New York: Random House, 1982.

Montaigne, Michel de. *Essays*. Trans. Donald Frame. Stanford: Stanford University Press, 1958.

Thomas, Lewis. *The Medusa and the Snail*. New York: Viking, 1979.

Thoreau, Henry David. *Walden*. Ed. J. Lyndon Shanley. Princeton: Princeton University Press, 1973.

White, E. B. *Essays of E. B. White*. New York: Harper, 1977.

Woolf, Virginia. *A Room of One's Own*. New York: Harcourt, Brace and World, 1957.

From Outside, In

Barbara Mellix

Two years ago, when I started writing this paper, trying to bring order out of chaos, my ten-year-old daughter was suffering from an acute attack of boredom. She drifted in and out of the room complaining that she had nothing to do, no one to "be with" because none of her friends were at home. Patiently I explained that I was working on something special and needed peace and quiet, and I suggested that she paint, read, or work with her computer. None of these interested her. Finally, she pulled up a chair to my desk and watched me, now and then heaving long, loud sighs. After two or three minutes (nine or ten sighs), I lost my patience. "Looka here, Allie," I said, "you too old for this kinda carryin' on. I done told you this is important. You wronger than dirt to be in here haggin' me like this and you know it. Now git on outta here and leave me off before I put my foot all the way down."

I was at home, alone with my family, and my daughter understood that this way of speaking was appropriate in that context. She knew, as a matter of fact, that it was almost inevitable; when I get angry at home, I speak some of my finest, most cherished black English. Had I been speaking to my daughter in this manner in certain other environments, she would have been shocked and probably worried that I had taken leave of my sense of propriety.

Like my children, I grew up speaking what I considered two distinctly different languages—black English and standard English (or as I thought of them then, the ordinary everyday speech of "country" coloreds and "proper" English—and in the process of acquiring these languages, I developed an understanding of when, where, and how to use them. But unlike my children, I grew up in a world that was primarily black. My friends, neighbors, minister, teachers—almost everybody I associated with every day—were black. And we spoke to one another in our own special language: *That sho is a pretty dress you got on. If she don' soon*

43

leave me off I'm gon tell her head a mess. I was so mad I could'a pissed a blue nail. He all the time trying to low-rate somebody. Ain't that just about the nastiest thing you ever set ears on?

Then there were the "others," the "proper" blacks, transplanted relatives and one-time friends who came home from the city for weddings, funerals, and vacations. And the whites. To these we spoke standard English. "Ain't?" my mother would yell at me when I used the term in the presence of "others." "You *know* better than that." And I would hang my head in shame and say the "proper" word.

I remember one summer sitting in my grandmother's house in Greeleyville, South Carolina, when it was full of the chatter of city relatives who were home on vacation. My parents sat quietly, only now and then volunteering a comment or answering a question. My mother's face took on a strained expression when she spoke. I could see that she was being careful to say just the right words in just the right way. Her voice sounded thick, muffled. And when she finished speaking, she would lapse into silence, her proper smile on her face. My father was more articulate, more aggressive. He spoke quickly, his words sharp and clear. But he held his proud head higher, a signal that he, too, was uncomfortable. My sisters and brothers and I stared at our aunts, uncles, and cousins, speaking only when prompted. Even then, we hesitated, formed our sentences in our minds, then spoke softly, shyly.

My parents looked small and anxious during those occasions, and I waited impatiently for our leave-taking when we would mock our relatives the moment we were out of their hearing. "Reeely," we would say to one another, flexing our wrists and rolling our eyes, "how dooo you stan' this heat? Chile, it just too hy*ooo*-mid for words." Our relatives had made us feel "country," and this was our way of regaining pride in ourselves while getting a little revenge in the bargain. The words bubbled in our throats and rolled across our tongues, a balming.

As a child I felt this same doubleness in uptown Greeleyville where the whites lived. "Ain't that a pretty dress you're wearing!" Toby, the town policeman, said to me one day when I was fifteen. "Thank you very much," I replied, my voice barely audible in my own ears. The words felt wrong in my mouth, rigid, foreign. It was not that I had never spoken that phrase before—it was common in black English, too—but I was extremely conscious that this was an occasion for proper English. I had taken out my English and put it on as I did my church clothes, and I felt as if I were wearing my Sunday best in the middle of the week. It did not matter that Toby had not spoken grammatically correct English. He was white and could speak as he wished. I had something to prove. Toby did not.

Speaking standard English to whites was our way of demonstrating that we knew their language and could use it. Speaking it to standard-English-speaking blacks was our way of showing them that we, as well as they, could "put on airs." But when we spoke standard English, we acknowledged (to ourselves and to others—but primarily to ourselves) that our customary way of speaking was inferior. We felt foolish, embarrassed, somehow diminished because we were ashamed to be our real selves. We were reserved, shy in the presence of those who owned and/or spoke *the* language.

My parents never set aside time to drill us in standard English. Their forms of instruction were less formal. When my father was feeling particularly expansive, he would regale us with tales of his exploits in the outside world. In almost flawless English, complete with dialogue and flavored with gestures and embellishment, he told us about his attempt to get a haircut at a white barbershop; his refusal to acknowledge one of the town merchants until the man addressed him as "Mister"; the time he refused to step off the sidewalk uptown to let some whites pass; his airplane trip to New York City (to visit a sick relative) during which the stewardesses and porters—recognizing that he was a "gentleman"—addressed him as "Sir." I did not realize then—nor, I think, did my father—that he was teaching us, among other things, standard English and the relationship between language and power.

My mother's approach was different. Often, when one of us said, "I'm gon wash off my feet," she would say, "And what will you walk on if you wash them off?" Everyone would laugh at the victim of my mother's "proper" mood. But it was different when one of us children was in a proper mood. "You think you are so superior," I said to my oldest sister one day when we were arguing and she was winning. "Superior!" my sister mocked. "You mean I'm acting 'biggidy'?" My sisters and brothers sniggered, then joined in teasing me. Finally, my mother said, "Leave your sister alone. There's nothing wrong with using proper English." There was a half-smile on her face. I had gotten "uppity," had "put on airs" for no good reason. I was at home, alone with the family, and I hadn't been prompted by one of my mother's proper moods. But there was also a proud light in my mother's eyes; her children were learning English very well.

Not until years later, as a college student, did I begin to understand our ambivalence toward English, our scorn of it, our need to master it, to own

45

and be owned by it—an ambivalence that extended to the public-school classroom. In our school, where there were no whites, my teachers taught standard English but used black English to do it. When my grammar-school teachers wanted us to write, for example, they usually said something like, "I want y'all to write five sentences that make a statement. Anybody git done before the rest can color." It was probably almost those exact words that led me to write these sentences in 1953 when I was in the second grade:

> The white clouds are pretty.
> There are only 15 people in our room.
> We will go to gym.
> We have a new poster.
> We may go out doors.

Second grade came after "Little First" and "Big First," so by then I knew the implied rules that accompanied all writing assignments. Writing was an occasion for proper English. I was not to write in the way we spoke to one another: The white clouds pretty; There ain't but 15 people in our room; We going to gym; We got a new poster; We can go out in the yard. Rather I was to use the language of "other": clouds *are*, there *are*, we *will*, we *have*, we *may*.

My sentences were short, rigid, perfunctory, like the letters my mother wrote to relatives:

> Dear Papa,
>
> How are you? How is Mattie? Fine I hope. We are fine. We will come to see you Sunday. Cousin Ned will give us a ride.
>
> Love,
> Daughter

The language was not ours. It was something from outside us, something we used for special occasions.

But my coloring on the other side of that second-grade paper is different. I drew three hearts and a sun. The sun has a smiling face that radiates and envelops everything it touches. And although the sun and its world are enclosed in a circle, the colors I used—red, blue, green, purple, orange, yellow, black—indicate that I was less restricted with drawing and coloring than I was with writing standard English. My valentines were not just red. My sun was not just a yellow ball in the sky.

By the time I reached the twelfth grade, speaking and writing standard English had taken on new importance. Each year, about half of the newly graduated seniors of our school moved to large cities—particularly in the North—to live with relatives and find work. Our English teacher constantly corrected our grammar: "Not 'ain't,' but 'isn't.'" We seldom wrote papers, and even those few were usually plot summaries of short stories. When our teacher returned the papers, she usually lectured on the importance of using standard English: "I *am;* you *are;* he, she, or it *is,*" she would say, writing on the chalkboard as she spoke. "How you gon git a job talking about 'I is,' or 'I isn't' or 'I ain't'?"

In Pittsburgh, where I moved after graduation, I watched my aunt and uncle—who had always spoken standard English when in Greeleyville—switch from black English to standard English to a mixture of the two, according to where they were or who they were with. At home and with certain close relatives, friends, and neighbors, they spoke black English. With those less close, they spoke a mixture. In public and with strangers, they generally spoke standard English.

In time, I learned to speak standard English with ease and to switch smoothly from black to standard or a mixture, and back again. But no matter where I was, no matter what the situation or occasion, I continued to write as I had in school:

> Dear Mommie,
>
> How are you? How is everybody else? Fine I hope. I am fine. So are Aunt and Uncle. Tell everyone I said hello. I will write again soon.
>
> Love,
> Barbara

At work, at a health insurance company, I learned to write letters to customers. I studied form letters and letters written by co-workers, memorizing the phrases and the ways in which they were used. I dictated:

> Thank you for your letter of January 5. We have made the changes in your coverage you requested. Your new premium will be $150 every three months. We are pleased to have been of service to you.

In a sense, I was proud of the letters I wrote for the company: they were proof of my ability to survive in the city, the outside world—an indication of my growing mastery of English. But they also indicate that writing was still mechanical for me, something that didn't require much thought.

Reading also became a more significant part of my life during those early years in Pittsburgh. I had always liked reading, but now I devoted more and more of my spare time to it. I read romances, mysteries, popular novels. Looking back, I realize that the books I liked best were simple, unambiguous: good versus bad and right versus wrong with right rewarded and wrong punished, mysteries unraveled and all set right in the end. It was how I remembered life in Greeleyville.

Of course I was romanticizing. Life in Greeleyville had not been so very uncomplicated. Back there I had been—first as a child, then as a young woman with limited experience in the outside world—living in a relatively closed-in society. But there were implicit and explicit principles that guided our way of life and shaped our relationships with one another and the people outside—principles that a newcomer would find elusive and baffling. In Pittsburgh, I had matured, become more experienced: I had worked at three different jobs, associated with a wider range of people, married, had children. This new environment with different prescripts for living required that I speak standard English much of the time, and slowly, imperceptibly, I had ceased seeing a sharp distinction between myself and "others." Reading romances and mysteries, characterized by dichotomy, was a way of shying away from change, from the person I was becoming.

But that other part of me—that part which took great pride in my ability to hold a job writing business letters—was increasingly drawn to the new developments in my life and the attending possibilities, opportunities for even greater change. If I could write letters for a nationally known business, could I not also do something better, more challenging, more important? Could I not, perhaps, go to college and become a school teacher? For years, afraid and a little embarrassed, I did no more than imagine this different me, this possible me. But sixteen years after coming north, when my youngest daughter entered kindergarten, I found myself unable—or unwilling—to resist the lure of possibility. I enrolled in my first college course: Basic Writing, at the University of Pittsburgh.

For the first time in my life, I was required to write extensively about myself. Using the most formal English at my command, I wrote these sentences near the beginning of the term:

> One of my duties as a homemaker is simply picking up after others. A day seldom passes that I don't search for a mislaid toy, book, or gym shoe, etc. I change the Ty-D-Bol, fight "ring around the collar," and keep our laundry smelling "April fresh." Occasionally, I settle arguments between my children and suggest things to do when they're bored. Taking telephone messages for my oldest daughter is my newest (and sometimes most aggravating) chore. Hanging the toilet paper roll is my most insignificant.

My concern was to use "appropriate" language, to sound as if I belonged in a college classroom. But I felt separate from the language—as if it did not and could not belong to me. I couldn't think and feel genuinely in that language, couldn't make it express what I thought and felt about being a housewife. A part of me resented, among other things, being judged by such things as the appearance of my family's laundry and toilet bowl, but in that language I could only imagine and write about a conventional housewife.

For the most part, the remainder of the term was a period of adjustment, a time of trying to find my bearings as a student in a college composition class, to learn to shut out my black English whenever I composed, and to prevent it from creeping into my formulations; a time for trying to grasp the language of the classroom and reproduce it in my prose; for trying to talk about myself in that language, reach others through it. Each experience of writing was like standing naked and revealing my imperfection, my "otherness." And each new assignment was another chance to make myself over in language, reshape myself, make myself "better" in my rapidly changing image of a student in a college composition class.

But writing became increasingly unmanageable as the term progressed, and by the end of the semester, my sentences sounded like this:

> My excitement was soon dampened, however, by what seemed like a small voice in the back of my head saying that I should be careful with my long awaited opportunity. I felt frustrated and this seemed to make it difficult to concentrate.

There is a poverty of language in these sentences. By this point, I knew that the clichéd language of my Housewife essay was unacceptable, and I generally recognized trite expressions. At the same time, I hadn't yet mastered the language of the classroom, hadn't yet come to see it as belonging to me. Most notable is the lifelessness of the prose, the apparent absence of a person behind the words. I wanted those sentences—and the rest of the essay—to convey the anguish of yearning to, at once, become something more and yet remain the same. I had the sensation of being split in two, part of me going into a future the other part didn't believe possible. As that person, the student writer at that moment, I was essentially mute. I could not—in the process of composing—use the language of the old me, yet I couldn't imagine myself in the language of "others."

I found this particularly discouraging because at midsemester I had been writing in a much different way. Note the language of this introduction to an essay I had written then, near the middle of the term:

> Pain is a constant companion to the people in "Footwork." Their jobs are physically damaging. Employers are insensitive to their feelings and in many

49

cases add to their problems. The general public wounds them further by treating them with disgrace because of what they do for a living. Although the workers are as diverse as they are similar, there is a definite link between them. They suffer a great deal of abuse.

The voice here is stronger, more confident, appropriating terms like "physically damaging," "wounds them further," "insensitive," "diverse"—terms I couldn't have imagined using when writing about my own experience—and shaping them into sentences like, "Although the workers are as diverse as they are similar, there is a definite link between them." And there is the sense of a personality behind the prose, someone who sympathizes with the workers: "The general public wounds them further by treating them with disgrace because of what they do for a living."

What caused these differences? I was, I believed, explaining other people's thoughts and feelings, and I was free to move about in the language of "others" so long as I was speaking *of* others. I was unaware that I was transforming into my best classroom language my own thoughts and feelings about people whose experiences and ways of speaking were in many ways similar to mine.

The following year, unable to turn back or to let go of what had become something of an obsession with language (and hoping to catch and hold the sense of control that had eluded me in Basic Writing), I enrolled in a research writing course. I spent most of the term learning how to prepare for and write a research paper. I chose sex education as my subject and spent hours in libraries, searching for information, reading, taking notes. Then (not without messiness and often-demoralizing frustration) I organized my information into categories, wrote a thesis statement, and composed my paper—a series of paraphrases and quotations spaced between carefully constructed transitions. The process and results felt artificial, but as I would later come to realize I was passing through a necessary stage. My sentences sounded like this:

This reserve becomes understandable with examination of who the abusers are. In an overwhelming number of cases, they are people the victims know and trust. Family members, relatives, neighbors and close family friends commit seventy-five percent of all reported sex crimes against children, and parents, parent substitutes and relatives are the offenders in thirty to eighty percent of all reported cases.[12] While assault by strangers does occur, it is less common, and is usually a single episode.[13] But abuse by family members, relatives and acquaintances may continue for an extended period of time. In cases of incest, for example, children are abused repeatedly for an average of eight years.[14] In such cases, "the use of physical force is rarely necessary because of the child's trusting, dependent relationship with the offender. The child's cooperation is often facilitated by the adult's position of dominance, an offer of material goods, a threat of physical violence, or a misrepresentation of moral standards."[15]

The completed paper gave me a sense of profound satisfaction, and I read it often after my professor returned it. I know now that what I was pleased with was the language I used and the professional voice it helped me maintain. "Use better words," my teacher had snapped at me one day after reading the notes I'd begun accumulating from my research, and slowly I began taking on the language of my sources. In my next set of notes, I used the word "vacillating"; my professor applauded. And by the time I composed the final draft, I felt at ease with terms like "overwhelming number of cases," "single episode," and "reserve," and I shaped them into sentences similar to those of my "expert" sources.

If I were writing the paper today, I would of course do some things differently. Rather than open with an anecdote—as my teacher suggested—I would begin simply with a quotation that caught my interest as I was researching my paper (and which I scribbled, without its source, in the margin of my notebook): "Truth does not do so much good in the world as the semblance of truth does evil." The quotation felt right because it captured what was for me the central idea of my essay—an idea that emerged gradually during the making of my paper—and expressed it in a way I would like to have said it. The anecdote, a hypothetical situation I invented to conform to the information in the paper, felt forced and insincere because it represented—to a great degree—my teacher's understanding of the essay, *her* idea of what in it was most significant. Improving upon my previous experiences with writing, I was beginning to think and feel in the language I used, to find my own voices in it, to sense that how one speaks influences how one means. But I was not yet secure enough, comfortable enough with the language to trust my intuition.

Now that I know that to seek knowledge, freedom, and autonomy means always to be in the concentrated process of becoming—always to be venturing into new territory, feeling one's way at first, then getting one's balance, negotiating, accommodating, discovering one's self in ways that previously defined "others"—I sometimes get tired. And I ask myself why I keep on participating in this highbrow form of violence, this slamming against perplexity. But there is no real futility in the question, no hint of that part of the old me who stood outside standard English, hugging to herself a disabling mistrust of a language she thought could not represent a person with her history and experience. Rather, the question

51

represents a person who feels the consequence of her education, the weight of her possibilities as a teacher and writer and human being, a voice in society. And I would not change that person, would not give back the good burden that accompanies my growing expertise, my increasing power to shape myself in language and share that self with "others."

"To speak," says Frantz Fanon, "means to be in a position to use a certain syntax, to grasp the morphology of this or that language, but it means above all to assume a culture, to support the weight of a civilization."* To write means to do the same, but in a more profound sense. However, Fanon also says that to achieve mastery means to "get" in a position of power, to "grasp," to "assume." This, I have learned—both as a student and subsequently as a teacher—can involve tremendous emotional and psychological conflict for those attempting to master academic discourse. Although as a beginning student writer I had a fairly good grasp of ordinary spoken English and was proficient at what Labov calls "code-switching" (and what John Baugh in *Black Street Speech* terms "style shifting"), when I came face to face with the demands of academic writing, I grew increasingly self-conscious, constantly aware of my status as a black and a speaker of one of the many black English vernaculars—a traditional outsider. For the first time, I experienced my sense of doubleness as something menacing, a built-in enemy. Whenever I turned inward for salvation, the balm so available during my childhood, I found instead this new fragmentation which spoke to me in many voices. It was the voice of my desire to prosper, but at the same time it spoke of what I had relinquished and could not regain: a safe way of being, a state of powerlessness which exempted me from responsibility for who I was and might be. And it accused me of betrayal, of turning away from blackness. To recover balance, I had to take on the language of the academy, the language of "others." And to do that, I had to learn to imagine myself a part of the culture of that language, and therefore someone free to manage that language, to take liberties with it. Writing and rewriting, practicing, experimenting, I came to comprehend more fully the generative power of language. I discovered—with the help of some especially sensitive teachers—that through writing one can continually bring new selves into being, each with new responsibilities and difficulties, but also with new possibilities. Remarkable power, indeed. I write and continually give birth to myself.

Black Skin, White Masks (1952; rpt. New York: Grove Press, 1967), pp. 17–18.

Autobiographical Memory and Sense of Place

Rockwell Gray

One's sense of personal identity depends upon the recapture in memory of the key places in which one's
life has taken place. The phrase itself—"taken place"—is a kind of pun:
we live by occupying, by taking possession of, a succession of places.
Human life is always concretely circumstantial. All experience is *placed*
experience. Thought and deed, taste and judgment, occur within the constraints and enabling conditions of highly specific settings. Though philosophy tends to suppose that thought is disembodied and of universal
purport, even our most sublime ruminations are shaped and colored by
the anchoring truths of body, climate, and cultural environment. However
tolerant and catholic our views, we hold them within a perspective
shaped by many collective conditions and by each person's finally unique
sense of identity. One's vantage point—the angle from which he must see
the world—is not of course fixed or constant, but we can see no more
than our horizon of expectations permits. It provides the frames of reference and the enabling presuppositions of our acts and utterances, indeed
the very manner in which we apprehend experience.

For each of us, the world begins and develops in a network of forms and
beliefs which antedate our appearance on earth, making human life in-
conceivable and indescribable as an abstract course. And as every river
needs its bed, so every existence requires its successive "standpoints."
This term may seem too static for the kinetic and metabolic process of
living, yet it is apposite after all, for we must always literally stand (or sit
or lie) somewhere in order to be in the world at all. In short, we cannot
know who we are without knowing where we have been; and recall of all
those now absent places is necessary to a full sense of dwelling in the
present. To dwell is to be embedded, and to be embedded is to belong

through a history of having belonged in many places before. The remembered, re-placed past in all its restorative concreteness must buoy up the present in order that our lives not glide down the shallow stream Thoreau remarks in one of his great mystical images: "Time is but the stream I go a-fishing in. I drink at it; but while I drink I see the sandy bottom and detect how shallow it is. Its thin current slides away, but eternity remains." The autobiographer too fishes in the time-stream and mounts it toward its source, seeking depth by artistically recasting the life he more heedlessly lived the first time around.

Yet the world of our beginnings, as of our later journeys forth, is never wholly grasped or attained. All we can expect is to seize it from the ground we occupy, extrapolating its unknown features from the particular shore of its vastness we ply. Strange indeed is our capacity to bear within us sketches of the whole that are never to be completed. In the lines of Czeslaw Milosz,

> Consciousness enclosed in itself every separate birch
> And the woods of New Hampshire, covered in May with green haze.
> The faces of people are in it without number, the courses
> Of planets, and things past and a portent of the future . . .
> Then one should extract from it what one can, slowly,
> Not trusting anybody. And it won't be much, for language is weak.[1]

However limited, the patterns of individual experience are carried within us from our earliest perceptions of an ordered world. While many of its features are generic, conditioned by the rhythms of a larger collective experience, each of us puts his own stamp on the "raw materials" of existence, each has a distinct version of "where it all began," and each crafts a unique story of ensuing development, success and failure. As Margaret Laurence notes of the Canadian prairie town of her childhood in the 1930s, "Because that settlement and that land were my first and for many years my only real knowledge of this planet, in some profound way they remain my world, my way of viewing. My eyes were formed there."[2] To recover that place in autobiography meant, for her, to cognize the validity not only of private experience but of the larger enclosing sphere as well:

> This was my territory in the time of my youth, and in a sense my life since then has been an attempt to look at it, to come to terms with it. Stultifying to the mind it certainly could be, and sometimes was, but not to the imagination. It was many things, but it was never dull.
> The same, I now see, could be said for Canada in general.[3]

Patriotism, she realizes, is rooted in one's claims on local place; we learn to belong to a region, or even a nation, only by extension from more immediate experience.

All later experience remains bound, in some degree, to such beginnings. The cosmopolitan viewpoint is a kind of sophisticated fiction developed in later life, for all transcendence of the limitations of place is enacted in the highly particular terms which early define what each of us means by "the world." To grasp a life in all its rounded complexity, seeing it as it has been seen from the perspective which constructed it, one must be able to re-envision the various physical settings of the existential drama. The old metaphor of the world as a stage and man as the player is apropos: we know ourselves by rehearsing and incorporating what has happened in the many loci of our days. What I do and what befalls me together constitute my history and, to a large extent, my person. This is far more dependent on context and surrounding circumstances than is indicated by the traditional concept of autonomous individual selfhood. No moment of our lives can be understood apart from such specificity. In that sense, there was and is no purely objective place. For the cartographer, yes, the town I lived in as a child may be entered on the map, but for me it will always exist on the inner map of experience and memory. Through evocation of childhood roaming and of all my later residences and wanderings in the world, I recreate the angle of vision which rendered each place meaningful.

Yet there is more to a life than any rendition of place, however subtle, can suggest, for I also define myself by recalling my thoughts, my utterances, my relationships, and the products of my mind and hands. These expressions too are colored by my sense of place and by all the conditions geography imposes, providing a powerful, encompassing substratum for my sense of identity. If, for example, I ask myself why I currently live in a small town in the western piedmont of the Allegheny Mountains between Johnstown and Pittsburgh, Pennsylvania, I must answer in terms of the successive moves which brought me here and the motivation for them. Yet, in practice, my sense of my life's flow is less orderly and sequential than that, for memories of space traversed and time spent are conflated and brought to bear on the present in a highly personal, idiosyncratic manner. My pleasure or displeasure in a particular landscape or interior carries within it roots deep in my first years of life. As we do not see landscape and the natural world without instruction from art—without the perceptual frames and visual conventions regnant in our culture—neither do we respond to any place without the informing presence of many remembered places and experiences layered palimpsest-like in consciousness.

55

When I delight in the long slope of a pasture bordered by windbreaks of poplar and birch in a rolling, hilly countryside, I call upon many different times when I have been in similar settings or seen them represented in art. One of my earliest recollections of such a composition of elements comes from the illustrations by Harrison Cady for the animal stories of Thornton Burgess. Bobby Coon, Jimmy Skunk, and Peter Rabbit all lived amongst undulating meadows bordered by stone walls and birch-studded woodlands. The skies, ordinarily blue, were graced by the puffy, drifting cumulus clouds I still associate with simple peace and well-being. It was a cozy world to contemplate, despite frequent contretemps in the lives of the animal folk. Its likeness to the meadows and walls I already knew in a semi-rural New England town of my boyhood helps account for the acuity and durability of this memory, though it may just as well be that my early delight in softly pastoral beauty was in fact first shaped by Cady's illustrations.

Patterns of personal taste and aesthetic response carry a deep history. Last fall, as I walked my young daughter to lunch across the campus where I teach, the brilliantly lit yellow of a lambent, turning maple suddenly fixed my sense of that place in terms of another, earlier one. This luminous tree in western Pennsylvania fused with others like it on the rustic village green of Nelson, New Hampshire, a tiny town I had known in my early twenties and had had placed for me more deeply by May Sarton's *Journal of a Solitude,* composed during a period of residence there. Just before lunch I had been teaching my students to read Loren Eiseley's "The Brown Wasps," an essay about the dependence of all animals on a highly specific sense of home territory. Only man, of course, can articulate this dependency and raise it to a symbolic status, but other creatures in the essay (a mouse, pigeons, the titular wasps) also know the yearning for and return to familiar domain. Eiseley tells of a tree he planted as a child with his father, who believed that when the boy grew old he would live in the house under the grown tree and recall their planting it together. It was to be a bond between generations. The family left that house while Loren was still a young boy, but he carried within the image of the growing, then presumably grown tree through six decades of life. The assumption that it was still there, in the Nebraska back yard, gave him a unique sense of rootedness in the world. Late in his life, he returned to the old childhood residence and was jolted to see no tree at all. What had happened to it he could neither know nor imagine. He realized then that he had nurtured the tree in memory, where it would continue. What counted was his symbolic connection with the original "sacred" ground and the shared task of planting.

The golden maple of my campus carried my thoughts further into the matter of place. It helped me feel more at home in an area to which I had very recently moved by anchoring the present in deep affective domain. Though my connection to Nelson was based almost entirely on my vicarious experience with Sarton's account of settling into an old farmhouse in the town, I had read her journal at a time when I felt particularly adrift in the world. Hence, what I perhaps felt most essentially upon seeing the golden maple was the balm of a quiet fall weekend, some years before I married, when I had fantasized a home for myself by reading through *Journal of a Solitude*. Yet there was more: it seems likely the maple carried me back beyond that weekend, and beyond the even more distant memory of an afternoon or two spent on the Nelson green, to the trees of childhood in fall. Great maples and elms dominated and sheltered our neighborhood in that time. The turning of the leaves in my southern New England town was always followed by the wonderful ritual of raking and burning them. As we helped my father in this task, we dove and buried ourselves in the great massed piles and danced through the milky, acrid smoke. Shared task, shared play—the festival of leaves gets close to my deepest sense of being on earth. Yet the elms and maples of that street, victims since of blight and beetle, are no longer there. Their only place now is in memory, and my return to them must be through autobiographical reconstruction. Like Eiseley in his return to the Nebraska house, I discovered in that maple the symbolic articulation of my deepest sense of place. The tree itself, like the American elms consubstantial with my youth, was only one motif in the slowly evolving web of images and themes that express my larger sense of personal space, my strategy for taming a wide and alien world.

Like many men and women today, hardly knowing where home is any longer, I have had to build myself a composite sense of place. This primary task of modern autobiographical memory is especially salient in America, where constant mobility exacerbates the already complicated search for a clear sense of identity. Any study of the controlling patterns of autobiography must emphasize its function in our current culture as an antidote to anonymity, disconnection and uprootedness. In the pursuit of our own life stories (and vicariously in the consumption of those of others), we seek to distinguish ourselves from the crowds of persons who appear all too much like us. But, mobile and other-directed as so many of us are, we tend to confuse our identities with our itineraries or our ascent on some professional ladder of success. When the lack of deep connection to a place and its traditions forces us to ask where we actually are, we are also asking who we are. Having moved four times in the last eight years, I recently entered a phone booth and saw afresh the oddity of sorting place names according to state and area code. There was Pittsburgh at "412," the area into which I had recently moved, and Milwaukee at "414," the area I had just left. And there were all the other locations abroad in the land with numbers of no use to me and names that didn't even conjure an image: Davenport, Sacramento, Grand Forks, Mobile, Abilene, Raleigh, Harrisburg. They belonged to my cognitive map in only the most peripheral way.

Later that summer, listening to the autobiographical vignettes with which fellow vacationers on an Atlantic beach introduced themselves, I realized that Americans, more insistently and radically than most other peoples, substitute some form of quick "guerrilla" autobiography for a sense of community and continuing place. Instead of clear, coherent stories, one hears snatches of personal history proffered as tags of identity. The self-presenter fires off those bits of his past which will render him or her quickly and superficially familiar to unknown others. In this manner, the autobiographical impulse has a vital social function, though the "histories" so deployed have little communicative force or staying power. We might call this conversational activity "pseudoautobiography," though the term begs the point that the loose, anecdotal nature of many published autobiographies is hardly more authentic. In fact, there is no single prescribed form which guarantees us the real thing. The issue is more one of intention, motive, and purpose. A letter or set of letters, a conversation or an ongoing dialogue, may be more genuinely autobiographical in spirit than many an autobiography self-announced. Despite the fragmented, decontextualized nature of the bits of stories given in lieu (and in search of) an established sense of personal identity, such a form of self-presentation may tellingly reveal the conditions of life in our society.

Since middle-class American lives, for all their actual variety, often seem homogeneous in their essential structure, the absence in our experience—and thus in our stories—of a deep sense of place is reflected in the facility with which we recognize each other as fellow joggers, book-club members, or health-food "freaks." Shared patterns of consumer taste link us in a vaguely friendly blur of familiarity, while the deeper-lying differences among us, as well as the profounder reaches of common experience, are excluded from many of our encounters. Yet, though autobiographical reflection and memory may suffer from the effects of rapid mobility, homogenized experience and the attrition of traditional structures of home and family, these very conditions intensify our interest in personal history. I need to evoke the past in each of its settings—to re-view myself in a succession of cultural and physical contexts—in order to meet the threat of shallowness or excessive immediacy in the present. The reduced or "immediate" self of the person who conveys little sense of roots in the past—whose self-presentation, for example, more resembles a curriculum vitae than a richly furnished story—bears comparison with the "one-dimensional," "other-directed," or "narcissistic" personalities various commentators have seen as characteristic of our culture. Such "anti-autobiographical" models are of course ideal types, for no human life is as bereft of relationship to the personal and collective past as pessimistic culture critics often suggest; and precisely autobiographical memory serves as an antidote to such self-reduction, making present again layers of past life that have receded for lack of articulation or a mnemonic structure of association.

The personal past can indeed be known again, often with a sweetness and fullness it lacked the first time around, but it must be drawn patiently out of the neglect into which the wash of preemptive practical concerns sweeps it. Even when not wholly neglected, it may have been buried under a clichéd set of tag-memories or covered by a slick pattern of familiarity. The work of recovery—the cultivation of reveries upon the past—counters the dominance of sheer change, which is our shibboleth and, ultimately, our bugaboo. Meditation on that resultant loss of the past has produced the best of nineteenth- and twentieth-century autobiography, an anxiety-ridden genre which reflects our dual quest for stability and renewal. Its finest modern exemplars are responses to the experience of uprooting and displacement, attempts to anchor our loose, fluid identities, so susceptible of moulding by the shifting peer groups and environments through which we restlessly move.

In much modern literature, in fiction fully as much as in autobiography, the pointed hunger to recapture the past as an act central to one's search for identity testifies to the trauma of disconnection from our points of origin. Deprived of the simpler givens of social and cultural identity more familiar to earlier ages and cultures, we suffer from extreme individuation unsupported by the guiding ethos of tribe or locale. As we find our lives bound to a linear progression through secularized, non-teleological time, we revolt, as Mircea Eliade has suggested in *Cosmos and History,* against the spectacle of personal and collective history endlessly unfolding forward. Our autobiographical need to re-create the past thus invokes the myth of eternal return, for simple movement through worldly time, bereft of any final judgment or prospect of paradise, is too harsh a prospect for most. If we cannot have eternity, we may at least achieve the next best thing by recasting our lives in the order of art, where truth may be clearer and meaning more complete than anywhere else in our experience.

Central to this process is the celebration of the revered places which have formed the person. Such re-creation is actually coextensive with the power of memory, rooting it in the stability of spatial order. As Maurice Halbwachs has noted:

Feelings and reflection, like all other events have to be resituated in some place where I have resided or passed by and which is still in existence. Let us endeavor to go back further. When we reach that period when we are unable to represent places to ourselves, even in a confused manner, we have arrived at the regions of our past inaccessible to memory. That we remember only by transporting ourselves outside space is therefore incorrect. Indeed, quite the contrary, it is the spatial image alone that, by reason of its stability, gives us an illusion of not having changed through time and of retrieving the past in the present. But that's how memory is defined. Space alone is stable enough to endure without growing old or losing any of its parts.[4]

The house I lived in as a child of ten may be demolished, and hence preserved only in my mental image of its rooms and surroundings. That degree of change I can assimilate, though often with difficulty: but if the entire neighborhood and even the surrounding landscape itself have been radically altered or destroyed, I may suffer a kind of amnesia about that phase of my life, or indulge in free-ranging fantasy in lieu of accurate recall. Grounded as even our highest mental life is in bodily placement and sensory apprehension of the physical world, we can neither think nor remember without reference to physical contexts. If, for example, I wish to recall the years of my earlier life spent in Chile two decades ago, I begin by invoking images of the apartments I rented in Santiago, the parks and boulevards where I strolled, and the restaurants where I ate. Similarly, I recall the assassination of John F. Kennedy in close conjunction with images of the Chilean coffee shop where I was sitting when the ominous and still confused news from Dallas was first bruited about. My initial sense of the significance of his death will always be fused with remembered images of anxious Chilean faces clustered in that little café.

Besides needing to reimagine the landscapes and locales of our history, we literally carry much of the past with us as we move from one place to another. My library, for example, not only defines the topography of my intellectual concerns over the years, but recalls to me the many cities and bookshops in which I purchased its thousands of volumes. The furniture around me, much of it passed on by my and my wife's families, also bespeaks earlier places of residence, patterns of taste, and family rhythms and rituals. Articles of clothing, sets of dishes and glassware, wedding gifts, paintings, photographs, tool chests, and mementoes of earlier travels all carry the potential of stirring memory and structuring autobiographical recall. Yet even the most emotionally loaded items—photograph albums, say, or precious heirlooms—often fail to prompt the past into lively presence, just as a literal return to a favorite childhood spot may be less meaningful than the recreation of that place in memory. We have all had the expectation of great insights and profound emotions upon returning to the beloved house, neighborhood or landscape, charged, through years of memory-work, with symbolic power. Sometimes, doubtless, the return is deeply affecting, but more often we find ourselves unable to re-create the emotion-charged perspective of other years. The surest way back, then, is through the wiles of art. Joyce, separated by clever choice from Dublin at the outset of his adult life, wove the sense of his native city intricately through almost every line he wrote. Mann's *Buddenbrooks,* too, is steeped in the atmosphere of the author's native Lubeck; Rilke's work is imbued with the presence of Prague, Paris, Rome, and the Duino castle on the Adriatic; Buenos Aires looms in much of Borges's poetry and prose; old Frankfurt permeates Goethe's *Dichtung und Wahrheit;* and the counterposed cities of Boston and Ávila establish the dialectic within which George Santayana traced his dual sense of identity in a three-volume autobiography.

In "The Brown Wasps," Eiseley's contrast between the needs of insects to return to destroyed nests and man's need to make symbolic order of physical space suggests that humans have built their worlds of memory and imagination from a highly evolved form of the animal's sense of territoriality. While migratory birds and herd animals cover hundreds or thousands of miles in cycles of departure and return, humans echo that impulse in their far more complex efforts to define the meaning of "home." Our highly developed sense of native realm—doubtless a fusion of culture and instinct—may well be founded in infantile recognition of object permanence. As babies, we learn that the mother who has just disappeared into the other room is actually there and will return: she has not ceased to be simply by virtue of her physical absence. Grasping this lesson, little children prepare themselves to build an entire symbolic universe in thought. Their later ability to create art, tell stories, or fictionalize their own experience will partake of the powers fostered in that crucial early stage wherein they establish a new cognitive relationship to the physical world, learning that absent persons and things may be invoked through the power of language and visual imagery.

But if we gradually succeed in carrying an ever more extensive personal universe in our heads, our psychic growth keeps roots in some tangible and localized ground. Young persons who early learn to trust the relative permanence of key persons and places around them nonetheless retain a strong "conservative" desire to have things remain in their appointed places. After mastering the familiar territories of their room, neighborhood, or town, they are reluctant to see their bedroom furniture radically changed, or the fields and woods down the street broken by bulldozers for the construction of new homes. As adults they may carry into later life something of this same concern that things once known remain in their original setting. In myth and religious ritual, the adult expresses the need to give or restore order to the cosmos which children enact in their passion for ritualized games, stories, jokes, and play. Yet, always, in youth and older age, the passion to design an ordered world depends, like that of Eiseley's wasps, upon renewed connection with the physically familiar. Symbolic animals though humans be, they still yearn with their animal "cousins" for the very smell and feel of home.

As adults grow older and likely move away from earlier dwelling places, they need to know tacitly that they are still there, providing connection with a meaningful past which includes the assurance of a continuous world of culture and tradition. The verifiable, continued existence, say, of one's birthplace and hometown, along with the familiar streets and haunts of childhood, serves metonymously to confirm one's link to an earlier life. The life of one's youth is authenticated, we might say, by the mute witness of the things among which it took place. Halbwachs observes:

> Auguste Comte remarked that mental equilibrium was, first and foremost, due to the fact that the physical objects of our daily contact change little or not at all, providing us with an image of permanence and stability. They give us a feeling of order and tranquility, like a silent and immobile society unconcerned with our own restlessness and changes of mood. In truth, much mental illness is accompanied by a breakdown of contact between thought and things, as it were, an inability to recognize familiar objects, so that the victim finds himself in a fluid and strange environment totally lacking familiar reference points. So true is it that our habitual images of the external world are inseparable from our self that this breakdown is not limited to the mentally ill. We ourselves may experience a similar period of uncertainty, as if we had left behind our whole personality, when we are obliged to move to novel surroundings and have not yet adapted to them.[5]

This hunger for placement may extend beyond the immediate settings of neighborhood or hometown to encompass an entire state or region. It may even include our efforts to stitch together far-flung wanderings across the globe, or, in very recent times, to see our existence on earth as a "local" history taking place in a corner of the apparently empty universe. A recent photograph of the earth viewed from a space satellite showed me the curve of continents blurred by overlying clouds and the sweep of starry dark beyond the rim of the globe. In this perspective, the central valley of Chile was always, in sidereal terms, only a step away from my childhood home in Rhode Island, vaguely localizable in the photograph by reference to the outward curve of New England and Cape Cod in the northeasterly reaches of North America. Conceived in cosmic terms, my *Wanderjahren* in *finis terrae,* thousands of miles from familiar terrain, actually took place in a neighboring precinct of this temperate, sheltering earth. I can see that the drama of distant removal from native realm happened upon what now appears a little stage. However much mortals trek about this planet, we now know as never before that our odysseys are but modest ventures on a soil incomparably more hospitable to us than the great stretches of interstellar emptiness. The scale of the traumatic journey from home has expanded radically. Where one once felt lost and nostalgic after crossing the neighboring hills, or even bordering oceans and continents, it is now the voyage into outer space which chills our marrow. Still, our heartstrings need intimate anchoring in more immediate local space, and the new cosmic perspective, graphically available to us in an unprecedented way, might even cause each of us to cleave all the more passionately to his dear bit of this rare green globe.

Sitting this morning at a worktable in central New Jersey, where I am merely a weekend visitor, I spin the desk globe before me to rehearse, as one would say a rosary, the touchpoints of my travels. Tracing lines between the various cities, I muse over their distance from each other. New names confuse me ("Sri Lanka" for old "Ceylon"), until I notice the earlier appellation in parentheses below. Closing my eyes, I can recite backward over the years the names that mark my travels, recalling each place in order and remembering the physical approaches to and departures from them. If I imagine that I shall never have the time or opportunity to return to certain of them, I am saddened. Certain places begin to seem recessive or moribund in my experience. In most cases, I imagine that I will in fact find the occasion to return. But, what then? Must I go back every few years to each of the places I have ever known? The process entails an infinite regress, impossible to imagine as I proceed to know new places all the time. There must inevitably be a growing number of them never to be seen again. Fortunately, we need not actually return to the very place itself, since a new setting will often reconnect us with old familiar ones long behind or deep within us. Thus, in New Mexico the dusty brown churchyard enclosed by a eucalyptus grove and overlooking fields of corn stretching toward bare, rocky mountains returned me instantly to many similar settings I had known years before in Spain, Mexico, Argentina, and Chile. It was not exactly like any of the others, but it shared with them all some common essence and certain roughly comparable features.

A ramble under the arching trees there in Chimayo triggered a flow of memory which made present the forgotten weeks and years lived in the kindred landscapes of other lands. They had dropped from active memory because our capacity to bear simultaneously in mind multiple realities is rather limited. Yet, in happy moments we transcend this limitation: the New Mexico churchyard restored the lost places, however briefly, in the first moment I knew it.

Similar to that case is our discovery of meaning in many areas of life. When I read a new book and encounter familiar lines of reasoning or clusters of imagery, my entire "web" of associations with other books, to which I shall probably never return, is set in vibration. The new experience of reading becomes a kind of allusive rereading of past texts. These, in turn, shed light on the present reading. Here one discovers that the way forward and the way back are one and the same. Analogously, autobiography is not simply a process of tracing our way from the present back into the past, or from the past forward, but rather a frame of order which places past and present into dialectic relation with each other.

Of all the touchpoints we find in our world-wandering, whether of face or place, inscription or ritual or familiar sound, some stand out above others as the "hot points" of our affective life. Some, that is, become sacred, while others remain profane. The key symbolic places, precincts of charged meaning we will never forget, become the spinal column of our autobiographical structure. But, unlike the shrine marking the epiphany of a deity, they are sacred only to individual memory. For me, there is a short section of the Atlantic coast in southern Rhode Island, a stretch of beach that looks toward Block Island, ten miles south in mid-ocean. As I write these lines this summer day, I have, as in other summers, returned to this bit of littoral laminated with intimate memories. I first knew it as a child 35 years ago, staying with my family in a tiny summer cottage on the beach. Both recalling and actually visiting the spot bring the unfolding of previously unplumbed layers of memory. I return, now and *in illo tempore,* to the long sweep of beach and dune and breakwater. Sheltered by the curve of coast and the semi-circular rock barrier enclosing the entrance to their harbors lie the twin fishing villages of Galilee and Jerusalem. Today, fishing boats, pleasure craft, and offshore ferries make their way in and out of the passage to open ocean exactly as they did decades before. I see my little brother, as then, suddenly appear, running to the top of the dune covered with coarse beach grass behind our box of a cottage with the flat sundeck roof. He dashes out several times daily at the sound of the whistle from the lumbering passenger ferry bound to or from Block Island, racing to his vantage point to salute the old steamer's passage.

64

Through the stream of August days, fog and sun and seawind, we amble or race or play ball along the edge of the water. Atlantic storms sometimes push great breakers onto these shores. Then, when water is dull red and dark purple with churning masses of seaweed, and the waves mount in ominous silence above us before their effervescent collapse, my brothers and I plunge and sport like dolphins, riding the rollers to shore, letting ourselves be tossed and bounced off the bottom before we are carried, quick flotsam, onto the beach. Some clear August mornings we entertain ourselves beachcombing or walking to the end of the breakwater, picking our way over massive blocks of granite tumbled into the sea. Later, we dally at the dock by the fish market to watch lobsters harvested from the "pots," whose bright buoys bob all along the rocks. Under the dock, children's eyes descry the eerie spider crab, the blue crab, starfish, and jellyfish and a profusion of empty shells in the muck. To this same cottage and shoreline I have returned, decades later, with my own family. Now my present life with them is buoyed up for me by the momentum it receives from living, many-layered memory.

The pursuit of personal history entails such recreation of the emotional as well as the physical space in which a period of life was lived. Invoking the affective perspective, with its record of attention and disattention, attraction and repulsion, one conjures up the aura surrounding that space, the poetic penumbra bestowed upon it by imagination. The memory of a cozy bed next to a window with a pleasant outlook may stir a rich cluster of associated moods and images out of the past; and the cue provided by the key spatial image often initiates a narrative line, or a series of narrative fragments, that further orders our recovery of the past. By remembering, for example, where we have been most comfortable or felt most sheltered, or by recapturing an especially beloved countryside or landscape, we elaborate and distill our particular patterns of taste and perception. These lines of memory begin, usually, in highly specific, even ritualized "bits" of remembrance: by stumbling, apparently at random, upon the memory of a windy winter evening when I hiked from the Spanish village of El Escorial, the site of Philip II's great monastery-mausoleum, to a much tinier village along the road to Ávila, I start to recapture the romantic mood that governed my wanderings during a year of study in Spain. A sickle moon was in the sky of fading light, a sharp wind whipped groves of roadside poplars, the road itself almost empty of traffic. I found my way in advancing dark to the cozy fire of a family that rented a guest room to occasional travelers. On yet another winter night in another village, near Guadalajara, I slept in the garret-like room of an old widow with whom I had shared a frugal supper and a crackling fire of dry twigs and branches at an open hearth. We talked over tea of her memories of the Spanish Civil War and of her long-dead husband, a veteran of the struggle. That night I slept soundly under two comforters in an ice-cold room at the top of the stairs. I think that room, that house, and that old woman are a variation on the arch-memory of summer nights spent at my grandmother's summer house in southern Rhode Island, looking out over stone walls and pastures to the Atlantic. By connecting these memories of widely separated times and places, I sketch in my personal map of comfortable settlement in the world.

Apparently discrete and isolated memories are bound into clusters by personal patterns of meaningful association. With such patterns, I build up over years the profile and the ultimately ineffable mark of "my life." On my cognitive map, for example, the name "Antonio Machado" often recalls a capacious, huge-windowed old classroom at Pembroke College in Providence, where, as a senior at Brown University, I took a class in "Modes of Literature." The professor was an elegant, learned Spanish emigré, who wrote on the board one day the Spanish name for which I had no reference. I recall this now, I suppose, because I have just invoked the Castilian villages and linked them tenuously with the sensibility of childhood. Now, thinking of that heady class in Pembroke Hall, and of my first acquaintance with the name of one of the greatest Spanish poets, I trace in further detail my mnemonic map, defining more closely a developing sensibility eager for poetic knowledge of the world. The connections may seem obvious enough in retrospect: the first memories were of the open roads of Spain and the wayside villages which sheltered the dreamy wanderer; the second were of my Spanish mentor. The common denominator would seem to be Spain; but the additional recall of Machado provides a further link, for he was the great poet of the beautifully barren open stretches of Castile and of its dusty, poplar-lined roadways, the poet I read most during that winter of walking the villages.

Were I to take this nucleus of radiating memories further, I would explore the relation of poets to the landscapes they sing, the affinity I felt for Hispanic culture, the open road as a theme in literature and in my life, and even the simple appeal of an old sampler that hung on my grandmother's wall: "Let me live in a house by the side of the road and be a friend to man." I do not know where these vaguely associated themes end. Perhaps I would also develop a list of all the beds and bedrooms in which I have spent comfortable nights, a kind of history of my waking and sleeping. Such a web of allusive memory, comprehending disparate moments, settings and texts, brings meaning to apparently unconnected experiences, converting the maze of existence into coherent autobiographical territory. Mnemosyne, mother of the muses, presides over the transmutation of life into art. Working metaphorically and metonymously, autobiography becomes a form of heightened, integrated reflection upon selected facets of one's past. In the words of one psychologist,

> Memory is attention which endures, which envisions both backwards and forwards, which can shine upon deep recesses filled and perhaps half-forgotten long ago; it is made up of intuitions as well as representations, feelings perhaps but faintly perceived, odors, sights, sounds, hesitancies, judgments— all the thoughts that go into the making up of mind. . . . What we call memory is a vast process, billions of acts of attention. . . . The great act of attention is all-inclusive; the more of a life that is remembered and brought to bear upon the present moment in living expression, the higher the grade of being.[6]

Selecting certain past odors, sounds, sights and images for prolonged attention, creative memory illumines and elaborates the crucial way stations of our lives. In some such fashion, every human being possesses an affective map of the settings that have most nourished and shaped him. From innumerable instances, we may choose for illustration the Scots poet Edwin Muir's story, exemplary both in its blend of unique record and universal meaning, and in its feeling for the vibrant fragment as much as the ordered pattern of memory. In the opening two chapters of *An Autobiography,* he re-creates his Orkney Island childhood, from which he was abruptly severed as if from Paradise itself. In the subsequent account of his odyssey through major cities of the world (London, Prague, Dresden, Rome, etc.), he traces a spiritual and geographical journey representatively modern in its chronicle of dislocation and wandering. In a tone characteristic of his generation, Muir bears witness to a time of vast cultural and political change. Born on the Isle of Wyre in 1887, he lived through the two World Wars (in neither of which he fought), and died in 1959. His autobiography falls into two parts, "The Story and the Fable," published in 1940, and the longer *An Autobiography,* published in 1954. The elapsed time between these two accounts is treated succinctly in the chapter "Interval":

> The generation to which I belong has survived an age, and the part of our lives which is still immobilized there is like a sentence broken off before it could be completed; the future in which it would have written its last word was snatched away and a raw new present abruptly substituted; and that present is reluctant now to formulate its own sentence, from the fear that what it has to say will in turn be cut short by yet another raw present.[7]

Muir's account is organized in terms of place names, moving from Wyre to the town of Garth on a neighboring island, then to the big world in Glasgow and London. (The story moves through widening concentric circles of travel and experience.) In the twenties he goes abroad to Prague, later lives in several other European cities, and becomes director of the British Institute in Rome a few years before his death. Much like him, a number of restless British literary travelers between the two wars, driven by an urge to escape the confines of their native island culture, produced a remarkable body of autobiographical travel literature. Cosmopolitan in spirit, they transcended the narrower, more pragmatic colonialist spirit which had lured many of their countrymen abroad in an earlier day. Like many of these writers (Greene, Lawrence, Huxley, Durrell, Waugh, Norman Douglas, Robert Byron, et al.), Muir made travel and the sense of place central to rumination on the meaning of his life. Yet—also like many of the others—he was not writing a travel book in the usual sense, for his journeys were, more clearly than for many of his peers, the outward form of a soul's development, the story of education and self-discovery—a kind of *Bildungsautobiographie*.

In leaving the Orkneys and the ways of his father and ancestors behind, Muir enacted the classic modern journey away from a surer, simpler identity toward what could only be an approximate, unfinished sense of self. Gradually and partially, with great frustration, he gained self-knowledge on the road. Very major aspects of his sensibility came clear only relatively late in his life. Advancing by fits and starts, he groped his way on a kind of circular quest, for he eventually returned to Scotland in old age as Warden of Newbattle Abbey College. But his life was, in another sense, a one-way movement into a destiny he only vaguely divined, even at the end of his testament:

> Some kind of development, I suppose, should be expected to emerge, but I am very doubtful of such things, for I cannot bring life into a neat pattern. If there is a development in my life—and that seems an idle supposition—then it has been brought about more by things outside than by any conscious intention of my own.[8]

The idea that a pattern of development might be an "idle supposition" is a radical one too little invoked by autobiographers, who generally need a central metaphor in order to complete their tales. But, facing his mysterious and fragmented life, Muir refused teleological movement, admitting that memory eluded and betrayed him. Writing of a season spent thirty years earlier in the Austrian alps, he remarks:

Time wakens a longing more poignant than all the longings caused by the division of lovers in space, for there is no road back into its country. Our bodies were not made for that journey; only the imagination can venture upon it; and the setting out, the road, and the arrival: all is imagination. We long most for the places in time where we were happy. . . . Yet our memories of a place, no matter how fond we were of it, are little more than a confusion of lights on a ground of maternal darkness. I remember the Sonntagberg by a sudden rush of spring flowers, a silver thread of water on a mountainside in sunset light, and only then to be seen, a patch of turf so quiet and clean that the light seemed to be more still there, a peasant woman shearing a sheep which she held affectionately on her knee, kissing its nose now and then to comfort it, and two snakes fighting so furiously in the middle of a mountain stream that they were swept, still fighting, over a cataract.[9]

These luminous fragments are the *signa* of his identity. However broken and jumbled they may appear, they illumine the core of his sensibility. With them, he takes into himself the essence of that lyrical spring and summer decades before.

The imaginatively transformed image cannot, finally, restore the key places to us or return us to them. As Muir notes, "our memories are real in a different way from the real things they try to resuscitate."[10] In dreams, imagination and the creation of art, they take on talismanic power, working toward the deeper end of psychic integration. Such memories become our means of deciphering and constructing a sense of identity: I am the person who remembers this moment, view, encounter or place, and who binds them all together in a unique whole; no one else remembers exactly what I do of a certain city in a certain year; I cannot know why I summon up or am invaded by particular memories, but I can keep an attentive vigil over their passage through my mind. Reflecting similarly on the occasions for poetry, Robert Penn Warren begins his "Minneapolis Story,"

Whatever pops into your head, and whitely
Breaks surface on the dark stream that is you,

May do to make a poem—for every accident
Yearns to be more than itself, yearns,

In the way you dumbly do, to participate
In the world's blind groping rage toward Truth. . . .

The truth he invokes might be understood as the light shed upon human destiny as a whole by the intentions and dreams of individual lives as mirrored in autobiography. And just as Warren's poem goes on to develop a highly particular place in the rest of the poem—a snowy pre-Christmas evening near Hennepin Avenue in Minneapolis "long years ago"—so each tracing of our destinies is done on some slate of the world's surface. There, among the objects, structures, and sites of our resolutely physical embeddedness in this life, we find and create the objective correlatives of our life's hidden course.

Notes

1. Quoted in Stanislaw Baranczak's review of *Unattainable Earth*, in the *New York Times Book Review*, July 6, 1986, p. 9
2. "Where the World Began," in Arthur M. Eastman et al., eds, *The Norton Reader*, fifth edition (New York: Norton, 1980), 11.
3. Laurence, 14.
4. *The Collective Memory*, trans. Francis J. Ditter and Vida Yazdi Ditter (New York: Harper and Row, 1980), 157.
5. Halbwachs, 128.
6. Frank Barron, "Diffusion, Integration, and Enduring Attention in the Creative Process," in Robert W. White, ed., *The Study of Lives: Essays on Personality in Honor of Henry A. Murray* (Chicago: Atherton Press, 1963), 236.
7. *An Autobiography* (New York: Seabury Press, 1968), 194.
8. Muir, 280.
9. Muir, 224.
10. Muir, 225.

Part Three

History, Criticism, and Appreciation

The Emergence of the Essay and the Idea of Discovery

Michael L. Hall

Perhaps my title should have been, "The Idea of Discovery and the Emergence of the Essay." But I hope the order on which I have settled will reflect the proper emphasis in the discussion that follows. This is, after all, an essay on the emergence of the "essay" as a new genre. But in other respects the question of emphasis is less important. Both the emerging "essay" and the "idea" of discovery are associated with something taking place throughout Europe in the sixteenth and seventeenth centuries: an awakening to the impact of Renaissance discoveries, particularly in the observational sciences of astronomy and geography. My thesis, simply stated, is that the essays of Michel de Montaigne and Francis Bacon as well as later examples by John Donne and Sir Thomas Browne—different as they are in their formal qualities—exhibit not only similar rhetorical strategies but also a common attitude, a spirit of exploration; that in certain important respects the essay emerged in the late sixteenth and early seventeenth centuries as a product of the Renaissance "idea" of discovery and in response to it.

But the "idea" of discovery is not the same thing as discovery itself. We have heard it said, for example, that in 1492 Columbus discovered America, but the event was not as simple as that statement suggests. We generally do not find something unless we have some "idea" of what we are looking for. Columbus was looking for a new trade route to the East, not a new world. It took other voyages and the insights of other explorers such as Amerigo Vespucci before the knowledge began to form and sink into the European consciousness that Columbus had found a "new world." And if we think for a moment, perhaps we can begin to com-

73

prehend with Edmundo O'Gorman the impact that this "discovery" must have had on European thought and on received notions not only about geography but about other kinds of knowledge as well.

Similarly, Copernicus did not immediately address the profound religious and cosmological implications of his hypothesis that the earth was not stationary but revolved around the sun. What he hoped to establish was a simpler (and certainly more aesthetically and mathematically pleasing) way of accounting for astronomical phenomena by taking the sun as the center around which the earth and the planets revolved. Only many years later (after contributions by others such as Kepler and Galileo) would astronomers regularly assume that the Copernican theory correctly represented the movement of the planets. Throughout the seventeenth century, laymen and philosophers alike disputed the mounting scientific evidence, and poets such as Donne and Milton seem to have had it both ways.

We should begin by recalling the familiar commonplace that the Renaissance was an age of discovery and invention—an age marked by the appearance of such new things as the mariner's compass, printing, the telescope, new lands, and new stars as well as by the recovery of much of the wisdom of the past, the restoration of lost languages, and the editing and dissemination of lost texts. A few key dates may be helpful. In addition to Columbus's voyage of 1492, we should remember that Gutenberg's Bible was published sometime after 1454, that Luther's ninety-five theses were nailed to a church door in 1517, and that Copernicus's *De Revolutionibus Orbium Coelestium* appeared in 1543. The full impact of these events, and of many other similar ones that accompanied them, was still being felt throughout the sixteenth century and well into the seventeenth. Not until 1580 did Francis Drake become the first Englishman to circumnavigate the world, and not until 1610 did Galileo publish his *Siderius Nuncius*, with its revelations of mountains and craters on the moon and spots that moved across the face of the changeless sun.

Even so, within a relatively brief span of time, the ancient model of an ordered universe, which for centuries had seemed unassailable, was challenged and overthrown by Renaissance astronomers; the face of the earth itself was altered by Renaissance voyages. Nor was this spirit of discovery limited to the sciences alone, to knowledge of earth and stars. In the late sixteenth and early seventeenth centuries, it manifested itself as a new mode of thought and discourse. Essayists as diverse as Montaigne and Bacon, or Donne and Browne, turned their attention to the examination of received opinions, to a search for inward truths as well as outward. The

74

new discoveries in geography and astronomy required rethinking the past and reexamining old assumptions about the earth and the heavens, but they also made necessary a reassessment of the place of men (and women) in the new conception of the universe that was beginning to emerge from the ruins of the older order. Renaissance writers sometimes looked backward as well as forward. Discovery and recovery were often intertwined as philosophers and poets tried to put their world back together, to reestablish relation and coherence. When we turn to the literature of the Renaissance and seventeenth century, we detect something more than excitement over specific discoveries or inventions; we find a growing sense of discovery as an "idea" influencing a wide range of Renaissance thought and expression: from Thomas More's utopian vision to Francis Bacon's scientific method and, finally, to the emergence of the essay, a new genre written in a new style of prose.

II

One of the more unsettling and at the same time thought-generating discoveries was the New World. America, even before it was clearly recognized as a new world, captured the imagination of the Renaissance not simply with promises of wealth and empire, though these were strong inducements to exploration and settlement, but also with visions of the golden age and the earthly paradise. We can see this association even in the first letter of Columbus describing what he saw on his first voyage. He marveled that in the month of November trees were "as green and lovely as they are in Spain in May." And he continued, "the people of this island, and all the other islands which I have found and of which I have information, all go naked, men and women, as their mothers bore them" (Jones 14–15). These inhabitants appear to Columbus totally innocent and guileless. Clearly, ideas both of the biblical paradise and of the classical golden age came to mind as he searched for familiar formulas to convey impressions of the tropical regions and native populations he encountered on his voyage.

Because of the association between the New World and paradise or the golden age, the discovery of America had a profound effect on Renaissance thought. Early accounts of the newfound land in Hakluyt's *Principal Navigations, Voyages, and Discoveries of the English Nation* and in Sir Walter Raleigh's *History of the World* abounded with references to "the golden age" and "the Paradise of Eden" (Hakluyt 8:305;

Raleigh 46). The New World became an embodiment of an ancient ideal of human perfection. Montaigne's remarks in his essay "Of the Caniballes" are perhaps the clearest evidence of what I am suggesting. With his usual penetration and overstatement, Montaigne observes that the discovery of the New World has made the speculations of philosophers and poets obsolete: "For me seemeth that what in those nations we see by experience, doth not only exceed all the pictures wherewith licentious poesie hath proudly imbellished the golden age, and all her quaint inventions to faine a happy condition of man, but also the conception and desire of Philosophy. They could not imagine a genuitie so pure and simple, as we see it by experience; nor ever beleeve our societie might be maintained with so little art and humane combination" (1, 30, 164).

The method of Sir Thomas More's *Utopia* (1516) had already, to some extent, supported Montaigne. The fictions with which More constructed his humanist fantasy rely heavily on details which link *Utopia* to the literature of discovery as much as to the dialogues of Plato. Raphael Hythloday, we recall, is a Portugese navigator who has sailed with no less an explorer than Amerigo Vespucci himself. But the sense of the New World as an ideal vision is even stronger in Francis Bacon's *New Atlantis* (1627), written some 100 years after More's *Utopia*. Though the *New Atlantis* too is an island discovered by European voyagers, Bacon's fantasy world is very different from More's humanistic vision. The *New Atlantis* is more than a Utopia; it offers a glimpse of the kind of future which Bacon and his followers imagined—a world transformed by the discoveries of science and technology rather than by humanism.

III

We come, then, to the new philosophy. Bacon connects the New World and new sciences not only in *New Atlantis* but elsewhere. His essay "Of Plantations," for example, presents a practical program for planting colonies and for systematically exploiting the new American lands. And in his *Novum Organum*, which displayed on its title page an engraving of a galleon sailing through the pillars of Hercules (the limits of the ancient world), Bacon remarks: "We must, therefore, disclose and prefix our reasons for not thinking the hope of success improbable, as Columbus, before his wonderful voyage over the Atlantic, gave reasons of his conviction that new lands and continents might be discovered besides those already known; and these reasons, though at first rejected, were yet proved by subsequent experience and were the causes and beginnings of the greatest events" (*Novum* 1, 92). There is a similar use of the image of discovery in the concluding remarks to the *Advancement of Learning*. There Bacon observes; "Thus have I made as it were a small globe of the intellectual world, as truly and as faithfully as I could discover; with a note and description of those parts which seem to me not constantly occupate, or not well converted by the labour of men" (*Works* 3:490).

In these examples Bacon invokes the image of the voyage of discovery to describe scientific exploration; the "small globe of the intellectual world" resembles the larger globe then being mapped by Renaissance voyagers. Of course, not every Renaissance author was as optimistic as Bacon. For some the new discoveries, particularly in astronomy, were disturbing, as John Donne's well-known comments in the *First Anniversarie* attest:

> And new Philosophy cals all in doubt,
>   The Element of fire is quite put out;
>   The Sunne is lost, and th'earth, and no mans wit
>   Can well direct him, where to looke for it. . . .
>   Tis all in pieces, all cohaerence gone;
> All iust supply, and all Relation.
>   [P.73, 11. 205–14]

The new philosophy, more than the New World, offered a serious challenge to the Renaissance worldview. The new stars sighted by Tycho Brahe and Johann Kepler, the new cosmology of Copernicus, Kepler, and Galileo, destroyed more than the authority of Aristotle; they undermined the very nature of Renaissance science and religion. After Copernicus, and certainly after Kepler and Galileo, Renaissance scientists were no longer satisfied merely with "saving the phenomena" within traditional patterns of explanation: they were ready to alter the patterns themselves in light of new discoveries.

In fact, the idea of discovery looms large in Bacon's description of his new method of science. The new induction, as he called it, was intended to supplant the tautologous system of Aristotle and the scholastics, with its reliance on the logic of the syllogism, and to break away from the dominion of classical authority. Bacon proposed, instead, a mode of invention grounded in experience rather than argument. In the *Novum Organum* his indictment of the old philosophy is succinctly stated: "Even the effects already discovered are due to chance and experiment, rather than to the sciences; for our present sciences are nothing more than peculiar arrangements of matters already discovered, and not methods for discovery or plans for new operations" (1, 8). In a later aphorism he continues: "The present system of logic rather assists in confirming and

rendering inveterate the errors founded on vulgar notions than in searching after truth, and is therefore more hurtful than useful" (1, 12).

I am suggesting that the discoveries of the New World and the new stars
and all of the other new things which seemed to be coming to light in the
sixteenth and seventeenth centuries helped inform an idea of discovery
which obtained not only in the sciences but in other areas of knowledge as
well. Truth in any realm is no longer something acquired by assimilating
received views but something which one must seek out for oneself and
experience, like an explorer charting new lands. The key word in this
discussion, it seems to me, is "experience," and it applies to inward journeys of self-discovery as well as to the ventures of outward-bound exploration. In his essay "Of Experience," Montaigne asserts, "I study my selfe
more than any other subject. It is my supernaturall Metaphisike, it is my
naturall Philosophy," and goes on to add, "Out of the experience I have of
my selfe, I finde sufficient ground to make my selfe wise, were I but a
good proficient scholler" (3, 13, 970–71). In the face of conflicting claims
and uncertainty about the nature of human knowledge, there is a tendency among Renaissance and seventeenth-century authors to look inward, to explore the interior landscape, to seek paradise within, to move
in true Renaissance fashion from macrocosm to microcosm. One thinks
of Donne's remark in his *Devotions upon Emergent Occasions:* "Stil
when we return to that Meditation, that *Man is a World,* we find new *discoveries*" (Meditation 8, 40).

IV

If the main lines of this discussion seem clear, let me sketch in more clearly the links between the idea of discovery and the emergence of the essay
during this same period as a distinct, new prose genre. It was surely no
accident that this new genre, this new mode of inquiry, along with a new
style of prose, should appear at this particular moment in European history. In an age fascinated by the implications of the new philosophy and
the discovery of the New World, the essay provided a kind of prose composition particularly suited to the examination of conventional wisdom,
the exploration of received opinion, and the discovery of new ideas and
insights—a kind of written discourse which allowed the author to think
freely outside the constraints of established authority and traditional rhetorical forms. We may also find the same idea in the background of the
revolution in prose style which occurred in the late sixteenth and early

seventeenth centuries, when Ciceronianism, long associated with the discredited doctrines of the old philosophy, was overthrown by writers such as Montaigne and Bacon, who sought a rhetorical style which would portray in language, as Montaigne put it, "the progress of my humours, that every part be seene or member distinguished, as it was produced" (680).

Montaigne, who published his first book of *Essais* in 1580, tells us explicitly what he perceives to be the essential qualities of his new kind of prose composition, a genre which represents a definite break with the elaborate rhetorical conventions of other forms of writing. Essays, he says, are not supposed to be the products of art or study, but are intended to be spontaneous, tentative, open-ended, and even unfinished. For example, in his essay "Of Friendship," he describes his compositions as "antike workes, and monstrous bodies, patched and hudled up together of divers members, without any certaine or well ordered figure, having neither order dependencie, or proportion, but casuall and framed by chance" (1, 27, 144). The prose style of the essay also suggested tentativeness, openness, and spontaneity. Both in France and in England, the early essayists tended to reject the artificial symmetry of Ciceronian prose, its balanced clauses and studied formality, preferring to portray in language the actual process of the mind seeking truth (Croll 51–101, 167–202; Williamson 11–31). Such a style was ideally suited to the essay, itself a tentative and unstructured exploration of a topic in which matter, according to Montaigne, is more important than words: "It is for words to serve and wait upon matter, and not for matter to attend upon words. . . . I would have the matters to surmount, and so fill the imagination of him that harkneth, that he have no remembrance at all of the words." He then declares his preference for "naturall, simple, and unaffected speech . . . so written as it is spoken, and such upon the paper, as it is in the mouth, a pithie, sinnowie, full, strong, compendious and materiall speech, not so delicate and affected, as vehement and piercing. . . . Rather difficult than tedious, void of affection, free, loose and bold, that every member of it seeme to make a bodie" (1, 25, 134).

The essay, then, was regarded as tentative and spontaneous, written in a style which reflected the movements of the author's mind as he meditated on a subject (Pebworth, "Not Being"). But we should notice other qualities in the new genre. One is the frequent quotation from and allusion to authorities, a generic trait probably related to the practice, so popular among Renaissance humanists, of keeping commonplace books. These collections of favorite passages and familiar quotations from ancient and modern authors were often supplemented with personal observations by the collector and gathered together under topical headings as in Ben Jonson's *Timber; or, Discoveries Made upon Men and Matter,* in which we find headings such as *Fortuna* and *Consilia* and *De bonis et malis.* (It is worth noting that Seneca and Plutarch were among Jonson's favorite ancient authors, as they were for both Montaigne and Bacon.) Another related quality is the subversion of received opinion and even of accepted rational processes of thought, or at least of the deductive process which depends on established authority for its major premises and axioms. In fact, commonplace books often collected conflicting and even contradictory passages from the ancient authorities, a practice which Bacon recommends in his *De Augmentis Scientiarum* and often employs in his essays. Finally, there is the tension between the private, interior world of the essayist meditating on some topic and the public world of his audience or readers, the rhetorical tension between the writer and his book.

V

As I have noted elsewhere, all of these qualities may be clearly observed in the essays of Montaigne ("Drawing"). The many quotations from and allusions to classical authors, along with anecdotes from history and Montaigne's personal experience, are not deployed as proofs or as undisputed authority presented to confirm a single thesis but are assembled as conflicting cases and contradictory evidence. In the essay "Of Sadnesse or Sorrowe," for example, Montaigne begins by declaring himself free of this passion, describing it as a "foolish and base ornament" (1, 2, 6) and agreeing with the Stoics who reject it as base and cowardly. But the examples and quotations which he cites no more support this thesis about the nature of passion than its opposite. He repeats the story of *Psamneticus* (Psammenitus), a king of Egypt who endures the degradation of his daughter and execution of his son without display of emotion but breaks into tears at the sight of "a familiar friend of his haled amongst the captives" (6). Then he recounts the similar case of a prince who receives the news of the death of his elder and younger brothers with "unmatched countenance and exemplar constancie" but is transported when he learns of the death of a servant and abandons himself "to all manner of sorrow and grief" (6–7). From these examples, Montaigne remarks, some have concluded that excess of grief leads to the passionate release of emotions.

But in the case of Psammenitus we have the king's own testimony that he showed his sorrow at the sight of his friend held captive "because this last displeasure may be manifested by weeping, whereas the two former exceed by much, all meanes and compasse to be expressed by teares." Montaigne adds the examples of the painter who portrayed Agamemnon with a veil over his face at the sacrifice of Iphigenia, "as if no countenance were able to represent that degree of sorrow," and of the poets who say that Niobe was changed to stone from excess of grief (7). At the same time, quoting classical authority all the while, he dilutes the impact of these explanations by remarking that love may have a similar effect and, likewise, excess of pleasure and even excess of shame.

We quickly note that Montaigne does not stay close to his topic (sorrow and sadness), nor does he argue a thesis—that he is not subject to this passion. Instead, he explores the topic by presenting examples from lore and literature, but the examples prove nothing and are, in fact, contradictory, open to various interpretations. His conclusion, that he is "little subject to these violent passions" because he hardens his "apprehension" by daily doses of discourse, seems almost a nonsequitur (9). Certainly, it does not follow from his examples, though these may be the method of his physic. Instead, what we encounter when we read Montaigne are what Barry Waller has called "repeated strategies of disorientation" (506–507).

The relationship between the essayist and the reader is an important part of Montaigne's subversive rhetoric. He wants us to feel that we are reading his own private thoughts, presented as they occur to him without the intervention of art or design (see 2, 37, 680). In his preface, "The Author to the Reader," Montaigne expresses the desire to stand "naked" before us: "I desire therein to be delineated in mine owne genuine, simple and ordinarie fashion, without contention, art or study: for it is myself I pourtray." He even goes so far as to suggest that the reader will have no interest in so personal, "so frivolous and vaine a subject" and therefore dismisses us and bids farewell. But we recognize, of course, that all of this is part of Montaigne's rhetorical technique, the same technique which labels the essays themselves as tentative, spontaneous, and open-ended. He hopes to remove the barriers between author and reader, but he also wants us to lower our critical resistance, to forget ourselves for a moment and enter into the private world of the author. The sincerity, the honesty of his observations, like the roughness and openness of his style, must be seen as part of the art which conceals "art or study."

In an often quoted passage from "Of Giving the Lie," Montaigne acknowledges the tension between the private and the public aspects of the essay, between the interior world of a mind meditating and the exterior world of books and readers: "In framing this pourtraite by my selfe, I have so often beene faine to frizle and trimme me, that so I might the better extract my selfe, that the patterne is thereby confirmed, and in some sort formed. Drawing my selfe for others, I have drawne my selfe with purer and better colours, then were my first. I have no more made my booke, then my booke hath made me" (2, 18, 602). The notion that the essay is a record of spontaneous thought, an honest and even artless representation of the essayist thinking to himself, is a rhetorical fiction that Montaigne recognized more openly as he increasingly saw his essays in terms of a book and a reading public. Moreover, the nature of the genre creates this tension between private and public. The act of writing, even without publication, introduces art and rhetoric; as soon as an author commits his private thoughts to paper, they are no longer merely "antike workes" or the play of a mind thinking but literary artifacts with syntax, grammar, and rhetoric directed toward some reading "public," whether that public is limited to the author himself (and possibly to a small circle of intimate friends) or includes the vast unknown audience of readers who may walk in off the street and purchase his book. The introduction of an audience, however defined, implies, even necessitates, rhetorical strategy and posturing. As Montaigne acknowledges, in drawing himself for others he has drawn with "purer and better colours"; he has availed himself of art and rhetoric. But more than that, the act of writing itself has colored not only his words, but also his thoughts, his actions, his being: "I have no more made my booke, then my booke hath made me." He might almost have said, "I have no more influenced my readers, than my readers, through the prospect of my writing to them, have influenced me."

The rhetorical technique of the essay is somewhat dialectical in that it involves both author and reader in an implied dialogue—or at least in heuristic, cooperative exploration of a subject—that leads to moments of revelation though not necessarily to any final synthesis. And the shared experience of author and reader is central to the genre's rhetorical appeal; it is also an important part of all the other qualities we have observed: the tentativeness, openness, and spontaneity; the roughness of style; the reference to authority and persistent questioning of received opinion; the tension between private and public worlds. It is not sufficient to say that the essay is an explorative genre or that it is a form of meditation and discovery through discourse. We must also acknowledge that the essayist marshals rhetorical strategies with the intention of conveying to a reader the experience of personal exploration and discovery.

VI

Francis Bacon's methods were different, but his intentions were similar. In the first book of *Advancement of Learning* (1605), Bacon appears to echo Montaigne: "Here therefore is the first distemper of learning, when men study words and not matter; . . . for words are but the images of matter; and except they have life of reason and invention, to fall in love with them is all one as to fall in love with a picture" (3:284). In the second book he describes the object of his new inductive method: "Knowledge that is delivered as a thread to be spun on, ought to be delivered and intimated [insinuated], if it were possible, *in the same method wherein it was invented:* and so is it possible of knowledge induced" (3:404). He advocates the use of aphorisms, which "cannot be made but of the pith and heart of sciences" and which, "representing a knowledge broken, do invite men to inquire further," abjuring the examples and fluid transitions of connected discourse and presenting dispersed particulars (405).

More than any other seventeenth-century English author, Bacon demonstrates the direct relationship between the new mood of discovery in science and learning and the art of discourse, notably the part played by the new knowledge in the rejection of Ciceronianism and its replacement by an anti-Ciceronian style variously labeled plain, Senecan, or Attic. The new philosophical discourse for which he called was to be one that would imitate in writing not so much *the* process of discovery as *a* process of discovery, carefully re-presented to the reader, allowing the reader to experience the movement of the author's mind and to examine the premises upon which his conclusions are founded. In *Valerius Terminus, of the Interpretation of Nature,* Bacon observes "that . . . it is not a thing so easy as is conceived to convey the conceit of one man's mind into the mind of another without the loss or mistaking, specially in notions new and differing from those that are received. That never any knowledge was delivered in the same order it was invented" (3:248).

Scholars have long known that Bacon's essays, first published in 1597, then expanded and revised in 1612 and 1625, were a part of his scientific program, his Columbian voyage in quest of "new lands and continents," his description of the "small globe of the intellectual world" (see Ronald S. Crane and Stanley E. Fish, for instance). In them he attempts to reach a varied audience with writings on subjects of practical interest. Even essays on themes which from the titles ("Of Truth," "Of Death," "Of Atheism," and so forth) would appear more speculative than practical, Bacon writes in a pragmatic, if not a Machiavellian, manner. His philosophical statements about the nature of truth, for example, are a soft kernel of familiar platitudes surrounded by hard insights.

The essay "Of Truth" begins by describing the attraction of lies: "But it is not only the difficulty and labour which men take in finding out of truth, nor again that when it is found it imposeth upon men's thoughts, that doth bring lies in favor, but a natural though corrupt love of the lie itself" (6:377). Later he adds, "this same truth is a naked and open daylight, that doth not show the masks and mummeries and triumphs of the world, half so stately and daintily as candlelights." Finally he remarks rather cynically: "Truth may perhaps come to the price of a pearl, that showeth best by day; but it will not rise to the price of a diamond or carbuncle, that sheweth best in varied lights. A mixture of a lie doth ever add pleasure" (6:377). After such a beginning, the philosophical tone that follows seems somewhat sanctimonious: "But howsoever these things are thus in men's depraved judgments and affections, yet truth, which only doth judge itself, teacheth that the inquiry of truth, which is the presence of it, and the belief of truth, which is the enjoying of it, is the sovereign good of human nature" (378). But these concessions to philosophy are pale indeed in the glaring daylight of the remarks that issue when Bacon passes from "theological and philosophical truth, to the truth of civil business": "It will be acknowledged, even by those that practice it not, that clear and round dealing is the honour of man's nature; and that mixture of falsehood is like allay in coin of gold and silver; which may make the metal work the better, but it embaseth it" (378). Bacon's image of falsehood as the alloy used in coining gold and silver is interestingly ambiguous. Although the statement ostensibly supports truth over falsehood, the image itself undercuts that support and recalls the usefulness of "allay" which, though it "embaseth" the gold and silver, makes the coin more practical as currency. Rhetorically this assertion hidden in a statement suggesting the general acceptance of the high value placed on "clear and round dealing" casts a shadow of doubt upon those earlier philosophical platitudes. By remarking parenthetically that the truth is valued "even by those that practice it not," Bacon insinuates into the minds of his readers the suggestion that such high talk is the lip service that everyone, even the most corrupt, pays to the good. But there is a further rhetorical objective. Having brought us down to earth, Bacon has made us properly receptive to his final admonitions, which, though high, are also practical: "There is no vice that doth so cover a man with shame as to be found false and perfidious" (378–79). This Bacon knew at first hand, and it is worth noting that he mentions specifically the shame that follows being "*found* false and perfidious" (my emphasis). But further-more, Bacon notes, the judgment of men will be followed by a final judg-ment hereafter. Here he quotes (or at least alludes to) Montaigne's "Of Giving the Lie": "If it be well weighed, to say that a man lieth, is much to say, as that he is brave towards God and a coward towards men." Bacon has shifted from arguing that truth is its own reward to arguing that falsehood can get us into serious trouble, both on earth and later on as well. The second proposition does not exclude the first, but by acknowl-edging, at least through implication, the conflicting values of accepted wisdom, Bacon manages to engage our attention and cause reflection, perhaps even further inquiry. Without ever stating it, the essay puts for-ward yet another platitude: honesty is the best *policy*.

This unstated theme seems hardly accidental. We should recognize that policy, the prudent application of moral knowledge, most concerns Bacon in the *Essays*. His intention is not to discover the nature of truth but to "instruct and suborn action." Writings which instill practical wisdom, "Georgics of the mind," Bacon insists in *The Advancement of Learning,* "are no less worthy than the heroical descriptions of virtue, duty, and felicity" (3:419). Thus he detects two categories of moral knowledge: "the Exemplar or Platform of Good, and the Regiment or Culture of the Mind: the one describing the nature of good, the other prescribing rules how to subdue, apply, and accommodate the will of man thereunto" (419). The essays clearly fall within the second category. As I have said, even an essay such as "Of Death" illustrates such accommodation. Though his prin-cipal purpose appears to be to dispel the "natural" but otherwise "weak" and exaggerated fear of death by adducing contrary evidence and inter-jecting a good deal of gallows humor, Bacon's practical advice prescribes action: "He that dies in an earnest pursuit is like one that is wounded in hot blood; who for the time, scarce feels the hurt; and therefore a mind fixed and bent upon somewhat that is good doth avert the dolours of death" (6:380). "Of Atheism" similarly "suborns" action rather than con-templation. Bacon begins with an expression of faith: "I had rather be-lieve all the fables in the legend, and the Talmud, and the Alcoran, than that this universal frame is without a mind" (6:413). But though he pres-ents a series of strong arguments against it, his purpose is not wholly the refutation of atheism, and his conclusion avoids altogether the issue of *true* religion, asserting only the practical necessity for *some* religion.

We can see that Bacon's *Essays* are written in a rhetorical style which encourages us to examine them critically as aphoristic expressions of wisdom; but more important, the rhetoric is intended to move us to action, to subdue, apply, and accommodate our wills unto the good. The *Essays* display the interaction of rhetoric and the method of discovery. A truly philosophical discourse presents the actual movement of the mind in the process of thinking, searching for truth. The best method for expressing such a movement, according to Bacon, is the disjunctive method of dispersed aphorisms, the method of his *Novum Organum*. But the "duty and office of Rhetoric is to *apply Reason to the Imagination* for the better moving of the will" (3:409). In the *Essays* the aphoristic method is subtly transformed into a rhetoric of discovery intended to challenge received notions and provoke examination of them, to recreate the experience of discovering truth. At the same time, these transformed aphorisms are also carefully ordered so that the good might appear reasonable and practical.

Bacon's practical and sometimes aphoristic essays have always seemed very different from Montaigne's loose, open-ended explorations. Yet though their styles and methods may seem different, both Montaigne and Bacon share a skeptical attitude toward received opinions and ancient authority, and both essayists employ in their essays a rhetoric of discovery intended to engage the reader in a personal journey of exploration. Both rely on rhetorical techniques which are subtly subversive, which purposely confound the reader and often lead to active and cooperative inquiry in the place of straightforward assertion or rational instruction, to open exploration and the discovery of new insights rather than to closed argument or resolved debate. Finally, both essayists often subvert their own arguments and call into question the familiar forms of human reason.

Montaigne and Bacon were not the only essayists to employ a rhetoric of discovery. That the essay might be considered a journey into the unknown, a voyage of discovery, John Donne makes clear in his *Essays in Divinity* (1611?) when he invokes images of journeys and voyages to describe the process of his discourse. In one instance, passing from meditation on God's mercy to a more difficult consideration of his power, Donne remarks: "For thus long we have been in the Harbour, but we launch into a main and unknown Sea, when we come to consider his *Power*" (79). And in another passage, when Donne finds himself entangled in a discussion of Moses as the "first Author," he resorts to an elaborate simile:

> Therefore, as in violent tempests, when a ship dares bear no main sayl, and to lie stil at hull, obeying the uncertain wind and tyde, puts them much out of their way, and altogether out of their account, it is best to put forth such a small ragg of sail, as may keep the barke upright, and make her continue neer one place, though she proceed not; So in this question, where we cannot go forward to make *Moses* the first Author. [13]

In one sense Donne's was a journey among the Scriptures themselves, and he turns to the Bible for his authority: "Search the Scriptures because in them ye hope to have eternal life" (6). But at the same time he is, somewhat in the manner of Montaigne and Bacon, conducting a "search of learning" through the commentaries of the church fathers and books by other learned men. And when he apologizes, with almost equal portions of wit and humility, for infringing on anyone's copyright, his imagery suggests the activities of Renaissance explorers and trading companies (like the Virginia Company, from which he had sought preferment in 1608/9): "But because to such as I, who are but Interlopers, not staple Merchants, nor of the company, nor within the commission of Expositors of the Scriptures, if any licence be granted by the Spirit to discover and possesse any part, herein, it is condition'd and qualified as the Commissions of Princes, that we attempt not any part actually possess'd before, nor disseise others" (32). Donne's image here of the essayist as interloper captures something essential to the new genre, something we detect in Bacon and Montaigne as well—the essayist as amateur, though in this particular case, of course, Donne is thinking of himself as someone lacking a license to preach, someone who is merely essaying in the preacher's art.

I have written at some length about Donne's essays elsewhere ("Searching"), so let me turn finally to Sir Thomas Browne. The idea of discovery and the image of the New World appear in yet another form in his *Hydrotaphia; or, Urne-Buriall* (1658). In the opening paragraph Browne remarks: "That great Antiquity *America* lay buried for thousands of years; and a large part of the earth is still in the Urne unto us" (*Works* 1:135). By describing America as an uncovered antiquity, similar to those ancient urns recently turned up in Norfolk, the ostensible occasion for his essay, Browne identifies the newfound land and the recently uncovered human remains, adding that there are further mysteries still to be discovered, or perhaps we should say "uncovered" or "recovered." Our concentration focuses on the urns and their contents: the unknown parts of the earth or the dust of some ancient men. The emphasis leads naturally into the essay, the next paragraph of which begins with the primordial man, Adam, "made out of an extract of the Earth" (135). Browne's America metaphor is suggestive and consciously so, I would argue. He remarks that "Nature hath furnished one part of the Earth, and man another" (135). If we make the proper associations when we read that "a large part of the earth is still in the Urne unto us" (135), it takes only a small leap of the imagination to recognize that Browne is playing on two meanings of the word "earth": the world and man, "made out of an extract of the Earth" (135).

It is appropriate for Browne to commence with an image of discovery, for his method of meditation relies on the process of discovery. His elaborate and often perplexing exploration of human attitudes toward death and immortality, of the rites and superstitions surrounding burial, is a necessary preparation for the revelations of the final chapter of *Urne-Buriall*, the often anthologized chapter 5. The first four chapters Browne characterizes as a record of vain hopes, empty ceremonies, and confused intimations which are finally replaced by the realized knowledge of the Christian resurrection: "The superior ingredient and obscured part of our selves, whereto all present felicities afford no resting contentment, will be able at last to tell us we are more than our present selves; and evacuate such hopes in the fruition of their own accomplishments" (1:164). This is an interesting use of the word "evacuate," suggesting that the resurrection will somehow empty these vain hopes and leave only the experience of true immortality (see 169). There is no way to persuade us through reason, for reason itself has led men to such vanities. Thus Browne observes: "Happy are they, which live not in that disadvantage of time, when men could say little for futurity, but from reason" (163). Therefore Browne relies on the experience of discovery. By articulating with nearly exhaustive completeness the vain hopes of the past, whether founded on reason or superstition, he intends to demonstrate the futility of such beliefs. And once we have been emptied of error, we are prepared to receive the truth revealed in his fifth chapter, the true belief of Christianity.

The method of discovery employed by Browne in *Urne-Buriall* approximates in many respects Bacon's method of philosophical discourse; the early chapters seem to be objective observations on the variety of human attitudes toward death and burial. But that objectivity is only apparent. What at first appears to be a process of exploration is actually an evacuation. The encyclopedic completeness of Browne's exposition purges the mind of moral vanity, a necessary preparation for the revelation of the final chapter. Both Bacon and Browne employ a rhetoric of discovery, though Bacon's discoveries are in the great world of scientific knowledge and civil affairs, Browne's in the little world of the human soul; one is an outward quest for truth, the other an inward, meditative quest. Browne evokes the image of discovery to turn our thoughts in, toward ourselves. In *Urne-Buriall* that great Antiquity *America* becomes an emblem of self-knowledge rather than knowledge of the world.

Let me conclude with a final example from Browne's earlier work *Pseudodoxia Epidemica* (1646), a vast collection of "Enquiries into Vulgar and Common Errors" which very probably began as a collection in commonplace books. In his preface, "To the Reader," Browne uses the image of America and discovery in a context even more reminiscent of Bacon's usage than in *Urne-Buriall*. He compares the great world of knowledge and vulgar errors that he is about to explore to a "Labyrinth" in which "we find no open tract, . . . but are oft-times fain to wander in the America and untravelled parts of Truth" (*Pseudodoxia* 2:5). Interestingly, Browne also appears to invoke a pre-Copernican image of heavenly motion when he describes his inquiries into received notions: "and therefore in this *Encyclopaedie* and round of Knowledge, like the great and exemplary Wheeles of Heaven, we must observe two Circles: that while we are daily carried about, and whirled on by the swing and rapt of the one, we may maintain a natural and proper course, in the slow and sober wheel of the other" (3). But despite his lapse regarding the new astronomy (a lapse borne out by his apparent reluctance to embrace the "hypothesis of Copernicus" in Book VI, chapter 5), Browne's collection of personal opinions and observations on the learning of his day are, as Robin Robbins has noted very definitely, in the tradition of Bacon's great plan in *The Advancement of Learning* (1, xxviii–xxxiv, and 2, 1180). As Ted-Larry Pebworth has demonstrated rather convincingly, *Pseudodoxia Epidemica* is indeed a collection of essays very much in the mode of Montaigne and Bacon and may, moreover, be an important step in the development of the more scientific essays of Robert Boyle (*Wandering*, 176).

I will bring my own exploration to a close by pointing out that Browne's collection of his own thoughts and various bits of information and misinformation in *Pseudodoxia Epidemica* is perfectly in keeping with the method of the seventeenth-century essay from Montaigne and Bacon onward. Certainly, the collections of minor English essayists belong to this tradition: the works of William Cornwallis, Robert Johnson, and Daniel Tuvill. But I would also include a work such as Robert Burton's *Anatomy of Melancholy,* where, despite the elaborate structure of his partitions, Burton's method and attitude are explorative, a mixture of digressions, allusions, and equivocations that finally leave his book as open-ended and unfinished as Montaigne's. In certain respects all of these essayists were responding to the idea of discovery, to the notion that the world was in flux and that knowledge was no longer fixed by authority but in a state of transition. Recent doubts about the quality of human knowledge had encouraged writers such as Montaigne and Bacon and others such as Donne and Browne (and even Burton) to make a small globe of their intellectual world and chart the progress of their humors as they attempted to experience the world anew, to discover what was known and yet unknown and, if not restore order and coherence, at least wander a bit in the America and untraveled parts of Truth.

Works Cited

Bacon, Francis. *Novum Organum*. Great Books of the Western World. 54 vols. Chicago: Encyclopaedia Britannica, 1952.

_____. *The Works of Francis Bacon*. Ed. James Spedding, R. L. Ellis, and D. D. Heath. 14 vols. London, 1857–74.

Browne, Thomas. *The Works of Thomas Browne*. Ed. Geoffrey Keynes. 4 vols. Chicago: University of Chicago Press, 1964.

_____. *Sir Thomas Browne's "Pseudodoxia Epidemica."* Ed. Robin Robbins. 2 vols. Oxford: Oxford University Press, 1981.

Crane, Ronald S. "The Relation of Bacon's *Essays* to His Program for the Advancement of Learning." In *Essential Articles for the Study of Francis Bacon*, ed. Brian Vickers. Hamden, Conn.: Archon, 1968.

Croll, Morris W. *Style, Rhetoric, and Rhythm: Essays by Morris W. Croll*. Ed. J. Max Patrick, Robert O. Evans, and others. Princeton: Princeton University Press, 1966.

Donne, John. *Devotions upon Emergent Occasions*. Ed. Anthony Raspa. Montreal: McGill-Queens University Press, 1975.

_____. *Essays in Divinity*. Ed. Evelyn M. Simpson. Oxford: Oxford University Press, 1952.

_____. *John Donne: The Anniversaries*. Ed. Frank Manley. Baltimore: Johns Hopkins University Press, 1963.

Fish, Stanley E. "Georgics of the Mind: The Experience of Bacon's *Essays*." *Self-Consuming Artifacts: The Experience of Seventeenth Century Literature*. Berkeley: University of California Press, 1972.

Hakluyt, Richard. *Principal Navigations, Voyages, and Discoveries of the English Nation*. 12 vols. Glasgow: Hakluyt Society, 1903–1905.

Jones, Howard Mumford. *O Strange New World: American Culture: The Formative Years*. New York: Viking Press, 1964.

Hall, Michael L. "'Drawing Myself for Others': The *Ethos* of the Essayist." *Explorations in Renaissance Culture*, 7 (1981):27–35.

_____. "Searching and Not Finding: The Experience of Donne's *Essays in Divinity*." *Genre*, 14 (1981):423–40.

Montaigne, Michel de. *Essays*. Trans. John Florio. New York: Modern Library, 1933.

O'Gorman, Edmundo. *The Invention of America: An Inquiry into the Historical Nature of the New World and the Meaning of Its History*. Bloomington: Indiana University Press, 1961.

Pebworth, Ted-Larry. "Not Being, but Passing: Defining the Early English Essay." *Studies in the Literary Imagination*, 10 (1977):17–27.

_____. "Wandering in the America of Truth." In *Approaches to Sir Thomas Browne: The Ann Arbor Tercentenary Lectures and Essays*, ed. C. A. Patrides. Columbia: University of Missouri Press, 1982.

Raleigh, Sir Walter. *The History of the World*. London, 1614.

Waller, Barry. "The Rhetoric of Friendship in Montaigne's *Essais*." *New Literary History*, 9 (1978):507.

Williamson, George. *A Senecan Amble: Prose from Bacon to Collier*. 1951. Reprint. Chicago: University of Chicago Press, 1966.

Johnson's Rambler *and Its Audiences*

Paul J. Korshin

S amuel Johnson's reputation in his own time owed much to his fame as an essayist. Of the many short writings that he contributed over a career of more than forty years to magazines, journals, and reviews, those that solidified his fame more than any other are undoubtedly the ones collected in *The Rambler* (1750–52). This work is probably the most famous and successful of all the series of periodical essays that sought to imitate *The Spectator* of Addison and Steele, but unlike the earlier work, it is not a collaboration but almost entirely the product of one writer's imagination. When, a few years after Johnson's death, the *Encyclopaedia Britannica* first included an essay about Johnson's life and career, its author, George Gleig, stressed the centrality of *The Rambler* to Johnson's reputation. This substantial essay would stay in the *Encyclopaedia,* almost without change, for more than a half century until 1856, when the editors of the *Britannica*'s eighth edition decided to replace it with something more up-to-date. To this end, they commissioned Thomas Babington Macaulay to present Johnson's achievement to the mid-Victorian audience. Macaulay had high literary pretensions but little firsthand acquaintance with eighteenth-century literature, so that his effort to provide a balanced view of Johnson is more than slightly prejudiced. He admits that *The Rambler,* which sold slowly at first, became very popular after a few years. As to its literary qualities, Macaulay writes,

> A large party pronounced the style perfect, so absolutely perfect that in some essays it would be impossible for the writer himself to alter a single word for the better. Another party, not less numerous, accused him of having corrupted the purity of the English tongue. The best critics admitted that his diction was too monotonous, too obviously artificial, and now and then turgid even to

absurdity. But they did justice to the acuteness of his observations on morals and manners, to the constant precision and frequent brilliancy of his language, to the weighty and magnificent eloquence of many serious passages, and to the solemn yet pleasing humour of some of the lighter pages. On the question of the precedence between Addison and Johnson, a question which, seventy years ago, was much disputed, posterity has pronounced a decision from which there is no appeal. Sir Roger, his chaplain and his butler, Will Wimble and Will Honeycomb, the Vision of Mirza, the Journal of the Retired Citizen, the Everlasting Club, the Dunmow Flitch, the Loves of Hilpah and Shalum, the Visit to the Exchange, and the Visit to the Abbey, are known to everyone. But many men and women, even of highly cultivated minds, are unacquainted with Squire Bluster and Mrs. Busy, Quisquilius and Venustulus, the Allegory of Wit and Learning, the Chronicle of the Revolutions of a Garret, and the sad fate of Aningait and Ajut.

It matters little, perhaps, that Macaulay, in his ignorance of eighteenth-century literature, overlooked the fact that *The Spectator* was the work not just of Addison but of several collaborators as well. Nor does it matter much that Macaulay erred in his belief that some of the more memorable creations in the pages of *The Spectator* were also collaborative efforts and not the work of Addison alone. The famous Will Honeycomb, for instance, is the invention as much of Richard Steele and Eustace Budgell as of Addison. As for the large parties of contemporary critics whom Macaulay imagines as issuing opinions about the style, content, and diction of *The Rambler*, of course they scarcely existed, either; moreover, Johnson made his own extensive revisions not once but twice in that very diction.

What is significant about Macaulay's reading of *The Spectator* and *The Rambler*, just over a century after the conclusion of Johnson's work, is that such an influential writer should so trivialize the eighteenth-century periodical essay as to assume that the fame of a series like that of Johnson should be based on its introduction of memorable characters rather than on important intellectual qualities. Evidently Macaulay judged the success of the eighteenth-century periodical essay by the closeness of its resemblance to the Victorian serial publication of novels. With *The Spectator*, consequently, a reader could follow the exploits and opinions of a set of characters over a period of many installments, a quality which Macaulay found admirable. Johnson provides no such luxury in *The Rambler*. Yet despite such a central misunderstanding of the intellectual force of *The Rambler* and Johnson's other major works, Macaulay's essay would remain in the *Encyclopaedia Britannica*, without revision, until the eleventh edition of 1910. Furthermore, doubtless because the eleventh edition made relatively few changes, Macaulay's effective dismissal of Johnson has remained in the collective subconscious of English readers of the essay until the middle, even the late, twentieth century.

Thus to speak of the audience, to say nothing of the "audiences," of *The Rambler* may seem at first to be a waste of time, for largely thanks to Macaulay, the reputation of this work, Johnson's longest single literary effort, has simply been that it did not attract many readers. We usually measure a literary work's importance and influence by the sheer number of its readers, either in a brief period of time, as with bestsellers, or over a span of many years, as with a classic. In neither of these ways does *The Rambler* appear to have much chance of contention. After all, as students of eighteenth-century England have long known, Johnson undertook to write *The Rambler* as a twice-weekly series of essays, what we are accustomed to call periodical essays, and that very fact of the work's existence defines its miscellaneity: it is a collection of small works rather than a coherent whole. While Johnson wrote these essays, according to the usual view, his real literary and hence intellectual involvement centered on his *Dictionary* (1755), which absorbed his primary attention. Indeed, his preoccupation with the *Dictionary* is evident in *The Rambler* with the constant appearance of hard or "philosophick" words, words that he was obviously busy collecting and defining in his lexicographical labors and whose presence in his essays serves to make them dull, perhaps unreadable. Certainly this heavy, even humorless approach to his varied subjects kept his audience so small that the matter of a wide readership and appeal is hardly worth considering. And even if the subject were worthy of our attention, we cannot escape the fact that the essays that compose *The Rambler* are not beautifully crafted literary gems but careless productions that Johnson habitually dashed off hastily and never bothered to revise, as if he were the Daniel Defoe of literary essayists. Johnson's lack of intellectual engagement with his collection of essays is further evident in the fact that he abruptly ended the series at about the time of his wife's death: his personal concerns weighed so heavily upon him that he simply could not go on with the work. Every one of these erroneous propositions receives support from the highly prejudiced view of Johnson that Macaulay's evaluation of 1856 promoted.

But our assumptions about *The Rambler* are often the result of hearsay evidence that derives from the writings of Johnsonian biographers and memoirists—Macaulay is not the only offender—whose acquaintance with Johnson was nonexistent or started long after he had completed his classic collection. It is certainly true that *The Rambler* is his longest work: in the two years of its publication (March 1750 to March 1752), he wrote almost all of its 208 issues (only four essays are by other writers, while three more contain brief contributions from friends). In contrast, virtually every other English series of periodical essays had contained frequent and often substantial contributions from several writers; the best-known such collection, *The Spectator,* had been a collaboration of several people, and most authors of lesser-known series had accepted work from many other writers. Johnson's other long work, his collected *Lives of the English Poets* (1779–81), would include at least one life by another writer (the life of Edward Young is almost wholly by Herbert Croft) and would simply reprint one biography that Johnson had published nearly forty years earlier (the life of Savage). It is extremely difficult to demonstrate that his work on the *Dictionary* preoccupied him during the early 1750s to the point where *The Rambler* commanded no more than his idle hours. I think that this notion derives from Boswell's assurance, in his *Life of Johnson,* that during 1750–52 Johnson was chiefly occupied with his *Dictionary.*

Whether there is a reflection of Johnson's lexicographical work in his use of philosophical words or terms in *The Rambler* is also hard to prove. It is true, as W. K. Wimsatt noted almost fifty years ago, that there are several hundred "philosophick" words scattered about *The Rambler,* but a few hundred words (most of them used just a few times and the majority just once) form a very small fraction of a work that comprises more than 300,000 words—about 0.1 percent of the whole. Nor can we be certain that a few philosophical words render such a long work unreadable. Johnson's philosophick diction may have seemed difficult to a Yale graduate student writing a dissertation in the late 1930s—W. K. Wimsatt— but, when we consider this diction in the context of the milieu of the early 1750s, words such as "adventitious," "adscititious," "cathartick," "obtund," and "papilionaceous" are not very unusual. Johnson opposed coinages of new words anyway, and while some of his diction may seem hard to us today, almost all of it occurs with some degree of regularity in contemporary journalism, especially in the technical essays on scientific subjects that the editors of the monthly magazines liked to include in every issue. Indeed, on the few occasions when Johnson introduces recondite jargon, as he does in his essays on Milton's versification, he apologizes for it in advance and carefully explains every strange word. That the difficulty of the language made *The Rambler* dull or humorless is another unprovable assumption. The work is hardly a jestbook, to be sure, but anyone who regards *The Rambler* as dull has no acquaintance with contemporary sermons (all of Johnson's readers did have such an acquaintance, for sermons are the single most common literary genre in eighteenth-century England) and ignores Johnson's many contrived letters from fictitious correspondents and his numerous character sketches.

Both Boswell and Mrs. Thrale offer the information that Johnson's custom was to complete his essays for *The Rambler* at the last possible moment, even while the printer's devil lingered in the room waiting for the copy, and this apparently damning evidence has helped to condemn *The Rambler* as a species of journalism to which Johnson did not devote much thought. But neither Boswell nor Mrs. Thrale was acquainted with Johnson at the time he wrote *The Rambler*. Boswell was ten years old and Hester Lynch Salusbury (later Mrs. Thrale) nine when Johnson started the work, in 1750. The hearsay evidence that each presents about his habits of composition is so fragmentary and derivative that we may dismiss it as worthless. Besides, a reading of *The Rambler* in its entirety—an exercise that most of his contemporary biographers seem not to have contemplated—reveals internal evidence for the lengthy gestation of at least one-third of the essays, whether in the form of many accurate quotations, allusions to forthcoming essays, or the suggestion of some kind of research. We may further distance *The Rambler* from Johnson's lexicographical efforts by noting that, of the many hundreds of literary allusions that he makes in the course of the work, only about 10 percent relate to English authors whom he might have been reading as sources for usage and quotations in the *Dictionary*. And finally, as to Johnson's abrupt termination of *The Rambler* just after Mrs. Johnson's death, we might want to remember that Elizabeth Johnson had been in failing health for several years and that her death may not have been as sudden as a romantic view of the situation might imply. I think that there is further internal evidence in the work itself to suggest that Johnson had some plans regarding the scope of the complete series of *The Rambler* and that what may seem to be an abrupt conclusion was in fact a deliberate closure that he had in fact been contemplating for weeks or even months.

The Rambler thus merits serious consideration as a literary work, but the sort of attention that we give such a miscellaneous collection has always been rather uncertain. It is clear that Johnson took it seriously, far more so than he did most of his other works, if we judge by the kind of revisions that he gave it not once but twice. The first collected edition of 1752 contains a number of his changes, and the fourth collected edition of 1756 contains literally thousands of alterations, not by any means exclusively minor ones. The nature of the audience for such a work is clearly significant. The original folio issues seldom had a press run of more than

500 copies or so. Even if we assume a large readership for the original serial issues, there were only a few thousand readers of *The Rambler* between 1750 and 1752. But we also know that the contemporary journalistic press readily reprinted—perhaps "pirated" is a better word— works that publishers deemed likely to attract readers (as Johnson himself observes in several of the essays, "the presses of England are open"), and *The Rambler* was one of the collections of essays most widely treated in this way. Indeed, earlier collections of periodical essays like *The Tatler* and *The Spectator* had smaller audiences than did Johnson's work, for there were no magazines or newspapers in the early decades of the century to perform the work of reprinting. When we have a complete census of reprintings, abridgments, and piracies of all *Rambler* essays, we will have a better idea of its original audience, but I think it fair to say that the work's first audience was unprecedentedly large for a series of periodical essays in the mid-eighteenth century.

Johnson himself, of course, never uses the word "audience," since he made a clear distinction between a body of people who heard a work read or performed (auditors) and a body of people who read the work to themselves (readers). He once mentions the possibility of an author's hearing his work being read aloud in a coffeehouse or a tavern; otherwise, he speaks of his audience only as his "public" or his "readers." It is worthy of note that Johnson refers to his readers rather seldom for an eighteenth-century periodical essayist; Addison and Steele, in contrast, speak in a great many *Spectator* papers of what their readers have communicated to them, what they have overheard in public places, and so on. But Johnson almost never brings up such topics. Since he always refused to print correspondence, although he does occasionally refer to letters from readers with a good deal of ironic humor, he had no need to cater to the tastes of particular readers. Besides, the intellectual milieu of the 1750s differs radically from that of Addison and Steele. Johnson was a professional man of letters; Addison and Steele were literary dilettantes for whom literature was an avocation. Johnson did not depend upon a small coterie in London for his audience, since the means of book distribution at midcentury permitted a man of letters to develop a wide public. Thanks to the improvement of the country's road system and the growing efficiency of the post office, a letter or journal sent from London to Oxford or Cambridge would reach its destination overnight (just as it does, perhaps, today); even Scotland was at most three days away (and the post office observed no holidays in the eighteenth century). Hence *The Rambler* is not a series merely for a London circle. As the evidence of the work itself shows,

Johnson intended to reach, and knew that he was reaching, a public far beyond the capital, for he includes a number of essays that are specifically about the country, something that *The Spectator* rarely did.

I have referred to the "audiences" of *The Rambler,* for the work differs somewhat from most other literature in having several bodies of readers, each different from the other. *The Rambler's* first audience consisted, we must assume, of the people who bought or otherwise obtained the original issues of the periodical. Complete sets of all 208 issues are so rare that, I suspect, very few people purchased the entire work in its original form. When I say "very few," I mean a figure in the hundreds; the press run for the original issues, as I have noted, seldom exceeded 500 copies. The reprinting of selected issues in London and provincial newspapers, a kind of selective anthologizing, obviously made *The Rambler* familiar to thousands of other people, but we can make only random speculations about who these readers were. All that we can say for certain about the original audience for *The Rambler* is that its members perceived the work sequentially, as a series of essays whose order and relationship to each other were not necessarily clear, no matter how coherent the subject matter.

The second audience of the work consists of the readers who did not read the essays as they originally appeared but who first made an acquaintance with the work as a complete collection. In other words, *The Rambler's* second audience includes everyone who has ever read Johnson's collected works since 1752. In this case, of course, I refer to the entire work, not to selected essays that may have appeared in anthologies. Indeed, since Johnson's periodical essays have always reached a wide audience through this medium, there is even a third audience for *The Rambler* consisting of readers who have read only a few well-known essays like the one on prose fiction (No. 4), the screech owl essay (No. 59), or the one on biography (No. 60). The comments of Macaulay in the *Encyclopaedia Britannica* tend to suggest that he may actually belong to this third audience himself. But the second audience is clearly the most important. In Johnson's own century, this group was very large, for after the completion of the original run of *The Rambler* in March 1752, there were more than three dozen editions of the work by 1800, plus at least seven more complete reprintings as part of Johnson's collected works, or roughly an edition every year until the end of the century. In the nineteenth century, the popularity of *The Rambler* would appear to have declined somewhat, as Macaulay concluded (in 1856), since there were only about three dozen separate editions plus another twenty full reprintings in collections of Johnson's works, or about one edition every two years.

However, nineteenth-century editions are larger than those of the eighteenth century, are on cheaper paper, and cost less than earlier collections, so I think we can be sure that Johnson's periodical writing reached an even wider audience in the century after his death than it did while he was alive.

The perceptions of *The Rambler*'s second audience clearly differed from those of his primary readers. First of all, these later readers did not perceive the essays as a periodical or an interrupted series. Rather, this second audience saw *The Rambler* as a coherent literary work, with translations of the Greek and Latin mottoes and other quotations, clear interconnections among various essays that have similar subjects, and—later in the eighteenth century—even a table of contents (which one of Johnson's editors added, so it has no authorial mandate) that defines and sometimes erroneously categorizes each essay according to its subject matter. That the thumbnail descriptions in the table of contents, ubiquitous in all editions after Johnson's death, are almost always too highly focused and are thus often rather misleading must have affected the perceptions of later readers. For example, No. 134, one of Johnson's few statements on his methods of composition, the table of contents describes as "idleness an anxious and miserable state." No. 114, Johnson's great attack on capital punishment, the author of the table of contents blandly describes as "the necessity of apportioning punishments to crimes." And No. 90, an important trail-breaking study of Milton's versification, the contents calls "the pauses in English poetry adjusted." Anyone who used the table of contents, then, as a guide to the contents of *The Rambler,* must inevitably have wondered why Johnson gave his essays such inaccurate titles or perhaps why Johnson, in his writings, had the strange habit of wandering so far from his announced topic. We may count ourselves fortunate, perhaps, that the text of *The Rambler* has, until the recent Yale edition of Johnson's works (a production of the 1960s) been relatively impervious to annotation.

It is foolish to speculate about what does not exist, and so I will not try to imagine how readers might have perceived a work like *The Rambler* that happened to be accompanied by a commentary like that of George Birkbeck Hill on Johnson's *The Lives of the English Poets*. Yet the relatively pristine state of Johnson's text for most of the book's history has meant that his second audience has been relatively unhampered by dispensational readings and scholia; readers of *The Rambler* have had to make up their own minds about the work's many and various meanings. The matter may seem a small one, but when we compare Johnson's classic collection with the reading that we would give to an ancient author such as Cicero or Catullus, the difference acquires significance. By 1500, for example, the text of Catullus's poems had already acquired about 1,000 pages of commentary, in folio. Since annotation has come late to *The Rambler*—and we have the sparse, nonprescriptive notes of the Yale editors—we can be sure that the interpretations of its audience have been more independent, less guided, than those of readers of other famous essays, like *The Spectator* or Bacon's *Essays Civil and Moral*.

A further perception of *The Rambler*'s second audience that was probably not shared by the work's original readership concerned Johnson's guidance as to appropriate moral behavior or attitudes. The work's audience, as we know, read the work as a series of ephemera, and ephemera are by their very nature writings that we readily discard. When we find incomplete runs of the first edition of *The Rambler*, it is most common to find that the lacunae are at the start of the run, not in the last two-thirds of the series. Evidently after *The Rambler* caught on and acquired a steady following, people were less likely to throw away individual issues. The physical impression of the work as a collection, as four or six bound volumes, may seem of slight importance to us today, accustomed as we are to books in the familiar codex form, but for Johnson's eighteenth-century readers a steady repetition of the work's many editions helped to establish *The Rambler*'s nonephemeral quality and to affirm its importance. New editions of a well-known work are not exactly repetitions, either, for each one in reality covers a new territory and reaches a different audience from that of its predecessors. People who already owned one edition of *The Rambler*, in other words, would not be likely to acquire another edition, unless there were some especially strong claim on the title page that the work had been fully revised and was entirely new. Such was never the case with Johnson's essays, for after the edition of 1756, Johnson made no further revisions, and his publishers made no claims to suggest that later editions were in any way new in content. So the existence of *The Rambler* in a steady succession of multivolume editions helped to classicize it and gave it an aura of authority. Johnson's second audience partook of this quality; his original readers could not savor it. Hence the further the stream flowed from its source, somewhat paradoxically, the more authority Johnson's periodical writings acquired. The more famous we consider a man of letters to be as his reputation grows over the years, the more authoritative later generations of readers consider his writings to be.

This process becomes evident when we compare an early comment from Johnson's second audience with another that dates from some forty years after the work's beginning. In 1759, the first instance, Oliver Goldsmith writes about *The Rambler* in an issue of *The Bee.* This is the issue in which Goldsmith conceives of "the fame machine." In a dream vision, Goldsmith watches the coachman of this machine as he turns away prospective riders who do not qualify for a seat in the coach. One of the passengers is Johnson himself, who clambers up carrying a stack of folios. The coachman rudely shoves the volumes out, causing Johnson to object, "What, not take in my dictionary!" But the coachman notices a little book protruding from one of the author's pockets and asks what it is. Johnson answers, "A mere trifle, it is called the Rambler." The coachman at once replies, "The Rambler! I beg, sir, you'll take your place; I have heard our ladies in the court of Apollo frequently mention it with rapture." And all this for only one volume of *The Rambler* (the early editions, as I noted, had four or six volumes)! My second instance is the commentary that Boswell offers about *The Rambler;* it dates from 1791 and is quite different. Boswell makes no suggestion that Johnson's essays may have amused a feminine audience. Actually, he goes so far as to suggest that Johnson ridiculed women's intelligence because the characters of women that he introduces are so silly. Clearly, we ought not to take seriously Boswell's abilities as a literary critic. But Boswell stresses aspects of *The Rambler* that do not show up in Goldsmith's account: the work's profound veneration for Christianity, its instructive qualities, its generous benevolence toward "every consolation which our state affords us," its preference for the sun of revelation over the twilight of pagan philosophy. Boswell is not mistaken to present *The Rambler* in this light. He is merely revealing how the work's second audience, over time, adjusted its perceptions of the work to the prevailing image of Johnson as a profound man of letters, a major presenter of philosophical truth. *The Rambler,* of course, is not ostensibly a work of Christian apologetics, and indeed, Johnson quotes pagan authors about ten times more often than he cites writers associated with Christian theology and traditions. That Boswell stresses the work's active religiosity shows what about Johnson was important to his second audience in the 1790s. Thanks largely to Boswell, in fact, the second audience of *The Rambler* has stressed ever since the work's religious didacticism instead of the entertaining qualities that Goldsmith's jehu mentions. Between Goldsmith and Boswell there are many other notable discussions of Johnson's essays that show that his readers gradually came to think less of him as a wit and more of him as a philosopher.

Johnson, as I observed above, does not talk about his public often enough for us to be sure of his sense of audience. Most of his references reflect upon his letters from various readers or refer to what he saw as his lack of popularity. There is an affected irony—an authorial strategy—

about most of these comments, as when Johnson observes, in his final issue, No. 208, "I have never been much a favourite of the publick, nor can boast that . . . I have been animated by the rewards of the liberal, the caresses of the great, or the praises of the eminent." We know, on the contrary, that Johnson received a great deal of attention from the intellectual community of his day for *The Rambler;* even before he ended the original series the first collected edition was in progress. Johnson gives us a better sense of his popularity with his readers when he is less preoccupied with rhetorical posing, as in No. 56, an essay on the fine art of giving offense. Here, in the midst of a long presentation of affronts both accidental and deliberate, he confesses:

> I am afraid that I may be taxed with insensibility by many of my correspondents, who believe their contributions unjustly neglected. And indeed when I sit before a pile of papers, of which each is the product of laborious study, and the offspring of a fond parent, I, who know the passions of an author, cannot remember how long they have lain in my boxes unregarded, without imagining to myself the various changes of sorrow, impatience, and resentment, which the writers must have felt in this tedious interval.

The public nature of Johnson's apology for ignoring his correspondents— an eighteenth-century essayist was expected to engage in exchanges of letters with those who wrote to him—suggests that his audience was larger than we may have surmised, but it also shows that Johnson operated his literary enterprise according to different rules from what may have obtained before. That is, he did not consider that he had an obligation to reply to those who wrote to him with advice, questions, and so on. He was not to be considered on a par with some mid-eighteenth-century John Dunton, the reputation of whose *Athenian Mercury,* in the 1690s, derived from his willingness to answer any and all queries, however absurd. Johnson would have had other reasons to want to break with the tradition of Dunton, whose periodical publications included *The Rambler's* namesake—*The Night Walker; or, Evening Rambles in Search after Lewd Women* (1696–97). So the rules of literature had changed, and *The Rambler,* by virtue of Johnson's treatment of his readers, was evidence of the change.

We find Johnson reflecting on the nature of his audience in another way, I think, namely in his many discussions of literary fame. One of the best of these appears in No. 106. Here Johnson talks about the vanity of human hopes, well expressed by the evidence of a public library, which contains many mighty volumes which are now "scarcely known but by the catalogue." The learned, Johnson says, "often bewail the loss of ancient writers whose characters have survived their works; but perhaps, if we could now retrieve them, we should find them only the Granvilles, Montagues, Stepneys, and Sheffields of their time, and wonder by what infatuation or caprice they could be raised to notice." That Johnson can speak with such absolute certainty of the lesser status of a clutch of Restoration writers tells us how confident he is that he is not, in fact, one of the Granvilles, Montagues, Stepneys, or Sheffields of the mid-eighteenth century. We can also sense his certainty that, in the public libraries of the future, no one will ever be able to say that *The Rambler* was scarcely known but by the catalogue. Here Johnson is speaking not just to his primary audience but, with a sure sense of his accomplishment thus far in his series of essays, to posterity, to that second audience which he must have known even then his work would have.

The portion of *The Rambler's* second audience that it is most difficult to trace is not those who read it as a collection of 208 essays but rather those readers who, as a reflection of the work's original public, who knew it only as a series of essays that appeared twice a week, have become acquainted with Johnson through the pages of an anthology. Anthologizing of eighteenth-century periodical essays started in the 1780s, and the first such collections obviously had wide appeal as guides to self-education and as texts for schools. Indeed, the anthologizers of the late eighteenth century, like those of the present century, were most often schoolteachers or educators of some sort. These men, who include such respectable minor writers and essayists as Vicesimus Knox and W. F. Mavor, plundered the entire field of eighteenth-century periodical literature to assemble their collections. In an age with only a modest idea of the nature of literary property, the essay was an ideal subject for the anthologizer—there were no permissions fees to pay—and, we would expect, the favorites included *The Spectator* and *The Rambler*. The two series are more or less equally represented in contemporary anthologies; since *The Spectator* contains more than five hundred numbers, this parity shows that Johnson's work was already more popular than that of Addison and Steele. Once again demonstrating the paucity of Macaulay's knowledge, the anthologists almost invariably select *Spectator* papers that are exemplars of light social criticism, but the selections from *The Rambler* are always essays that deal with philosophical and ethical subjects.

These early anthologies had a wide audience, for some of them survive in dozens of editions. Vicesimus Knox's *Elegant Extracts in Verse and Prose*, which Knox first published in the 1780s (and which later he changed to two volumes, one of verse and one of prose), was still being printed fifty years later. The various editions of *Elegant Extracts* include a number of essays from *The Rambler* printed without abridgment save for the removal of Johnson's Greek and Latin mottoes and most of the classical quotations in the texts themselves. By the time that Macaulay wrote his critical and largely unfavorable analysis of Johnson for the *Encyclopaedia Britannica*, several hundred editions of a number of different anthologies had reprinted about one-fourth of *The Rambler* as individual essays in an untold number of copies. So when Macaulay assured his readers in 1856 (and those on through 1910 as well) that "an allusion to [Johnson's] Rambler . . . is not readily apprehended in literary circles," he was seriously mistaken. He went even further, however, in his erroneous generalizations: "But though the celebrity of the writings may have declined, the celebrity of the writer, strange to say, is as great as ever. Boswell's book has done for him more than the best of his own books could do." Undoubtedly Boswell's biography had done much for Johnson's reputation by mid-Victorian times but, practically unnoticed by those who frequented Macaulay's "literary circles," Johnson's periodical essays, the most easily anthologized of works, continued to flourish. The leaders of the literary world seldom trouble to read schoolbooks, miscellanies, abridgments, and the other materials that bring high culture to a popular audience and to young students. It is evident that Macaulay, for one, did not even know that such collections existed. But Johnson's *Rambler* essays have for centuries played a large role in schools. The formation of modern schools and departments of English in the late nineteenth century created a new need for collections of the classics of English literature, and here, too, we find, *The Rambler* in popularity outstrips any other collection of eighteenth-century essays. And the first selection devoted solely to Johnson's essays, George Birkbeck Hill's *Select Essays of Dr. Johnson* (1899), includes about one-fourth of the entire *Rambler* among its total of seventy-seven of Johnson's essays. So we can say with assurance, I think, that Johnson's second audience includes a large subcategory of readers, largely hidden from the gaze of literary historians, who read selections of his *Rambler* essays for the purpose of self-improvement or as part of their education.

The evidence that Johnson knew what sort of literary property he had in *The Rambler* appears strongly at the end of No. 106:

> There are, indeed, few kinds of composition from which an author, however learned or ingenious, can hope a long continuance of fame. He who has carefully studied human nature, and can well describe it, may with most reason flatter his ambition. Bacon, among all his pretensions to the regard of posterity, seems to have pleased himself chiefly with his essays, "which come

home to mens business and bosoms," and of which, therefore, he declares his expectation, that they "will live as long as books last."

For Johnson to tell his original readers, his primary or first audience, that Bacon prized his essays most of all his works, is a declaration to them—and to us, his second audience—that he expected them to compare *The Rambler* not to collections of eighteenth-century periodical essays, not to Addison, but to England's most famous collection of essays, those of Bacon himself. And we, his second audience, know that he was right.

"Ecstasy & Eloquence": The Method of Emerson's Essays

Robert Atwan

L ate in life Emerson set down a rather melancholy remark in his journals: "Why," he asks himself, "has
never the poorest country college offered me a professorship of rhetoric? I
think I could have taught an orator, though I am none" (Matthiessen, 18).
The thought of Emerson as an American Quintillian (or as a modern
director of composition), however, does not quite succeed. Emerson, of
course, *was* a fine orator—one of the most effective and innovative of his
age. But perhaps the reason no college ever offered him a position as a
rhetoric teacher was that he came to have very little use for rhetoric, either
as a method of oratory or as a method of written composition.

In his career Emerson shifted from a Unitarian preacher who delivered
sermons to a professional Lyceum speaker who delivered lectures. As he
did so, his tolerance for traditional rhetorical structures grew less and
less. In his famous "Divinity School Address" of 1838, it is clear that his
growing difficulties with Christianity are in large part closely connected
with attitudes toward speech and language. Here, as so often in Emerson,
his uneasiness over conventional religion seems inseparable from his uneasiness over rhetorical conventions: he says of Jesus that "the idioms of
his language, and the figures of his rhetoric, have usurped the place of his
truth; and churches are not built on his principles, but on his tropes"
(Porte, 1980). As a direct attack on the current state of preaching—of
religious rhetoric, if you will—the address was so offensive to the faculty
that Emerson was not invited back to Harvard for nearly thirty years.

It is no surprise that, six months after this address, Emerson, entirely
dissatisfied with the pulpit, preached his last sermon. He had instituted a
series of public lectures several years earlier. As his circuit widened, the

lectures had begun to provide him with a moderate income. He was enthusiastic about the possibilities of the Lyceum. "A lecture," he noted in his journal for July 1839, "is a new literature" (Gilman, vii, 224). A few months later, he attempted to describe this "new literature" more thoroughly. Under a journal entry headed "Eloquence" and "Lyceum," Emerson wrote:

> Here is all the true orator will ask, for here is a convertible audience & here are no stiff conventions that prescribe a method, a style, a limited quotation of books, & an exact respect to certain books, persons, or opinions. No, here everything is admissible, philosophy, ethics, divinity, criticism, poetry, humor, fun, mimicry, anecdotes, jokes, ventriloquism. All the breadth & versatility of the most liberal conversation, highest lowest personal local topics, all are permitted, and all may be combined in one speech; it is a panharmonicon,— every note on the longest gamut, from the explosion of cannon, to the tinkle of a guitar. Let us try, if Folly, Custom, Convention & Phlegm cannot hear our sharp artillery. Here is a pulpit that makes other pulpits tame & ineffectual—with their cold mechanical preparation for a delivery the most decorous,—fine things, pretty things, wise things, but no arrows, no axes, no nectar, no growling, no transpiercing, no loving, no enchantment. Here he may lay himself out utterly, large, enormous, prodigal, on the subject of the hour. Here he may dare to hope for ecstasy & eloquence. [Gilman, vii, 265]

As usual with Emerson, the mood did not last long. A few months later, in February 1840, he notes: "These lectures give me little pleasure. . . . I have not once transcended the coldest selfpossession. . . . I dared to hope for ecstacy & eloquence. A new theatre, a new art, I said, is mine" (Gilman, vii, Journal E, 338). And he goes on to paraphrase his expectations from his earlier journal entry, ruthlessly turning every harsh critical remark he made about the pulpit back to bear on his own lectures. Here was no exciting "new literature" but more of the same literary customs and conventions.

Though Emerson's sermons and lectures would hardly serve as models of tight rhetorical organization ("I found when I had finished my new lecture that it was a very good house, only the architect had unfortunately omitted the stairs" [Matthiessen, 23]), they nevertheless contained the expected homiletic enumerations or divisions, and they developed according to a logical progression of ideas. John Jay Chapman observed how the lectures differed from the essays: "It is noticeable that in some of Emerson's important lectures the logical scheme is more perfect than in his essays" (Barzun, 162). Chapman, however, attributes this difference to Emerson's peculiar methods of composition; he so consistently revised and reworked his journal entries into his finished writing that the "logical scheme became more and more obliterated" (Barzun, 162).

This not uncommon critical view assumes a rather careless Emerson and an accidental incoherence of composition: the essays would have been more orderly if only Emerson had been more orderly in his method. Yet I have come to see the rhetorical disorganization—the obliteration of logical schemes—as precisely what Emerson was striving for in his "search for a form" (F. O. Matthiessen's phrase; Matthiessen, 14). And I see the major essays not as sloppier versions of his major lectures—or as convenient distillations from his journals and lectures—but rather as his successful discovery of the suitable form. "Emerson had his message," Henry James noted, "but he was a good while looking for his form" (James, 6). Not finding his "new literature" in sermons and lectures (or, I should add, in poetry), he finally found it in 1840 in the essay.

William James said that "Emerson's mission culminated in his style, and if we must define him in one word, we have to call him Artist" (William James, 454). Emerson is truly an artist, and his art is the art of the essay. Great essayists are perhaps rarer than great poets or novelists, and Emerson ranks among the very few masters of the genre—with Montaigne, Francis Bacon, and Samuel Johnson. I say so mainly as a reminder, since Emerson is often regarded as everything *but* an essayist. In the critical literature we can readily find Emerson the philosopher, the moralist, the literary critic, the lapsed theologian, the failed poet, the culture hero, the great national genius who set the agenda for all subsequent American literature. But only rarely is Emerson viewed as an essayist—the way Montaigne, say, is invariably considered. Scarcely a study of Montaigne fails to concentrate its critical attention on Montaigne's relation to the essay. Yet even recent studies that attend closely to Emerson's language tend to divorce that language from its genre, leaving us with an Emerson of brilliant detached sentences, an Emerson who is all style and no form. Much contemporary criticism thus supports the remark of Henry James that it was Emerson's "singular power" to be "a striking exception to the general rule that writings live in the last resort by their form" (James, 32).

I prefer to look therefore now not at Emerson's prose—which has been the subject of abundant and often superb critical discussion—but at Emerson's essays and in particular at what he imagined the essay could be and do. Emerson had long been an avid reader of essays—indeed most of his favorite works of literature were essay collections—Plutarch's *Morals* (to which he wrote a preface in 1870); Montaigne, whom he adored and about whom he wrote one of his finest essays; and, of course, Francis Bacon. Yet despite—or perhaps because of—all these great models, Emerson came to the essay slowly, even reluctantly. He saw it, as many writers have before and since, as a lesser literary form (in our time, E. B. White complained that to be an essayist is to be "a second-class citizen" [vii]). Emerson admitted sadly to Carlyle in that critical year 1839, "I do not belong to the poets, but only to a low department of literature, the reporters; suburban men" (Matthiessen, 48). Like many highly creative people, Emerson tended to devalue what he could most naturally do, and only when he found a way to reimagine the essay, to reinvent it for himself in terms that offered more aesthetic challenges than anything he had previously encountered in literary composition, could he then throw the full extent of his genius into the form.

Emerson's decision to begin seriously writing essays in 1840 seems clearly related to his increasing discontent with the literary possibilities of sermons and lectures. As brilliant as Emerson was in these forms, he needed a vehicle that would allow him to give his creativity full rein, to take risks with conventional structures and logical organization, to turn traditional rhetoric inside out. He was, as we have seen, disappointed that his lectures did not provide the "new literature" that he had hoped would serve as the outlet for his creative ambitions. But perhaps what he wanted to achieve in the lecture could be achieved in another form, one that did not entirely depend on what he clearly regarded as the necessary rhetorical compromises of public speaking. The essays of 1840 represent that "new literature." There Emerson waged his war against rhetoric and took unprecedented risks with whatever is conventionally meant by verbal communication.

Since "ecstacy & eloquence" could not be found in the lecture, as he had hoped, Emerson sought them in the essay "Ecstasy & Eloquence." The words ripple through all of Emerson's writing and ultimately form the major contours of his thought. I will return to the 1839 journal entry to examine the importance that these terms bear to any consideration of Emerson as an essayist. He is speaking here, remember, of his high hopes for his lectures. I see in his statement, however, the literary expectations that he will soon bring to the essay.

Emerson hopes to find a form in which "everything is admissible, philosophy, ethics, divinity, criticism, poetry, humor, fun, mimicry, anecdotes, jokes, ventriloquism." He wants breadth and versatility that will permit in one speech the full range of topics contained in the "most liberal conversation." He then introduces a remarkable image for the form he is seeking. "It is," he says, "a panharmonicon,—every note on the longest gamut, from the explosion of cannon, to the tinkle of a guitar."

Emerson is picturing here an actual musical instrument, one he may have heard in Boston some years earlier. The strange instrument was the creation of a rather notorious German inventor, Johann Maelzel—a musician, mechanical genius, shifty businessman, and maker of many popularly exhibited automatons. Maelzel conned America in the 1820s with the famous automaton chess player that Edgar Allan Poe eventually exposed. First exhibited in Vienna in 1804, the panharmonicon gradually grew to be an entire automatic orchestra consisting of flutes, drums, trumpets, cymbals, strings, triangle, clarinets, violins, and cellos. The whole ensemble was activated by weights acting upon a pinned—we would now say programmed—cylinder. Between 1813 and 1814, Maelzel induced Beethoven to compose several scores for the instrument in the hope that both men would make a killing by taking it on tour; instead, in the end they nearly killed each other. Beethoven's scores were appropriately martial; thus Emerson's imagery: "Let us try if Folly, Custom, Convention & Phlegm cannot hear our sharp artillery." The panharmonicon was perfect for battle pieces. Beethoven composed his Wellington Symphony for the instrument.

Emerson was clearly affected by Beethoven's martial themes. He had a lifelong obsession with Napoleon, and the essays themselves—with strife as one of their leading tropes—often have the ring of spiritual battle pieces. But my interest in the panharmonicon as an image of the essay form has less to do with the kind of music it rendered than with the nature of the instrument itself. For here indeed was "every note on the longest gamut" but without musicians. Here was an instrument without a performer, art without a human presence. (This feature may explain, too, why the automaton orchestra would better suit the invisible essayist than the visible lecturer.) The depersonalized nature of the self-performing artifact also led to its greater potential as an Emersonian vehicle for both ecstasy and eloquence.

Eloquence for Emerson was not a matter of smooth and decorous speech; the term suggested for him instead a wide variety of articulation, which is perhaps the reason that the panharmonicon, with its strange medley of sounds ("every note on the longest gamut"), appealed so vividly to him. In a letter to Carlyle in 1841, he writes: "I imagine an eloquence of infinite variety,—rich as conversation can be, with anecdote, joke, tragedy, epics and pindarics, argument and confessions" (Slater, 308). In 1849, once again wistfully imagining himself as a composition teacher, he notes in his journal: "I think if I were professor of Rhetoric,—teacher of the art of writing well, to young men, I should use Dante for my textbook." Dante, he claims, "knew how to throw the weight of his body into each act" (Whicher, 318). Emerson is thinking of Dante's *De Vulgari Elo-*

quentia—an essay that Kenneth Burke claims "operates in the realm where poetic and rhetoric cross" (167–69)—and especially Dante's paradoxical notion of "nobil volgare eloquenza," the notion of the nobility of common speech, the "natural" speech we learn in our infancy. Dante, says Emerson, "knows 'God damn,' and can be rowdy if he please, and he does please." In its variety and its "vulgarity," we can see how the popular panharmonicon—banging and tooting and clanging and tinkling away to everyone's delight and amazement—offered Emerson a fitting image of the all-embracing eloquence he was seeking.

How far Emerson had come in his views on eloquence can be seen in an 1825 journal entry, where he also uses a musical metaphor for prose composition. In trying to understand his response to musical performance, he borrowed a term from painting:

> He that searches analogies in art & life will discern something akin to what in painting is called *keeping,* in many corners where 'tis unlooked for. For tho' mine ear is untaught by nature or art in the mysteries of music yet I have found my guess that such performance was good or bad, on more than one occasion borne out by competent hearers when my only means of forming a judgment was the observation that there were abrupt transitions from loud to soft sounds without the just degree which might be termed the *keeping* of music. A skilful critic will readily see the justice of the application of this figure to any composition also whether in verse or prose. [Gilman, II, 321]

Sheldon W. Liebman has observed in a fine essay on the development of Emerson's theory of rhetoric that this passage, with its concern for clear and smooth transitions, shows Emerson to be still under the spell of Hugh Blair's enormously influential *Lectures on Rhetoric and Belles Lettres* (1783). By the late 1830s, however, Emerson no longer shared Blair's views on composition, and his writing had begun to reflect a deliberate use of "abrupt transitions" (Liebman, 187–88). This rejection of rhetorical decorum played a significant part in his transformation of the essay into a less conventionally rhetorical literary genre. His essays of the 1840s were as much out of "keeping" with Blair's rhetorical principles as were Beethoven's late quartets with the harmonies of eighteenth-century chamber music. Not surprisingly, one of the most insightful essays on Emerson was written by Charles Ives.

By "ecstasy," Emerson means more than an exalted state of feeling. He often uses the word in its literal sense of "a standing apart" or of "standing outside of oneself." Interpreting Swedenborg's mystical visions, Emerson wrote: "The ancients called it *ecstasy* or absence—a getting out of their bodies to think" (Emerson, 663). (Matthiessen, who refers to this passage, also notes that Donne's "Exstasie" was one of Emerson's favorite poems [68].) For Emerson this literal ecstatic state is intimately connected with the relations between speaker and audience. In his first journal reference briefly comparing lecture oratory to the panharmonicon (July 5, 1839), he claims, "Only then is the orator successful when he is himself agitated & is as much a hearer as any of the assembly" (Gilman, 224–25). The speaker—much like Whitman's ecstatic speaker in "Song of Myself"—is thus transported outside himself into an amorphous identity that radically blurs any convenient rhetorical distinction between the writer and his audience: "I celebrate myself, / And what I assume you shall assume, / For every atom belonging to me as good belongs to you."

These momentary dissolutions of the personal speaking self—the instrument without the performer—occur throughout Emerson's essays and amount to what I consider to be his major contribution to the genre. How does an essayist such as Emerson go beyond the limits of Montaigne's "naked" self? He plunges deeper into creation and invents a "transparent" self. He is not satisfied with simply creating various personalities or with being an inconsistent eccentric or with adopting that favorite of essayistic modes the self-congratulatory confession—these were all conventional personae of the familiar essay even by Emerson's time. "The great," he said, "always introduce us to facts; small men introduce us always to themselves" (Matthiessen, 9). As his panharmonicon image suggests, Emerson strove in his compositions for the elimination of the individual ego. Thoreau justly observed that Emerson's essays seemed like "unembodied" voices (Matthiessen, 10).

Emerson's best description of the ecstatic nature of his essays is contained in one of his finest pieces of writing, "The Method of Nature." An address delivered some five months after the publication of his first collection of essays in 1841, this oration deals almost entirely with the relation of the ecstatic state to thought and literature, and in its indirect way serves—along with the remarkable essay on Montaigne—as Emerson's most comprehensive commentary on his own literary method.

For Emerson, ecstasy *is* nature's method, and if I understand him correctly, he means that nature's genius—the ultimate model of all genius—consists in a total disregard of will, intention, particular ends, or final cause. Wanting to examine how far nature's antiteleological method is "transferable to the literary life" (Emerson, 118), Emerson contrasts ecstasy with intention: "Nature can only be conceived," he says, "as existing to a universal and not to a particular end, to a universe of ends, and not to one,—a work of *ecstasy*, to be represented by a circular movement, as intention might be signified by a straight line of definite length" (120). To write according to a natural method—to live, as Emerson puts it, "a life of discovery and performance"—means to abandon our respect for the work of art and concentrate only on the art. If the writer would imitate nature's ecstatic method, he must eliminate from his work all personal intention: "What is best in any work of art, but that part which the work itself seems to require and do; that which the man cannot do again, that which flows from the hour and the occasion, like the eloquence of men in a tumultuous debate?" (Emerson, 125). To prod our minds into working in a natural way, however, means more than drifting into "free-writing" or spontaneous literary process. Emerson is not proposing anything so simple. He demands that the writer suspend all effort at effect, all conscious intention toward a compositional goal, toward all rhetorical aim.

True eloquence, then, for Emerson becomes antithetical to rhetoric. Rhetoric exists as intention, as a deliberative means to an effect, as a method of achieving a compositional purpose. Eloquence can occur only when the writer has the presence of mind—or rather the ecstatic absence of mind—to abandon the patterns and formulations of rhetoric and create instead a "new literature" that would truthfully record the multiform and simultaneous method of nature. For Emerson, rhetoric depends upon talent, eloquence upon genius. Rhetoric gives us the expected; eloquence surprises.

"When we have broken our god of tradition, and ceased from our god of rhetoric, then may God fire the heart with his presence," Emerson says in "The Over-Soul" (Emerson, 328). Emerson's essays represent the enactment of his radical disengagement from both literary customs and conventional rhetoric. To immerse ourselves in the essays is to experience a constant shattering of rhetorical organization: definitions seem to alter or dissolve with the movement of syntax; systems of classification are outright ridiculed; logical transitions and connections are erased; examples, illustrations, and quotations sometimes undermine the points they are meant to support; chains of cause and effect are consistently interrupted. Emerson rarely narrates; seldom offers lengthy descriptions; almost never explains; does not care to build a tightly argued case for anything.

If Emerson has a dominant rhetorical mode, it is exhortation. But whereas most persuasion seeks an audience's identification or conversion, Emerson's essays—like Robert Frost's poetry—seem to work against any manipulative form of communication, seeking rather, as Frost says in "The Most of It," not "its own love back in copy speech / But counter-love, original response." As Chapman suggests, Emerson's aim was not persuasion but agitation, a method that favored his notorious inconsistency and self-contradiction. "Do not," Emerson says, "set the least value on what I do, or the least discredit on what I do not, as if I pretended to settle anything as false or true. I unsettle all things" (Barzun, 167).

Matthew Arnold was correct when he criticized Emerson's essays for having "no evolution" (Konvitz, 71). The essays never take the form of cumulative argument, never develop an expository point, never assume an observable rhetorical shape. They do not, that is, evolve continuously or teleologically with a definite end or a final purpose in mind. To retain the biological metaphor, they proceed by saltation, by sudden movements and abrupt transitions. They demonstrate the creative process—to be sure—but this is not a process that leads ultimately to a product; it is rather a process that at all points shows itself at odds with the finished product. It is a process struggling against its completion. Like the panharmonicon, the essays make us eerily aware of an orchestra without a conductor, of a performance without performers. And like the panharmonicon, too, the music is mainly martial. To borrow Kenneth Burke's observations on Dante, the essays seem always to be carrying on a war between rhetoric and poetics, as though the world of writing were permanently divided between these two camps. Emerson speaks in "The Method of Nature" of "the form of the formless" (Emerson, 122), acknowledging in that address both our need for form and our resistance to it. All of his major essays show a strenuous pulling in two directions—rhetoric against poetry, line against circle, intention against ecstasy.

In an 1844 newspaper article on Emerson's essays, Margaret Fuller offered one of the most accurate literary predictions in the history of American criticism. After calling attention to Emerson's lack of "harmonious effect," she concluded that the essays "will lead to great and complete poems—somewhere" (Konvitz, 25). She clearly saw the course of American literature. Emerson's essays did not lead to a flowering of the essay form in America; in fact, they may have been a dead end. If the essay is the one genre that did not make a notable transition into twentieth-century modernism, the reason may be that Emerson's radical departures from conventional literary orderings had already taken it to that stage. After Emerson, the American essay (with the exception of Santayana's work) grew increasingly personal and moved far closer to rhetoric than to poetry. But recall his quest for a form in which "everything is admissible"—the image of that curious panharmonicon—and we can begin to hear the barbaric yawps, howls, minstrelsy, and jazz tunes, the ecstatic rhythms of American eloquence in our great long poems.

Works Cited

Barzun, Jacques, ed. "Emerson." In *The Selected Writings of John Jay Chapman.* New York: Minerva Press, 1968.

Burke, Kenneth. *A Rhetoric of Motives.* Berkeley: University of California Press, 1969.

Emerson, Ralph Waldo. *Essays and Lectures.* Ed. Joel Porte. New York: Literary Classics of the United States, 1983.

Gilman, W. H., et al., eds. *The Journals and Miscellaneous Notebooks of Ralph Waldo Emerson.* Boston: Harvard University Press, 1960–77.

James, Henry. "Emerson." *Partial Portraits.* Ann Arbor: University of Michigan Press, 1970.

James, William. "Address at the Centenary of Ralph Waldo Emerson" (1903). Cited in *The James Family: A Group Biography,* ed. F. O. Matthiessen. New York: Vintage Books, 1980.

Konvitz, Milton R. *The Recognition of Ralph Waldo Emerson.* Ann Arbor: University of Michigan Press, 1972.

Liebman, Sheldon W. "The Development of Emerson's Theory of Rhetoric, 1821–1836." *American Literature,* 41 (May 1969), pp. 187–88.

Matthiessen, F. O. *American Renaissance.* New York: Oxford University Press, 1941.

Slater, Joseph. *The Correspondence of Emerson and Carlyle.* New York: Columbia University Press, 1964.

Whicher, Stephen E. *Selections from Ralph Waldo Emerson: An Organic Anthology.* Boston: Houghton Mifflin, 1957.

White, E. B. *Essays of E. B. White.* New York: Harper and Row, 1977.

William Hazlitt and His "Familiar Style"

Nancy Enright

> Coming forward and seating himself on the ground in his white
> dress and tightened turban, the chief of the Indian Jugglers
> begins with tossing up two brass balls, which is what any of us
> could do, and concludes with keeping up four at the same time,
> which is what none of us could do to save our lives, not if we
> were to take our whole lives to do it in. Is it then a trifling power
> we see at work, or is it not something next to miraculous?
>
> —"The Indian Jugglers" (*Works*, VIII)

The wonder and admiration that William Hazlitt felt
for the Indian jugglers and tightrope walkers grew
perhaps out of his devotion to *balance* in the area of writing. For Hazlitt
defines the essay according to the terms of what he calls "the Familiar
Style." This style consists of a balancing act between various extremes and
opposites.

In his essay "On the Familiar Style" (*Works*, VIII, 242), Hazlitt delin-
eates the terms of his definition, responding to attacks against his "underformality." Criticized for vulgarity and lack of polish ("On the Familiar
Style") and called a "slangwhanger" (Chesire 101–102), Hazlitt defends
himself by explaining the difference between a Familiar Style and mere
lack of style. He insists that creating the balance between a proper structure and style on the one hand and a pleasing naturalness on the other
requires hard work and much skill: "It is not easy to write a familiar
style. . . . There is nothing that requires more precision and, if I may so
say, purity of expression, than the style I am speaking of" ("Familiar
Style," *Works*, VIII, 242).

Hazlitt clearly describes the two barriers the good essayist must not
cross, overformality and underformality, in order to achieve this proper

balance, a balance not maintained in his *Liber Amoris* or in his letters and journal. The Familiar Style "utterly rejects not only all unmeaning pomp, but all low, cant phrases, and loose, unconnected, slipshod allusions" ("Familiar Style," *Works,* VIII, 242). The essayist must be direct and clear without being offensively blunt or overly emotional. Of course, what might have offended Hazlitt's nineteenth-century audience and what would alienate twentieth-century readers differ considerably, and realistically a writer can never achieve a perfectly accessible and fully audience-directed style. However, as an ideal toward which one aims, the balance between over- and underformality is an important goal for the essayist who wishes to avoid merely ventilating emotion or writing to a limited clique of readers. The Familiar Style is informed not by censureship or "policing" of expression but rather by a sensitivity to clarity and an awareness of audience.

This distinction is clearly seen when Hazlitt's discussion of a particular concept in an essay is compared with his treatment of it in another form of writing, such as one of the letters in his *Liber Amoris.* This work, decidedly not an essay, consists of a series of conversations, written in script form, between Hazlitt's thinly veiled persona, H, and a young lady named Sarah Walker; it also includes letters to her, less often from her, and, most often, to friends about her. In one such letter Hazlitt describes his passion in the following words: "The barbed arrow is in my heart—I can neither endure it, nor draw it out; for with it flows my life's blood" (Letter 7, *Liber Amoris* II, 138 *Works,* VIII, 124). Contrast the preceding example with the following discussion of passion in one of Hazlitt's essays: "Passion is the undue irritation of the will from indulgence or opposition; imagination is the anticipation of unknown good; affection is the attachment we form to any object from its being connected with the habitual impression of numberless sources and ramifications of pleasure. The heart is the most central of all things" ("On Novelty and Familiarity," *Works,* XII, 310). Note the distancing of tone and the control evidenced in the essay, though both essay and letter describe passion. Or again, examine another example, the subject of which is disappointment in love, taken from Hazlitt's essay "On Great and Little Things," in which the tone and voice are certainly personal. Hazlitt is obviously discussing something deeply important to him, but the frenzy and the clichés, evident in the letter, are gone, replaced by more objective, distanced tone and vocabulary: "To see beauty is not to be beautiful, to pine in love is not to be loved again—I always was inclined to raise and magnify the power of Love" (*Works* VIII, 236–37). Hazlitt's choice of words in the essays is prompted not by his emotional need to ventilate, as it is, at least to a greater degree, in the letter, but by a desire to communicate an idea to his audience in the clearest, most accessible way he can. One might argue that the comparison is weakened by the fact that in the letter Hazlitt is talking about a personal passion, whereas in the essays he is discussing passion in general, though in the second passage the context is an indirect reference to Sarah Walker. However, even when he is specifically describing his own negative emotions, his sense of failure and disappointment toward the end of his life, in his essay "On the Pleasure of Hating," he avoids what might be called the vulgarity and the lack of control evidenced, not inappropriately so, in the letters, the journal, and even the *Liber*. In the essays, the balance is maintained: "Mistaken as I have been in my public and private hopes, calculating others from myself and calculating wrong; always disappointed where I placed most reliance; the dupe of friendship, and the fool of love; have I not reason to hate and to despise myself? Indeed I do; and chiefly for not having hated and despised the world enough" (*Works*, XII, 136). Compare the preceding paragraph to the following excerpt from a letter to P. G. Patmore in the *Liber* concerning Sarah Walker. Hazlitt's persona, H, laments, "To what a state am I reduced, and for what? For fancying a little artful vixen to be an angel and a saint, because she affected to look like one, to hide her rank thoughts and deadly purposes. Has she not murdered me under the mask of tenderest friendship?" (*Liber Amoris* II, Letter 9, *Works*, VIII, 127). Or again, compare the excerpt from the essay "The Pleasure of Hating," quoted earlier, with the following expression of identical feelings of failure and general disillusionment in Letter 8 of the *Liber:* "I am pent up in burning and impotent desires which can find no vent or object. I am hated, repulsed, bemocked by all I love" (26, *Works*, VIII, 125). Both letter and essay express the same depth of despair, but the wildness, the sense of cathartic expurgation through the process of writing itself, is controlled in the essay, as it need not be in the letter. And Hazlitt's personal letters go beyond those in the *Liber*, which, as Robert Ready observes, are themselves edited to fit the overall theme and structure of that work and given "a good deal more coherence" than "some of the disconnected ravings we find in the original letters" (Ready 54). Note, for example, the following excerpt from this personal letter from Hazlitt to P. G. Patmore: "I would give a thousand worlds to believe her anything but what I suppose. *I love her, Heaven knows* [italics Hazlitt's]. W. H. You say I am to try her after she agrees to have me: No: but I hate her for this, that she refuses me, when she could go to—[several words obliterated] aye, and with a grave air,—I'm mad! so much for sentiment" (*Works,* IX, 273). These letters offer an even more striking contrast with the essays. They remind me of the sort of writing composition that students do when told to "free-write" or to write in their journals. Ideas and perhaps deep feelings are flung out on paper, and only later do they achieve coherence and clarity in essay form. The sense of balance in the Familiar Style allows writers to express their deepest emotions but always with an awareness of their audience's sensibilities; when an essayist remains merely self-indulgent and ambiguous or disorganized, he or she has not gone far enough with revision or editing for clarity's sake.

Audience awareness also demands careful word choice, leading to writing that is precise, another attribute of the Familiar Style which also involves balance. Though the essayist need not be as technically precise, perhaps, as the scientist, philosopher, or theologian must be, he or she needs to choose words with greater care than does the conversationalist. Hazlitt says: "Out of eight or ten words equally common, equally intelligible, with nearly equal pretensions, it is a matter of some nicety and discrimination to pick out the very one, the preferableness of which is scarcely perceptible, but decisive" ("On the Familiar Style," *Works*, VIII, 243). For example, notice the use of the word "dalliance" in the following excerpt from "The Pleasure of Hating": "Pleasure asks a greater effort of the mind to support it than pain, and we turn, after a little *dalliance*, from what we love to what we hate" (emphasis mine). Hazlitt could have conveyed virtually the same sentence meaning with several other words— "while," "time," "flirtation"—but "dalliance" conveys just the right sense of short, fleeting time combined with a sense of something being loosely and playfully held. Again, note the use of the word "governed" in "Conversations as Good as Real III" (*Works*, XX, 295): "A man's understanding often had no more influence over his will than if they belonged to two different persons; nor frequently so much, since we sometimes consented to be *governed* by advice, though we could not control our passions if left to ourselves" (emphasis mine). In the context, the word "governed" denotes influence; however, "governed" also implies a sense of authority and of force not found in the word "influenced" and is thereby connected with the term "control" used in the next phrase. Hazlitt saw this ability to choose the precisely correct word as his strong point (Nabholtz 98); Hazlitt states, "I only used the word which seemed to me to signify the idea I wanted to convey, and I did not rest until I got it" ("Letter to William Gifford," *Works*, IX, 30; quoted in Nabholtz).

This precise use of words helps to give the Familiar Style its quality of being like "heightened conversation." Again, the sense of balance is important. While Hazlitt asserts, "To expect an author to talk as he writes is ridiculous" ("Characteristics," *Works*, IX, Letter 281, p. 208), he says that a good essay should give the effect of conversation in terms of voice and personal expressiveness while heightening this effect with the precise use of appropriate words. Says Hazlitt, "To write a genuine or truly English style, is to write as anyone would speak in common conversation, who had a thorough command and choice of words, or who could discourse with ease, force, and perspicuity, setting aside all pedantic and oratorical flourishes" ("Familiar Style," *Works*, VII, 242). Nothing could sound more simple and "conversational" than the following statement from Hazlitt's essay "On Novelty and Familiarity": "I have spun out this Essay in a good measure from the dread I feel of entering upon new subjects" (*Works*, XII, 309). What could be more personal or appear more spontaneous than a writer's confession of a feeling of inadequacy about writing? However, a close reading will discover that the words "spun out" are indeed carefully chosen and implicitly metaphorical, suggesting a weaving of words and implying an analogy between spinner/craftsman and writer/craftsman. Or notice the key words in Hazlitt's description of the "newly ennobled" lady in "On Vulgarity and Affectation": "She rises into the air of gentility from the ground of a city life, and flutters about there with all the fantastic delight of a butterfly that has just changed its caterpillar state" (*Works*, VIII, 165). What words or phrases could better suggest the ephemeral quality of the state he is describing than "rises into air," "flutters," "fantastic delight," "butterfly"? The sentence is written in simple and clear English vocabulary, but the precisely chosen words "heighten" its effect.

Together with careful word choice, artful sentence structure also gives Hazlitt's Familiar Style the sense of being heightened conversation. Notice the parallelism in this highly personal and expressive yet carefully written excerpt from "A Farewell to Essay Writing" (*Works*, XVII, 314): "Beautiful Mask! I know thee! When I can judge of the heart from the face, of the thoughts from the lips, I may again trust myself!" Or note the similar use of parallelism in the following excerpt from "On Paradox": "With one party, whatever is, is right: with their antagonists, whatever is, is wrong" (*Works*, VIII, 147). The balance of the sentence structure unobtrusively gives the writing a poetic quality not usually found in ordinary speech while allowing it to retain its sense of naturalness and spontaneity.

Using the precise word in its proper context requires effort but not stultifying and excessive self-consciousness in a writer. Here again the balance of the Familiar Style avoids the extreme of overly rigorous precision of language. Like the Indian Juggler, the essayist must keep the equilibrium between naturalness of tone and carefully chosen vocabulary. While "the first word that occurs" is certainly not always the best, it may, says Hazlitt, "be a very good one; and yet a better may present itself on reflection or from time to time" ("Familiar Style, *Works*, VIII, 244). The good essayist is comfortable enough with subject and self to relax about vocabulary, allowing ultimately for better word choice. Hazlitt says a change in wording "should be suggested naturally . . . and spontaneously, from a fresh and lively conception of the subject" ("Familiar Style," *Works*, VIII, 244). Unlike the philosophical or scientific writer, the essayist of the familiar style need not rigorously labor over the technically correct term. The subject, as always, is key; if the words elucidate the subject as clearly as possible, the essayist has done his or her job. Even the general organization of the essay must be determined by the subject and not rigorously imposed upon it. As John Nabholtz points out, Hazlitt's essays are not amorphous, as some people have said, but organized naturally around subject and purpose rather than made to fit a rhetorical pattern. Says Hazlitt: "A clear and comprehensive mind is, I conceive, shewn, not in the extensiveness of the plan which an author has chalked out for himself, but in the order and connection observed in the arrangement of the subject and the consistency of the several parts" ("Reply to the Essay on Population," *Works*, I, 186–87; quoted in Nabholtz). Hazlitt makes this point very clearly in his description of the Familiar Style: "It is not pomp or pretension, but the adaptation of the expression to the idea that clenches a writer's meaning" ("Familiar Style," *Works*, VIII, 244). Therefore, the proper choice of words and the correct organizational pattern flow from the desire to communicate as easily and effectively as possible with one's audience. If that desire becomes tainted with the urge to impress or mystify, meaning becomes lost in the words instead of being expressed through them.

Using what Hazlitt calls "common words" in their clearest application will result in universality, another important quality of the Familiar Style. The desire to communicate something to an audience leads the essayist to avoid pretension on the one hand and slang or ambiguity on the other; once again, we see that balance is key to Hazlitt's conception of the essay. Words are chosen for the clearest exposition of the subject and are used in their most widely recognized meaning. Says Hazlitt, "A truly natural or familiar style can never be quaint or vulgar for this reason, that it is of universal force and applicability, and that quaintness and vulgarity arise out of the immediate connection of certain words with coarse and disagreeable, or with confined ideas" ("Familiar Style," *Works*, VIII, 242).

This distinction often arises in composition classes. If the teacher as well as the students can consistently remember the fulfillment of the goal of communication as the yardstick by which to measure all word choices, then much confusion may be avoided. Having taught composition on the college level for eight years, I know that many student writers need to see why it is important to choose words that their audience will clearly understand and to avoid words that will either alienate or confuse their readers. Thus the desire for clarity and universality, not for an overly pristine sense of formality, makes the use of slang words or colloquialisms generally inappropriate in a college essay though entirely appropriate in a letter, a journal, or ordinary speech. Words such as "hassle" (used as a noun) or "party" (used as a verb), for example, make perfect sense when used among student speakers, but in an essay intended for a general audience, these terms may be wrong. As Hazlitt puts it, a colloquialism "has a stamp exclusive and provincial" ("On Vulgarity and Affectation," *Works,* VIII, 162). A quality that Hazlitt finds particularly annoying is *affected* vulgarity, for like any other affectation, it falsifies writing: "Nothing is vulgar that is natural, spontaneous, unavoidable. Grossness is not vulgarity, ignorance is not vulgarity, awkwardness is not vulgarity; but all these become vulgar when they are affected and shown off on the authority of others, or to fall in with *the fashion* or the company we keep" ("On Vulgarity and Affectation," *Works,* VIII, 161). Colloquialisms often fit the above description, since they are frequently expressions in vogue, fleeting in popularity and changeable of meaning.

However, far from saying that informality is wrong in itself, Hazlitt himself uses slang, colloquialisms, and obscenity in his letters and journal but generally eschews such language in his essays, where his aim is the clarity and universality of the Familiar Style. Notice, for example, his use of the word "set" in the following excerpt from his journal notes during the period of his infatuation with Sarah Walker: "She then went out and gave one of her *set* [emphasis mine] looks at the door" (*Journals,* March 4, 1823). Hazlitt seems to have a special, personal meaning for the word "set"—appropriate for his journal but not for an essay, were he to use it in one without an explanation. In fact, he makes a point of saying that he avoids such a practice: "I never invented or gave a new and unauthorized meaning to any word but one single one (the term 'impersonal' applied to feelings) and that was in an abstruse metaphysical discussion to express a very difficult question" ("Familiar Style," *Works,* VIII, 244). Notice the contrast that Hazlitt stresses between language of the Familiar Style, which should always advance the audience's ease of understanding, and that of another sort of writing, here metaphysics, wherein technical precision must impose itself over audience accessibility. Another example of Hazlitt's use of terminology inappropriate for the Familiar Style is his calling Sarah Walker "a bitch" and "an artful little vixen" and other such appellations in his letters or journal while avoiding such terminology in the essays.

Of course, no writer can ever achieve a style that is totally universal. Like all of the qualities of the Familiar Style, its universality is also an ideal toward which the essayist aims; the essayist can never be completely and equally accessible to *all* audiences. However, the concept of universality can do much to help students and teachers go beyond the mere arbitrariness of what is considered "acceptable" or "unacceptable" for a formal essay as opposed to what is appropriate in preliminary free writing or journal writing. If the clearest communication possible with one's audience is the goal in the essay, as Hazlitt suggests, the decision about which phrase works and which one does not becomes simplified. And student writers, understanding the *reason* why certain colloquialisms or slang words are considered inappropriate for a specific audience or type of assignment, can avoid the mistaken idea that all such informal language is bad *in itself* when used in the proper context.

This understanding can alleviate the confusion into which some student writers fall as they try to avoid informality, which they have been taught to do without understanding why, by using an excessively formal and inflated style. The result is writing in what Hazlitt calls "the florid style . . . the reverse of the familiar" (*Works,* VIII, 246). While the Familiar Style "is employed as an unvarnished medium to convey ideas," the Florid Style "is resorted to as a spangled veil to conceal the want of them" ("Familiar Style," *Works,* VIII, 246). Unfortunately, the latter problem is more difficult to correct than the former. To such writers, the pageantry of words seems impressive, and often they cannot understand exactly what the writing teacher (or editor) finds objectionable. However, Hazlitt says such writers are guilty of another sort of "vulgarity" which is perhaps even worse than that which they are trying to avoid: "Gentility is only a more select and artificial vulgarity" ("On Vulgarity and Affectation," *Works,* VIII, 157). The root problem in both cases is falsehood, "taking manners, actions, words, opinions on trust from others, without examining one's own feelings or weighing the merits of the case" ("On Vulgarity and Affectation," *Works,* VIII, 157). As with all of the other attributes of the Familiar Style, the key here is once again to convey the subject in the most direct and honest way possible, maintaining the balance between a confusing overformality and a limiting colloquialism. An inflated style, like a "vulgar" one, as Hazlitt calls it, impedes honest communication.

Hazlitt notes a further solution for this problem of artificiality in his discussion of the naturalness of the Familiar Style. For Hazlitt, the source of all good writing is Truth: all that is real, expressed in words as it is experienced in the heart of the writer. For him, any other sort of writing is mere "pride and ignorance—pride in outside show . . . and ignorance of the true worth and hidden structure of both words and things" ("Familiar Style," *Works*, VIII, 247). In his essay "On Novelty and Familiar Things," Hazlitt states, "That the tongue or the pen or the pencil can describe the workings of nature with the highest truth and eloquence without being prompted by or holding communication with the heart . . . I utterly deny" (*Works*, XII, 298). One cannot *pretend* to a Familiar Style; one must be speaking from the heart. In Hazlitt's words, "What we impart to others we have within us" ("Novelty and Familiar Things"). The writing teacher and the student writer both experience the frustration of reading and producing, respectively, works that proceed from a desire for a grade, a desire to imitate "textbook style" writing, a desire to please; however, if students can be guided toward producing works that on one level or another proceed from the heart, they will have moved a long way toward becoming serious and interesting writers. Any essayist, guided by Hazlitt's principles of the Familiar Style, can move in the direction of writing that fits Harold Bloom's description of Hazlitt's literary essay: "It must be experiential; it must be at least somewhat empirical or pragmatic; it must be informed by love of its subject; above all it must follow no method except the personality of the critic himself" (Bloom 8).

Hazlitt's Familiar Style of essay writing can therefore be defined as *a means for the mind to express the feelings of the heart,* as it is stirred by nature, that is, anything and everything. Yet it must do so in a manner that retains the balance, the sense of audience awareness, that distinguishes self-expressiveness from mere self-indulgent expression. The Essay, with its adaptability and limitless range of potential subjects, is the perfect vehicle for such expression. Its possible subject matters are vast because the capacity of the human mind to interpret and experience its surroundings is vast. "What a Proteus is the human mind!" exclaims Hazlitt; "All that we know, think of, or can admire, in a manner becomes ourselves" ("On Personal Identity," *Works*, XVII, 274). Hazlitt's own essays, particularly when they are contrasted with his other writings, exhibit the Familiar Style he advocates in their clarity, their universality, their naturalness, and, most important, their balance. Though Hazlitt humbly contrasts his ability as a writer with the dexterity of the Indian Juggler, his Familiar Style is a valiant attempt to reproduce as well as to define, through "the inefficiency and slow progress of intellectual compared to mechanical excellence" ("Indian Jugglers," *Works*, VIII, 79), something of the balancing act he so admired.

Works Cited

Bloom, Harold. "Introduction." In *Modern Critical Views: William Hazlitt,* ed. and introd. Harold Bloom. New York: Chelsea House, 1986.

Chesire, Ardner R., Jr. "William Hazlitt: Slangwhanger." *Wordsworth Circle,* 7 (1976):101–102.

Hazlitt, William. *The Complete Works in Twenty-One Volumes: Centenary Edition.* Ed. P. P. Howe. After the edition of A. R. Waller and Arnold Glover. New York: AMS Press, 1967.

————. *The Journals of Sarah and William Hazlitt, 1822–1831.* Ed. Willard Hallard Bonner. *University of Buffalo Studies,* vol. 24, no. 3, February 1959.

Nabholtz, John R. "Modes of Discourse in Hazlitt's Prose." *Wordsworth Circle,* 10 (1979):97–106.

Ready, Robert. "The Logic of Passion: *Liber Amoris.*" In *Modern Critical Views: William Hazlitt,* ed. and introd. Harold Bloom. New York: Chelsea House, 1986.

The Essay as Aesthetic Ritual: W. B. Yeats and Ideas of Good and Evil

Charles O'Neill

Virginia Woolf claims that the essay "should lay us under a spell with its first word, and we should only
wake, refreshed, with its last" (*CEII* 41). These words apply literally to
the essays of William Butler Yeats. Most often consulted as explanatory
material for the poetry and plays, Yeats's many essays exist in their own
right as unique examples of the modern essayist's art. I will consider
Yeats's early essays with a view to accounting for the "spell" they cast no
matter how often they are read.

At the end of his career, Yeats wrote, "As I altered my syntax I altered
my intellect" (*E&I* 530). This statement applies as much to his prose as to
his poetry. Yeats wrote essays throughout his life for many purposes: to
create audiences for his diverse interests, to explain his esoteric beliefs,
and to reflect on his art and on his life. The *Autobiographies* volume is
actually a series of more or less self-contained essays composed over
many years and in differing styles. From the luxuriant rhythms of his
earliest prose to the astringency of his last, Yeats's essays reflect not only
the evolution of a commanding literary sensibility but also the evolution
of the modern essay itself.

Ideas of Good and Evil collects the best and most suggestive of the
essays Yeats wrote between 1895 and 1903, from his thirtieth to his thirty-seventh year. In this period the poet was committed both to creating an
audience for Irish literature and to the symbolist aesthetic in art and
thought. These early essays differ from other modern essays and from
Yeats's own later work. Whether appraisals of other writers, reflections on
the nature of art, or investigations into occult ideas, the essays in *Ideas of*

Good and Evil employ symbolist thought and technique to suggest a version of "reality" in which the imagination—and not science—is the central good.

In his essay "Magic," Yeats asks rhetorically, "Have not poetry and music arisen, as it seems, out of the sounds the enchanters made to help their imagination to enchant, to charm, to bind with a spell themselves and the passers-by?" (*E&I* 43). For Yeats, the purpose of this spell or enchantment was nothing less than the transformation of the modern world. In the new age that symbolist art is heralding, the imagination will reassert its ancient authority over empirical reality. "I cannot get it out of my head," Yeats writes in 1895, "that this age of criticism is about to pass, and an age of imagination, of emotion, of moods, of revelation, about to come in its place" (197). Symbolist in manner and matter, the essays collected in *Ideas of Good and Evil* attempt to indicate, as much as Yeats's poems of the 1890s, the art of that "new age."

Kenneth Burke, in *Counter-Statement,* writes that "if the artist's 'revelations' are of tremendous importance to him, he will necessarily seek to ritualize them, to find a correspondingly important setting for them" (168). In the nineteen essays of *Ideas of Good and Evil,* Yeats attempts to "ritualize," through complex patterns of syntax and symbol, the "revelation" of the new age he anticipated. According to Burke, "Revelation is 'belief,' or 'fact.' Art enters when this revelation is ritualized, when it is converted into a symbolic process" (168). The early essays of Yeats are works of art: while announcing the "revelation" of a new age, they also, by means of evocative symbol and complexly cadenced prose, deliver that "revelation" in "ritual." The best of these essays go beyond the traditional rhetorical ends of the form to enter the nonparaphrasable realm of poetry. From the great mass of his early essays, book reviews, and journalism, Yeats selected only those works which, in manner as well as matter, announce a new age.

Yeats, with his avowed hostility to objective truth, logic, "the restraints of reason" (*E&I* 195), and a corresponding faith in subjectivity, intuition, and revelation, works without many of the traditional tools of the essayist in designing his "aesthetic rituals." In an essay entitled "The Moods," Yeats explains: "Literature differs from explanatory and scientific writing in being wrought about a mood, or a community of moods, as the body is wrought about an invisible soul; and if it uses argument, theory, erudition, observation, and seems to grow hot in assertion or denial, it does so merely to make us partakers at the banquet of the moods" (*E&I* 195). This brief essay, only a paragraph in length, replaces argument by a patterned repetition of words and phrases in the manner of a poem. It is, in effect, a "spell" that Yeats seeks to cast over his readers. The nineteen essays together constitute "a community of moods" that persuade by suggestion and evocation. Yeats writes, "Everything that can be seen, touched, measured, explained, understood, argued over, is to the imaginative artist nothing more than a means, for he belongs to the invisible life, and delivers its ever new and ever ancient revelations" (E&I 195). Thus as an imaginative artist Yeats comes to the essay, employing symbolist thought and technique to deliver this "revelation."

The beliefs that organize and motivate *Ideas of Good and Evil* are presented most succinctly in the essay "Magic." Yeats declares, "I believe in the practice and philosophy of what we have agreed to call magic," and he then lists three articles of faith or "doctrines": "(1) That the borders of our mind are ever shifting, and that many minds can flow into one another, as it were, and create or reveal a single mind, a single energy. (2) That the borders of our memories are as shifting, and that our memories are a part of one great memory, the memory of Nature itself. (3) That this great mind and great memory can be evoked by symbols" (E&I 28). The essay "Magic" treats, in detail, the poet's own efforts to evoke "spirits" by means of magical symbols. "I cannot now think symbols less than the greatest of all powers," Yeats writes, "whether they are used consciously by the masters of magic, or half consciously by their successors, the poet, the musician and the artist" (E&I 49). All artists, in other words, work in the same essential manner and to the same end: casting spells to evoke the "great memory," they thereby enchant their audiences. Yeats claims, "If I can unintentionally cast a glamour, an enchantment, over persons of our own time who have lived for years in great cities, there is no reason to doubt that men could cast intentionally a far stronger enchantment, a far stronger glamour, over the more sensitive people of ancient times, or that men can still do so where the old order of life remains unbroken" (E&I 42). With *Ideas of Good and Evil*, Yeats will announce the imminent return of the "old order of life."

Yeats took the book's title from William Blake. According to Yeats, Blake "announced the religion of art," the one "true" religion of the modern world. "In our time," Yeats writes, "we are agreed that we 'make our souls' out of some one of the great poets of ancient times" or out of such modern poets as Blake, Shelley, or Wordsworth (IGE 111). The role of the artist in this "soul-making" is that of a priest: "We who care deeply about the arts find ourselves the priesthood of an almost forgotten faith, and we must, I think, if we would win the people again, take upon ourselves the method and the fervour of a priesthood" (IGE 203).

In such a religion of art, the "ideas of evil" would include rhetoric, allegory, the will, reason, Nature, and time; those of "good" would include revelation, symbol, imagination, art, and Eternity. The central "good" is, of course, the imagination. The goal of such a faith would be "to come at least to forget good and evil" in what Yeats calls "an absorbing vision of the happy and unhappy" (*E&I* 129). The imagination, in these terms, is beyond good and evil.

If William Blake is behind much of the matter of this volume, Walter Pater inspired its manner. In his 1918 poem "The Phases of the Moon," Yeats recalls "that extravagant style / He had learned from Pater" (*P* 164, 26–27). He employed that style in his fiction and essays of the 1890s. In *The Renaissance,* Pater, following Buffon, noted that "'the style is the man'—and it is his plenary sense of what he really has to say, his sense of the world" (412). Hating what he called "that straight-forward logic, as of newspaper articles" (*E&I* 5), Yeats, when he deployed his own prose style most deliberately, dispensed with argumentation, "manifest logic," and "clear rhetoric" (8) in favor of evocation, poetic citation, and suggestive rhythm. Yeats can be seen as having turned his back on the three most popular modes of the nineteenth-century essay: the familiar essay (Hazlitt), the critical essay (Arnold), and the scientific essay (Huxley). In this, he followed Pater, who, in his essay on "Style," insisted that a writer is "vindicating his liberty in the making of a vocabulary, an entire system of composition, for himself, his own true manner" (398).

Pater's sinuous, allusive prose style was perfectly suited to Yeats's symbolist aesthetic. Late in his career, Yeats printed a passage from Pater's description of the Mona Lisa as free verse, contending that it was a poem, one which had arisen "out of its own rhythm" (*OBMV* vii). For Yeats, poems often did arise, not from ideas, but from rhythms, and the acoustic singularity of a cadence or phrase frequently led him to an insight not consciously intended. In like manner, Yeats felt that Pater's subtly cadenced prose rhythms were able to transform a rhetorical description into a poetic incantation. It was the "extravagant style" he needed for his own early prose.

Yeats's debt to Pater goes well beyond the influence of the latter's prose rhythm. In essays written throughout his long career, Yeats practices what Pater, in the preface to *The Renaissance,* calls "aesthetic criticism" (71). Pater required the "aesthetic critic" to ask: "What is this song or picture, this engaging personality presented in life or in a book, to me? What effect does it really produce on me?" (71). The essays on art and artists collected in *Ideas of Good and Evil* examine their subjects for the sake of what they mean to Yeats and, specifically, to his sense of an imminent "revelation." Yeats's essays are examples of what Pater calls "the literature of the imaginative sense of fact" (395). The artist, for Pater, transcribes "not . . . mere fact, but his . . . sense of it" and concludes, "All beauty is in the long run only *fineness* of truth, or what we call expression, the finer accommodation to that vision within" (396). Yeats's "vision" in his early poems, stories, and essays was of a world about to undergo a complete change of mind, or "mood," and he accommodated his "speech" on the art and ideas of others to that personal "vision within." Throughout *Ideas of Good and Evil,* literary criticism, historical speculation, poetry, philosophy, the occult, and personal experience are woven together to illustrate what Yeats calls "the continuous indefinable symbolism which is the substance of all style" (*E&I* 155).

In an essay entitled "The Symbolism of Poetry," Yeats describes the change of style the "new age" will bring:

> With this change of substance, this return to imagination, this understanding that the laws of art, which are the hidden laws of the world, can alone bind the imagination, would come a change of style, and we would cast out of serious poetry those energetic rhythms, as of a man running, which are the invention of the will with its eyes always on something to be done or undone; and we would seek out those wavering, meditative, organic rhythms, which are the embodiment of the imagination, that neither desires nor hates, because it has done with time, and only wishes to gaze upon some reality, some beauty; nor would it be any longer possible for anybody to deny the importance of form, in all its kinds, for although you can expound an opinion, or describe a thing, when your words are not quite well chosen, you cannot give a body to something that moves beyond the sense, unless your words are as subtle, as complex, as full of mysterious life, as the body of a flower or of a woman. [*E&I* 163–64]

This singular sentence makes up what I would call an "aesthetic ritual"; the "revelation" of a "change of style" is delivered in the "ritual" of the sentence's incantatory cadences. Instead of argument or description, Yeats, following symbolist procedure, suggests this coming "change" with the "wavering, meditative, organic rhythms" of the sentence itself. From individual sentence to entire volume, *Ideas of Good and Evil* is as deliberately composed as the "sacred books of the arts" it anticipates: form and content are inextricably fused.

In an essay entitled "Symbolism in Painting," Yeats declares, "All art that is not mere story-telling, or mere portraiture, is symbolic, and has the purpose of those symbolic talismans which medieval magicians made with complex colours and forms, and bade their patients ponder over daily, and guard with holy secrecy; for it entangles, in complex colours and forms, a part of the Divine Essence" (*E&I* 148). As much as any symbolist poem, the essays in *Ideas of Good and Evil* are designed to "entangle," on the formal levels of sentence, essay, and collection, the "patient" reader as well as whatever "part of the Divine Essence" the poet can capture. For Yeats constructs both sentence and essay as "symbolic talismans" that require pondering before they yield a meaning.

Yeats's famous essay "On the Philosophy of Shelley's Poetry" can bring his essayistic strategies into focus. Written in a style of Paterian extravagance, it is a striking example of symbolist procedure applied to the essay form. Dispensing with logic, reason, and argumentation, and relying on evocation, suggestion, and incantation, the essay is a symbolic talisman that proposes the image of Shelley as a symbolist poet. All of the volume's themes are woven into this prose reverie: symbolism, magic, Irish folklore, and the "revelation" that Yeats hoped for. Yeats's "Shelley" is as much a creation of a Paterian "vision within" as Pater's own "Mona Lisa."

Like a familiar essay, it opens with a personal reminiscence: "When I was a boy in Dublin," Yeats writes, "I was one of a group who rented a room in a mean street to discuss philosophy" (*E&I* 65). Yeats then announces his "one unshakable belief": "I thought that whatever of philosophy has been made poetry is alone permanent" (*E&I* 65). After years of observing "dreams and visions," he is now "certain" that "the imagination has some way of lighting on the truth that the reason has not, and that its commandments, delivered when the body is still and the reason silent, are the most binding we can ever know" (*E&I* 65). This sequence of beliefs, which we recognize from other essays in the volume, serves as a prelude to the discussion of Shelley. Yeats's "imagination," then, sets the conditions in which Shelley will be seen. We can expect that when *Prometheus Unbound* is introduced, it will be seen as a Yeatsian "sacred Book." He writes of it: "I remember going to a learned scholar to ask about its deep meanings, which I felt more than understood, and his telling me that it was Godwin's *Political Justice* put into rhyme, and that Shelley was a crude revolutionist, and believed that the overturning of kings and priests would regenerate mankind" (*E&I* 65–66). Yeats, who felt that a new "revelation" would soon regenerate mankind and that Shelley was one of its prophets, uses these lines to dismiss academic criticism: it is the "scholar," and not Shelley, who is revealed to be crude; Yeats's "feeling" for the book is the "standard" of judgment.

Yeats then assimilates Shelley to his symbolist pantheon. By a careful selection of quotations from *A Defense of Poetry*, Yeats insists that Shelley exalts the imaginative faculty and denigrates reason, "the calculating faculty" (*E&I* 68). "The speaker of these things," Yeats writes, "might almost be Blake, who held that the Reason not only created Ugliness, but all other evils" (*IGE* 68). Yeats is, clearly, creating in Shelley a precursor in order to provide further proof that "all art that is not mere story-telling . . . is symbolic" (*E&I* 146).

After "proving" that Shelley was an early symbolist, Yeats concludes the first section of the essay by assimilating Shelley's work to his own world of Irish folk belief:

> I have re-read his *Prometheus Unbound* for the first time for many years, in the woods of Drim-na-Rod, among the Echtage hills, and sometimes I have looked towards Slieve ná nOg where the country people say the last battle of the world shall be fought till the third day, when a priest shall lift a chalice, and the thousand years of peace begin. And I think this mysterious song utters a faith as simple and as ancient as the faith of those country people, in a form suited to a new age, that will understand with Blake that the Holy Spirit is 'an intellectual fountain,' and that the kinds and degrees of beauty are the images of its authority. [*E&I* 77–78]

Shelley, Blake, Yeats himself, and the unlettered Irish "country people" are all united in receiving influences from what he calls here, with a nod to orthodoxy, "the Holy Spirit" but in the next paragraph the "great Memory" (*E&I* 79).

The longest sentence of the entire volume begins, "Alastor passed in his boat along a river in a cave" (81). It continues, paratactically, for thirty-four lines and draws on at least seven separate poems by Shelley in order to exhibit his recurring symbols. In the essay "Some Post-Symbolist Structures," Hugh Kenner notes that Yeats adopted Mallarmé's "syntactic legerdemain" in some poems of the 1890s. Kenner proves that Yeats's poem "He Remembers Forgotten Beauty" "proceeds by systematic digression from its formal structure" (388). And Kenner claims, "The effect is to move our attention as far as may be from the thrust of subject-verb-object. The structure is formal, elaborate, symmetrical, and syntactically faultless; and yet only by a very great effort of attention is the reader like to discover it is" (390). Yeats's prose, likewise, "proceeds by systematic digression"; in doing so, it creates true talismanic labyrinths, sentences to wander lost in, hypnotized by rhythm and word choice. We are finally convinced of the "truth" of the sentence, not by its logic or cogency, but by the elaborate formal "ritual" we have undergone to reach its end.

The conclusion of "On the Philosophy of Shelley's Poetry" reveals the true import of the essay. Here Yeats is imagining a Shelley born into a culture in which the older imaginative traditions are still in force:

I think too that as he knelt before an altar where a thin flame burnt in a lamp made of green agate, a single vision would have come to him again and again, a vision of a boat drifting down a broad river between high hills where there were caves and towers, and following the light of one Star; and that voices would have told him how there is for every man some one scene, some one adventure, some one picture that is the image of his secret life, for wisdom speaks first in images, and that this one image, if he would but brood over it his life long, would lead his soul, disentangled from unmeaning circumstance and the ebb and flow of the world, into that far household where the undying gods await all whose souls have become as quiet as an agate lamp. [*E&I* 94–95]

In this "talismanic sentence," Shelley's own images—the "caves and towers," "Star," and drifting boat—are the pretext for Yeats's own "critical creation." It is, in fact, a belief of Yeats's—that for every man there is "one image" which will redeem his soul from the entanglements of reality—that is being "revealed" in the "aesthetic ritual" of the sentence. Yeats's own beliefs, finally, and not "The Philosophy of Shelley's Poetry," are the real subject of this essay. Shelley's own work is judged inadequate throughout and nowhere more than in the concluding sentence. There Yeats writes: "But [Shelley] was born in a day when the old wisdom had vanished and was content merely to write verses, and often with little thought of more than verses" (*E&I* 95). With these abrupt words, the "spell" that the essay cast is broken, and we are left impatiently waiting for the day when the "old wisdom" will return.

The question that "The Philosophy of Shelley's Poetry" asks—and it is the question posed by *Ideas of Good and Evil* as a whole—might be "How does the Great Memory work in the modern world?" Yeats's answer is that it works through symbols. But as an "answer" impossible of "proof," it is given through suggestion and repetition. Yeats's "dialogue" with Shelley, with his symbols considered as "philosophy," can extend only so far; Shelley is not Yeats, and the "dialogue" is finally internal.

If, as I have claimed, each essay in *Ideas of Good and Evil* is a "mood," the entire volume makes up what Yeats calls "a community of moods" (*E&I* 195). Whatever the ostensible subject of each essay, they have a common style, content, and purpose. All, in some degree, seek to announce a "revelation"; each does so by "ritualizing," with rhythm and symbol, its contents. On receiving the volume, Yeats's oldest friend A. E. (George Russell) wrote to the poet: "I did not think I would like the book so well as I do for I had only read one or two of the essays before, but read together they throw a reflected light on each other and the book has a perfect unity" (Jeffares 132). In a reverie on the future of the arts entitled "The Autumn of the Body," Yeats concludes with the prophecy:

> I think that we will learn again how to describe at great length an old man wandering among enchanted islands, his return home at last, his slow gathering vengeance, a flitting shape of a goddess, and a flight of arrows, and yet to make all these so different things "take light from mutual reflection, like an actual trail of fire over precious stone," and become "an entire world," the signature or symbol of a mood of the divine imagination as imponderable as "the horror of the forest or the silent thunder in the leaves." [*E&I* 195]

In this passage, the images are from Homer, the quoted phrases from Mallarmé: the oldest Western poetry and, as of 1903, the newest, are drawn together by Yeats as embodiments of that "invisible life" which, he believes, perpetually "delivers its ever new and ever ancient revelations" (*E&I* 195).

The essays in *Ideas of Good and Evil*, like poems, finally resist paraphrase. Their intricate thematic, syntactical, and sonic patterns, sometimes descending into obscurity, often rising into poetic lucidity, make them works of art. Their contribution to the later poetry of Yeats has been, I believe, overlooked. In managing the syntactical complexities of his talismanic sentences and in the sudden "leaps" of poetic and intuitive "logic" the essays make, Yeats went a long way toward the intricate stanzas and sharp contrasts of his finest poetry.

Essays are written for many reasons: to describe, to persuade, to inform, to record personal impressions. Yeats himself had these as goals but felt compelled to work toward them in his own way. He declared: "The scientific movement brought with it a literature which was always tending to lose itself in externalities of all kinds, in opinion, in declamation, in picturesque writing, in word-painting . . . , and now writers have begun to dwell upon the element of evocation, of suggestion, upon what we call the symbolism in great writers" (*E&I* 155). The symbolist essay, as Yeats developed it in this volume, seeks to persuade and inform by "suggestion" and "evocation," to make his readers susceptible to an imminent "revelation" by involving them in the "aesthetic rituals" of sentence and essay. It is not a direction that most other essayists of the twentieth century have followed.

Yeats himself changed the direction of his prose. When reading the proofs of *Ideas of Good and Evil*, he had a meeting with the young James Joyce, who made him self-conscious and doubtful about the "generalizations" the books contained. Yeats then wrote, but did not publish, an "introduction" containing these criticisms. He did, however, write a letter to A. E. which casts light on his formal and thematic intentions:

> I am no longer in much sympathy with an essay like "The Autumn of the Body," not that I think that essay untrue. But I think that I mistook for a permanent phase of the world what was only a preparation. The close of the last century was full of a strange desire to get out of form, to get to some kind of disembodied beauty, and now it seems to me the contrary impulse has come. I feel about me and in me an impulse to create form, to carry the realization of beauty as far as possible. [*Letters* 402]

Yeats's "strange desire to get out of form" helped create the incantatory rhythms and the subjective development of these early essays.

If Yeats himself became disenchanted with the millenarian aspirations of *Ideas of Good and Evil*, the essays in which he elaborated them still possess the power that Virginia Woolf sought in the modern essay: "It must draw its curtain around us, but it must be a curtain that shuts us in, not out" (*CEII* 50). These symbolist essays of Yeats enable us, reading them, to participate in an "aesthetic ritual" while we ponder, in the prose itself, a poetic "revelation."

Works Cited

Burke, Kenneth. *Counter-Statement.* 1931. Berkeley: University of California Press, 1969.

Jeffares, A. Norman, ed. *W. B. Yeats: The Critical Heritage.* London: Routledge, 1977.

Kenner, Hugh. "Some Post-Symbolist Structures." *Literary Theory and Structure.* Ed. Frank Brady, John Palmer, and Martin Price. New Haven: Yale University Press, 1973.

Lentricchia, Frank. *The Gaiety of Language: An Essay on the Radical Poetics of W. B. Yeats and Wallace Stevens.* Berkeley: University of California Press, 1968.

Pater, Walter. *Walter Pater: Three Major Texts.* Ed. William E. Buckler. New York: New York University Press, 1986.

Symons, Arthur. *The Symbolist Movement in Literature.* 1899. Reprint. New York: E. P. Dutton, 1959.

Woolf, Virginia. "The Modern Essay." *Collected Essays, II.* New York: Harcourt, 1967.

Yeats, W. B. *Autobiographies.* London: Macmillan, 1955.

_____. *Essays and Introductions.* New York: Macmillan, 1961.

_____. *Ideas of Good and Evil.* 1903. New York: Russell and Russell, 1967.

_____. *The Letters of W. B. Yeats*. Ed. Allen Wade. New York: Macmillan, 1955.

_____. *The Oxford Book of Modern Verse, 1892–1935*. Chosen by W. B. Yeats. Oxford: Clarendon Press, 1936.

_____. *The Poems*. Ed. Richard J. Finneran. New York: Macmillan, 1983.

_____. *Uncollected Prose by W. B. Yeats*. Vol. 1. Ed. John P. Frayne. New York: Columbia University Press, 1976.

"Inferences Made Afterwards": Lawrence and the Essay

Duane Edwards

"Bitzer," said Thomas Gradgrind. "Your definition of a horse."
—CHARLES DICKENS, *Hard Times*

An essay is subjective, and so it cannot be trusted as much as a novel. And the "article" is even worse. Relying heavily on other people's ideas, it is not spontaneous. Also, being preconceived, it may do no more than justify a mental attitude or satisfy a personal need. So while the novelist may, at times, be "a dribbling liar," at least he writes a novel, "the highest example of subtle inter-relatedness that man has discovered" (Lawrence, *Phoenix*, 528). Being interrelated rather than absolute, that part of a book which is a novel cannot lie or be a lie. Instead, it is a "first creation." At the moment of inception, it is the process of discovery for the author. Like a flower, it is only what it is, in living relationship to its creator.

The same cannot be said for the typical essay. The subject of an essay is the author. At times we may not think so. Reading D. H. Lawrence's very beautiful "Flowery Tuscany" for the first time, I felt that I was surveying the Italian countryside through the informed, sensitive lens of an expensive camera. I saw what Lawrence calls the "rush of flowers": the narcissus, asphodel, myrtle, and hyacinth; the purple violet, the silvery pink almond blossom, the red tulips like poppies; the blue, thick, rich meaningful grape hyacinths, the peach blossom which "reveals itself like flesh"; the red-mouthed daisies "in sheets," the "lovely thick softness" of the cherry tree, "the early purple orchid, ruddy and very much alive"; the "odd yellow tulips, slender, spiky, and Chinese-looking" (50–55). But I was fooled. I did not see the flowers as they were; I received Lawrence's

137

impression of *meaningful* grape hyacinths, of a tulip which is, absurdly and beautifully, *like a poppy*, of a daisy with *a red mouth*.

Lawrence was not lying about what he saw so feelingly, nor was he creating. Instead, he saw what others could not see, and he wrote about it—in an absolute manner. That is, the author *is* the middle of his subject, is in the midst of the living flowers, looking out. And no one is looking in. No one is at the edge of the tulip field, shouting, "Damn it, Lawrence, you're wrong; the tulips aren't like poppies, they're like pale hands." So his account of flowers is absolute and may even be a lie.

Since Lawrence wrote first-rate poems, great short stories, the best travel literature in the English language, plays that work well in performance, volumes of fine letters, and novels, it is surprising that he wrote many essays. I am glad that he did. Placed alongside the novels and stories, the essays remind us that "essay" and "novel" are ideal categories. Like Plato's circles and squares, they exist only in the mind. Yet the categories are useful. They raise questions about what objectivity is, how an idea differs from a thought, what an article is, and why Lawrence wrote essays to begin with.

Why *did* Lawrence write essays? The obvious answer is that he needed the money, but he wrote for more than the money. He wrote to express his "mental attitude," his ideas, the ideal portion of his being, what is extrapolated from experience. Commenting on this passage in *Fantasia of the Unconscious*, he wrote

> This pseudo-philosophy of mine—"pollyanalytics," as one of my respected critics might say—is deduced from the novels and poems, not the reverse. The novels and poems come unwatched out of one's pen. And then the absolute need which one has for some sort of satisfactory mental attitude toward oneself and things in general makes one try to abstract some definite conclusions from one's experiences as a writer and as a man. The novels and poems are pure passionate experience. These "pollyanalytics" are inferences made afterwards, from the experience. [57]

At a glance this passage seems to refute my claim that novels are more objective than essays. After all, Lawrence calls novels "pure passionate experience" and calls his own essay an "absolute need" for "some sort of satisfactory mental attitude." And the common assumption is that ideas and mental attitudes are objective, while feelings are subjective.

Nothing could be farther from the truth unless, like Humpty Dumpty, we choose the meanings of our own words. Consult the dictionary where "objective" is defined as "existing independent of mind." Or consult a dictionary of literary terms in which an essay is defined as "a subjective and stimulating treatise." Or consult Lawrence himself, who wrote about ideas and thoughts, essays and novels, fiction and nonfiction.

As a young man Lawrence wrote three pieces called "A Chapel among the Mountains," "A Hay Hut among the Mountains," and "Once." The first two, the "mountain" pieces, seem to be nonfiction and the third seems to be fiction, but it is impossible to say that Lawrence intended them so. What *is* certain is that he and Frieda actually made a trip to the Tyrol, the setting of the "mountain" pieces, and so it is tempting to assume that the events of the first two pieces are drawn from his own life.

An autobiographical basis alone is not enough to make these pieces essays. After all, the best fiction often contains bits, fragments, and even entire slices of real life. But in the two pieces that seem to be essays, nothing has a life of its own, in relationship to the narrator. Instead, everything comes at the reader from one perspective: the narrator's. He observes and records the events and keeps them under his control. Another character, a woman named Anita, is present too and could disrupt the pleasant flow of conversation and events, but the narrator will not allow her to do so. In fact, she seems to exist at his discretion. She does not resist, and she does not startle. And when she speaks, he becomes feeble and yielding. On one occasion, he even fails to answer her, so the conversation can go nowhere—except where the narrator wants it to go. As a result, Anita's existence in the essays seems arbitrary.

So does the ending of the second essay, an ending which Lawrence erased, without detracting from the essay, and which the editors of *Phoenix,* II, reproduced, without adding anything to the essay. And so does the path, which becomes a road. It is in the essay not because of the vital connection with the characters or the setting but because the narrator needs it to go from one place to another.

Exerting such careful control, the narrator does not exist in relationship to Anita or in relationship to the events of the essay. As a result, he does not become distinct from his author. Instead, he and the author are synonymous, and he is at the center of the events he records. But he refuses to become involved in what he presents, and so he remains a mere chronicler. He even admits as much when, inside the chapel, he studies "a pale blue picture . . . , where a woman lay in bed, and a baby in a cradle not far away," and then adds

> I looked at them. And I knew that I was the husband looking and wondering. G., the husband, did not appear himself. It was from the little picture on his retina that this picture was reproduced. He could not sum it up, and explain

it. . . . But at least he could represent it, and hang it up like a mirror before the eyes of God, giving the statement even if he could get no explanation. And he was satisfied. And so, perforce, was I, though my heart began to knock for knowledge. [*Phoenix*, II, 33]

In brief, the events in the first two pieces, like the blue scene on the canvas, are projections of the narrator's memory; they are not the creation or even the recreation of experience itself. In fact, the narrator, left out of the experience he describes, feels a lack; his heart begins to knock for knowledge, he says.

Such is not the case with "Once," which is a story. Again, the unnamed narrator and Anita are featured, but this time she resists him and, in fact, says what he does not want to know. It is as if his heart has knocked so loudly for knowledge that a door is opened, finally, but the narrator cannot choose the door, nor can he know what is on the other side. Yes, he can accept quite readily that "she began to take lovers" when her marriage failed. After all, he wants to be part of that series. So he defines her promiscuity as "the courage to live, almost joyously." But once he lets the other lovers through the door and encourages her to talk about a one-night stand with a young German aristocrat who is the standard by which she measures all of her lovers, he cannot control his emotional response. He becomes irritated at first and then angry. And the incident is not merely a scene regarded from the point of view of a very perceptive observer; instead, it is part of a story. The two characters exist in relationship to one another and to the author. Whatever would emerge in such a situation does emerge—despite the author. He learns what he would rather not know about Anita and about himself—that she is pathologically narcissistic, that she has known only sensations with a man, that she has "felt the lack" of love during lovemaking; and that all of these characteristics attract him to her. Writing an essay, the narrator could not have gained this knowledge; he would have to have had it beforehand.

For Lawrence, fiction generally and the novel especially *are* experience itself. This statement does not mean that fiction is independent of its author. In fact, Lawrence believed that "an author should be in among the crowd, kicking shins or cheering on to some mischief or merriment" (Letter: June 22, 1925). But an author is not the subject of his novels; neither are his ideas or his personal feelings. Certainly his ideas and feelings may be *included* in a book but always in relationship to everywhere else in the book, or the book will not be a novel, will not be art, will not be "pure passionate experience."

In contrast, essays are "inferences made afterwards, from the experience." Since "the desire to abstract some definite conclusions" from experience is an "absolute need" (*Fantasia*, 57), this desire should not be condemned or denigrated. Nevertheless, it should be recognized for what it is: a subjective comment on experience itself and thus, to a degree at least, a distortion of what is.

There is a pattern. A person makes love, stops making love, and begins to think about what he did, but he is no longer doing it. Time is a knife which passes between experience and ideas, making it impossible for the two to be congruent. And in the postcoital gloom or peacefulness, a person may be experiencing something different from passion, something which must be explained, justified, or at least reacted to, like the shouts of an angry husband in the hall. At that moment ideas become dangerous. They can support or justify anything and may be lies.

Nevertheless, ideas are important. We must have them, Lawrence says, if only to dislodge from the mind fixed ideas that we already have. Besides, when we think, we do not have *only* ideas, that is, we do not always abstract from experience; sometimes we have thoughts. Like an idea, a thought is part of consciousness which has "two bodies of knowledge: the things [a person] tells himself, and the things he finds out" (*Phoenix*, 732). The former is an idea, the latter a thought.

"Man is a thought-adventurer," Lawrence says, suggesting that thoughts are both inevitable and desirable; they are part of what makes us human and makes us satisfied as humans. "But by thought we mean, of course, discovery. We don't mean this telling himself stale facts and drawing false deductions which usually passes as thought. Thought is an adventure, not a trick" (*Phoenix*, 732). Like adventures, some thoughts are more pleasing (or more pleasant) than others. In sweet novels, only certain thoughts are allowed: those that the reader expects or the author mentally prefers. But a sweet novel is not a novel at all, being preconceived and formulaic and self-gratifying. In fact, sweet novels remind us that Lawrence was right when he said that a book is a "perfect place to tell lies in" (*Phoenix*, 731).

But a novel is merely a book unless, of course, it is a record of mental attitudes only or an autobiography without passion, interpretation, or interrelatedness. However, if it reveals "true and vivid relationships" and the author "honours" his relationship to the book, that is, if the author is "true to the flame" in himself *and* imparts his own quickness and aliveness to his story, he creates not simply a novel but a great one (*Phoenix*, 530; *Phoenix* II, 425). Doing so is not easy. It means giving up all the sweetness that readers crave and authors prefer to the thoughts that emerge when a first creation occurs. Old ideas that are comfortable must die; new thoughts that disturb and repel must be born. But it also means new life, for a "novel as a tremulation can make the whole man alive tremble" (*Phoenix, 575*).

Kangaroo was supposed to be a novel but remained an essay which behaves, at times, like a novel. The chapter called "The Nightmare" behaves like a novel when it reveals the unsuspected depth of Somers's revulsion for the war and the whole human race. So do Somers's arguments with his wife when, attempting to be lord and master, he enters into a vivid relationship with Harriet, who demolishes him and his fixed ideas. Generally, however, *Kangaroo* is the vehicle which Lawrence uses to transport what he already knows about himself from one place to another: from England to Australia, from one part of his conscious mind to another. Unable to perform the artist's job of making the unconscious conscious, Lawrence could not write a novel. Consequently, after only six weeks, he set the manuscript aside.

The Plumed Serpent is a novel; the center holds and everything is interrelated. As a result I like Lawrence's "Mexico novel." In fact, I consider it a great work of art. But not everyone agrees with me. Critics have called it Lawrence's "sick experience" (Vivas, 69) and "the only cynical and heartless book Lawrence ever wrote" (Moynihan, 90). Even Harry T. Moore, Lawrence's advocate and biographer, speaks of its ridiculous extremes, dubs it a "magnificent failure," and, speaking for many, writes: "The final effect is one of superb music with a foolish libretto" (*The Priest of Love,* 504). Other critics are equally harsh. They do not like what Don Ramon says, they do not approve of the execution of the prisoners, and they do not like such passages as "Last year the peons had murdered the manager of one of the estates across the lake. They had stripped him and left him naked on his back, with his sexual organs cut off, his nose slit and pinned back, the two halves, to his cheeks, with long cactus spines" (*Plumed Serpent,* 110). Like Kate *in* the novel, some readers *of* the novel would rather not know that "people, outwardly so quiet, so nice," can smile sweetly during the day and, at night, cut off a man's genitals and slit his nose. In brief, they do not want to learn the lesson of the Holocaust. So they extrapolate from the novel, condemn what they extrapolate, and ignore its relation to the rest of the novel.

A well-known scholar wrote to me recently and said that he did not like the Lawrence who wrote *The Plumed Serpent* and other works of the "late" period. My rejoinder is this: the Lawrence who wrote about Don Ramon and Kate and Quetzalcoatl is the Lawrence who wrote everything that has his name on it. It is true that he made discoveries as he wrote and that these discoveries enabled him to change. In writing *The Plumed Serpent,* for example, he discovered that man is a moral animal and a murderer; that savages and saints "are all of one blood stream." These thoughts affected him, made him physically ill in fact, but, essentially, he remained the coal miner's son who, as a man, looked over the Haggs where he had enjoyed himself as a boy and realized that he was still that boy. People dislike not Lawrence of the late period but what he discovered.

Lawrence knew, of course, that people would not judge his great stories as works of art, at least not at first. Instead, they would be pleased or revolted by bits broken off from the novels. But this problem did not deter him. "If there is a loathsome thought or suggestion," he wrote, "let us not dispatch it instantly with impertinent righteousness; let us admit it with simplicity, let us accept it, be responsible for it" (*Phoenix*, 677). Practicing what he preached, he expressed his own anti-Semitism often and loudly, in letters and in speech, until he purged himself. And he let his characters express what is loathsome: Paul Morel hastens his mother's death, Ursula canes Vernon Williams until he is trembling flesh, and Mellors says that he could kill lesbians. Such incidents are ugly but true: they are what each character would say and do at that time and in that place. They fit. And since they fit, they are parts of relationships which are "true and vivid" although not sweet, and each novel that *is* a novel becomes "a moral work," that is, it affects readers; it changes them or at least makes change possible; it refines their morality.

Some people respond to Lawrence's novels as if they are essays, that is, they assume that the novels are more subjective than "The Reality of Peace" or "Art and Morality." Either Lawrence *is* Birkin, or Paul Morel, or Don Ramon, or Cipriano, or Cipriano and Ramon, or Ursula, or Birkin-Ursula, or else the whole novel is Lawrentian. He himself believed that he should be "the felt but unknown flame . . . behind all the characters" (*Phoenix*, II, 419), that is, that a novel should not be an account of an author's life. Yes, he used incidents from his own life and from the lives, letters, and conversations of his friends, but in doing so, he had to put them into a new relationship. At such times, they took on a life of their own, apart from their author but in relationship to him. That is, relationships in a novel become a first creation; they exist for the first time; they, not the author, are what the novel is. So Lawrence is not Birkin; he is not Don Ramon. In fact, personally (as a person) he is not in the novels.

There are times when I wish Lawrence were in the novels, buttoning his gloves, for example, or blowing his nose when the cold wind comes down from the Rockies and frosts the tips of his beard. But he is not there. He is, however, in the essays, and they are generally sweet and subjective. Yes, they tell us many things; what Lawrence believed consciously, how he

143

behaved among ordinary people, and what interested him. But the essay is less reliable than the novel; it is more subjective.

This statement does not mean that essays are packs of lies. In fact, at times Lawrence speaks so sincerely in an essay that the gap between the essay and the novel seems to have closed. In his "Introduction to *Memoirs of the Foreign Legion*," for example, Lawrence could have told himself what he wanted to hear. After all, his refusal to continue giving money to the chubby, charming parasite named Magnus contributed to his suicide. But Lawrence avoids sweetness and admits that he *had* said, "Yes, he must die if he cannot find his own way." And after expressing his respect for Magnus "for dying when he was cornered," he adds:

> It is this betraying with a kiss which makes me still say: "He should have died sooner." No, I would not help to keep him alive, not if I had to choose again. I would let him go over into death. He shall and should die, and so should all his sort: and so they will. There are so many kiss-giving Judases. He was not a criminal: he was obviously well-intentioned: but a Judas every time, selling the good feeling he had tried to arouse, and had aroused, for any handful of silver he could get. A little loving vampire! [*Phoenix*, II, 354]

This passage is so devoid of sentimentality, so rich in sentiment, and so sincere that we feel it has been tested in relationship; that it is a thought and not an idea; that it is true.

At the same time, there is no doubt that the speaker is Lawrence: the voice is personal, there is no context within which Lawrence's view can be tested and, possibly, refuted, there are no vivid relationships. So Lawrence's "Introduction" is an essay, but it is not a pack of lies. Instead, it is an account of what Lawrence consciously believed.

Knowing what anyone—especially a novelist—consciously believes is important. It facilitates communication or at least starts an exchange of views, even when lies are told. Besides, my experience is that a novelist is more likely than his critics to know what he believes. As a result I am glad Lawrence wrote essays. Reading them, I learn what he consciously believed about women, submission, independence, equality, democracy, sex, consciousness, the unconscious, relationships, social roles, niceness, the novel, ideas, thoughts, syphilis, flowers, dead birds, Susan the cow, Rex the dog, Alfred the rabbit, the Lawrence family, Maurice Magnus, porcupines, red trousers, hunting, England, matriarchy, Red Indians, and even Rowbotham, the man who bit off Rex's superfluous tail for "a quart of the best and bitter." For me, what Lawrence says about each of these subjects is always interesting and is sometimes a path into the more difficult works, the novels. Occasionally the path does not go anywhere or rushes to the edge of a precipice, but even then it is valuable. The idea floating free of a context is an absolute; it has nothing to do with living things such as a novel, a flower, a horse, or an actual person. So it is not much good as an idea, but it does underscore how important it is for an idea to find a context, to exist in relationship to characters, situations, and other ideas, and in doing so to lead to discoveries—and to become part of "what is," always, of course, in connection with Lawrence, who is in the essays, making inferences.

Something must be said about Lawrence's presence in the essays, if only to dispel some assumptions: that the "real" Lawrence is in the novels and that the real Lawrence was a brooding genius compelled, most of the time, by black moods. Yes, Lawrence *did* have a dark side. He shouted at Frieda in public and sometimes struck her; he wrote a letter which caused Bertrand Russell to contemplate suicide for twenty-four hours; he turned suddenly on his friends, calling John Middleton Murry "a dirty little worm" and Frieda "the devouring mother"; he condemned entire groups of people: Jews, Italians, homosexuals, Mexicans, Englishmen. Then, surpassing even himself, he wrote: "I have decided the human race is a mistake" (Letter: July 28, 1929). But these moods passed quickly most of the time. Besides, there were the other Lawrences: the ones who cooked and cleaned, listened to the robins and the finches, made dresses for little girls and gowns for women, played charades, rowed his own boat, rode horseback in New Mexico, fished with the peasants in Italy, admired the vegetables and lobsters in the marketplace, discussed sex with Compton Mackenzie, gave chocolate to a little girl, responded to flowers and the Rockies, taught a little girl her lessons, repaired his shirts, wove a straw hat, stuck Norman Douglas with a luncheon bill (Douglas had done the same to him earlier), put his few belongings on the back of an ass and trudged with Frieda through five miles of drifts and over a wild river, and, on Mackenzie's thirty-seventh birthday, showed up unexpectedly with a bottle of wine and Mackenzie's typewriter under his arm. (I am grateful to Leo Hammalian for citing so many of these incidents in *D. H. Lawrence in Italy.*)

In the novels, where is this Lawrence, or as he would say, where are these Lawrences? And where is the Lawrence whose "gentleness and . . . eager friendliness . . . made people like him" as a child (*The Priest of Love*, 26) and who caused Edith Sitwell to claim that *everyone* fell in love with Lawrence or Frieda, compelled Douglas to describe him as a person who was, by nature, blithe, prompted even his mother-in-law to call him lovable, and inspired scores of invitations. (The list sounds like something from the society page: Henry Savage, Lady Raleigh, the Gibsons, the Abercrombies, Mrs. Jackson, the Huntingdons, the Cochranes.) The answer is that Lawrence is everywhere and nowhere. As the subject of the novels, he does not exist; as the life, the quickness, and the spirit of the novels, he is everywhere.

It matters that essays are more subjective than novels and that ideas are not thoughts. After all, articles are essays which are often choked with ideas, and many important people write articles. In college, professors also teach young people how to write essays and, in advanced literature classes at least, how to write articles. And the assumptions about essays must affect how teachers write and what they teach.

In his glossary of literary terms, M. H. Abrams expresses some of these assumptions. An article is a formal, impersonal essay written by an authority. Not so the informal essay, which is, he says, personal and intimate and written in "a relaxed, humorous, self-revelatory, and sometimes whimsical fashion" (33). Although Abrams does not say so explicitly, he implies a contrast: an article is objective, an essay is not. And unwittingly he underscores a second contrast: an article is boring; an essay is not. In my view, the two contrasts are related. The article is often boring because the essayist tries too hard to be objective.

There are, of course, degrees of subjectivity. The journal writing of freshmen is the most subjective form of prose. Designed to enable students to put words down on paper in order to overcome their fear of writing, journal writing is an account of what a student already knows, expressed in a form with which he is at least comfortable. So it teaches him nothing; in fact, playing with dead ideas in a way that approximates rambling, the freshman journal writer remains caught in the present moment, the present state of knowledge. He flounders, and may drown, in the sea of his own subjectivity.

A skillful writer of articles is far less subjective but is never as objective as the book he is writing about when that book is a novel. *Potentially,* the article is a means of dissolving fixed ideas about books and authors and events which are so complex that a few ideas, no matter how artfully arranged, will never pin them down. And often articles are accounts of the opinions of other scholars and literary precedents. These accounts may be useful; they may provide new ways of looking at an old subject. But they *may* have very little to do with the object they purport to study: the novel or the body of poems. To begin with, the precedents cited by literary critics may, like legal precedents, be bad ones; then, too, while an author may resemble Blake and Nietzsche, he is neither. So using other people's opinions or citing literary precedents does not automatically result in objectivity: in seeing the novel as it is.

Obviously we all need other people's opinions, and we need to find fresh ways of looking at a novel to which we have become accustomed, so we need essays and need to establish that any great thinker has a context and originates, to some degree, in other people's works. Indeed, after overcoming the disappointment of discovering that Lawrence learned so much from Blake, Whitman, and Nietzsche, there is the excitement that comes from seeing Lawrence as part of a great heritage, both literary and philosophical. But we make a mistake if we assume that we are objective to the extent that we cite other people's opinions and cite precedents. And we make another mistake if we assume we are objective if we simply stick to the facts. Remember Bitzer in *Hard Times*. Called upon to give a boy's definition of a horse, he answered: "Quadruped. Graminivorous. Forty teeth, namely, twenty-four grinders, four eye-teeth, and twelve incisive. Sheds coat in spring; in marshy countries, sheds hoofs, too." Factual and accurate, he is also boring. And he says nothing about what any one horse is, in reality. We see, then, that it is not enough to be what is generally *called* objective. We must find a way of putting our ideas into relationship with other people's ideas and with whatever we are studying. Only then will we make discoveries and respond to novels and poems, and to other people, in their objective beauty.

Works Cited

Abrams, M. H. *A Glossary of Literary Terms*. New York: Rinehart, 1957.

Lawrence, D. H. *Fantasia of the Unconscious*. New York: Viking Press, 1962.

_____. *Phoenix: The Posthumous Papers of D. H. Lawrence*. Ed. Edward D. McDonald. New York: Viking Press, 1936.

_____. *Phoenix*, II. Ed. Warren Roberts and Harry T. Moore. New York: Viking Press, 1968.

_____. *The Plumed Serpent*. New York: Random House, 1954.

Moore, Harry T. *The Collected Letters of D. H. Lawrence*, II. New York: Viking Press, 1962.

_____. *The Priest of Love*. New York: Farrar, Straus and Giroux, 1974.

Moynihan, Julian. *The Deed of Life: The Novels and Tales of D. H. Lawrence*. Princeton, N.J.: Princeton University Press, 1963.

Vivas, Eliseo. *D. H. Lawrence: The Failure and the Triumph of Art*. Bloomington: Indiana University Press, 1960.

The Whole Achievement
in Virginia Woolf's
The Common Reader

Georgia Johnston

I n this study I will consider essays that an author has deliberately placed together, not essays placed together by an editor (for a course reader) or a teacher (for a class), although some of my ideas may apply to those collections as well. For example, many teachers may group essays according to theme or style so that a class of students, reading them in organized progression, will perceive distinctions and similarities more readily than if the essays had not been so related. As a parallel, I will hypothesize that the writing of essays as a group expands an author's ability to highlight subtleties of theme and style, allowing the author to guide a reader, whether didactically or unobtrusively, more easily toward that author's philosophy or theory. In addition, I will ask how reading essays as a group changes a reader's experience of individual essays; perhaps the reader (like the student) becomes attuned to a similarity of style and content, heightening the power of both content and style to persuade.

As my title suggests, I will use Virginia Woolf's first volume of essays, *The Common Reader* (*CR*), to move these concerns from the abstract to the specific. Since I am the first critic to discuss the essays in *The Common Reader* as parts of a thematically whole work, I will also show how both logical progression of content and similarity of style encourage this type of reading. Conversely, analyzing the essays in toto will highlight both that progression and that stylistic integrity.

When *The Common Reader* was published in 1925, reviewers treated the book as a collection of separate essays, not as a thematic whole. Edgell Rickword, for example, writes bluntly: "There is no explicit link between the literary essays which make up this volume and to be just to Mrs. Woolf it would be necessary to criticize each of them separately." Instead of doing so, Rickword treats neither volume nor single essays with serious attention. He asks, condescendingly, "What, in fact, does all the present fuss about literature amount to? It is the disease of an age" (153).

H. P. Collins (also in 1925) recognizes that Woolf focuses on personal lives of various figures, but he misses the larger critical connections that, for Woolf, bind writers, critics, and readers. Woolf, he says, "avoids both the most penetrating kinds of analysis and the *philosophical* synthesis; she inclines rather to a semi-creative interest in men and women which makes the final impression of her criticism less pure, less inevitable, than it might be" (156). Collins also attacks Woolf's methods: "She never willingly accepts any impersonal standards of aesthetic value. None the less, we believe that to Mrs. Woolf—to anybody—definite comparison or judgement would be impossible had she not, willy-nilly, absorbed something of the courage of others' convictions—dogmas, if you must" (156). Collins insists that Woolf never willingly accepts impersonal standards but that she has somehow "absorbed" dogmas from others, implying that Woolf's work is uninspired and unoriginal. She is "semi-creative," not "penetrating" (a quality particularly valuable for this male reviewer).

These criticisms respond in part to Woolf's methods, which seemed more fictional than critical to many early critics because Woolf presents her subjects as people with full lives, not as dryasdusts. She presents their sensory experiences. For instance, we observe the duke's household with Lady Dorothy Neville: "She had seen the troops of highly decorated human beings descending in couples to eat. She had . . . observed the Duke himself dusting" (*CR* 196). Woolf combines unexpected metaphorical description with domestic activity, leading us to expect soldiers (logical in a duke's household) when she writes "troops" and "highly decorated." In consequence, readers resee the couples descending the stairs and reconnect the culturally masculine to the culturally feminine. Woolf also uses metaphor to empathize with her subjects' positions. For example, Lady Dorothy "was confined rather to a bird-cage than to an asylum; through the bars she saw people walking at large, and once or twice she made a surprising little flight into open air. A gayer, brighter, more vivacious specimen of the caged tribe can seldom have existed" (197). Woolf follows imagined quotidian activity and metaphor with philosophy—"one is forced at times to ask whether what we call living in a cage is not the fate that wise people, condemned to a single sojourn upon earth, would choose" (197). Each fictional technique supports the next, so that, if the reader doubts the imagined progression at any point, the case is lost, but, if not, the results seem as plausible as birth and death dates.

Though factual and precise about dates, quotations, and other reference points associated with the critic, Woolf's essays stress people and the unprovable parts of their lives—feelings, thoughts, motives—over the provable facts. Woolf presents her historical figures as if they could be our neighbors or our relations no matter how distanced their fame has made them. She humanizes. I think that, if Collins had read the essays as a whole work, he would have appreciated Woolf's fictional methods as creative tools reconstructing historical texts, rather than criticizing those methods as final products.

All these reviewers, paying close attention to Woolf's fictional methods, emphasize that the essays in *The Common Reader* combine the critic and artist. None looks at Woolf's theory about the usual distance that critics create between writer and reader, which is implicit in her use of these methods. Instead, H. I'A. Fausset writes that Woolf "has discovered how to write for the newspapers without ceasing to be an artist and how to exalt criticism into a creative adventure" (151), and Arnold Bennett (Woolf's pronounced enemy) called *The Common Reader* an "agreeable collection of elegant essays" (189). Though these phrases seem to be praise, sexist terms such as "creative adventure" and "elegant essays" imply that Woolf's essays are not serious critical writings.

Woolf, however, despite early reviewers' judgments, was a serious essayist. Following the example of her father, Leslie Stephen, she began her writing career as an essayist. In one of her earliest pieces, "The Decay of Essay-writing" (1905), she extols the virtues of the essay as having a "shape" that allows "what you cannot with equal fitness say in any other" (166). By the time she began collecting essays for *The Common Reader,* she had deliberately experimented with that shape in order to examine form and content again, this time to create a fuller literary form. During the book's conception, for example, she considered placing the essays within a larger format, a format she called "Otway conversation." Andrew McNeillie explains that this structure would be "the conversation between a fictitious, book-loving Penelope Otway—a true common reader—and her friend" (*CR* xii). Woolf writes that the conversations would be "a setting" and would "make a book" (*A Writer's Diary* 57) of the individual essays. She worries that "this might be too artistic; it might run away with me; it will take time" (57). Later, Woolf would think about using a similar device in a projected essay-novel, *The Pargiters,* in which fiction and essays would alternate and expand the scope of each other. Though in 1935 she dropped the essay portion to retain the novel *The*

Years, in the earlier *Common Reader* Woolf decided to dispense with fictional gel; the essays would stand alone.

Early in Woolf's work on the volume, she writes that "the collection of articles is in my view an inartistic method" (*A Writer's Diary* 57), contrasting one idea (a collection of unconnected essays) to a second possibility (a "too artistic" volume including Otway conversation). The third option—a volume of essays connected by their own content—materialized. As Woolf predicted, fiction became the "prevailing theme." In addition, the language of her diary entries suggests the book that would emerge: words and phrases such as "current," "shape the book," "get a stress upon some main line," and "embedding" (57) emphasize a conceived whole, not an edited volume of separate essays. That she excised some of the essays from the original list that she drew up in August of 1923 (*A Writer's Diary* 58) and added more essays that she wrote between 1923 and 1925 reinforces a reading of *The Common Reader* as a planned whole. Sometimes, too, endings of essays lead to beginnings of next essays, as if the transitions were those of chapters, not separate essays. As an example, I quote the ending of "Notes on an Elizabethan Play": "Meanwhile, as if tired with company, the mind steals off to muse in solitude; to think, not to act; to comment not to share; to explore its own darkness, not the bright-lit-up surfaces of others. It turns to Donne, to Montaigne, to Sir Thomas Browne, to the keepers of the keys of solitude" (57). Woolf describes the mind, in the above lines, as turning to solitude and, among others, Montaigne. As does the mind, so does the essay volume; the next essay, "Montaigne," begins with the proposition that Montaigne is alone (solitary) in writing a picture of himself. Woolf further expands the concept of solitude by exploring the difficulties of communicating the "life within," separated from the "life outside" (59). And "if we ask this great master of the art of life to tell us his secret, he will advise us to withdraw to the inner room of our tower" (61). Indeed, from a beginning mental solitude in "Notes on an Elizabethan Play," Woolf extends the word "solitude," in "Montaigne," to ability, to spirit, and to physical isolation.

How does Woolf's construction of a volume rather than a collection affect a reading experience? Thematically the essays lead one to another. For instance, the reader, analyzing the essays in order, can see that the first three essays study the reader. "The Common Reader," the short first essay, describes Dr. Johnson's "common reader," a reader outside an elite academy of critics and scholars. The second essay, "The Pastons and Chaucer," appropriates the abstraction of that common reader, a reader who becomes the concrete John Paston, the reader who reads Chaucer because

Chaucer gives him pleasure and takes him beyond his life's limitations. The third essay, "On Knowing Greek," again emphasizes the common reader by suggesting that common readers would profit from knowing Greek and raises the common reader to the level of Greek characters like Antigone and Ajax and Electra (27), Penelope and Telemachus and Nausicaa (38).

The next two essays study writing. Taking sixteenth-century writing beyond an elite reader, "The Elizabethan Lumber Room" and "Notes on an Elizabethan Play" teach the value of Elizabethan writing for any reader. The next four essays, "Montaigne," "The Duchess of Newcastle," "Rambling round Evelyn," and "Defoe," study particular writers and how they, differently, connect writing to fame. For Montaigne, pleasure comes from beauty in writing, while the duchess proclaims, "All I desire is fame" (69). "Rambling round Evelyn" shows that keeping a diary, as John Evelyn did, can be valuable because it brings him fame after his death. In contrast to John Evelyn, whose writing we value because it shows him as an example of many men, Defoe stands out as "the founder and master" "of the school of Crabbe and Gissing" (94). History has given Defoe the fame that the Duchess of Newcastle so desired.

These studies of writers and their desires act as preliminaries to essays that study what makes a text valuable. In essays from "Addison" to "George Eliot," Woolf criticizes and applauds various writers to the extent that they present what life is really about. She instructs readers to read behind the "monument" (95) or "tomb" (96) that critics may construct over writers and their texts, and she privileges everyday life (141). "Everything," she writes, "is the proper stuff of fiction" (154).

Woolf begins to suggest that critics, instead of discovering textual value in the writers' texts, create rules to inscribe textual value. In "The Russian Point of View," we read, "Our estimate of their [the Russian texts'] qualities has been formed by critics who have never read a word of Russian" (173, 174). In other words, unqualified critics have dictated value. By the time readers reach "The Patron and the Crocus," Woolf is asking, as writers must, "How to write well?" (210). In Woolf's system, this question has its necessary corollary for us: How to read and critique well? These essays question elitist critics' formation of a canonical system and, with Bloomsburian rebelliousness, suggest that such a system limits what writers will write.

As the above synopses indicate, *The Common Reader*'s subthemes change from (1) a study of the reader, to (2) a study of writing, to (3) a study of happiness and of fame connected to writing (or why people write), to (4) a study of a text's value, to (5) a study of canon formation.

Finally, the volume analyzes (6) the critic and the critic's function. Because "the only advice they [the critics] can offer is to respect one's own instincts" (232), the last essays build a system in which the common reader is common critic. For example, with a vision encompassing the passing of eras, "The Modern Essay" predicts the canonical question: what of Conrad will survive his age? The next essay, "Joseph Conrad," answers that Conrad's "books . . . will come to mind and make such questions and comparisons seem a little futile" (230). In "How It Strikes a Contemporary," the final essay, we read, "To believe that your impressions hold good for others is to be released from the cramp and confinement of personality" (238). In total, these last essays make "futile" a critical system based on authorities' perceptions; these last essays give the common reader the task of being the common critic and, perhaps, even the common writer.

Throughout *The Common Reader,* Woolf labels the present as a time when, because of limited view, critics cannot pinpoint true value as well as the common reader can. By personifying "the common reader" as John Paston in her second essay, Woolf reconsiders even a canonical classic like Chaucer's stories because, with John Paston, we re-place the stories in their imagined Present. Since John Paston reads Chaucer's stories when they are young, not through a veil of critical esteem, he can value Chaucer's stories only for the quality they add to his life, not for the label of mastery they have in the twentieth century. Paston brings to his reading a value system that some may call naive when compared to the critics', for Paston values what he reads because it affects him, not because it should affect him.

The concept of reading joins the volume's ending and beginning. The last essays discuss the critics' inefficacy to judge, with the result that both book and writer in critics' hands become dead (hidden behind a "monument"), while the first essays illustrate how common readers value a book and how, if that book produces change, it is alive. Reading the essays sequentially highlights the chronological movement of *The Common Reader* and suggests that common readers have given critics responsibility to judge merit. Conversely, by reading the last essays as a group and then returning to the first, we perceive that Woolf has, from the beginning, given a solution for the pomposity and false authority of critics; she takes from the pundit and returns reading to the common reader. When we read the volume as a whole, circularly, the last essay, "How It Strikes a Contemporary," informs the first, "The Common Reader," as if Woolf had conceived of the volume as a loop.

From diary entries and from transitions leading essay to essay, we can tell that Woolf intended this collection of essays to have a thematic progression. In addition, work by such recent critics as Michele Barrett (9–18) and Kathleen Klein suggests the possibility of at least one unifying theme. In their analyses of the whole body of Woolf's criticism, each suggests that Woolf highlights the traditional discrepancy between economic states of female authors and male authors. For example, Kathleen Klein documents Woolf's awareness of the discrepancy and compares Woolf's presentations of female and male writers. She demonstrates that Woolf discusses the "correlation" between male writers on a horizontal plane, as the writers represent and focus a particular historical period. In contrast, Klein suggests, Woolf exposes an additional vertical "correlation" when she discusses women's writings: "Since the usual historical sources and facts are inadequate to properly place women, Woolf begins to create a new historiography. . . . women felt the limitations rather than the opportunities of the age" (Klein 238). Suggestive of women's lack of privacy that men could, perhaps, more easily secure is Woolf's image of Jane Austen "sitting in her private corner of the common parlour" (CR 136). Suggestive of women's constricted movement is Woolf's stress on all the women writers' lack of exposure. Woolf considers how new friends, travel, and visits to London would have benefited Jane Austen's and Charlotte Brontë's sensibilities and their writings.

If Klein's conclusions (about Woolf's nonfiction in general) apply to *The Common Reader,* then Woolf has unified the volume by repeatedly emphasizing a theory about economics and writing. *Common Reader* essays on female writers, such as Jane Austen, George Eliot, the Duchess of Newcastle, and the Brontës, would need to present patterns. In fact, Woolf does suggest the obstacles those writers had to overcome. Woolf nudges us to think of the deprivations. The literary, for example: "She became . . . the authoress of a novel called *Pride and Prejudice,* which, written stealthily under cover of a creaking door, lay for many years unpublished ("Jane Austen," CR 137). Or for Charlotte Brontë, the social: "In that parsonage, and on those moors, unhappy and lonely, in her poverty and exaltation, she remains" (CR 155). Or for George Eliot, the lack of encouragement: "One recollects that she never wrote a story until she was thirty-seven, and that by the time she was thirty-seven she had come to think of herself with a mixture of pain and something like resentment" (CR 169). For each of these female writers, Woolf describes deprivation, achievement despite limitation, and our loss because greatness would have been even larger if these writers' situations had not been compromised by "sex and health and convention" (CR 172).

In contrast, when Woolf discusses a male writer such as Addison, Defoe, or Conrad, she shows the critical system's vigor in promoting him. For instance, she writes, "The temptation to read Pope on Addison, Macaulay on Addison, Thackeray on Addison, Johnson on Addison [fn.] rather than Addison himself is to be resisted, for you will find . . . that Addison is neither Pope's Addison nor anybody else's Addison, but a separate, independent individual still capable of casting a clear-cut shape of himself upon the consciousness . . . of nineteen hundred and nineteen" (97). She places Conrad in the "ranks of novelists" (230) studied in the all-male curriculum of the schoolboy (223) and Defoe, as I mentioned earlier, in the "school of Crabbe and of Gissing" (94). She suggests, for all three novelists, a web of supportive fellow artists.

When we read the essays as a whole volume, images of women's disadvantages recur. Woolf's patterned positions on men and women writers suggest that, because women were compromised by gender and all the limitations that gender imposed, their writing suffered (Barrett 9–10). Klein shows that Woolf used images to connect the luxuries of power and money to men. Her example, Woolf's "The Elizabethan Lumber Room," that *Common Reader* essay connecting a lushly furnished room with men's writing, promotes my study. Rooms and money (and women's lack thereof) become symbolic of position (and women's lack thereof) in society. Like the other criticism that Klein discusses, *The Common Reader* as a whole enforces images (and their absences) that show Woolf's continuous contrast of gender's effects (Klein 231–48).

In addition to progression of theme and unifying patterns of content, the volume gains a unity through style. When read as a whole, *The Common Reader* creates a persona quite like the "Angel in the House," Woolf's own depiction of the Victorian epitome of pure and modest womanhood ("Professions for Women" 149–54). Woolf herself, in "A Sketch of the Past," reevaluates *The Common Reader*: "When I re-read my old *Common Reader* articles I detect it [the Victorian manner] there. I lay the blame for their suavity, their politeness, their sidelong approach, to my tea-table training. I see myself handing plates of buns to shy young men and asking them, not directly and simply about their poems and their novels, but whether they like cream as well as sugar" (129). Woolf's metaphorical connection of style to manners is not unique to this section of autobiography, though she did not always connect her style to "tea-table training." For instance, in "Mr. Bennett and Mrs. Brown," she suggests that "a convention in writing is not much different from a convention in manners" (110). The parallel with writing suggests that writing conventions change as the relation between author and audience changes. In her metaphoric scene, Woolf, through gender, divides herself (the critic) from the "shy young men," whom she presents as both writers (novelists and poets) and audience (of her manners and, therefore, her critical book). Because the progressing theme of *The Common Reader* promotes a change in how reader and writer relate, one wonders if one of Woolf's aims in critical writing was to change, like the outdated Victorian manner, outdated and disparaging expectations of gender roles.

Phyllis Rose emphasizes Woolf's gender when she astutely observes that Woolf, by using the "persona," deliberately evaded the traditional critical stance: "Her persona for [all her] criticism, uniting all the essays [not only *The Common Reader* essays] is that of a woman, neither professional critic or scholar, moderately informed, who is modestly, earnestly, trying to illuminate life through the reading of books" (Rose 42). Because the persona presents a modest voice, Woolf gains the trust of readers such as Bennett, who lambasted some of her novels, and Collins, so that they deemed her elegant instead of radical. Even when Woolf castigates Wells, Galsworthy, and Bennett, she pads her complaints with compliments ("But Mr. Bennett is perhaps the worst culprit of the three, inasmuch as he is by far the best workman" [*CR* 147]) and concessions ("We have to admit that we are exacting, and, further, that we find it difficult to justify our discontent by explaining what it is that we exact" [*CR* 148]). By being polite and earnest, Woolf's persona is able to infiltrate subversive positions about the canon without opening the volume to overt attacks from the very critics Woolf denounced. Her progressing theme about the difference between the common reader and the critic, her recurrent statements comparing men's and women's differing status within the powerful literary apparatus, give the "Angel of the House" persona poignancy even when it is effective. Woolf of 1925 was not so clearly attacking as in 1929, when she dissected Professor von X (*A Room of One's Own* 31–35).

Because the earlier volume's persona disguises its critical functions beneath the stylistic, some of Woolf's later twentieth-century critics believe that she intentionally manipulates her audience. For example, Phyllis Rose asserts that the persona "can be seen as a defiantly feminine response to authoritarian, abjuring omniscience and an ironic turning to account of her own lack of advantages" (Rose 42). Barbara Currier Bell and Carol Ohmann also note Woolf's persona in their article covering all of Woolf's criticism, and they attempt to reverse critical prejudice of it: "[Woolf] writes in a way that is said to be creative, appreciative, and subjective. We will accept this description for the moment but will later enlarge on it, and even our provisional acceptance we mean to turn to a compliment" (363). In contrast to earlier critics' adjectives, Bell and Ohmann assert that Woolf deliberately writes "unpretentiously." Woolf avoids posturing in an "authoritarian" mode as an "eminence" or "lecturer," they continue, because Woolf, by "asserting . . . a community, . . . create[s] a community" (364). For them, Woolf's volume reveals the power of writing that gives invisible ideas substance. Woolf's writing thus humors and sympathizes, persuades without bludgeoning. It reveals, for Bell and Ohmann, rather than an Angel of the House, the democratic common reader as the basis of Woolf's broadly appealing persona.

The Common Reader read as a whole reiterates the success of Woolf's persona. On the first level, the volume's persona, with elements of both "Angel of the House" and Common Reader, presents stylistic consistencies. On a second level, images, metaphors, and thematic repetitions and progressions complicate a reader's understanding of gender power structure and, as a result, economic institutions. Although we can read any one of the essays in *The Common Reader* out of the context of the volume, we can also, with profit, read the volume as a whole. In consequence, our understanding of content—particularly Woolf's questioning of authority to decide literary value—becomes more informed. The larger context of all the essays together then shapes our understanding of style—particularly Woolf's use of images and of persona to emphasize her theories. By making each essay one part of a larger vision, Woolf, in *The Common Reader*, has used the limiting form of the essay as one might use one poem in a book of poems and has reached beyond that chosen form.

Works Cited

Barrett, Michele. Introduction. In *Women and Writing*, by Virginia Woolf. New York: Harcourt, 1979.

Bell, Barbara Currier, and Carol Ohmann. "Virginia Woolf's Criticism: A Polemical Preface." *Critical Inquiry*, 1 (1974):361–71.

Bennett, Arnold. From "Another Criticism of the New School." In *Virginia Woolf: The Critical Heritage*, ed. Robin Majumdar and Allen McLaurin. Boston: Routledge and Kegan Paul, 1975.

Collins, H. P. Review from *Criterion*, July 1925. In *Virginia Woolf: The Critical Heritage*, ed. Robin Majumdar and Allen McLaurin. Boston: Routledge and Kegan Paul, 1975.

Fausset, H. I'A. Initialed review from *Manchester Guardian*, May 1925. In *Virginia Woolf: The Critical Heritage*, ed. Robin Majumdar and Allen McLaurin. Boston: Routledge and Kegan Paul, 1975.

Klein, Kathleen Gregory. "A Common Sitting Room: Virginia Woolf's Critique of Women Writers." In *Virginia Woolf: Centennial Essays*, ed. Elaine K. Ginsberg and Laura Moss Gottlieb. Troy, N.Y.: Whitson, 1983.

Rickword, Edgell. Initialed review from *Calendar,* July 1925. In *Virginia Woolf: The Critical Heritage,* ed. Robin Majumdar and Allen McLaurin. Boston: Routledge and Kegan Paul, 1975.

Rose, Phyllis. *Woman of Letters: A Life of Virginia Woolf.* New York: Oxford University Press, 1978.

Woolf, Virginia. "Mr. Bennett and Mrs. Brown." *The Captain's Death Bed and Other Essays.* New York: Harcourt, 1950.

_____. *The Common Reader.* Ed. Andrew McNeillie. New York: Harcourt, 1984.

_____. "The Decay of Essay-writing." *Academy and Literature,* February 25, 1905, pp. 165–66.

_____. "Professions for Women." *The Death of the Moth and Other Essays.* London: Hogarth, 1981.

_____. *A Room of One's Own.* New York: Harcourt, 1929.

_____. "A Sketch of the Past." In *Moments of Being,* ed. Jeanne Schulkind. New York: Harcourt, 1976.

_____. *A Writer's Diary.* Ed. Leonard Woolf. New York: Harcourt, 1953.

The Modernist Essay: The Case of T. S. Eliot—Poet as Critic

J. P. Riquelme

"The triumph is the triumph of style. . . . Vague as all definitions
are, a good essay must have this permanent quality about it; it
must draw its curtain round us, but it must be a curtain that
shuts us in, not out."

—VIRGINIA WOOLF, "The Modern Essay"

"Criticism is no more to be judged by any low standard of
imitation or resemblance than is the work of poet or sculptor."

—OSCAR WILDE, "The Critic as Artist"

The modernist essay emerges as part of the reaction
against Matthew Arnold that is characteristic of
Modernism. Arnold expresses his sense of the secondary function of criticism in his famous 1864 lecture at Oxford on "The Function of Criticism
at the Present Time." There he asserts that the "aim of criticism" is not the
passing of judgment, though it is judgment's precursor, but the achieving
of accurate perception through procedures exercised by a "disinterested
curiosity." The critic strives "to see the object as in itself it really is." The
most forceful early counter to Arnold's attitude toward criticism as less
independent and less worthy than creation comes from Oscar Wilde in
his volume *Intentions* (1891), especially in the essay in dialogue form,
"The Critic as Artist," originally published as "The True Function and
Value of Criticism: with Some Remarks on the Importance of Doing
Nothing." For Wilde, criticism's aim is to see the object as it is not, and
this aim is never disinterested and never just a procedure. And it need not
be pursued through the style of high seriousness that Arnold adopted. By
both assertion and example, Wilde makes claims for criticism that are at
least as wide-ranging and, in the results, at least as successful as any we

encounter nowadays. With the combined force of Ruskin and Pater as precursors to aid him, Wilde is able to create a crucial, liberating turning point in late nineteenth-century English letters. Wilde heralds the essay's importance as a literary form that would become the sibling of Modernist poetry and fiction in the first half of the twentieth century, but one that academic literary criticism continues largely to neglect. Despite this relative neglect, a surprising number of essays written by Wilde's Modernist descendants—Yeats, D. H. Lawrence, Eliot, Pound, Virginia Woolf, Jorge Luis Borges and Samuel Beckett, among others—have achieved the status so many contemporary critics desire for their works in prose: the status of being recognized as literature.

The Modernist essay is not easy of definition, and that is one of its characteristics, for it is not produced by an academic writer interested in adhering to the conventions of argumentation and decorum practiced by a community of established literary critics. The refusal of adherence takes on a variety of stylistic manifestations, markedly different from those of conventionally expository and interpretative literary critical essays. Because of its multiplicity and difference, the Modernist essay cannot be conveniently fitted either into the category of literary criticism or into literary criticism's categories. In part out of lack of another term, we call it an *essay* because it is a relatively short work in prose, but neither a short story nor a scientific or quasi-scientific report. Generally, it is a commentary dealing with art or literature whose function is not primarily expository and whose mode of procedure is not necessarily strictly logical. Its function is to help make possible the creation of a new kind of artwork, of which it may itself be an example and not just a precursor. Our response upon encountering an example of the form may resemble Samuel Beckett's in "Three Dialogues," where he says, "I don't know what it is, having never seen anything like it before." On this unashamedly flexible and general account, even a portion of another text, such as the "Scylla and Charybdis" episode of *Ulysses,* if taken in isolation from its fictional context, could be considered a Modernist essay. In this case, the episode is, in fact, one of the precursors of Beckett's "Three Dialogues," which is both essay and literary text masquerading as an interview. The clear distinctions between genres have largely disappeared.

I take as an exemplary Modernist essay, but by no means as a paradigm—this particular literary form always refusing to conform to any prescriptive pattern—, T. S. Eliot's "Tradition and the Individual Talent." Several reasons stand behind the choice. Eliot has consistently been the most badly treated of the major Modernist writers by the contemporary neo-Romantic reaction against Modernism that, in one of its forms, wishes to see the emergence of a creative criticism. Such a creative criticism has already been achieved in this and other Modernist essays. In addition, this specific essay is quite possibly the most widely anthologized literary essay of the twentieth century. It was so widely anthologized by 1964 that Eliot complained of its omnipresence in the preface to the reissuing of *The Use of Poetry and The Use of Criticism*, a volume that he hoped might provide anthologists with other material. The essay has now become so familiar to us that we take it largely for granted. It has been put to rest—buried as a dead part of the tradition—by our excessive contact with it. To read the essay as if it were readily intelligible, that is, under our control, is a serious failure of literary understanding, for such a reading is unable to recognize the continuing and permanent nature of the essay's radical qualities. It is not merely revolutionary in a specific historical situation that has now passed; it is perpetually revolutionary because of certain curious and compelling features of style.

Eliot's achievement as an essayist has been considerably misunderstood by those who claim that his reformulations of the English poetic tradition failed to turn back through logical argument the assertion that the poems of Dryden and Pope were, in Arnold's catchy phrase, "classics of our prose." Eliot was, in fact, not involved in redefining the canon only by means of conventional literary critical argumentation. In addition, through his *writing practice,* he changed our understanding of the possibilities for expression in prose. He answered Arnold in effect by taking the writing of prose seriously. For Eliot, who sees the real possibility of something coming into being, something that transforms the way we think in the present, thereby transforming the past, the *critical* project is indistinguishable from the *poetic* one. That something new need not be limited to poetry; it may well occur through and as prose.

In his writing practice Eliot implicitly rejects the simplistic association of literary forms with separable functions of mind. Prose need not be seen as a mimetic manifestation of critical, rational thinking, for it can involve a mixture in which creative and critical have indissolubly merged. Such prose may at times be both necessary to the creating of poetry and in many ways identical to it as to function and certain aspects of style. One function of prose so conceived is to act as both evidence and occasion for the bringing of new work into existence, perhaps quite different work implicated in the writing of the prose, but even the prose work itself as that something new. The style of such new work, whether in verse or in prose or possibly in both, strives to reach a maximal intensity, expressing and evoking a meaning and experience that could not be otherwise expressed and evoked. Section two of part five of *A Portrait of the Artist as a*

Young Man, in which Stephen Dedalus writes his villanelle, would be an example of a work that uses both verse and prose in order to represent the verse's creation. That representation embedded in prose is itself an example of the truly new text, though in this case it is a work of fiction. If the prose is really new, then the technical means employed to reach the necessary intensity will vary from other works. "Tradition and the Individual Talent" involves the creating of something new in both ways: as one of the precursors of *The Waste Land* and simultaneously as that poem's prose counterpart, going beyond the conventional literary essay to reach the status of literature. The essay reaches that status because, despite its ostensible familiarity, the more closely we look at its argument, organization, and even sentence structure, the stranger it becomes.

We can see this strangeness especially clearly at the end of the essay, in the oft-quoted concluding sentence of part III:

> And he [the poet] is not likely to know what is to be done unless he lives in what is not merely the present, but the present moment of the past, unless he is conscious, not of what is dead, but of what is already living.

At the beginning of this final section, only a single paragraph in length, Eliot claims that the essay "proposes to halt at the frontier of metaphysics or mysticism, and confine itself to . . . practical conclusions." But it does not halt at the frontier of what might be expected in the style and structure of a literary essay in the Arnoldean tradition. It crosses that frontier most prominently in the final sentence. We might recall at this point the distinction Eliot makes briefly in the concluding pages of "The Use of Poetry and the Use of Criticism (1933) between poems that have "'meaning'" in order "to satisfy one habit of the reader, to keep his mind diverted and quiet, while the poem does its work upon him" and those other poems, presumably Modernist ones, that pursue different possibilities entirely through the attenuating of meaning in the ordinary sense. The conclusion of "Tradition" also pursues those different possibilities. This is not to say that the sentence is nonsense, but it goes beyond the making of ordinary sense because of its resonance and complexity, generated by repetition and contrast within the sentence and within the essay at large. The repetition and contrast within the sentence are clear enough. They are part of the reason we do not grasp any simple, determinate significance when we read or hear the whole sentence and attempt a semantic interpretation: it is too complicated to be taken in all at once. But the sentence also does not yield an easily restatable meaning when we break it into parts for analysis, for it is organized antithetically, by contrasts that work through both multiple repetition and multiple antitheses. If we follow the to-and-fro, fro-and-to shifting, our engagement is decidedly temporal, in a way that does not result in a meaning that can be grasped instantaneously in overview.

Both grammatically and logically, the sentence is a multiple antithetical construction. The basic construction clearly announces an apparently controlling contrast through the use of "not" in counterpoint to "unless" and "but." Eliot uses constructions involving such contrasts regularly in the other essays collected in *The Sacred Wood*, for example, in the short pieces grouped under the rubric "Imperfect Critics." None of these other sentences, however, achieves a comparable complexity of structure and implication, for in "Tradition," the negation by contrast is repeated and then repeated again. Each repetition, which is also a contrast, modifies our sense of all the others. The contrast between "not likely to know" and the first dependent clause beginning with "unless" seems clear enough and easily graspable, until we reach the relative clause, "what is not," used as a substantive within the dependent clause, for the second "not" repeats the first one literally at the same time as it stands in contrast to it in context. The complications increase when we discover that the second "not" is linked to the "but" that follows shortly. Now, not just "not," but "not . . . but" repeats the whole "not . . . unless" construction while it also forms a part of it. And the antithesis with reversal is repeated again in the second, parallel subordinate clause, with its "unless . . . not . . . , but." When we compare the parallel dependent clauses, the contrasts that are also virtually repetitions proliferate. "What is not . . . but" is matched, but not repeated in form or meaning by "not of what is . . . , but of what is. . . ." "Merely the present" and "the past" occupy the same respective positions in the first as "what is dead" and "living" do in the second. The repetitions create alignments of meaning where semantically a contrast would otherwise stand. The connotations and the repetitions in structure, together with variations and reversals, combine to make each contrast and each repetition modify the possible meanings of their counterparts and antitheses in other parts of the sentence. In the other essays of *The Sacred Wood*, the constructions employing "not" and "but" generally function as part of Eliot's effort to achieve the sort of balanced judgments through pointcounterpoint that he praises in his commendation of Samuel Johnson as a model for critics in the "Introduction." The wildly complicated construction at the end of "Tradition" has little to do with balance, unless we understand that concept anew, dynamically, as an uneasy equilibrium produced by antitheses in interaction.

Such an analysis can help clarify the sentence's potentially dizzying effect on the reader, but it does not provide a clue to its meaning that can be applied semantically to produce a convincing, explanatory translation. The analysis suggests instead that the sentence's meanings are in flux, though not necessarily haphazardly so. It complicates rather than simplifies our sense of the reading process, which we now realize involves an encounter with multiple antitheses in a series of repetitions. Tropologically, we can describe the construction as a rhetorical process of transformation structured as a chiasmus within a chiasmus. We have a repetition and reversal, as in chiasmus, with the complication that the repetition and reversal have also been repeated in such a way as to include reversals. To use a German word, which Eliot himself employs in his essay on Massinger to describe some lines by Tourneur and Middleton, we find "meanings perpetually *eingeschachtelt* into meanings." The word evokes something like the fitting of Chinese boxes inside one another. Or we might think of anastomoses, the way veins in plants and animals merge with other veins through a system of tiny, articulating connections. This is a special kind of sentence in Eliot's prose, though by no means unique, whose resonance and appeal arise in part from syntactical and semantic complexities crafted into a rhythmic sequence of contrasts within contrasts. Such complexities can set us into a kind of mental activity in response that is not often engendered by a literary essay. But the sentence from "Tradition" exerts a special *concluding* force, because it has the rest of the essay as prelude and context. The essay has already given us, through the two analogies of parts I and II, a double antithetical structure, like the structure of meaning we are able to realize through our enactment and enact through our realization of the ending's syntactical and rhetorical play. In addition, through the shifts in style and focus from part to part, a stylistic pressure and thematic dissonance have built up that are brought to fulfillment by the reversals within reversals of the final sentence.

The large structure of the entire essay is reflected in the ending. The congruence amidst and by means of heterogeneous complications between whole and part gives the essay a great deal of its special force. It does so because the whole-to-part relationship of synecdoche is combined inextricably with the disjunctive, dialectical interplay of irony. Part reflects whole but only by reflecting the whole as an uneasy interaction of parts. This conjoining of synecdoche with irony amounts to a Modernist critique and revision of Organicist attitudes. As in the sentence, the parts of the essay may be said to overlap, that is, to interact, and to be in parallel at the same time as they differ significantly. The overlap is indicated in a straightforward way at the end of the first two parts, when the focus is shifted toward what will be developed in the part to come. The essay is structured like a complex sentence in which two segments, parts I and II, are set in parallel at the same time as they stand in antithetical relationship to one another. This structure of simultaneous contrast and parallelism is most obvious in Eliot's use of analogies in place of more conventional argumentation to make his case, which, bluntly stated, is a case against Romanticism as a tradition that had become a moribund cliché still refusing to die. Eliot carefully chooses his analogies to propose antithetical alternatives to conventional Romantic ones; that is, the alternatives are at once antithetical to the conventions and to one another. How fair Eliot is to Romanticism is not at issue here, for the essay is not working in service to balanced judgment but in service to an impulse to write that must express itself in new ways.

Eliot's strategy is to attack Organicist visions of both literary history and literary creation, which he sees as the debased, unusable tradition of Romantic thinking. In part I, he rejects the notion that literary history, and by implication history in any form, is teleologically oriented, developing with a clear direction like an organism either growing or evolving toward a higher state that carries with it in some direct way the stages that have preceded. In place of growth and evolution, he describes a model that also has an organic aspect but not the same one. This aspect is something like homeostasis. Literary history is not to be thought of as growing and improving gradually in a foreseeable direction but as simply changing in response to new stimuli on the way to achieving again temporary homeostasis. This conception of history as involving mutation, or disruption, and eventual homeostasis rather than continuous growth stands in contrast to both the ideology of Imperialism—that is, of Social-Darwinism—and the tenets of Marxism, with their common heritage of teleological views of history. The other aspect of Organicism that Eliot rejects is the notion of the poet's mind as sensitive plant. Here his choice of analogy from *inorganic* chemistry, the catalyst that remains unchanged in the chemical reaction though it enables it, is antithetical to the conventional Romantic conception of the poet's role.

With the introduction of the second analogy, the complications, like those of the sentence's construction, arise, for this analogy is built around an inorganic process, while the first one is still basically organic, though not teleologically so. Both analogies challenge by implication the debased Romantic conventions, but they also reflect through the antithesis of organic with inorganic a sensitivity to an abiding dissonance. As Eliot understood, such dissonance accompanies any serious attempt to conceptualize about history and mind together rather than about one or the other separately. The recognition that this and related dissonances are incapable of being assimilated smoothly into any conceptual system relying primarily on one kind of rhetorical figure, as Organicism relies on synecdoche, forms another, perhaps the boldest, aspect of the position Eliot takes against Romanticism and its heritage. The essential role of contradiction in the critique of Romanticism, understood as aligned with Organicist attitudes toward history and mind, helps explain and justify the complexity of the essay's final sentence.

The intensity that the style of "Tradition" reaches in its ending belies the clear distinction many critics have tried to make between Eliot's work as poet and his work as critic. In his well-known essay, "Poetry and Drama" (1951), Eliot formulates in one way the stylistic ideal he strives for, here with specific reference to his attempt to write verse drama:

> . . . if our verse is to have so wide a range that it can say anything that has to be said, it follows that it will not be "poetry" all the time. It will only be "poetry" when the dramatic situation has reached such a point of intensity that poetry becomes the natural utterance, because then it is the only language in which the emotions can be expressed at all.

Achieving this ideal of a flexible style is also one goal of Eliot's work three decades earlier in both verse and prose. We can reformulate Eliot's statement for this earlier, and in certain regards more general, context pertaining to the relationship of prose to verse: If our prose is to have so wide a range that it can say anything that has to be said, it follows that it will at times come close to being "poetry." It will only do so when the critical situation has become critical in another sense; when the issues and the argument reach a point of such intensity that prose of the usual sort is left behind, because then the new style is the only one in which the necessary complexity can be expressed at all. The fact that Eliot continued working in both poetry and prose throughout his career points to his abiding interest in developing a range of styles. Within that range, the wide latitude in style and the resulting possibility of new juxtapositions and combinations of styles make possible the simultaneous representation and evocation of aporia. This evocation is one of the goals of the flexible style. As in the ending of "Tradition," the style communicates the grounds for its own intensity by reflecting in its movement the contradictory structure of the dissonance as source. Because of that movement, the essay remains permanently outside what we can call, following Beckett, "the domain of the feasible."

The Modernist essay, for which I have taken "Tradition and the Individual Talent" as primary example, is a literary form that cannot justifiably be evaluated by a mimetic standard. This is true in at least two senses. It is not merely a reflection of either some ostensible object of study or of a faculty of mind that we might just as well call reason rather than the critical faculty. It moves beyond the function of critical exposition and outside the control of the conventionally assumed Arnoldean constraints of both the object and reason. Its power inheres largely in its style, which it draws round us, shutting us in, not out, by giving us an experience of meaning that goes beyond semantics. We can say of Eliot, as of other writers of Modernist essays, what Eliot said of F. H. Bradley: "Certainly one of the reasons for the power he still exerts, as well as an indubitable claim to permanence, is his great gift of style." Eliot's most original contribution as a critic is his prose style, through which he responds effectively to the Arnoldean distinction in value between poetry and prose. In reading "Tradition and the Individual Talent," we can experience the aporia of the title when the essay's structure and style evoke in us the interplay of reciprocal relations in a continuous process of exchange. This process in itself is not wholly describable by means of the formulation of reason yoked to the thematic semantics of critical exposition. We can come close to an adequate description in one way by comparing its images and structure to those of some Modernist poems. We encounter, to our surprise and against our expectation, because the form is prose but not fictional, a phenomenon closer to Yeats's "Byzantium" and "Those images that yet / Fresh images beget" than to anything Matthew Arnold was able to write in either prose or verse. The triumph is the triumph of style.

The Husbandry of the Wild

Sherman Paul

F orewords are usually last words, commentary on the work done. In respect to what has been accomplished they are placed first in order to open the text, to provide a way in. It seems appropriate, then, in talking about *A Sand County Almanac,* to begin with Aldo Leopold's introductory sentences, to hear how he says what he has to say.

> There are some who can live without wild things, and some who cannot. These essays are the delights and dilemmas of one who cannot.
>
> Like winds and sunsets, wild things were taken for granted until progress began to do away with them. Now we face the question whether a still higher "standard of living" is worth its cost in things natural, wild, and free. For us of the minority, the opportunity to see geese is more important than television, and the chance to find a pasque-flower is a right as inalienable as free speech.
>
> These wild things, I admit, had little human value until mechanization assured us of a good breakfast, and until science disclosed the drama of where they came from and how they live. The whole conflict boils down to a question of degree. We of the minority see a law of diminishing returns in progress; our opponents do not.

These sentences exemplify one of Leopold's best styles, an easy, open, straight-on, vernacular, spoken style. Every declaration is measured and firm but not contentious; ingratiating, rather, as prefatory statements should be, even though from first to last what is set out, characteristically, is polarized, a matter of opposition and conflict. This is a personal style, not the objective style of scientific work, for example, Leopold's *Game Management,* which begins with a definition against which his achievement in *A Sand County Almanac* may be measured: "Game management is the art of making land produce sustained annual crops of wild game for recreational use." Leopold's personal style belongs to what, in his large archive—how did one who sat so long at a desk have time for field-work?—it belongs to what are called "philosophic and literary writings." This is a separate category in keeping with two critical distinctions, *leisure* (as against *work*) and *country* (as against *land*), both, in turn, related by a sense of adventure and "defiance of the contemporary."

Almost all of Leopold's philosophic and literary writings required revision. The easy style didn't come easy; its artfulness was earned by attending to style as attentively as he attended to all serious matters. Leopold was always a writer, but this doesn't mean, as we sometimes say, that he was a natural writer. He had to learn to write, and in doing so travelled a long way from the occasional humorous scribbling of such early publications as *The Pine Cone* and the forceful and certain field despatches of the enthusiastic forester. It does not detract from his achievement, then, to note in the first sentence—"There are some who can live without wild things, and some who cannot"—to note here, as elsewhere, that he mingles with his own voice the voice of E. B. White. The voices, say, of Thoreau and Muir, great writers whom he acknowledges, were not contemporary; there were profound historical reasons that prohibited their direct appropriation, one of them the diminishment of the singular that much besides ecology fostered, the awareness, as with White, that all a writer who speaks *in propria persona* can serve up is one man's meat. White, incidentally, brought out his essays under that name in 1942, essays written during his retreat to a salt water farm in Maine. About this time Leopold proposed a Christmas book of essays that did not include many "shack essays," as those in the almanac section were called, or take its title from the round of things he did on the sand county farm he purchased in 1935.

Especially resonant of White in this opener are the way of speaking and what is said. There is, for example, the political terminology, the insistence on freedom and inalienable rights that belonged to a time of domestic and global strife—the Great Depression and World War II. An unobtrusive terminology ("cost," "progress," "'standard of living'") introduces an important economic perspective. A scientific perspective also enters, with the word *science*, unquestioned here, a discloser of evolutionary and ecological knowledge, and not, as Leopold knew, an agent of economic forces, the "mechanization" he refers to, the "diminishing returns" he recognizes. Leopold, himself a scientist, pits *ecos*/ecology against *econ*/economy, and by way of the former, which he hoped would teach us to love the land and have community with it, rallies to his side the power of *eros*. He answers a question that seems to me to be implicit in some of the questions ("*How do you grow a lover?*"; "*How do you grow a poet?*") asked by Robert Kroetsch in *Seed Catalogue: How do you grow a lover of the land?*

Leopold pits a subversive science—ecological understanding is both subversive and moral, subversive because moral, which is why Paul Goodman considered it the fitting science for writers—against the dismal science of getting and spending, knowing that subversives like himself are a minority, belong to the margins, as Wendell Berry again reminds us. Hence, with little chance of victory, he settles for amelioration ("a question of degree") and writes in the spirit of accommodation. More than anything, this connects him with White—as in this instance it also connects him with Lincoln at Gettysburg. This is evoked by "now we face the question whether . . ." and "whole conflict." The ecological crisis—*crisis* in a medical sense, the pathology evident to anyone willing to see it and especially to someone trained to see it and, in addition, the owner of a worn-out farm—the ecological crisis, as he knew from the asperity of his work on the Wisconsin Conservation Commission, might very well find an analogue in civil war. At the outset of the *Almanac* Leopold makes this connection and reads in terms of *the* Civil War the present irreconcilable (irreconciled) conflict of man and land.

White's accommodation is spelled out in the title of his book: it grants that one man's meat is another man's poison, that my satisfactions need not be yours. You are not deprived of television (just beginning to transform our lives when Leopold cited it) because I hanker after geese. But is this live-and-let-live resolution of the conflict the case in the crucial opening sentence? *There are some who can live without wild things, and some who cannot.* This may be read as saying that it is possible to live without wild things, that one may choose to live a meager life of this kind even though living with wild things is richer. The antithesis of the sentence is also compromised by that fact that its restricted meaning plays against our knowledge that, ultimately, we cannot live without wild things— without the wild, to which, we inevitably recall Thoreau saying, we owe the preservation of the world.

To introduce *wild* in the first sentence and insist on it in the first sentences of the subsequent paragraphs confirms Leopold's genius. The minority for whom he speaks now includes Thoreau ("Life consists with wildness") and Muir (whose remark, "In God's wildness lies the hope of the world," echoes Thoreau) and many others, chiefly the "radical amateurs," as Stephen Fox calls them, who comprise the militant moral tradition of conservation or, in Donald Worster's phrase, "the party of conscience." White's accommodation is characteristic, Leopold's is not. Like

Thoreau in "Walking," an essay in significance to be paired with "Civil Disobedience," Leopold wishes to make an extreme statement. "I wish to speak a word for Nature," Thoreau says, "for absolute freedom and wildness . . . to regard man as an inhabitant, or part and parcel of Nature. . . ." Such concern for the wild allows no compromise.

The accommodation of the foreword is rhetorical, the good sense of a writer who, having lost immediate battles, wants to be heard, even, as he suggested, in the *Reader's Digest,* the magazine equivalent of any number of popular forums—garden clubs and PTAs, for example—that he addressed. The difficulty of placing his book and an editor's skeptical reception of his "philosophical reflections"—nature-writing was welcome but not challenging ecological thought, which one publisher's reader found "fatuous"—all this, as well as the counsel of a former student, may have prompted Leopold to discard an earlier foreword notable for the polemical force of its autobiographical witness.

This foreword, in the revision of 31 July 1947, is a major document, and new editions of *A Sand County Almanac,* the first edition wisely enlarged to include some complementary essays from *Round River,* should add it. Nothing of Leopold's that I have read is so summary, filled as it is with salient thoughts that he says were "the end-result of a life-journey." There is something conclusive here, and in the reiterated *during my lifetime,* that evokes a journey's end and asks us to consider his book as testamentary. These thoughts—"These essays," he now begins, "deal with the ethics and esthetics of land"—these thoughts are final. This may explain his willingness to express once more his "discontent with the ecological *status quo*"—that is, with the economic uses of science and the impotence of the conservation movement—and it may explain the unusual presence of the personal, even the need to confess his sin.

Leopold's enthusiasm for hunting—he had hunted from boyhood in Iowa, coming to nature-study in this way, and the shack was purchased for a base-camp—this enthusiasm, and the very enterprise of game management, have always disturbed me. I share Muir's view of both, that hunting is "murder business" and that protective measures such as game management arise because "the pleasure of killing is in danger of being lost from there being little or nothing left to kill. . . ." Leopold's defense of hunting as an ethical discipline as against the wantonness of sport doesn't convince me. So I was happy to find that Leopold, after twenty years, admits that the predator control he fostered was "ecological murder." He participated, he says, in "the extinguishment of the grizzly bear," in his mind the wilderness itself; he was "accessory to the extermination of the lobo wolf" and rationalized it "by calling it deer management." Having done this he contributed to the "erasing [of] the wilderness" practiced in the name of range conservation, for once a wilderness area has been proclaimed and the predators killed to increase the game, logic (of a bureaucratic kind) requires roads to enable the hunters to "harvest" the game, and access destroys the wilderness.

I mention this folly because he does in the narrative of his career and because the education of Aldo Leopold may be said to begin here, in his official capacity as a forest ranger and chief of operations in the Forest Service in Arizona and New Mexico. Leopold makes the point of noting that he is a "research ecologist" and that in appraising his work we should remember that his predecessors, Thoreau, Muir, Burroughs, Hudson, and Seton, "wrote before ecology had a name, before the science of animal behavior had been born, and before the survival of faunas and floras had become a desperate problem." Few writers, he says, "have dealt with the drama of wild things since our principal instruments of understanding them have come into being." He is one of them, a scientist by training, and, of course, a professional, an expert, in the service of government and university—the University of Wisconsin, which had fitted Muir for his joyous exploration of nature and had created a professorship of wildlife management for Leopold.

Leopold's education, at least in this summation, was disenchanting largely because of its institutional character. The crucial lesson belongs to the 1920s, when he worked for the Forest Products Laboratory in Madison, and found "the industrial *motif* of this otherwise admirable institution . . . little to [his] liking." At this time, he would have us believe, he took the trips to the Sierra Madre Mountains that taught him that "land is an organism" and that hitherto he "had seen only sick land"—trips he actually took a decade later. As a result of his *work* at the Laboratory, he claims that he wrote, among other philosophic essays, "The Land Ethic," a composite work incorporating earlier attempts to set out an ecological ethic that was actually written in 1947 or 1948; and as a result of his *leisure* in the mountains, he wrote "Song of the Gavilan" and "Guacamaja," sketches in *A Sand County Almanac* that he placed with his trip to the unspoiled delta of the Colorado, thereby associating healthy land (wilderness) with his youth. The reasons for these departures from chronology are profoundly autobiographical and tactical. He asks us to see these writings in relation that we may better realize the complexity and unity of his thought, its grounding in experience—how the man who appreciated *country* ("the personality of the land, the collective harmony of its soil, life, and weather") troubled over *land* ("the place where corn, gullies, and mortgages grow"), how *leisure* entailed habits of *work*.

The shack journals that he kept at the farm, for example, do not contain thoughts so much as records of work done and things seen. There are few initial compositions of the kind that allow you to read the journals of Thoreau and Muir, simply records, neat, schematic, and indexed, the data-keeping of a scientist, such brief daily entries as the Forest Service requires. Yet, even as the journals make us wonder how such data was transformed into essays, they tell us how much there is to see, how rich the field of attentions—that his record is one of familiarization, the requisite participation that enables one to inhabit a place. Leopold methodically employed science to this end, in order, in Heidegger's term, to *dwell.* This is why he says of the last episode of his narrative, the purchase of the farm, that his "education in land ecology was deflected. . . ."

Deflected at first seems curious, but the import of Leopold's story turns on it. We may understand its use by recalling his initial dismay at the destruction of the land and the doubts he early had about "man in the role of conqueror." The ethics and esthetics of land have become his concern because, as he says in the juxtaposed sentence, "During my lifetime, more land has been destroyed or damaged than ever before in recorded history." Science, he finds, has encouraged rather than halted this destruction (of land bureaus, agricultural colleges, and extension services, he notes that "no ethical obligation toward land is taught in these institutions"), and his own scientific education, making him aware of what is invisible to others, has penalized him by isolating him, forcing him to live alone in "a world of wounds." "An ecologist," he says, "must either harden his shell and make believe that the consequences of science are none of his business, or he must be the doctor who sees the marks of death in a community that believes itself well, and does not want to be told otherwise." Leopold's education, accordingly, involved the concurrent growth of perception and conscience, a crisis, moreover, of scientific conscience, and prompted him, like the good doctor in Ibsen's play, to become an enemy of the people.

Ethics and *esthetics* enter his vocabulary where hitherto agronomic terms had been prominent. *Esthetics* identifies his thought with the preservationist concern for something more important than profit and marks his subscription to the tradition of nature-writing in which we find Thoreau and Muir—the "arcadian" tradition as against the "imperial" tradition, to borrow Donald Worster's way of distinguishing the opposing strands of ecological thought. The beauty Leopold saw in the natural world exercised esthetic judgment, the subjective certainty of right and wrong, and demanded ethical action. For him, beauty in nature was not a genteel satisfaction, never estheticized or ideal; it was a summons, a reminder of obligation. So having bought the farm, a week-end place fifty miles from Madison, a place of leisure not of work, he fulfilled a wish more clamorous than the desire to hunt: the wish to own land, not to have it as a possession or resource but to have it as a responsibility, to become a participant in its life, a citizen "in a community of which soils and waters, plants and animals are fellow members, each dependent on others, and each entitled to his [and her] place in the sun." The democracy of this community probably owes something to the Wisconsin Idea, which arose in opposition to the ruthless pioneering exploitation of which the abandoned farm was a testimony. Still, the point of Leopold's practice of the "land ethic" is that individuals, citizens, a last resort in bureau-ridden society, must enact it, and, equally important, that restoration must become their work. This goal is wonderfully put by what was actually done at the farm: "the husbandry of wild things on our own land." Such husbandry, as Wendell Berry to some extent exemplifies it on his farm, has "feminine" connotations of nurture and care; it is not the work of man the conqueror, and it stands against the unsettling of America. The husbandry of wild things is a valuable radical idea and should not be confused with the gentrification more frequently hoped for by week-enders who have purchased abandoned farms. This idea provides the unity that seemed questionable in Leopold's book. "These essays," he says, "are one man's striving to live by and with, rather than on [or off] the American land." This idea is their meat, answering to the dismay Muir expressed when he said that "most people are *on* the world, not in it—have no conscious sympathy or relationship to anything about them. . . ." Because of this idea, *A Sand County Almanac* is Leopold's most important and deservedly prized work.

II

A Sand County Almanac did not immediately find a shape for this conviction. The small volume that Leopold proposed in 1941 did not have the three-part structure of the book that was accepted in 1948, and published posthumously in the following year. Some shack essays, as we saw, were included, but there was no almanac, and there were none of the didactic essays that comprise the last section. The book lacked its present framework of significance; its argument was not yet structural.

Most of the essays belonged to what is now Part II ("Sketches Here and There") and the volume took its title from one or another of them:

Marshland Elegy and Other Essays or *Thinking Like a Mountain and Other Essays*. These are fitting titles because the essays celebrate the several biota Leopold had known, some historically of a frontier time, others primordial, of the Pleistocene, in almost every case to end in threnody, with a sense of loss, even of doom, equalled, I think, only by Faulkner in "The Bear," the central ecological fable of *Go Down, Moses*, published in 1942. *Once lost, forever lost* is what these essays tell us—that, as Leopold knew, "the creation of a new wilderness in the full sense is impossible."

What was possible, the rearguard action he had taken, was not sufficiently represented in this version of the book, although "Great Possessions," the working title of *A Sand County Almanac*, suggests it. In this shack essay he says of his farm, "I am the sole owner of all the acres I can walk over," and in this Thoreauvian spirit adds, "not only boundaries . . . disappear, but the thought of being bounded." Place has given him cosmos. There is no indoors in *A Sand County Almanac:* he is outside, *in* the world, at home in intimate space, dwelling with all that is "in a house," as Muir said of similar experience, "of one room." When I think of Leopold, two images of him always come to mind, neither of the horseman, hunter, or canoeist, nor for that matter of the scholarly professor. The first image is of the early riser sitting outdoors on a rough-hewn bench heating coffee over the fire, with every sense taking in the morning world; the second is of the watcher who, having cleared a swath, sits near the shack awaiting the sight of deer—the deer that for him, as for George Oppen whose words I cite, cry faith *in this in which.*

The idea of an almanac, or at least the need to concentrate on it, was suggested by an editor. It may have been congenial because some early installments had been directed to farmers and published in a booklet, *Wild Life Conservation on the Farm*, in 1941. At this time, Leopold made an unusual entry in the shack journal:

> What we hear of conservation is mostly what transpires in the parlor of land-use. This is a factual account of what happens in the kitchen. The particular kitchen of which I speak is one of the sand counties of Wisconsin. . . .

He had used the parlor-kitchen figure to a different end in *Game Management*. Now it accords with the remarks on land-use at the conclusion of "Cheat Takes Over," also completed in 1941:

> I found the hopeless attitude [of ranchers] almost universal. There is, as yet, no sense of pride in the husbandry of wild plants and animals. . . . We tilt windmills in behalf of conservation in convention halls and editorial offices, but on the back forty we disclaim even owning a lance.

The reviews of the published book were neither as attentive nor as stringent as the reader's report of Alfred Etter, a professor at Washington University. This report, coming two months after Leopold's death, was not significantly acted on except for the change of title. "Sauk County" became "Sand County": a little known place yielded to a familiar biota. But *almanac* did not, as Etter suggested, yield to *seasons*, a more agreeable disposition of the material because he felt in several instances "the obligation of a calendar [to be] unfortunate." This is just: the materials are disproportionately distributed and sometimes lack calendrical necessity. Had Leopold lived to revise the manuscript, he might, Etter thought, have replaced the "weak links" and managed a tour de force. But in its present form he found the almanac diffuse and its essays "considerably less potent than those of the second and third Parts." He meant by this that they lacked "keen intellect," and what he called their "vague impression" was associated with the most frequent comment on the writing in this part— that it was "a little too sweet." Etter believed that this detracted from "the Professor's personality"—diminished the force of the man who was known professionally for his forthright integrity, a man, we might add, in many ways representative of an ideal type of his time. Thus, to reiterate, as Etter does, "The total effect of the Professor's personality [and presumably of the book as well] would be increased by the elimination of flowery or delicate words which inevitably find their way into writings on these subjects." Reviewers were not troubled by this; several were naturewriters and were not as sensitive as Etter to the ways in which sentimentality may compromise scientific ecology.

What Etter saw is there but of little consequence in light of what he didn't see: the three-part dialectical play of the book. Leopold himself explains this in the foreword as a movement from an account of seeking "refuge from too much modernity" and trying to reclaim "what we are losing elsewhere," to an account of previous experiences that taught him "the company is out of step" (a way of speaking he sometimes used to characterize himself), to an exposition of the ideas that would enable the company to "get back in step"—where *back*, surely, is a crucial word. Each part, he might have pointed out, has its own compositional unity and function and presents a different aspect of the author. Beginning in the present, the book treats simple, undemanding rural pleasures, the week-end activities of the husbandman of wild things. Then it recovers the past when, as adventurer, Leopold had known wild biota—recovers this in present recollection and therefore with a sense of loss. The conclusion, again in the present, belongs to the professor for whose different demanding discourse Leopold (the artist) has set the stage. The three parts might

also be designated *Thoreau, Muir,* and *Leopold,* for the participatory seasonal record, if not the family activity, recalls *Walden,* the double ply of
adventure and conservation recalls any number of Muir's books (written
in recollection), and Leopold, their successor, brings both forward in the
uncompromising upshot of the conclusion where his divergence from the
managerial conservation of Gifford Pinchot, in which he had been
trained, also shows the extent of his education.

The dialectic of this structure serves the deepest instructional purpose
of the book. "See or go blind," Gary Snyder's injunction in *Myths &
Texts,* names it—see things and their relations. Luna Leopold, in the pref-
ace to *Round River,* speaks of his father's "lifetime of developing perception" and this is what is artfully set out in such a way as to foster ours.
And not only perception but the action it entails. Consciousness, as the
French know in having one word for both, awakens conscience. To see
and refuse to act is to go blind, is not to follow the way perception opens.
The professor and the husbandman are active men. Like Thoreau and
Muir before him and Snyder after him, Leopold speaks for an unac-
knowledged constituency, for the wild, the silent world (Ponge's phrase).
Like them, he is a figure, the exemplar of his own thought, and this gives it
authenticity.

The almanac need not be complete nor detailed in order to be useful.
We do not need to know what to observe but only to observe, to be the
hunter in "The Deer Swath," the last shack essay, written in 1948 and
published in *Round River*—the hunter who has learned the "the world
teems with creatures, processes, and events," that every ground, whether
city street, vacant lot, or illimitable woods, is hunting ground. An almanac reminds us to keep our eyes open to the seasonal, annual, and annular
aspect of things; it fosters the idea of cycles, the recurrences that are the
wonder and delight of the seasons, the "cycles of beginnings and ceasings"
Leopold notes at the outset, that representation of reality, the round river,
"the never-ending circuit of life." Much of the data in the shack journals
pertains to phenology, the science, according to Webster's dictionary, of
the relations between climate and periodic biological phenomena, such as
the migrations and breedings of birds, the fruiting of plants, and so on.
Phenology is a contraction of *phenomenology,* the observation of just
those phenomena, as in Thoreau's "Kalendar," that enable us to antici-
pate nature. But the rootword is also worth remembering because perceptual experience roots us in the world.

In a study of the rhetoric of *A Sand County Almanac,* Peter Fritzell says
that the almanac is composed of "perceptual situations." These situations
might also be called "events," a term from Whitehead's philosophy of

organism in keeping with Leopold's awareness of process. Susan Flader, the preeminent student of Leopold, speaks of "the person and the place," a phrase evoking the postmodern poetics of the poet-in-the-field, and nothing covers the poetics of the almanac so well as William Carlos Williams' dictum, "No ideas but in things." Thoreau begins the year with the thawing clay of the railroad cut, with the melting ice of the pond and the return of geese, and Leopold marks March with the last. But perhaps in eagerness to begin, to set things in motion, he attends a January thaw, tracking a skunk in the snow much in the way Thoreau tracked a fox. There are several morals to be drawn from this simple act of going outdoors to look (his motion of beginning, simple because winter has abstracted the landscape): that little is as good as big because what matters is relation; that participating in nature, economic as he reports it in the case of mouse, hawk, rabbit, and owl, is by virtue of this very act of mind more than economic; that the "pathetic fallacy" of taking the perspective of each creature is not in fact sentimental unless granting biotic equality to all things is sentimental; that observation and meditation are inextricable because, as Heisenberg teaches, observation alters what is observed, and because, as Emerson says, "man is an analogist, and studies relations in all objects."

The analogies Leopold draws work both ways, but most often the "animal analogues" serve, as in Amer-indian medicine, as instructive "analogies to our own problems." The mouse, for example, who has everything "neatly organized" to satisfy its needs, finds that "the thawing sun has mocked the basic premises of the microtine economic system." For the mouse the thaw is a catastrophe of the kind that destroys civilization—a catastrophe as much of natural happening (nature is violent, and the communal life of organisms is prompted by climatic change) as of tunnel vision and reluctance to change. The mouse may be said to illustrate an evolutionary lesson out of Veblen.

Leopold is speculatively present but not omniscient. He would accept Emerson's definition of the poet as the integrator of all parts if it did not seem willful, if it acknowledged the mystery of harmony ("the great orchestra") and represented the ego as necessary only to seeing (hearing) the integration. That he heard the great orchestra is not literary fancy, and distinguishes him, as it did Thoreau, from those who only see the world. The form Leopold used to compose his observations is itself instructive of this: an ideogram of six fragments presenting a complex event called "thaw," a multiphasic occurrence that bespeaks community because whatever exists in the same space belongs there and plays its functional part, however unwillingly, whether for good or ill, with everything else.

An ideogram does not impose form so much as assume that the reality it represents is united in ways beyond our understanding; it asks us to look for relationships. It is the mode, in this instance, of someone who has learned humility.

The almanac may be diffuse, but in taking us over the ground, much as Thoreau and Muir do, Leopold allows us to share his experience. We come to know the place, and learn some of its ecological lessons. One of the most important concerns evolutionary and historical time. The latter is truly *time*, the furious linear assault of progress that Lévi-Strauss says, in *Tristes Tropiques*, betrayed the paradisal promise of America. In one of the most cunning essays, Leopold tells time in terms of sawing down a shattered oak. He reads back from the present, as we must do in order to know our places; reads cultural or human geography in Carl Sauer's way to show us how man in the landscape disturbs its ecological stability, diminishes its power of self-renewal, and visibly alters it. The immigrant road that passes the shack made the Westward Movement possible. It is the archetypal road, the great destroyer of wilderness, precursor of the railroad whose iron, Hart Crane said, "always . . . dealt cleavage." Thus, to read back is to realize that settlement was also an unsettling of a climax culture, that the economic waste of wild life, forest, and marsh was prodigal, that only 80 years stands between the sawyer at the shack and Muir, who in 1865, wished to establish nearby a sanctuary for wild flowers and even then exemplified the "mercy for things natural, wild, and free" that Leopold believes we must now acquire.

There are many glimpses of paradisal (wild) America in Part II, "Sketches Here and There." Most notable are those of the Delta of the Colorado, explored by Leopold and his brother before its abundant wild life was supplanted by cantaloupes, the Sierra Madre Mountains, a haven of singing river and birds, and the mountain world of the Southwest, the place of "heroic" manhood where he was "on top" and "every living thing sang, chirped, and burgeoned." Here in the mountains, the initials he finds carved in the aspen tell of romance (as much an aspect of ecology as the peenting of the woodcock in Part I)—tell of "the glory of [his] mountain spring." For at this time he married Estella Bergere. Nothing perhaps marks his difference in temperament from Thoreau and Muir so much as this—as, say, the loving flourish of the dedication of the *Almanac* "to my Estella," where *my* does more than distinguish wife from daughter.

The exuberance of the writing belongs to youthful adventure and is measured by an elegiac counterpoint. It is also measured by the landscape of the enclosing frame, the marshland, initially of Wisconsin, long-since drained, and finally of Clandeboye in Manitoba, now threatened with extinction. "The marshlands that once sprawled over the prairie from Illinois to the Athabasca," Leopold concludes, "are now shrinking northward." And when they are gone we will no longer coexist with the Pleistocene, live "in the wider reaches of evolutionary time," and hear, as he also did in the green lagoons of the Colorado, the bugling of the cranes, "the wildest [because oldest] of living fowl." The fate of marsh and bird, of course, is as good an example of land-use and conservation as any. "A roadless marsh is seemingly as worthless to the alphabetical conservationist," he remarks, "as an undrained one to the empire-builders."

The section on Wisconsin links Parts I and II, and among other things provides an earth-history of the sand counties and a political history of the governmental efforts to remedy their poverty. The failure to improve the counties contrasts with Leopold's self-elected work of restoration in Part I—his effort "to rebuild," as he says in the foreword, "what we are losing elsewhere" in the way our land-use contributes to the downward wash to the sea of atoms once locked in stone and subsequently almost endlessly recycled in food-chains. We extinguish biota as well as species— the passenger pigeon is an example of the latter—and we cannot even keep a small portion of a river wild.

As an ecologist Leopold follows Whitman's advice to study out the land, its idioms and its men. "Illinois Bus Ride" is the best and briefest instance—and of the mordant-ironic style he reserves for the economic-minded and ecologically-mindless: farmers, agriculture and conservation experts, sportsmen and other nature-consumers. This is indeed the style of "keen intellect" and registers dismay. Recollection evokes it because Leopold is moved by what Bachelard calls reverie toward childhood, the very reverie of childhood that suggests to him that "growing up" is "growing down." He tells us in "Red Legs Kicking" that "my earliest impressions of wildlife and its pursuit retain a vivid sharpness of form, color, and atmosphere that half a century of professional wildlife experience has failed to obliterate or to improve upon." This—and much of the writing—confirms Edith Cobb's view of the ecological imagination of childhood, of the perceptual wealth that vouchsafes genius. This ecological imagination, in his account, is complemented by an equally vivid sense of the ethical restraint imposed by the act of killing. And later, when he shoots a wolf and watches the "fierce green fire dying in her eyes," he learns an ethical lesson of even greater ecological importance. He learns, as Buber had in answering the gaze of animals, that animals have being (are *Thou* not *It*) and have every right to biotic equality. Leopold acquires the foundation of his thought; for thinking like a wolf is as requisite as thinking like a mountain.

To think like a mountain is to think ecologically, in terms of relationships and land health, in ways, that is, that do not promote "dust-
bowls, and rivers washing the future to the sea." Reminded of *The Grapes
of Wrath* (1939), we recall the natural and social consequences of what
Steinbeck called "the system." Shortly after, in the phrase "peace in our
time," we are asked to remember the price of appeasement and are not
allowed to settle for that. Leopold shows us how he changed his ways—
conversion is the archetypal pattern of his book—and he writes in order
to change our ways, to build "receptivity into the still unlovely [unloving]
human mind." His book itself may be said to be ecological because it is
generous and generative, written in the spirit of gift exchange, the social
analogue of the cyclical transfer of energy; a fertile book, having "the
ability of the soil to receive, store, and release energy." Nearly 40 years
after its publication, because we have so little heeded it, its value may be
said to have increased. Leopold says that "the outstanding scientific discovery of the twentieth century is . . . the complexity of the land organism" and, as much as anyone, he made us appreciate its life. In doing so
he spoke of impending doom. He knew, as he says in the discarded foreword, that "our foothold is precarious, not because it may slip, but because we may kill the land before we learn to use it with love and respect."
Kill the land, as he had once killed predators! Destroy the very ground
under our feet!

The ethical bearing of Leopold's work is notable but what is not mentioned is his resistance to his own entropic vision. Jeremiad might have
served him, but he chose other literary forms and addressed us as citizens,
taking advantage perhaps of our predilection to think well of ourselves.
Neither *A Sand County Almanac* nor *Round River* is addressed to fellow
experts but to men and women of good will, the kind of people who, in
another time, began the conservation movement by forming the Sierra
Club. In "A Man's Leisure Time," the prefatory essay of *Round River,*
Leopold expatiates on hobbies (among them, his and his wife's hobby of
archery, which connects this essay to leisure at the farm)—expatiates on a
notion I found suspect until I recalled that the conservation movement, so
well described by Stephen Fox, had begun as a hobby and—this is
Leopold's strategy—must again become one, farther down the line than
vigilant protest, now in the leisure-time practice of the husbandry of wild
things. It may be quixotic to think, as he did, that the battle will be won
on the back forty, but some of us here apparently agree. In any case, like
some of his predecessors, he "created cultural value by being aware of it,
and by creating a pattern of growth." A cultural value because the problem involved *culture,* not only an errant agriculture but "how to bring

about a striving for harmony with the land among a people many of whom have forgotten there is any such thing as land, among whom education and culture have become almost synonymous with landlessness."

When Leopold sent off the earliest version of the book he told the editor that he didn't want to write "mere natural history," and that "field skill and ability to write [such as his] seldom occur in the same person." In saying this, he repudiated "amateur natural history . . . of the dickey-bird variety," the result of "ladies and gentlemen wander[ing] afield not so much to learn how the world is put together as to gather subject matter for tea-time conversation." To be sure, this is not what Thoreau did at Walden Pond, though in a sentimental age it was an outcome of the transcendentalists' correspondential vision of self and world that authorized a symbolical appropriation of nature in the interest of self. Natural history in Thoreau is also a mode of autobiography. Thoreau went to the woods to find *himself* in relation to nature, to the end of self-culture, soul-making. More than a century later, Leopold went to the farm as a trained scientist in order to recover a relationship to the land and further its health. The spiritual legacy of Thoreau and Muir belongs to his social idealism; he does not share their Idealist philosophy, and was better able to look at nature without looking at himself. He shares this stance toward reality with many contemporary poets and thinkers and finds his place with them because he believed that "the detection of harmony is the domain of poets" and because he gave some of them the legacy of *inhabiting*, of living in place. He stands with them also because the reference of his work is Western Civilization itself, its world alienation and landlessness, the necessity it is under to transform ego-thought into eco-thought. "To change ideas about what land is for," he wrote just prior to undertaking *A Sand County Almanac*, "is to change ideas about what anything is for." In doing this he did what Muir thought almost impossible: he obtained a hearing in behalf of nature from a standpoint other than that of human use. Moreover, he proposed a correlative action, not only the preservation of the wilderness but the husbandry of the wild, the *wildering*, John Stilgoe's resonant term for the irrepressible return of the wild, that any of us might foster on abandoned land. In Leopold's work the attitude toward what was once fearful—the presence and encroachment of the wilderness—has changed; his is not a howling but a singing wilderness, and a measure of health. Its ecological importance is recognized and it is encouraged. The wild returns as the predators do, in the interest of climax, of a complex, diverse, stable biota. Such wildering, I find, goes with *worlding*, another resonant term, this one Richard Pevear's, because the husbandry of the wild is a discipline of familiarization that enables us to live in the world.

I honor Leopold for these reasons. In studying him, I have come to recognize one of the few professors whose leisure-work (I join his polar words)—whose leisure-work, in the words of another great professor, has exemplary validity.

The Literary Achievement of Loren Eiseley

E. Fred Carlisle

I n October, 1947, Loren Eiseley published an essay titled "Obituary of a Bone Hunter" in *Harper's* magazine. This presumably autobiographical sketch related three incidents from the 1930s in which Eiseley failed to make the big find that would have made him famous. The first occurred in a cave near Carlsbad, New Mexico, when spiders turned him back. The second missed opportunity happened in a similar cave, and that time he turned back because of an egg in an owl's nest. The third involved an apparently crazy old man and a fragment of what might have been a fossil human jaw bone. Eiseley attributed these failures to the "folly of doubt," rather than to bad luck or limited scientific ability, and he concluded his account of "the life of a small bone hunter" by saying, "I have made no great discoveries." "There will be no further chances."

The finality of that seems odd coming from a man who had turned forty only a month before the essay appeared and who was on his way back to Penn to assume the chairmanship of the Anthropology department. But evidently, it continued to express something of Eiseley's belief about his career, for twenty-four years later, he included the "Obituary," virtually unchanged, in his autobiographical collection, *The Night Country.* "I have made no great discoveries." Well, in a strictly scientific sense, perhaps he did not. But as an estimate of his career, there is a great irony in that sentence, for Loren Eiseley did, in fact, make an extraordinary discovery when he came upon his true and original genius in the unique voice and vision of *The Immense Journey.*

In what he considered his favorite book, Eiseley told the story of human evolution, but his story was not science in the usual sense. He also included "a bit of his personal universe," and so the book became, as well, "the record of what one man thought as he pursued research and pressed his hands against the confining walls of scientific method in this time." In this unconventional record, Eiseley sometimes spoke extravagantly about miracles, the magic of water, and enormous extensions of vision. Like Thoreau, Eiseley wandered beyond certain professional and literary orthodoxies and tried to speak the truths he had discovered. As he said later in *The Unexpected Universe,* "I am trying to write honestly from my own experience." Like Emerson, Eiseley searched for an adequate geometry—a kind of new idiom or language—to express the mysterious and contradictory nature of experience that science had helped him discover.

With the 1957 publication of *The Immense Journey,* Eiseley completed a critical phase of his literary development. He had found a way to intertwine all the strands of his personal and professional life into a coherent whole. *The Immense Journey* tells one of the epic stories of science and simultaneously provides an imaginative exploration and an artful expression of it. In short, Eiseley intertwined autobiographical, scientific, figurative, and metaphysical elements into a new idiom and a unique vision, and that is the heart of his literary achievement.

The voice and vision were both firmly grounded in science. Without that experience and knowledge—and this is as necessary as it is obvious to say—Eiseley could never have become the original and accomplished writer he was. The facts of his scientific development and career are well known and require no summary here. His scientific *achievement* is less certain, but it was clearly substantial. Perhaps he did not succeed as either a researcher unearthing important new fossils and artifacts or as a theoretical anthropologist advancing and supporting new formulations for inadequately explained data. Nevertheless, he participated in field research of some significance; he had a remarkable command of his and related fields of knowledge; he published a great many important analytical and critical papers; he developed a great ability for exposing the inadequacy of others' work; he was in fact an excellent scholar and critic in his field—and later a significant historian of science. Eiseley became a very successful academic scientist, and that in itself is a notable achievement.

But even more than that, science shaped Eiseley's thinking about nature and human experience, and his writing about science influenced his later literary style. It is fascinating in itself, but not the point here, to trace his development as a writer of science and to see the modulation from a very conventional professional style toward the new idiom. But the most obvious literary foundation for his achievement, however, was the poetry and prose he published in the thirties and early forties.

In the ten years since his death, this earlier work has become better known and like the facts of his scientific career needs no lengthy review here. What is important to remember is that, at least indirectly, the work is autobiographical; it is firmly tied to place and to the historic and pre-historic pasts; and it reflects a questioning if not yet scientific mind. The poetry bears the mark of a distressing childhood and youth, as well as young adulthood, and it reflects Eiseley's attachment to place—the spaces extending from the prairie around Lincoln to the uplands of western Ne-braska and beyond. Besides its personal and confessional quality, the po-etry speaks, as well, of an entire region and people for whom struggle, poverty, and failure were a way of life.

As a young poet Eiseley developed considerable control, complexity, and subtlety in his work and achieved a level of sensitivity and maturity that extended the significance of his poetry beyond the experience of a particular young man and region. He wrote well in the mid-1930s. Never-theless, his work created no new poetic idiom, nor did it discover any new perspectives. The images, forms, and themes were all rather conventional. The development in his style reflected to some extent his increasing per-sonal confidence and stability, but Eiseley did not discover in poetry a way of moving beyond certain emotional and psychic resolutions or beyond certain literary conventions.

In science, by contrast, he seemed to find the order, system, and ide-ology he needed to insulate himself from the turmoil of his life. There, he discovered control and explanations that confirmed his experience, gave it wider significance, and enabled him to escape the relative isolation of a lyric poet. As a member of a professional community, he developed a style appropriate to the impersonal and analytic conventions of science. But that style then gave way to a more personal and fluent language. Eiseley was apparently trying to recover certain qualities of expression, feeling, and insight that he had developed as a poet but subdued as a young scien-tist, and was trying also to expand the potential meanings of his prose. This development—and it is apparent by the late forties—led in just a few years to what I am calling a new idiom.

This new mode or style can most clearly be characterized through the layers or dimensions Eiseley so artistically intertwined in *The Immense Journey*: science, autobiography, figuration, and metaphysics. The layer of science is very clear. It is realized in the story of evolution that Eiseley tells—a direct, informed account that gives the book its narrative and expository structure.

The autobiographical aspects are equally clear. From the first chapter on, Eiseley is telling two stories—one about evolution, the species history, and one about himself from his personal experiences as a fieldworker to his discoveries of significance and relationship. Autobiography constitutes part of what he calls the "unconventional record" of the book.

Figuration or metaphor is, first, the dimension that gives interest, texture, and impact to Eiseley's style. Such dramatic metaphors as "out of the choked Devonian waters emerged sight and sound and the music that rolls invisible through the composer's brain" compress time and radically connect different species in a powerful and meaningful way. Through them, Eiseley helps us see *our* place in the story—not just as its end but as beings still connected to its origins. The metaphoric dimension also enables him to relate the two histories. The "slit" which Eiseley describes in chapter 1 is but an example. Actual place, occasion for explanation and speculation, and metaphor for time and for Eiseley's situation in time, the "slit" helps intertwine all of the dimensions.

The metaphysical or speculative layer is associated most closely with the enormous extension of vision Eiseley speaks about. Although the later chapters seem more speculative than earlier ones, this layer is present throughout, as Eiseley's meditations about himself and time in the first chapter suggest.

In *The Immense Journey,* and in *The Firmament of Time* and *The Unexpected Universe,* Eiseley has made explicit and functional aspects of discourse and of experience that are at best implicit or invisible, and often absent, in the writing of most scientists or poets. This alone suggests that he is not simply a scientist who writes well about science or about human values; nor is he simply a popularizer (if he is one at all) who explains science to others; nor is he just a writer who makes "poetry" out of science, thereby changing it into something else. His achievement of a new idiom is more considerable.

In 1974, I characterized Eiseley's vision as a "heretical science," and while his way of thinking about science may seem less unusual today, there is no reason to think differently about the unorthodox character of that vision. I am not speaking about the themes of Eiseley's books and essays or of his ideas. Vision is something more basic; it informs and shapes ideas and themes. In the simplest sense, Eiseley discovered in *The Immense Journey,* and elsewhere, a greater and more comprehensive version of science than the usual or orthodox sense. It was in the words of Francis Bacon, a science "for the uses of life," and in a personal sense, it became a science for the uses of the self. It is science which *includes* the self.

Eiseley accepted evolution as a well substantiated scientific theory. His own professional work helped confirm or elaborate the theory and he studied and learned far more than he was able to observe directly. However, he also interiorized the theory, so that it functioned as a major structure for perceiving and comprehending experience. He dwelt in it, so to speak, and through it he made contact with reality. His research and travel, his scientific knowledge, and his belief in the modern theory of evolution gave his work perspective, shape, and authority, as well as content.

While Eiseley believed that scientific knowledge helps us understand the world, he could not forget that we are also often baffled by the natural world and limited and misled by our incomplete knowledge of it. Science liberates us with its knowledge and vision, yet it repeatedly redefines our limitations as it raises new problems and reveals new boundaries. He accepted the systematic structure of scientific method and knowledge, and they took him a long way. At the same time, he pressed against the narrow, confining limits of the very system he accepted, as he struggled to see through to the meanings hidden in nature. He tried to extend science so that it comprehended more, but he also tried to understand for himself. So no matter how far the instruments and structure of science carried him into nature, Loren Eiseley was still, in a sense, tracking himself—still seeking to establish *his* reality.

As a professional anthropologist, Eiseley searched widely for the origins of humankind. But that search extended naturally and logically to a search for the origins of himself in the fields and small towns of Nebraska and in the uplands of the ice age. It widened to a quest for himself as a solitary fugitive from the twentieth century and as one of a lonely and wandering species through time. It concentrated into a search for his inner self in the dark void and deep spaces within himself and in the evolution of the human brain—"in the windswept uplands of the human mind." Eiseley reached into the depths of time, of the earth, of life, and of himself—he classified *and* contemplated—in search of a more comprehensive science.

In *The Firmament of Time*, he writes "'The special value of science,' a perceptive philosopher once wrote, 'lies not in what it makes of the world, but what it makes of the knower.'" Loren Eiseley, however, did not reject one for the other. The one—the world—leads into the other—the self—for in one sense the self includes the world or holds some of the answers to it: "Man's quest for certainty is, in the last analysis, a quest for meaning. But the meaning lies buried within himself rather than in the void he has vainly searched for portents since antiquity." The value of the scientist's activity and knowledge rests in *their* value and meaning for the lived life—"for the uses of life."

Several writers believe that Eiseley's achievement is limited primarily to the personal or familiar essay—or to what he called the concealed essay. They quite reasonably associate Eiseley with the natural history essay in America and with authors like Henry Thoreau, John Burroughs, and John Muir, and, in the twentieth century, Aldo Leopold, Rachel Carson, Annie Dillard, and Lewis Thomas. There is no question that Eiseley was influenced by early nature writers, as he was by G. K. Chesterton. And Eiseley has made a significant contribution to the art. He must indeed be read and valued as an essayist. Nevertheless, his achievement exceeds that genre. Like Thoreau, Eiseley wrote at least one extraordinary book in which the artistry and meaning surpass the limits of the essay. In *The Immense Journey* certainly and perhaps in *The Unexpected Universe*—at his most successful in other words—Eiseley fused his essays into unified, coherent books in which the whole is greater than any sum of its parts.

And while Eiseley's finest books and essays certainly achieved what he attributes to the great nature writers, his vision nevertheless also exceeds theirs. In writing about Sir Francis Bacon, Eiseley said that "Words can sometimes be more penetrating probes into the nature of the universe than any instrument wielded in the laboratory." In saying this about Bacon, Eiseley seems to mean that words can be *scientific* instruments.

Words give the scientist a means to explain and interpret research and discoveries, and even here they are not altogether transparent. They are a medium which shapes the scientist's insights and therefore affects his meaning. But Eiseley means even more, for words function sometimes as the *primary* instrument of the scientist; they become the medium within which the scientist's knowledge and imagination operate in order to discover something of the nature of the universe. Words, I believe, functioned this way, scientifically, for Loren Eiseley.

Words also provide the great nature writers with a powerful instrument of insight and expression. Their contributions, however, are different. They add a dimension to science, "something that lies beyond the careful analyses of professional biology." Science requires their sensitivity and insight, for without it "we are half blind . . . we . . . lack pity and tolerance." These nature writers provide, apparently, a kind of synthetic vision. They write about nature *and* humanity. They see nature through frankly human eyes and try to express its beauty and meaning in human terms.

Now, certainly Eiseley did that, and in writing about the great nature writers, he may have been making a case for himself. But it is mistaken, I believe, to regard him simply as a nature writer who understood and

valued science—when in fact he was a scientist, and he was also a writer
—an artist. Because of this dual identity, his literary achievement was
distinct.

In *The Man Who Saw Through Time* Eiseley distinguishes between the
scientist and the artist in their great moments of creativity. Even though
both may experience the aesthetic joy of discovery and design, "a substantial difference still remains. For science seeks essentially to naturalize man
in the structure of predictable law and conformity, whereas the artist is
interested in man the individual." Eiseley believes that a person may be
both a scientist and artist, but somehow the two still remain separate;
their activities do not fuse into a single mode of creative activity. While the
discoveries of the great artist or scientist might give us a "new geography"—a new design for reality which in turn changes our world, their
domains for Eiseley are nevertheless distinct. The artist explores the interior—and draws the world and us within; whereas the scientist sometimes ventures to "remake reality."

The distinction seems sound enough. But perhaps in Eiseley's own case
the two ventures are not so different as he thought. Perhaps, *both* the
scientist and the artist discover and remake reality. The scientist may concentrate on the physical and chemical or organic and physiological constituents, and the artist may dwell on the emotional and psychological
constituents of reality. In our time, however, these domains are not always
so easy to separate, and sometimes they veer too close together for intellectual comfort.

Eiseley tried, I believe, to combine science and art as he explains them.
He concentrates on the individual and on humanity within the structure
of predictability (and unpredictability) defined largely by anthropology
and biology. In his writing the systematic activity and structure of science
merge with the search for the self within that structure. Science, then, is
simultaneously a pursuit of the self and an attempt to make increasingly
closer and closer contact with reality. The personal and universal dimensions of science merge in Eiseley's books, as the quest for knowledge of
reality and knowledge of oneself become one.

Eiseley realizes his unique voice and vision most fully in *The Immense
Journey* and in *The Unexpected Universe.* They are the heart of his literary achievement. Nevertheless, he wrote two other impressive books—
Darwin's Century, his major work in the history of science, and *All the
Strange Hours,* his remarkable autobiography. Both are memorable, and
from my point of view, they stand as complements to the books I value
most. The preparation of *Darwin's Century* certainly influenced and informed *The Immense Journey* and represents the scholarly and scientific

aspect of Eiseley's work. The autobiographical and figurative dimensions are clearly subdued. In *All the Strange Hours,* Eiseley subdued the scientific dimension of his work in order to excavate his personal life. Without these two books, Eiseley's literary achievement would be incomplete, certainly, but each in itself reveals only an aspect of his original genius. Without *The Immense Journey* and *The Unexpected Universe,* there would be no original—no literary achievement for the ages.

Public and Private Rhetorical Modes in the Essays of James Baldwin

James Cunningham

The world of James Baldwin's essays is indeed a world. However, the tendency to look upon his work as that of a personal essayist has the force of denying that his subjects are real. Behind this effect lies the popular American notion—with which much of Baldwin's work is at war—that the person is not real, that the self and the ego are synonyms. That the writer's subject is himself and the world and that the writer's business is that of looking at both as they really are should be well-established Baldwinian commonplaces by now. The alternative to this outlook is simply to fantasize about one or both. Baldwin understood that to regard time as something unreal or expendable is simply another way to fantasize. Thus the secret of being an American is to exercise daily and endlessly the power to forget the past. And if doing so is ever inconvenient, the next best thing is simply to falsify it.

The implication for understanding some important things about Baldwin's essays is that both their structure and their content will invariably involve storytelling or narrative that is both personal and retrospective as well as public or social. Society and the interior life and their interlocking relationship remain fundamental ingredients of what Baldwin the essayist has to say and the manner in which he usually says it.

I have always been fascinated by his use of anecdotes or vignettes to illustrate and argue and testify to what is difficult to convey any other way. While the value of experience is another commonplace of his work, the ingenuity with which the employment of narrative allows the reader to *experience* his expository meaning has always fascinated me as well. I used to simply write off this ingenuity as an inevitable result of his tendency to introduce fictional techniques into an otherwise discursive medium. The framework might be narrative, but the content was expository—or was it the other way around? In expressive writing—writing close to the self—it is more important to *show* than to *tell*. Every freshman student is taught this basic rhetorical axiom in composition class. Recalling instances from one's own experience also enhances a writer's credibility as someone with firsthand knowledge.

Baldwin certainly has the authority to discuss the ups and downs of the creative process. So when he demonstrates the problems and the breakthroughs involved in trying to construct a novel or a play and the mysterious role of memory, I will follow him very closely and intently. When his comments on the secrets of constructing dialogue become probing analyses of what he calls American incoherence or inarticulateness, and when, without missing a beat, he finds room for an anecdote or hypothetical example into which details of bodies in closets are deftly fitted, I give up trying to find my bearings in the discourse. I am simply under Baldwin's spell.

As a student of discourse types, however, I cannot resist applying theories of experts, such as James Moffett and James Britton, who try to classify types of expression. How does Baldwin's flair for dramatizing ideas by way of sensory detail or bold metaphor measure up, for example? How do his references to the writer as witness, a viewpoint which implies some kind of reporter, strike rhetoricians who consider description or storytelling the lowest of intellectual feats when compared with generalizing and theorizing and analogizing? Can accounts of personal experience handle rhetorical wonders such as these without abstract methods of seeing? And yet Baldwin seems to dance up and down the ladder of abstraction, while probing and generalizing and theorizing with all the ease and virtuosity one could wish—and still manages to remain at or return home to a familiar, flesh-and-blood observation like "trouble don't last always, nor does power."

I have been especially moved by the illusions of actual music or of performers at work in Baldwin's writing. This power to make musicians and their music making come alive on paper, come alive in words, is utterly awesome in his fiction but just as absorbing or revealing in the essays. As with so much of his recreatings of the lives and drives of artists, Baldwin's power to suggest the order of vision involved in being a performing artist, especially, attracts me to his many profiles of artists. The movie reviews come to mind, but so do pieces which try to explain the unpredictable ways of bringing characters or moments alive in the teeth of what simply cannot always be approached rationally. If glamor has a place in these discussions, it is usually simply a symptom of the isolation of the artist from the people or the interior forces which talent must tap for nourishment. Or glamor is treated as a symptom of the kind of fantasizing that is equally fatal to genuine creative effort.

It would certainly be strange if Baldwin's profiles of artists he knew intimately or whose careers he followed closely did not also contain at least some passages of self-revelation. It would be equally surprising if his introductory pieces to his four major essay collections failed to generalize and theorize about the nature of art or of society or of the relationship between the two. Nor should anyone be surprised to note how the personal and the intellectual content of these nonfiction pieces often assume the guise of one another.

Some people would say that reality and illusion also imitate each other. While the arts can be said to cultivate the illusion of reality, the deliberate cultivation of fantasy is another matter in Baldwin's view. The effort of Hollywood and Broadway, especially, to promote fantasy and to treat it as a synonym for the private life is the target of much of his film and theater commentary as well as his broader cultural criticism. In fact, the former is an illustration of the latter. And many of the artists whose work is exploited on behalf of such profit-making fantasizing are objects of his concern and wariness, if not compassion. In Baldwin's view, artists—whether performers or writers—are on a collision course with the fantasy industry which hires them, since they must use what they know about life in order to create the illusion of life on the screen, on the stage, or on the page.

Apart from the artists themselves, one of the most costly victims of the multimedia lying is the developing sensibility of the black child. To make us more sensitive to this damage, for example, is perhaps one of the reasons Baldwin traces his movie viewing in *The Devil Finds Work* all the way back to the age of seven. And while something other than benign neglect is at work here, the black child's need for a screen which corroborates his or her sense of reality collides head-on with that screen's principal business of corroborating white fantasies. In a *Look* magazine profile of Sidney Poitier, Baldwin elaborates on the problematic nature of the industry's compulsion to dishonesty, which black performers must outwit in order to smuggle bits of reality from their lives past the script writer:

> The industry is compelled, given the way it is built, to present to the American people a self-perpetuating fantasy of American life. It considers that its job is to entertain the American people. Their concept of entertainment is difficult to distinguish from the use of narcotics. . . . *And the black face, truthfully reflected, is not only no part of this drama, it is antithetical to it.* And this

puts the black performer in a rather grim bind. He knows, on the one hand, that if the reality of a black man's life were on that screen, it would destroy the fantasy totally. And on the other hand, he really has no right *not* to appear, not only because he must work, but also for all those people who need to see him. By the use of his person, he must smuggle in a reality that he knows is not in the script. [56]

The article concludes with an anecdote describing the morale boosting that Baldwin received from Poitier on the occasion of a book party for *Another Country.* It is worth quoting a passage because of its tone: "My publisher gave a party at Big Wilt's Small's Paradise in Harlem. Sidney came very early. I was ready to meet the mob, but I was scared to death, and Sidney knew, and he walked me around the block and talked to me and helped me get myself together" (57).

Besides contributing to the author's credibility as someone on intimate terms with the subject of his profile, and besides illustrating the point that artists need one another, the article underscores something important. The episode captures the quiet, unstated knowledge possible between people who have endured similar journeys. The key word here is *unstated.* Precisely this order of contact or interaction is deliberately kept out of screen depictions of black people, Baldwin seems to be suggesting. This point is repeatedly noted in his cataloguing of Hollywood's and Broadway's sins against both the black artist and the black audience. There is either outright falsification or simply silence.

But the notion of silence—which includes suggestions of apathy— brings to mind the walks around the block that occur throughout the essays. That these recollections are at once public and private, expressive and intellectual, is also a Baldwinian commonplace. Probably the one essay which sticks in my own memory, even in my sleep probably, is actually a printed speech from *Nobody Knows My Name.* And the title, "Notes for a Hypothetical Novel," alludes to an *Esquire* magazine symposium entitled "The Role of the Writer in America" and held at San Francisco State College in 1960. In the light of Baldwin's demonstration approach, one wonders what the other speeches were like. At any rate, my own testimony to what struck me upon first reading this piece when the book was published, and the one image or two that made such a lasting impression, may introduce a bit of redundancy here.

However, I am trying to demonstrate that the power behind the dominant force in a writer's imagination has the capacity to transfer to the imagination or memory of the reader, and that this power is no rhetorical accident. I remember the *picture* of a man in an open coat, stumbling down the street pursued by the jeering sounds of children, falling against the spikes of an iron fence, and hitting his head against one. The image of blood on his head and on the fence is prominent. And although he is drunk, he does not entirely resemble a wino. I also remember the puzzlement following Baldwin's admission that he had no idea why such a man held his imagination captive so long or how he might figure in some hypothetical novel, given the specifics of his life that Baldwin had to work with as material. Well, this fellow crops up in a 1964 essay, "Words of a Native Son," and this time an explanation of a sort is offered.

The other image I helplessly remember from the speech is a hypothetical closet with a hypothetical body in it, and the comically grim conversation which the murderer and his friend attempt while pretending that the dead mother is not in the closet. The increasing incoherence and the increasing panic—which are functions of one another—I dimly remember as the point and the point as a description of the special difficulty the American writer has of resurrecting talking Americans on the page or the stage or the screen.

"Words," also in *Nobody Knows My Name,* reads in much the same way as "Notes For," but instead of offering a hypothetical exercise in constructing a novel, it tackles the invention stage of a play—a hunt for a setting. The technical writing problem raised is not that of dialogue but of the physical details needed in building a stage character as opposed to a character like Ida from *Another Country.* In short, the ways of a playwright are contrasted with those of a novelist. In this context Baldwin pursues the issue of what he regards as American society's criminal silence in the face of the continued ruin of the young. Both the novel and the play, *Blues for Mr. Charlie,* deal with or turn on the figure of a dead youth. In describing the walk around the block, the same one in which he first encountered the stumbling, bleeding black man of his childhood, Baldwin is trying to reveal, in part, how writers stumble upon some of their own revelations or unsettling discoveries. He is attempting to share some connections he was able to make in order to suggest how imagination differs from fantasy and how the process of awakening people differs from that of trying to put them to sleep:

> But one afternoon in Harlem I understood something more about my story and about myself. My brother and some other people and my nephew were on the block where I grew up. It hadn't changed much in these last thirty-eight years of progress. And we also visited a funeral parlor nearby. A boy had died, a boy of twenty-seven who had been on the needle and who was a friend of my nephew's. I don't know why this struck me so much today, but it did. Perhaps because my nephew was there—I don't know. We walked to the

block where we grew up. There's a railing on that block, an iron railing with spikes. It's green now, but when I was a child, it was black. And at one point in my childhood—I must have been very, very young—I watched a drunken man falling down, being teased by children, falling next to that railing. I remember the way his blood looked against the black, and for some reason I've never forgotten that man. Today I began to see why. There's a dead boy in my play, it really pivots on a dead boy. The whole action of the play is involved with an effort to discover how this death came about. . . . All had a hand in it, as we all do. But this boy is all the ruined children that I have watched all my life being destroyed as we sit here, and being destroyed in silence. [399–400]

This piece, like the speech dealing with the creative process of constructing novels, ends with the same sobering insight and the same unanswerable challenge: we all must assume responsibility for what our country has become, as well as the responsibility for changing it. We must take the public fate of the young personally.

II

While the subject matter of introductions to collections such as *Notes of a Native Son* (1955) or *Price of the Ticket* (1985) hints at the range of topics that preoccupy Baldwin at a given period, the anecdotal or autobiographical content of these pieces offers a glimpse of the author's developing sensibilities and outlook. Thus this more personal material varies in scale and purpose. Preoccupations with the creative process and the trials of the artist, generational conflict between fathers and sons, the status of the interior life, or the price paid for overvaluing safety and success or for evading panic and rage must spring from somewhere. And that somewhere—the specifics of the author's life—is embodied in passages of personal recollection. In short, the public and private events to which Baldwin's introductions allude are anything but demonstrations of self-indulgence. Instead, they are crucial clues regarding the ways in which his perspective on these areas of discussion has evolved and why it comes to be intensified or how it comes to shift. Whether such pieces begin with the personal and end with the public is not really the issue. It is more important to note that Baldwin's structural movement resembles waves of expository and expressive material alternating with waves of exploratory or question-raising and argumentative material.

"Autobiographical Notes," the introduction to Baldwin's seminal work as an essayist, *Notes of a Native Son,* moves from an account of professional beginnings to public and literary issues and back again to a self-profile which concludes with one of his most stunning and provocative sentences: "I want to be an honest man and a good writer" (3). The only passage which rivals it in theoretical or aesthetic thrust is the one in which he articulates what amounts to his doctrine of experience: "One writes out of one thing only—one's own experience. . . . This is the only real concern of the artist, to recreate out of the disorder of life that order which is art" (7). His critical leanings as well as his iconoclasm reveal themselves, in part, in his view of the writer's task as involving the examination of attitudes and probes beneath the surface to "tap the source" (6). His role as cultural historian, and perhaps as psychologist, is embedded in his stress on the need to look back—individually and collectively—with a view to assessing one's past as a means of understanding the present and of dealing with unadmitted fears.

His iconoclastic disposition is revealed not only in his emphasis on the critical attitude but in the unsettling joke he insists lies in writing for the articulate black spokesman or intellectual—finding out that what has been called the "Negro problem" presents nothing to be articulate about. An anecdotal variation on this rude observation surfaces later in the profile piece on Norman Mailer, "The Black Boy Looks at the White Boy." There it is combined with the standard Baldwinian debunking of American notions of success and safety. Moreover, all of these topics can be subsumed structurally under the familiar trope of the Baldwinian journey. That Baldwin regards a journey unrecalled or unassessed as sheer folly is not only a clue to his radical status as a writer but a reminder that his introspective and retrospective outlook is mirrored in the structure of his essays as well—not to mention his fiction.

That the Baldwinian outlook and the price paid for it is a significant part of what he has to say is not as evident from the way these autobiographical notes are organized. This introductory essay has the look of a catalogue of miscellaneous items. Yet the tone shifts from the informative to the more probing and speculative. The first section brings the reader abreast of the writer's childhood and youth, professional beginnings and present perspective on the color problem, and describes insights into the craft and the hazards of writing. This section is related in a swift, telegraphic style. The self-disclosures are rendered in the spirit of both obligation and dismissal and take the form of allusions: his parents' reactions to his literary interests and activities, his earliest reading, his fellowships and the fate of his early writing projects, the link between his leaving the country for France and his completion of *Go Tell It on the Mountain*.

Only with the speculations on literary influence does the essay take off on its chief course—the relationship between the writer and society and between the writer and his cultural past or legacy. The allusion to Hemingway emphasizes the artist's need to last in order to get his work done and the identification of personal honesty with professional literary merit. But the final picture involves James Baldwin's vision rather than his topics; for the real subject matter underscored as Baldwinian turns out to be the business of acquiring a personal perspective on both the self and the world.

The essays in *Nobody Knows My Name* (1961), according to the sobering and mocking insights articulated in the "Introduction," are the hard fruit of hard questions posed for an expatriate writer at the crossroads— private and professional, temporal and spatial. And the traveler who speaks in this selection speaks in a tone that differs from the youthful, provocative one of "Notes." Here, the tone is more urgent and the revelations confided to the reader fewer but more unsettling. That Baldwin's language is especially memorable in this short, plain-spoken piece is due, in part, to his vivid and ironic orchestration of prison and travel imagery.

He gets a great deal of metaphorical mileage out of the figure of the haven dweller and dreamer whose will power is invested primarily in not waking up or traveling further with himself. This question-evading servant of self-delusion also serves as one of Baldwin's chief embodiments of American national character. The willful blindness attributed to this figure is the polar opposite of what is expected of the artist—to be a witness and a raiser of questions. The question of color, viewed by Baldwin as a means of obscuring "the graver questions of the self," is offered as an example of a false haven. Ingmar Bergman, the person to whom the introduction alludes as the antithesis of a self-deluding refuge seeker and who also serves as the subject of one of the major profile pieces in the book, illustrates Baldwin's premise that only by means of experience can a person connect with or profit from the experience of others. And the key to relating to our learning from other people is the questions which one's experience poses and which one must confront.

The Baldwin who emerges from more introductory pieces, the introduction written for the 1984 edition to *Notes* and "Introduction: The Price of the Ticket" is unclassifiable. He is at once more self-revealing and more discursive, more withering and more compassionate, more analytical and more sweeping in his generalizations, structurally more precise and more fluid. The framework is clearly that of personal narrative, but the center is discursive and analytical. If there is an overall tension, it is surely a mixture of the expressive and the exploratory, a blend of reverence and indignation. These are not brief, informal orienting pieces; these are full-length essays. And their language is charged to a surprising degree, given their function—like that of eccentric stretches of music.

Published only a year apart, these two essays illustrate one important lesson about Baldwin's use of personal experience in his nonfiction prose. Such accounts are always accounts of the world and the state of its moral and cultural health. The same is true of his portraits of artists and above all of his treatment of children and parents. This personal content demonstrates how he operates as a cultural and intellectual critic and chronicler. It also suggests why stylistic tone is so crucial. While his topical material serves as a key to what is on his mind, to treat him as merely a mind in pursuit of topics would be to neglect those intangibles which also control his imagination and thus to dictate what he makes of themes and concepts. In short, it would be to leave out what is most distinctive about his vision.

And speaking of vision, it helps to keep in mind that what a writer sees is largely a function of what the writer *has* seen, whether or not he or she chooses to remember it. In short, all writing is implicitly a report, whether the evidence from such a report is used to explore the self or to generalize about the world. Communicating this message is part of the burden of the following definitive passage from the introduction to *Nobody Knows My Name:* "But I still believe that the unexamined life is not worth living: and I know that self-delusion, in the service of no matter what small or lofty cause, is a price no writer can afford. His subject is himself and the world and it requires every ounce of stamina he can summon to attempt to look on himself and the world as they are" (12). This is one version of Baldwin's definition of the artist as essentially a witness. These words were published six years after the introductory piece to the first collection of essays and twenty-three years before the 1984 edition of *Notes of a Native Son.* Commenting on the two editions, Baldwin has occasion to do a bit of perspective juggling: "I had just turned thirty-one when this book was first published, and, by the time you read this, I will be sixty. . . . I remember many people who helped me in indescribable ways, all those years ago, when I was the popeyed, tongue-tied kid, in my memory sitting in a corner, on the floor. . . . I am, I suppose, a survivor" (xv). Baldwin's testimony in his final summing-up paragraph seems to line him up with all of the black spokesmen and leaders the country has always tried to dismiss as "extremists" and "fanatics": "What has happened, in the time of my time, is the record of my ancestors. No promise was kept with them, no promise was kept with me, nor can I counsel those coming after me, nor my global kinsmen, to believe a word uttered by my morally bankrupt and desperately dishonest countrymen" (*Notes of a Native Son* [1984], xvi). Given this stress on record keeping and broken promises, one might wish to retitle the essay: "Captive in the Promised Land" or "The Ancestors' Logbook."

If this is the record of an artist looking back over nearly sixty years, it is yet not all summing up. It is also the recalling of people who made a career possible or at least made it take the turns it took. One learns specifics about his activities during the two early return trips to this country, 1952 and 1954, the novels sold or completed, the experience of the student production of the first play, *Amen Corner*, at Howard University— Baldwin's first encounter with a university campus. Thus we learn that the first introduction was written between the house of the play's producer, writer Owen Dodson, and Baldwin's hotel, which was significantly named the Dunbar. We also learn that credit for the idea of the first collection of essays belongs to Baldwin's persistent and obviously far-sighted high-school buddy, writer Sol Stein. Baldwin's initial reaction was to dismiss the project on the grounds that he was "too young to publish my memoirs."

In his account of the resistance to this project, of his attempt to stand in the way of his own professional destiny, Baldwin casts himself as a type of haven dweller as well as a person struck by the novelty of a role he did not realize he had been playing:

> I had never thought of myself as an essayist: the idea had never entered my mind. . . . It has something to do, certainly, with what I was trying to discover and, also, trying to avoid. If I was trying to discover myself . . . , there was, certainly, between that self and me, the accumulated rock of ages. This rock scarred the hand, and all tools broke against it. Yet, there was a *me*, somewhere: I could feel it, stirring within and against captivity. The hope of salvation—identity—depended on whether or not one would be able to decipher and describe the rock. . . . The accumulated rock of ages deciphered itself as a part of my inheritance—a part, mind you, not the totality—but, in order to claim my birthright, of which my inheritance was but a shadow, it was necessary to challenge and claim the rock. Otherwise, the rock claimed me. [41]

In resorting to the extended metaphor of this dramatic and sphinxlike rock, the concrete details of a friend's challenge to publish an anthology of his nonfiction have been placed at a distance. Thus, what was launched as personal narrative has become, in a short space, a more generalized, schematic, or abstract account—but no less personal.

Of course, shifts among levels of generality are not only inevitable in communication but are also highly relative. The orchestrating of this movement is, perhaps, simply more conscious or deliberate among writers. Making the concrete general and the general concrete is certainly one way of describing common writing strategies. One method is made to reinforce the other. Some of the psychological dimensions of colonialism, or its ideological offspring, the notion of white supremacy, are handled in language that is laden with abstract nouns or personified abstractions named the Civilized and the Savage to denote victimizer and victim.

That their relationship is rendered in more concrete terms in the following passage is really just a matter of degree: "He is, practically speaking, the source of their wealth, his continued subjugation the key to their power and glory" (xiii). This passage is in the middle of a paragraph which ends with a fireworks display of blunt name-calling specificity: "Here, the Black has become, economically, all but expendable and is, therefore, encouraged to join the Army, or, a notion espoused, I believe, by Daniel Moynihan and Nathan Glazer, to become a postman—to make himself useful, for Christ's sake, while White men take on the heavy burden of ruling the world" (*Notes*, xiii). This is followed by a short, emphatic paragraph which builds on the implications of two short sayings or maxims which, with what has already been planted as doubts concerning any possible genuine change or progress in the conditions under which blacks have had to live in American society, add up to unanswerable indictment: "Well, *Plus ça change*. To say nothing, speaking as a Black citizen, regarding his countrymen, of *friends like these*."

The conditions alluded to here relate to the moral assumptions which Baldwin insists govern the thinking, and therefore the behavior, of his countrymen. The French saying, established in an earlier passage, brings its mocking force to bear on the useful recitals of evidence offered as signs of progress: "There have been superficial changes. . . . Morally, there has been no change at all and a moral change is the only real one. "Plus ça change," groan the exasperated French. . . . (The more it changes, the more it remains the same.) At least they have the style to be truthful about it" (xii–xiii). Whether Baldwin is conveying his experiences and reflections or his judgments, he makes constant use of what he has seen as a surviving witness and testifier. His testimony stems from the specifics of his own life and the lives known to him as well as from general observations on life contained in maxims or proverbs. The personal examples and the public expressions combine to serve as the basis for interpreting and assessing the larger record. Expression, exposition, and argument all have a role in arming the writer in the battle to make the self and world his subject.

"Introduction: The Price of the Ticket" has the distinction of harboring probably more of the people who helped Baldwin in "indescribable ways" than any other essay, certainly more than any other introductory piece. It is, if you like, a sort of showcase for some of the people who have acted as shaping forces in the essayist's life and work. Thus, these profiles offer another way of viewing the personal content of the nonfiction, the elements which keep it anchored close to the self.

The major figure in this particularly revealing account of a survivor saved by those who loved and valued him is a black painter in Greenwich Village. A political and intellectual running buddy who ends up in the river, a West Indian woman who owns the restaurant where Baldwin is a waiter, and the editor who launches him as a book reviewer are the co-stars. And while the restaurant owner and the sidekick clearly appear in the novels, all of them play the crucial role of mentors and models.

Beauford Delaney is cast in the role of a rescuer who materializes in the nick of time. He also comes across as a sort of Pygmalion mentor who opens an important door for the wider and deeper cultivation of Baldwin's intellectual and aesthetic sensibilities. Even more important, perhaps, is his role as a precedent-setting prototype: "Beauford was the first, walking, living proof, for me, that a black man could be an artist" (xi). Baldwin walks the reader into the sheer impact of this encounter with color and sound. His descriptions work as demonstrations of the kind of transforming and reorienting style and authority with which genuine artists relate to both the self and the world:

> I walked through that door into Beauford's colors—on the easel, on the palette, against the wall. . . . there *was* a fire escape which Beauford, simply by his presence, had transformed, transmuted into the most exclusive terrace. . . . I walked into music. Beauford never gave me any lectures. But, in his studio and because of his presence, I really began to *hear* Ella Fitzgerald, Ma Rainey . . . tell tales about Ethel Waters. And these people were not meant to be looked on by me as celebrities, but as a part of Beauford's life and as part of my inheritance. [x]

If such profiles offer the reader a glimpse of one source of Baldwin's uniquely sober and unsentimental view of artists as resources rather than superstars, they also underscore the reciprocal lifeline between the younger generation and the older: while the latter embodies the legacy of the former, the former represents the hope of the latter. And part of that hope involves what the Hemingway allusion at the conclusion of "Autobiographical Notes" stresses: the power to last, while pursuing one's lifeline-building work: "I repeat that Beauford never gave me any lectures, but he didn't have to—he expected me to accept and respect the value placed upon me. Without this, I might very easily have become the junky which so many among those I knew were becoming then, or the Bellevue or Tombs inmate . . . or the Hudson River corpse which a black man I loved with all my heart was shortly to become" (xii). The Eugene episode does serve as a vehicle for an account of Baldwin's introduction to the political Left, which, in turn, led him to a career as a journalist-essayist under such editors as Saul Levitas of the *New Leader* or Philip Rahv of *Partisan Review.* It also serves, by implication, to reinforce the grim picture of what can happen to that hope invested by the black community in the young in the absence of a Beauford Delaney. Eugene's fate is also made a part of the complicated background of Baldwin's decision to endure the life of an exile rather than adjust to what he saw as the cruel, willful absurdities of American life.

And part of the cruelty concerns what Baldwin constantly calls the *silence* of the American republic, given the ruined lives of the proverbial thousands who go under in each generation: "If I say that my best friend, black, Eugene, who took his life at the age of twenty-four, had been, until that moment, a survivor, I will be told that he had 'personal' problems. Indeed, he did, and one of them was trying to find a job, or a place to live, in New York. If I point out that there is certainly a connection between his death (when I was twenty-two) and my departure for Paris (when *I* was twenty-four) I will be condemned as theatrical" (xvii). So these intimate recollections are, in part, really arguments—living evidence which goes in the record book—in a case against American society as a place uniquely dangerous to the cultivation, not only of talent, but of the spirit, on which the individual self and its larger communal extension, the world, thrives.

Works Cited

Baldwin, James. "Autobiographical Notes." In *Notes of a Native Son.* Boston: Beacon, 1984.
———. *Nobody Knows My Name.* New York: Dell, 1981.
———. *The Price of the Ticket: Collected Nonfiction, 1948–1985.* New York: St. Martin's/Marek, 1985.
———. "Sidney Poitier." *Look,* June 23, 1968, pp. 50–57.

Part Four

Theory and Definition

Stretching the Limits of the Essay

George Core

I begin with the mundane and homely observation that one of the difficulties in participating in a conference devoted to the familiar essay is that you have to write a specimen of the genre: you cannot merely palm off—or dump—the usual rubbish that passes muster for an essay at the run-of-the-mill scholarly conference. The ordinary scholarly paper—the article—is as far removed from the essay as A. J. Liebling is from James Joyce. But both Liebling and Joyce write well, whereas your average scholar's prose, especially nowadays, is dreary at best. So much for my exordium. Now for a little history. I will try to keep it from being hopelessly literary.

I

The rise of the familiar essay in this country can be charted largely in the pages of a single magazine, and it will surprise no one when I say that the magazine is the *New Yorker*. In the fall of 1985 I published an issue of the *Sewanee Review* largely devoted to the *New Yorker* and to some of the major figures of its early history. One of the essays involved was "Modernism and Three Magazines: An Editorial Revolution" by Earl Rovit. In it Mr. Rovit argues that the *New Yorker, Time,* and the *Reader's Digest* all contributed significantly to modernism as we now know and understand it, particularly the transmission of information in the new world that emerged after World War I. And all developed distinctive formats and tones for conveying information. None of these magazines was engaged in strict reportage, as Rovit makes plain.

The distinctive contribution of the *New Yorker*—cartoons, newsbreaks, casual pieces, and even poetry and fiction aside, not to mention the magazine's distinctive format, with neat columns of print swimming strongly through high seas of advertising—lies in the realm of the essay. This is worth reconsidering, even though in recent times the magazine's venerable and recently retired editor, William Shawn, allowed many of his staff writers—especially the writers of profiles and book-length serials involving public issues—to become wordy and otherwise self-indulgent.

In the *New Yorker*'s salad days there were at least four great essayists working on the staff—E. B. White, who did more than any other person to establish the stylish tone of the magazine; James Thurber, who was probably the magazine's most famous and popular writer for most of his professional life; A. J. Liebling, who had the greatest range of the essayists involved and was the most learned and wily while superficially appearing to be the least sophisticated; and Joseph Mitchell, who is still connected with the *New Yorker,* but who has written little or nothing that has been published—at least under his own name—since his book on Joe Gould in 1965. I am deliberately neglecting other essayists whose stars are now blear—for instance, Frank Sullivan, S. J. Perelman, Robert Benchley, Wolcott Gibbs, and John Lardner. It would be stretching things to include such writers as Edmund Wilson, who were not primarily devoted to writing familiar essays.

Each of the writers in question wrote in many forms aside from the essay: you think immediately of Thurber's short stories and fables, of White's parodies and poems, of Liebling's critical articles on the press, of Mitchell's sketches in *My Ears Are Bent.* But each of these writers is essentially—quintessentially—an essayist; and in each case the writer's best essays often partake of the qualities of fiction.

I will not beat around the bush—or engage into providing a subtle inductive argument. My fundamental point is simple but worth restating: each of these essayists, in distinctive ways, moved the familiar essay toward fiction. Joseph Mitchell, who I sometimes think is the best of them as an essayist—even in some respects as a stylist—has in fact always called his essays *stories,* not reports or essays or memoirs or something else—*stories.* If you look in the author's note to *McSorley's Wonderful Saloon,* you will find that word; it reappears in the author's notes for *Old Mr. Flood* and *The Bottom of the Harbor.*

In the note to *Old Mr. Flood,* Mitchell, a taciturn man when it comes to his methods as a writer, becomes almost garrulous. He explains that "Mr. Flood is not one man; combined in him are aspects of several old men who work or hang out in Fulton Fish Market, or who did in the past." The author continues, making a sharp distinction: "I wanted these stories," he says, "to be truthful rather than factual, but they are solidly based on facts" (p. vii). (Had Alistair Reid's essays been presented in an equally honest light, his revelations about them a few years ago would not have been so controversial.)

In any case, as far as Mitchell is concerned, the bedrock providing the foundation for his essays is factual—a combination of scholarship and reportage, both of which are all but concealed, especially the scholarship. If you are interested in this aspect of the man whom Malcolm Cowley has called the paragon of reporters, read his "Joseph Mitchell: The Grammar of Facts" (1943) or Noel Perrin's "The Paragon of Reporters" (1983). Both Cowley and Perrin stress the factual side of Mitchell, a side that we see in all essayists worth their salt. Both also stress Mitchell's genius at depicting character, what Henry James would call "character expressed and exposed" (*The Future of the Novel,* p. 231); indeed Mitchell's skill at depicting reality springs from his inveterate interest in character, especially the characters of eccentric folk who often remind you of Dickens. Cowley clinches his clinically exact description of Mitchell's methods as a writer by observing: "You might say that he tries—often successfully—to achieve the same effects with the grammar of hard facts that Dickens achieved with the rhetoric of imagination." The *grammar of hard facts*— that is a phrase for us to conjure with. Perrin shrewdly amplifies Cowley's statement in saying, quite properly: "Part of Joe Mitchell's secret" is "that whatever he writes about he tends to know better than anybody else in the world" (p. 184).

For some years it has been rumored that Joseph Mitchell has another book in the making—probably a Mitchell Reader. I hope this rumor is true because such a book would naturally and inevitably bring him back into the eye of the reading public and make it plain that he is one of the great essayists of our time. Were I editing such a reader, I would probably make it a book of his essays in character, showing how he—to quote James again—has "the trick of investing some conceived or encountered individual . . . with the germinal property and authority" (*The Art of the Novel,* p. 44). For Mitchell, of course, those people are usually connected with what A. J. Liebling would unabashedly call low life or what some of us might be inclined to call little people, but in the author's note to *McSorley's* Mitchell calls this latter phrase "patronizing and repulsive" and says that there are no "little people" in his work. "They are as big as you, whoever they are," he adds. Some of these people—and the stories about them—appear in "Professor Sea Gull," his first account of Joe Gould; "Mazie," which Brooks and Warren thought plenty good enough to anthologize; in "King of the Gypsies"; and in "A Sporting Man," all from *McSorley's;* they also appear in the whole of *Mr. Flood* and in most of *The Bottom of the Harbor*. These and other pieces by Mitchell on New York City add up to an informal history of that great city, especially the waterfront, the Bowery, and other places outside the borough of Manhattan. The key to this history lies in the accumulated experience of the people about whom Mitchell has chosen to write. And, as James tells us, "a character is interesting as it comes out, and by the process and duration of that emergence; just as a procession is effective by the way it unrolls, turning to a mere mob if all of it passes at once" (pp. 127–28). A character like Mazie, whom Perrin has deliciously characterized as the tough-talking Mother Teresa of the Bowery, is emphatically one such germinal figure. Mazie is revealed largely through her conversation, and few authors deriving from any time or place and working in any literary mode can rival Mitchell for the exactness of his dialogue. Consider her closing speech. Mazie is speaking of the bums who occupy her days and nights and whom she mothers in a spirit of exasperation and affection: "To hear them tell it," she says, "all the bums on the Bowery were knocking off millions down in Wall Street when they were young, else they were senators, else they were the general manager of something real big, but, poor fellers, the most of them they wasn't ever nothing but drunks" (*McSorley's*, p. 36), says the Lady from Boston. One of her "clients," whom she calls Pop, says of himself: "I come from a devout family of teetotallers. . . . They was thirteen in the family, and they called me the weakling because I got drunk on Saturday nights. Well, they're all under the sod. Woodrow Wilson was President when the last one died, and I'm still here drinking good liquor and winking at the pretty girls" (p. 30). In that brief monologue we get the sad history of a protracted and largely wasted life.

A. J. Liebling's world has much in common with Mitchell's, but it is far broader, encompassing France, North Africa, Louisiana, the West, and still other places in addition to New York City. His range of subjects is also broader than Mitchell's. The most obvious difference between Joe Liebling and Joe Mitchell is that Liebling is often the protagonist of his essays, while Mitchell is never more than a bystander and is often invisible. In this sense John McPhee, the greatest of the present generation of *New Yorker* essayists, learned more from Mitchell's retiring ways than from Liebling's cheerful and unabashed egotism. McPhee, as I think his skillful editor William Howarth would agree, has also learned a vast amount about the use of fact from Mitchell.

Liebling's earmarks are the most distinctive of the writers we are considering with the possible exception of White. And let us not forget that each of these men has a strong and distinct signature. What are the elements of Liebling's signature? As I have already suggested, he has the same gusto for life, especially low life, that marks Mitchell's; and Liebling's collection of human instances is at least as broad as Mitchell's, but Liebling does not sink himself so deeply into the character of others as Mitchell regularly and naturally does. Fact is an important element in Liebling—but, again, it is not as extensive or essential as in Mitchell. Liebling regarded himself as a reporter, "a chronic, incurable, recidivist reporter," and he once said, "a good reporter, if he chooses the right approach, can understand a cat or an Arab." We may ask ourselves what approaches Liebling chose.

In certain ways Liebling pushes us still closer to fiction than Mitchell, in part because his facts are a good deal harder for the famous Checking Department of the *New Yorker* to verify.

In writing of himself and the press Liebling said: "Sinbad, clinging to a spar, had no time to think of systematic geography. To understand perfectly a new country, new situation, the new characters you confront on an assignment, is impossible. To understand more than half, so that your report will have significant correlation with what is happening, is hard. To transmit more than half of what you understand is a hard trick, too, far beyond the task of the so-called creative artist, who if he finds a character in his story awkward can simply change its characteristics." Liebling then adds: "Even to sex, *vide* Proust and Albertine. Let him try it with General DeGaulle." Liebling continues: "It is possible, occasionally, to get something completely right—a scene, or a pattern of larceny, or a man's mind. These are the reporter's victories, as rare as a pitcher's home runs" (*The Most of A. J. Liebling*, pp. 135–36).

If we look for a moment at a characteristic piece by Liebling, we can see what engages this writer's attention and affection. "Tummler," one of the best pieces that he ever published, deals with a con man named Hymie Katz, who, as one of his admirers says, "is a man what knows to get a dollar" (p. 106). Hymie's specialty is opening nightclubs; in between the flush times when one of his clubs is open and making money he plays the horses and runs various hustles of dubious legality; he is at his most imaginative and enterprising with the nightclub. Liebling quickly and surely gives us the facts involving such a business—especially how Hymie uses his money, which is all borrowed, to get the enterprise going. After explaining the various details Liebling says: "Despite all Hymie's forethought, exigencies sometimes arise which demand fresh capital." So the promoter then takes in partners. Liebling now writes of his hero: "He usually bilks his partners for the principle of the thing. He is not avaricious. Dollars, Hymie thinks, are markers in a game of wits as well as a medium of exchange. He refuses to let his partners keep any markers." Business goes nicely for a while, but as Liebling explains, "finally the creditors close in, or the entertainer either loses his brief vogue or goes on to a large club. Hymie returns to the horse-tipping business. He has written one more chapter in his saga" (p. 110). That saga, as Liebling deftly reveals it, includes Hymie's early life and an unforgettable vignette with his aged father (who when he comes out to meet his son locks the door of his jewelry shop from the outside so as to converse with his son safely on the sidewalk). What Liebling has presented in a 5,000-word essay might well be a picaresque novel.

Liebling's war reportage, with himself as a humorous observer of action that is often distinctly unhumorous, has novelistic qualities as well. Again the emphasis is on character, and like a fiction writer Liebling often concentrates on what James calls the "great central region of passion and motive, of the usual, the inevitable, the intimate." You find these qualities in "Quest for Mollie," "Madam Hamel's Cows," "My Little Louise," and many other pieces that he wrote about World War II. He told us much more about that war than any other reporter and probably any other writer, including various novelists, Hemingway among them. An essay such as "That Will Stay with You," published in 1949, could well be presented now as fiction. In it Liebling comes to an earned conclusion better than what you can find in most short stories as his protagonist, Marvin Bloom, a survivor of the carnage at Omaha Beach, asks a bartender: "Mac, did you ever see a deck covered with blood and condensed milk, all mixed together?" "No," replies the bartender, who adds: "Well, that'll stay with you" (p. 43). This image—of blood and condensed milk mixed together—is one of this reporter's victories. This piece, unlike the other war pieces that I have mentioned, does not appear in *The Road Back to Paris* or his other collections about World War II and returning to France. Instead it is derived from a long report, "Cross-Channel Trip," in which Liebling plays a considerable part; it is one of the best essays in *Mollie & Other War Pieces*. But Liebling the reporter does not appear as a character in "That Will Stay With You": he has disappeared.

All of this is to say that with Liebling we not only find the exact ear for dialogue and the profound interest in character, especially low-life characters, that characterize Mitchell's essays, but we also encounter other fictive qualities such as the controlling image. On occasion we even get the rudiments of plot.

With E. B. White we are confronted by still another breed of cat. In some ways White is the slyest and subtlest of the *New Yorker*'s writers. He offhandedly tells us more about the familiar essay than nearly anybody, including those who make heavy weather of the subject. "Only a person who is congenitally self-centered has the effrontery and the stamina to write essays," he writes in prefacing his selected essays. "Some people," he goes on to observe, "find the essay the last resort of the egoist, a much too self-conscious and self-serving form for their taste; they feel it is presumptuous of a writer to assume that his little excursions or his small observations will interest the reader" (pp. vii–viii). With such an author we may wonder how his essays may partake of fiction. Nevertheless they often do enter into the realm of fiction—and not merely when he is unwinding a grown-up children's story such as *Charlotte's Web*. "Death of a Pig," one of White's best and most characteristic essays, is in some respects a short story, an account of a comical and pathetic reversal in the usual pattern of buying a pig in the spring to fatten through the summer and butcher in the fall. White, by identifying himself with the pig, is able to present an unconventional parable, a melodrama, punctuated by moments of hilarity and pathos, about life and death. "The Death of a Pig" complements not only *Charlotte's Web* but what is White's most famous essay, "Once More to the Lake," which among other things is devoted to generational likenesses and indifferences as seen through the lens of memory. At the end of "Once More to the Lake," as you will remember, we are given an image of death and of life as White's ten-year-old son, Joel, buckles the cold soggy swimming trunks about his vital parts and his father, watching, feels a chill in the groin. It is a perfect image that compares with Liebling's image of blood and milk.

My own favorite of White's essays is the first part of "The Ring of Time," a superficially transparent allegory about the circus as a microcosm of life; the ring of time as presented here is a beautifully sustained image and symbol. White gives us at the same time a running commentary about his efforts as "recording secretary" or "writing man . . . charged with the safekeeping of all unexpected items of worldly or unworldly enchantment." The success of the moment—and of White's account of it—depends largely on the unrehearsed nature of the girl's ride as she stands easily on the back of a horse and turns around the ring. At this moment in her life, White tells us, "She believes she can go once around the ring . . . and at the end be exactly the same age as at the start" (pp. 143–45).

Again the image has fictive precision and rightness, and with a change here and there we might well have a short story—say, a tale turning on a conflict between the girl and her mother or the mother and the circus's manager.

213

The poetry of White's essays is obvious here, as it is in "Once More to the Lake," "The World of Tomorrow," "The Years of Wonder," most of the pieces in *One Man's Meat,* and many another essay. White is a poet of the city—of Manhattan—just as much as he is a poet of the country, particularly the salt water country in his part of Maine. White, following in the line of Thoreau, has done much to celebrate nature and in so doing to sound the alarm about what we are doing to the environment, a theme sounded in the work of many of the great American essayists of our century from John Muir to Loren Eiseley to Edward Hoagland and John McPhee. But White is a subtler reformer than most of these writers, especially Thoreau, as you will see in even an antiutopian essay such as "The Morning of the Day They Did It."

The element that you regularly encounter in White's essays, as in Mitchell's and Liebling's, one that strikes you as quintessentially fictive is scene. Scene is the sine qua non of fiction, as nearly anyone—perhaps even the most "advanced" theoretical critics of the present time—will readily admit who is not daft. Scene separates the true fiction-writer from the popular novelist, whether the latter writes thrillers or detective fiction or drugstore romance. The popular or pulp writer cannot write a scene if his or her life depends upon it: on that you may bet this month's mortgage payment and have a sure thing. Mitchell, Liebling, and White can; and that is especially true of Mitchell and Liebling. What this all boils down to is explained by James in the preface to *The Ambassadors:* "To report at all closely and completely of what 'passes' on a given occasion is inevitably to become more or less scenic."

James, in praising Turgenev, approaches scene from an entirely different perspective. Of course, as James, Percy Lubbock, and other critics have stressed, what is of first importance in fiction is "the dramatic incident or scene," and "to the scene . . . all other effect" should be "subordinated." (I quote Lubbock's *The Craft of Fiction.*) Yet James sees Turgenev's brilliance—what he calls the constant "element of poetry"—as depending upon "the mere particularized report" (*The Future of the Novel,* p. 232). It is that cumulative effect gotten through the closely observed and carefully chosen detail that characterizes the best essays of Mitchell, Liebling, and White.

What, then, you may ask, separates the best essays of these writers— say Mitchell's "Mazie," "King of the Gypsies," and *Old Mr. Flood;* Liebling's "Tummler," "Quest for Mollie," and "That Will Stay with You"; and White's "The Ring of Time," "Death of a Pig," "Once More to the Lake," "The Years of Wonder," and "The World of Tomorrow"—from fiction? The short answer is that often there is no definite line, as in Liebling's "That Will Stay with You," which you will recall my saying was dramatized from an earlier and more straightforward journalistic account of the same essential incident. Part of the answer is that your ordinary essay, no matter how good, doesn't have a plot in the usual sense that we apply that term to fiction. (Indeed, as White says in his foreword, "Most of my essays have no plot structure.") It may very well have all the constituents that I have mentioned—character presented in the round, cumulative use of related representative detail, the scenic element (including exactly rendered dialogue), a controlling image or extended metaphor—without being fiction in the traditional or classic sense; but it will probably lack the pattern of conflict, crisis, and resolution that is imbedded in the best fiction; and of course the author will usually be standing foursquare in the middle of the essay or off to the side of the action (but still unmistakably there)—and, of greater importance, the essay will be in large part about him or her and about the author's reaction to the action as it is told and interpreted.

All of this is to say that the familiar essay, as I have been measuring it, is finally closer to reportage on the one hand and to autobiography on the other than it is to fiction, even if, on occasion, the essayist strays from fact into making up details and into taking fictive license with his or her material.

To some of you—perhaps to all of you—I have mounted my hobbyhorse and ridden simultaneously and furiously off in all directions. What have you been driving at, you may quite properly ask? Or where does this leave us?

II

You will remember that I promised a little history of the rise of the familiar essay as seen through the *New Yorker*'s best essayists. I deliberately did not consider James Thurber, whose work is now fading badly; to some extent I scanted E. B. White, now the most famous of the four; I stressed two—Joseph Mitchell and A. J. Liebling who have been neglected, especially Mitchell.

What these writers and others nearly as good accomplished was to make the essay into an art form. They did this, on the whole, with no illusions. As late as 1977 White could say, with some asperity: "I am not fooled about the place of the essay in twentieth-century American letters—it stands a short distance down the line. The essayist, unlike the novelist, the poet, and the playwright, must be content in his self-imposed role of second-class citizen. A writer who has his sights trained on the Nobel Prize or other earthly triumphs had best write a novel, a poem, or a play, and leave the essayist to ramble about, content with living a free life and enjoying the satisfactions of a somewhat undisciplined existence" (p. vii). When White wrote those lines, he must have remembered his old friend Thurber's pretensions about winning the Nobel Prize for literature. Toward the end of his life Thurber thought of himself as the Henry James or Mark Twain of the *New Yorker* and whined about being neglected when in fact he had been lionized by T. S. Eliot and others. Then Thurber began believing his press notices.

Liebling, like White, never expected to be lionized. He enjoyed his position as a "mere" reporter and essayist, often poking fun at literary critics and other academic types, saying for instance, "I feel as naked as a critic without a fellowship, or a professor of communications without a grant" (*The Most*, p. 138) or using locutions like "as the boys on the literary quarterlies would say" (p. 231) often indulging himself in self-deflating jokes. One of the best of these jokes appears in a boxing sketch in which Liebling says: "I have been to the country myself. I went to a college in New Hampshire [Dartmouth]. But I seldom mention this, because I would like to be considered quaint and regional, like William Faulkner" (p. 35). In some respects Liebling was the Faulkner of American essayists, but in other ways Mitchell is even closer to that honor than Liebling.

In any event—to remount my hobbyhorse—these writers gave the informed general reader the familiar essay in all the forms that White mentions when he says: "There are as many kinds of essays as there are human attitudes or poses, as many essay flavors as there are Howard Johnson ice creams." "The essayist," White continues, "can pull on any sort of shirt, be any sort of person, according to his mood or his subject matter—philosopher, scold, jester, raconteur, confidant, pundit, devil's advocate, enthusiast" (p. vii). We see most of these poses in these writers—particularly Liebling, who fulfills them all.

All of this is well and good for the reader such as myself who repairs to the essay in the long innings of sleepless nights, but it is far better for the essayists who have inherited the mantels of White, Mitchell, Liebling, and Company—and who are trying to become worthy of their fathers and are too intelligent to think that parricide is the appropriate answer to what is now grandly called the Anxiety of Influence.

The leading essayists among us now, whether they be chiefly essayists or writers of another ilk, have profited immensely from the example of their immediate predecessors—note that I refuse to use Harold Bloom's term precursor—and can draw on that accumulated capital. One reason that ours is the Age of the Essay, as I have said in print once or twice and will now say again, is that such writers as Joan Didion, M. F. K. Fisher, John McPhee, Larry L. King, Edward Hoagland, Noel Perrin, Richard Selzer, Jane Kramer, Joseph Epstein, Roy Reed, Lewis Thomas, Carol Bly, and many another good essayist has profited by the examples of the writers we have been considering thus far. I do not mean to suggest that any of these writers is slavishly following in the paths of White, Mitchell, Liebling, and the rest; and I think it good that one can find first-rate familiar essays in a wide range of periodicals now—not merely in, say, the *New Yorker* or the *Atlantic* but also in the *Virginia Quarterly Review,* the *Yale Review,* the *American Scholar,* and other quarterlies. There are more good essayists now than fifty or even ten or twenty years ago, and their work is appearing in a greater variety of magazines. That development is all to the good. For some time the *New Yorker* came close to dominating the field so far as the familiar essay is concerned.

For anyone who is still with me and who wants to know my answer to the question Are any of our current essayists as good as Mitchell, Liebling, and White? I would say no; but some of them at their best—especially McPhee, King, and Epstein—come very close—and reasonably often—to rivalling these classic essayists. And why shouldn't they? For, as I have said, they have the example of this earlier generation. The same thing is beginning to look true for some of the best younger essayists in this country—and my list is by no means exhaustive. Indeed it is short largely owing to my own spotty reading. Robert Atwan could easily expand my list. I would call the names of Sam Pickering, Rob Schultheis, Alec Wilkinson, Mark Singer, and Bill Barich in this connection, knowing all too well that there are at least as many other good younger essayists.

These essayists have learned the essential secret that any good writer must always discover in order to be good and to find his or her own niche. This matter applies equally well to any other writer—but especially to the fictionist. The writer of fiction, long or short, most post himself or herself precisely in order to examine and dramatize the fictive country that is the individual writer's bailiwick. The same applies to the familiar essayist: once that writer finds the right post of observation or the right place on the stage, he or she can see the world in a fresh and distinctive way and can find the right tone in which to write about that world. If you look at some of the early work of the younger writers whom I have just mentioned—say Pickering's essays predating those in his first collection, *A Continuing Education,* or Wilkinson's *Midnights,* or Barich's *Laughing in the Hills,* you can see the author groping hesitantly toward finding his voice by searching for the precise place to pose himself. (Pickering has

217

found the right distance, the title of his new collection.) With Liebling or White that place, you will remember, is center stage; but with Mitchell it is just barely on the stage—or perhaps in the wings or even outside the theater. The familiar essayist today is often in the middle of things, and in this sense the familiar essay is often deeply autobiographical, as you would expect. But the world of the essayist is often simply a small part of the world outside that is being encountered, and the familiar essay of late has involved everything from the environment, as I have said, to matters seldom discussed in this way or from this vantage until recently—moonshiners, science and medicine, betting, life in England, cowboying, oranges, Monopoly, small hydroelectric dams, houses of prostitution, popular entertainers (including politicians), police work, and countless other subjects.

In general it is abundantly clear that the essay's limits have been extended and amplified in technical and substantive senses. All of this is obvious if you read but a few of the best essays published in the last five or ten years. You can read the *New Yorker* or other magazines or Robert Atwan's *Best American Essays* or the work as it has appeared in collections by the writers that I have mentioned.

In other words the familiar essay is alive and well. To my mind it is not merely alive and well but is flourishing. It is battening because this form of the essay is so constituted that it can bear additional bulk and weight without strain, provided that writers like McPhee and Selzer and Didion and Epstein continue to carry out their business as they already have done brilliantly. That business depends not only upon their having marshalled the various techniques that I have discussed but upon their marshalling the facts that will always provide the bedrock that must underlie any familiar essay. The best essays in this vein have always been bound to what E. B. White called the eloquence of fact; McPhee and the others have not forgotten that.

III

Throughout this essay I have quoted James, and I cannot resist using his language to point out a difficulty in my own presentation—what he would have called a misplaced middle, which is to say that my scrutinies of Mitchell, Liebling, and White—of the classic essay as it appeared in the salad days of the *New Yorker* magazine—have been too detailed in comparison to what has followed. You must therefore take the subsequent generalizations largely on faith.

What I have attempted to show—and I believe that I have shown—is that the best writers working regularly in the broad and deep vein that we are calling the familiar essay use the techniques of fiction as well as the techniques that we associate with the essay and upon which the essay always to some extent must depend, especially exposition and description.

Oddly enough, in recent fiction—especially the short story in its most popular forms today—the fiction writer often mechanically is using the techniques of the essay—particularly exposition—for his or her stories. Minimalism—the congeries of devices popularized—at first almost by accident—in the work of Raymond Carver, Ann Beattie, and other writers over the past decade depends largely on description and exposition. The result is a fiction that is founded on relentless exposition and that bulges with detail, often excessive detail devoted to arcane processes and to the superficial appearance of people and places. In the latter sense much contemporary fiction is old-fashioned, recalling Scott and Dickens and Hardy. The psychology tends to be primitive because the characters are often flat—shallow and uncomplicated. The action of the typical minimalist fiction entails a chronicle of everyday middle-class life and so in this sense it is often more nearly a report of mundane life than what appears in the best of our familiar essays.

That this situation is replete with irony I would be among the first to say. I am not announcing the end of the novel or the short story; I am talking about a particular form of fiction now in vogue that few critics have taken to task because they have failed to see beyond its apparent virtues—the dazzling surface of its maker's prose.

To see my point you need only read the annual anthologies of prize-winning fiction, especially *The Best American* series of the past few years.

IV

In his famous dictionary Samuel Johnson defined the essay as "a loose sally of the mind"; he also deemed it "an irregular, indigested piece, not a regular and orderly composition." White reminds us of the latter definition in the foreward to his selected essays. In any case we would be bound to consider it, for Johnson himself was no mean essayist. And, no matter how many definitions we consider, we will have to determine that the essay is impossible to define. For White it is a ramble through the basement or the attic of the essayist's mind. As Sam Pickering says, "the essay saunters, letting the writer follow the vagaries of his own willful curiousity. . . . The essay ruminates and wonders" (p. 9).

In this essay I have sauntered and meandered through the work of a few writers, examining aspects of their work that make it enduring—which is to say rereadable. We cannot legitimately ask more of literature than it stand the acid test of rereading.

As I have written elsewhere, the literature of fact—not the new journalism—has secured its place as a distinctive form of literature and mode of discourse in our time. The House of Literature has many mansions. The personal essay may not be the grandest of these, but it is solid and tight and respectable while providing a splendid view of human circumstance. In some respects the familiar essay is the most elastic, succinct, and engaging of all literary forms; and it is the linchpin that draws the grander forms of letters into a closer and more familial connection.

One of the most salutary aspects of the present-day literary scene is that the canon of literature has been opened up to include modes that have previously been neglected, and I think that the personal report is the most significant of these forms. If you ask me What about the nonfiction novel and how does it differ with what you have said about Mitchell and Liebling or you say How can you fail to give minimalist fiction its due, I can only helplessly reply, ladies and gentlemen, those are other stories—subjects for other essays, other rambles. This particular ramble is over. So much then for this particular instance of what White has called a mask and an unveiling.

Works Cited

Cowley, Malcolm. *The Flower and the Leaf: A Contemporary Record of American Writing,* ed. Donald W. Faulkner. New York: Viking, 1985.

James, Henry. *The Art of the Novel.* New York: Scribners, 1934.

_____. *The Future of the Novel,* ed. Leon Edel. New York: Vintage Books, 1956.

Liebling, A. J. *Liebling Abroad.* New York: Wideview Books, 1981.

_____. *The Most of A. J. Liebling,* ed. William Cole. New York: Simon and Schuster, 1963.

Mitchell, Joseph. *The Bottom of the Harbor.* Boston: Little, Brown, 1959.

_____. *McSorley's Wonderful Saloon.* New York: Duell, Sloan and Pearce, 1943.

_____. *Old Mr. Flood.* New York: Duell, Sloan and Pearce, 1948.

Perrin, Noel. "Paragon of Reporters: Joseph Mitchell." *Sewanee Review* 91 (Spring 1983): 167–84.

Pickering, Samuel F., Jr. *The Right Distance.* Athens: University of Georgia Press, 1987.

White, E. B. *Essays of E. B. White.* New York: Harper & Row, 1977.

The Skewed Path: Essaying as Unmethodical Method

R. Lane Kauffmann

There will always be much of accident in this essentially informal, this un-methodical, method.

—WALTER PATER

Is the essay literature or philosophy? A form of art or a form of knowledge? The contemporary essay is torn between its belletristic ancestry and its claim to philosophical legitimacy. The Spanish philosopher Eduardo Nicol captured the genre's uncertain status when he dubbed it "*almost* literature and *almost* philosophy" (207). The problem is hardly a new one. It goes back to what Plato called the "ancient quarrel" between poetry and philosophy, and more recently to the German romantic theorist Friedrich Schlegel, who called for a mode of criticism which would be at once philosophical and poetic. But today, when the status of critical discourse is up for grabs, reflecting the crisis of knowledge in the universities, the question of the essay takes on a new urgency. Now the predominant form of writing in the human sciences, it cannot avoid the challenge to define itself according to the prevailing standards of scientific knowledge and method.

Despite the essay's interdisciplinary prominence, it has fallen largely to literary critics and theorists to debate the generic status of the form. In Anglo-American letters, this debate is unavoidably filtered through the long-standing question of the nature and function of criticism. A century or so ago, Walter Pater and Oscar Wilde evoked criticism as art, while Matthew Arnold and others held it to the less glamorous role of mediating the great tradition. Nowadays, matters are less simple. The case for creative criticism is being made in North American universities by deconstructionists, a school of avant-garde theorists who challenge the conventional distinction between literary and critical discourse. Since, as Nietzsche observed, no discourse can escape rhetorical figuration, should criticism not give up the pretense of being a neutral metalanguage and join in the fun of writing, drawing upon the freedom and techniques available to all forms of expression?

The deconstructionist position is understandable as a reaction both to sterile academic criticism and to the scientist ethos of modern society. But the move to blur the distinctions between art and criticism is no more advisable now than it was a hundred years ago, when Wilde exhorted the critic to be an artist and flee the "dim, dull abyss of fact" (16). Indeed, the move is chancier now, because it may further undermine the already weak position of humanistic study in the universities and in society at large. By associating criticism with *l'esprit de frivolité*, deconstructionists may suppose that they are tweaking the nose of positivism. But they risk abandoning the field to positivistic method by trivializing other modes of inquiry. Whatever the intent, to insist that criticism and philosophy are not different in kind from literature is surely to weaken the essay's claim to be a legitimate medium of critical inquiry—a claim on which its future in the human sciences is bound to depend in large measure. Several important questions emerge in this regard. What are the cognitive and philosophical claims, and what is the methodological status, of the critical essay? Can these claims be honored without disowning the rhetorical flexibility and spontaneity long associated with the genre? Must one choose between the essay as literature and the essay as philosophy, or can it be both, to the detriment of neither? The aim of the present essay is to explore the answers given to these questions by several important modern theorists and to draw some conclusions as to the place of the essay in the contemporary human sciences.

I

Walter Pater may be credited with having rediscovered the essay as the "strictly appropriate form of our modern philosophical literature . . . ; the essay came into use at what was really the invention of the relative, or 'modern' spirit, in the Renaissance of the sixteenth century" (174–75). Pater's assumption that a continuous "modern" sensibility motivates the essay since Montaigne seems slightly anachronistic today. The serenity we find in Montaigne's writings (and to some extent in Pater's as well) is harder to come by nowadays. To be sure, the essay is still "an expression of the self thinking," as Alfred Kazin wrote in 1961 to introduce *The Open Form*. But the essaying self is much attenuated. One can no longer seriously pretend that the essay (or anything else) expresses "the individual's wholly undetermined and freely discovered point of view" (Kazin x). Since Marx and Freud, discovering one's point of view has come to mean discovering what determines it. One finds now a roughly inverse proportion between self-affirmation in a piece of discourse and the degree of philosophical seriousness accorded it. To read Montaigne now is to realize that the contemporary essayist travels under a more rigid protocol, within more carefully patrolled boundaries. Going through the disciplinary checkpoints of the knowledge industry, the essayist (the masculine pronoun will be used in this text) must declare his intentions. Are his writings subjective or objective? Opinion or knowledge? Classified as opinion, they may pass; few will take them seriously in any case. But if they claim to know something, they must be accompanied by the proper documents certifying their use of scientific method, and showing the fruits of its application. Whereas Montaigne wrote with one eye on the world and the other on himself, the modern essayist, *sub specie academiae,* works with one eye on the object of study while the other nervously reviews the methods by which he is authorized to know or interpret.

The unity of experience one encounters in Montaigne's writings was not given but achieved, forged in the midst of the civil and religious wars of the late sixteenth century. The medieval worldview was shattered, the Copernican revolution had begun, education and public life were chaotic, the wrenching paradigm shift toward modernity was under way (Barfield 14). Montaigne's serene individualism was anchored in the stoical and humanist traditions of *culture de l'âme,* combining self-cultivation and practical wisdom (Friedrich 322). Only this inner security can account for his exemplary "negative capability," the high tolerance for doubt and contingency which pervades his work.

Pater shrewdly identifies Montaigne's essays with the dialectic method of Plato's dialogues. Both forms, dialogue and essay, convey the flow of discursive reasoning, with or without the presence of an interlocutor. Both genres cut a circuitous path, approaching truth obliquely, registering the contingencies of occasion. The method of both genres is, for its genuine practitioners, "coextensive with life itself; . . . there will always be much of accident in this essentially informal, this unmethodical method" (Pater 185–86). Like Socrates, Montaigne has the wisdom of his ignorance; he knows that he knows not. Unlike Socrates, however, Montaigne is a true skeptic: he suspects that certain knowledge is unattainable through reason. Throughout his essays, he mocks human pretensions to systematic knowledge, whether in scholastic dogma, medicine, or humanist educational reforms. "I do not see the whole of anything," he informs us. "Nor do those who promise to show it to us" (Montaigne 219). The great scientific and geographical discoveries of the sixteenth century are for him only proof that we were once deceived by our certainties and will doubtless be so again. His only doctrine is the "docta ignorantia," "learned ignorance"—the wisdom that comes from accepting nescience and finitude as part of the human condition. This stance did not entail turning away from the pursuit of truth or learning; but Montaigne revels in the *quest* for knowledge, the pleasure of the chase, not its goal. He flouts the humanist equation of method with systematic presentation (Gilbert 69–73). As taught in the schoolbooks, the purpose of method was to facilitate knowledge by reducing all subjects to the bare essentials, thereby saving the student or reader from the idle *curiositas* of meandering authors and from the trouble of discovering the material for himself. Scorning the humanists' well-marked shortcuts, Montaigne preferred the crooked path of actual experience.

His use of the term *Essais* to name his writings was already a methodological choice (Friedrich 353–56). To essay is to experiment, to try out, to test—even one's own cognitive powers and limits. The word connotes a tentative, groping method of experience, with all its attendant risks and pleasures. Montaigne may digress from a topic but not from himself: "It is the inattentive reader who loses my subject, not I. . . . I seek out change indiscriminately and tumultuously. My style and my mind alike go roaming" (761). Montaigne cannot be dismissed as a self-absorbed humanist ideologue. To watch the self navigating a world in flux has little or nothing to do with narcissism and everything to do with close observation and critical reflection. "I do nothing but come and go. My judgment does not always go forward; it floats, it strays. . . . Nearly every man would say as much, if he considered himself as I do" (426). Long before Rimbaud's discovery that "je est un autre," Montaigne had recognized the decentered quality of selfhood. Long before Freud, he had debunked the uninterpreted self as a reliable foundation for knowledge: "Our dreams are worth more than our reasonings. The worst position we can take is in ourselves" (427). Montaigne appeals instead to mobility and chance. "I take the first subject that chance offers. They are all equally good to me. And I never plan to develop them completely" (219). His strategy of anticipated digression evokes the *ordo neglectus*, the insouciant style cultivated by the Renaissance man of the world (Friedrich 350, 359–64). He refers to himself ironically as "a new figure: an unpremeditated and accidental philosopher" (409). For Montaigne, there is no un-bridgeable gap between self and world; subject and object are one: "I am myself the matter of my book" (2). His essays constitute not only a mode of writing but a form of life; they are inseparable from the sentient self of the essayist.

His refusal to separate self from method, the living subject from the experienced object, places Montaigne on the far side of the epis-temological divide inaugurated by Sir Francis Bacon, for whom meth-odological self-renunciation was the necessary price of progress. Bacon conceived method as a way of screening out the passions and prejudices of the knowing subject, the better to enlist nature in the service of human ends. Though Montaigne did not foresee the imminent triumph of scien-tific method, his own "unmethodical method," grounded in the somatic self, is already an implicit critique of instrumental reason (Friedrich 153–55). Instinctively refusing to accommodate the constraints of systems, Montaigne rubs modernity against the grain. Or is it precisely this refusal which makes him our contemporary? Systems need the individual subject only as a foundational principle. They need only the subject qua rational being: "Je pense, donc je suis," wrote Descartes. To which Valéry would reply: "Parfois je pense, parfois je suis." Montaigne managed to think and to exist at the same time.

Notwithstanding Pater's invocation of a "relative" or "modern" spirit extending from Montaigne's century to our own, the intellectual condi-tions of the modern essay are no longer those of the essayist from Bor-deaux. Intervening is what Max Weber called the progressive rationaliza-tion or "disenchantment" of the world. The triumph of secular reason over religious authority, the social and political upheavals of western Eu-rope and the rise of the bourgeoisie, the expansion of printing and the public sphere—all of these things initially multiplied the possibilities of the individual. But with the advent of mass media and the commercialization of public discourse, along with the exponential increase and specializa-tion of knowledge and information, culture grew increasingly instrumen-talized. Thought became fragmented, the individual attenuated. The es-say moved away from the meditative self-portrait into more specialized forms. This process was not linear or uniform; it varied by national and cultural context. Sometimes it took the form of unbridled subjectivism: Karl Kraus rebuked the *feuilletonistes* of late nineteenth-century Vienna for their narcissistic impressionism (Janik and Toulmin 79–80). In En-gland, in contrast, the personal essay dropped out of sight between Lamb and Beerbohm, giving way to journalistic reviewing, in which the critic functioned as "the middle-man, the interpreter, the vulgariser" (Hunecker

151). The "habitual essayist," lamented Virginia Woolf, "must skim the surface of thought and dilute the strength of personality" (304). The tissues of experience had hardened; the essayist's dialogue with the world no longer flowed easily, as in Montaigne, through the prose membrane of the essay. Nor was this condition to be alleviated, *pace* Woolf, by "triumphs of style" or by "knowing how to write." The growing instrumentalization of culture affected not only the producers of essays but also their consumers, shaping the habits and expectations of the reading public. Surveying the previous half century of British essay writing, Woolf could still assert in the 1920s that the essay's sole purpose was to give pleasure (293). "Today tastes have changed," Auden would write a few years later, explaining the decline of the essay as a form of belles lettres by the diminished interest of modern readers in authorial subjectivity: "We can no longer derive any pleasure from the kind of essay which is a fantasia upon whatever chance thoughts may come into the essayist's head" (396).

Perhaps the best evidence of the specialization of modern thought is the rigid distinction usually drawn between the essay and systematic philosophy. Eduardo Nicol, an exponent of strict generic boundaries, defines the essay as a marginal genre of philosophy. In his view, the essayist's job is to speak of sundry issues in a nontechnical style to a general public, to illuminate particular phenomena against the background of ideas. The essayist and the true philosopher practice distinct modes of cognition: the philosopher methodically follows up the threads joining one problem to another rather than remaining attached, like the essayist, to the strand linking the single fact to an isolated problem or idea. Moreover, they stand in opposite relation to the genre as a medium of presentation: "For the born essayist, the essay is a way of thinking; for the born philosopher, the essay is an occasional form, a convenient way of setting forth his conclusions." While the philosopher rehearses his ideas in private before publishing them, the essayist's practice is "like a theatre of ideas in which the rehearsal and the final performance are combined" (Nicol 207–13; my trans.). Nicol does not deny the essay its place as a legitimate minor form; he insists only that the essayist accept the rules and lesser status of the genre and that he not try to claim the prestige of philosophy, the inherently superior calling. For the result would be chaos—a "confusion of genres." Nicol rebukes Jose Ortega y Gasset, the greatest Spanish philosophical essayist (and in temperament close to Montaigne) for just such a blurring of genres. Protesting the tendency of Ortega and his compatriots (especially Miguel de Unamuno) to make the self and its surroundings, rather than truth, the protagonists of their essays, Nicol lays down the law: "One must either serve the self or serve philosophy" (239). The choice is ultimately between ideology and science; between *doxa,* mere opinion, and *epistémé,* scientific knowledge (150). Nicol's distinction ratifies the alienation of thought from lived experience which Montaigne protested in his essays.

But the modern critical-philosophical essay—as instanced not only by Unamuno and Ortega but also by Walter Benjamin, Theodor W. Adorno, Roland Barthes, and Jacques Derrida, to name but a few—rebels against Nicol's law. Instead of bowing to philosophical systems, the essay—if one may adopt Adorno's device of personifying the genre to characterize the aims of its practitioners—refuses to subordinate its own impulses to norms handed down from above. It flouts the imperialism of scientific method while trespassing over the boundaries of the academic disciplines. At its most combative, modern philosophical essayism recalls Nietzsche's taunt in *Twilight of the Idols* that the will to system betrays lack of integrity (*Portable* 470).

II

Though it was Pater who first designated the essay as the "strictly appropriate form of our modern philosophical literature," it was Central Europeans schooled in the German Idealist tradition who did most to justify this designation. Thinkers in this tradition, from Lessing to Adorno, considered thought inseparable from its mode of presentation (*Darstellung*). The German romantics Schlegel and Novalis held that, through ironic self-reflection, "minor" genres such as aphorism, fragment, and essay could give form to speculative inquiry of the highest order (Lacoue-Labarthe and Nancy). Like the Idealism from which it derived, romantic essayism was largely eclipsed by the positivistic turn in European thought in the second half of the nineteenth century. By the turn of the present century, however, conditions allowed for the resurgence and fuller development of philosophical essayism (Luft 18–22, 100–21). Vitalist and aestheticist thinkers were in revolt against positivism and scientific method. Wilhelm Dilthey and Georg Simmel were trying to establish an independent methodology for the *Geisteswissenschaften* ("human sciences"). Along with Simmel, writers such as Robert Musil, Rudolph Kassner, and György Lukács were producing brilliant essays in cultural criticism.

In his 1911 collection, *Soul and Form,* Lukács, a young Hungarian critic, inquires into the plight of the modern essay, which he identifies with criticism (*Kritik*). How is it, he asks, that the writings of the greatest essayists, by giving form to a vital standpoint, or weltanschauung, man-

227

aged to transcend the sphere of science and attain a place next to art, "yet without blurring the frontiers of either"? How does such form "endow the work with the force necessary for a conceptual re-ordering of life, and yet distinguish it from the icy, final perfection of philosophy" (1)? Whereas the modern essayist uses the occasion of reviewing the works of others to formulate his essential questions, Plato, for Lukács the original and greatest essayist, needed no "mediating medium" and was able to pose his questions directly to life. Having lost Plato's golden age, when man's "essence" and his "destiny" were in harmony, the modern essayist finds no Socrates ("the typical life for the essay form") to serve as a vehicle for his own ultimate questions. The symbols and experiences drawn from other works do not suffice. The modern essay "has become too rich and independent for dedicated service, yet it is too intellectual and multiform to acquire form out of its own self," leading most critics to adopt a certain frivolity as their very "life-mood" (13–15). Lukács maintains that the essayist is by nature a precursor to a grand system, awaiting "the great value-definer of aesthetics, the one who is always about to arrive. . . . [the essayist] is a John the Baptist who goes out to preach in the wilderness about another who is still to come, whose shoelace he is not worthy to untie." But is the essayist then a mere harbinger who is rendered superfluous by the arrival of the grand system (16)? There is a deep ambivalence in Lukács's messianic longing for a system. His desire for wholeness (hardly uncommon in Central Europe on the eve of World War I) registers a partial protest against the fragmentation of modern life; but Lukács hesitates, sensing that such transcendence would involve sacrificing his individuality to a higher ideal. In this pre-Marxist phase of his work, Lukács concludes that the essay's unfulfilled longing is "a fact of the soul with a value and an existence of its own. . . . The essay is a judgment, but the essential, the value-determining thing about it is not the verdict (as is the case with the system) but the process of judging" (17–18).

The method of the modern essayist—that of commentary and critique—is no longer "co-extensive with life." He needs other works, other lives, to give meaning to his own. Indeed, as a specialist in cultural commentary, he has become a "mediating medium." Is it the essayist's destiny to find himself by losing himself? Not the way Lukács went about it—as one may observe by way of epilogue to his early theory of the essay. After becoming a communist in 1918 and participating in the Hungarian revolution, he went on in the 1920s to write *History and Class Consciousness,* the most influential work of Marxist philosophy since Marx. Placing Marxist theory under the aegis of the Hegelian category of totality, Lukács in effect opted for a secular version of the System he had heralded in messianic tones in his earlier work. Forced immediately to recant his Hegelian-Marxist synthesis, he nevertheless remained in the Party, which he regarded as his "ticket to history." Lukács's self-sacrifice to the idea of totality is mocked by the Stalinist system at whose service he placed himself, and his Marxist works are haunted by his earlier defense of the essay's fragmentary and solitary authenticity.

There is irony in the fact that his recanted work stimulated a countering, anti-Hegelian school of thought: the critical theory of the Frankfurt School, which used Lukács's own insights to criticize the totalizing pretensions of his Hegelian Marxism (Jay). The defense of the essay's philosophical legitimacy was continued by two members of this school: Walter Benjamin and Theodor W. Adorno. In the methodological introduction to his 1928 study of German baroque tragic drama, Benjamin draws a line between knowledge, which may be possessed, and truth, which may only be represented: "For knowledge, method is a way of acquiring its object . . . ; for truth [method] is self-representation, and is therefore immanent in it as form." Whereas philosophy as system "weaves a spider's web between separate kinds of knowledge in an attempt to ensnare the truth as if it were something that came flying in from the outside," Benjamin posits a nonacquisitive ideal for philosophy: truth as the representation of ideas. He sees in the discontinuous treatise or esoteric essay, which he compares to a mosaic, the proper form of this alternative philosophy: "Representation as digression—such is the methodological nature of the treatise. The absence of an uninterrupted purposeful structure is its primary characteristic. . . . The value of fragments of thought is all the greater the less direct their relationship to the underlying idea" (27–30). Thus began Benjamin's career of experimenting with fragmentary forms in criticism, forms displaying little or no "uninterrupted purposeful structure," ranging from treatise and commentary to surrealist pastiche, essay, and thesis. His "micrological" way of theorizing from particulars (the epithet is from Schlegel) had an ethico-ontological rationale. Benjamin saw his task as that of "redeeming" concrete phenomena from the refuse of history as they were abandoned by systems in their march to generalization. To this end, he used surrealist montage to light up cultural phenomena in a sudden "profane illumination." Whereas the pre-Marxist Lukács had assigned only provisional value to the essay's fragmentariness, Benjamin's prose experiments made fragmentation the heart of his method. Adorno, in turn, developed Benjamin's ideas into a full-scale theory of the essay. In his 1931 inaugural address at the University of Frankfurt, Adorno argued that the essay was the appropriate form for contemporary philosophy. Since traditional philosophy had failed in its effort to grasp the whole of reality through self-sufficient reason, it was time to give up stale systems and to rely instead on the essay as a more sensitive method of philosophical interpretation. The essay approached its objects in a spirit of "exact fantasy"—combining respect for the object's complexity with an element of imaginative freedom altogether lacking in systems. Fragmentary and experimental in form, the essay would be polemical in intent: "For the mind [*Geist*] is indeed not capable of producing or grasping the totality of the real, but it may be possible to penetrate the detail, to explode in miniature the mass of merely existing reality" ("Actuality" 132–33). Seconding Benjamin's endorsement of fragmentation as the essay's source of truth, Adorno's theory represents an unequivocal rejection of Lukács's Hegelian-Marxist validation of totality and system. Adorno's 1958 "The Essay as Form" presents his definitive theory of the essay as a critique of systematic method. The essay is said to reject the identity principle upon which all systems are based—the epistemological assumption that their network of concepts mirrors the structure of reality; that subject and object of cognition are ultimately identical. It also refuses the ontological priorities of systems—their privileging of the timeless over the historical, the universal over the particular (158). Instead of subsuming particular phenomena under first principles and hardened concepts, the essay form rhetorically mediates its own concepts, urging their "interaction" in the cognitive process while refusing to simplify that process. Proceeding in "methodically unmethodical fashion" (160–61)—Adorno echoes Pater, wittingly or not—the essay refuses to surrender its element of "fantasy" to the vain project of capturing the object within a rigid logical or conceptual framework. The essay observes a "pleasure principle" which mocks the stern "reality principle" of official thought (168–69). But it does not follow mere whim or fancy: "determined by the unity of its object" (165), the task of the critical essay, as Adorno notes elsewhere, is to follow "the logic of the object's aporias" ("Cultural Criticism" 32). Since the object—for Adorno, always part of social reality—is itself contradictory, "antagonistic," the essay is structured "in such a way that it could always, at any point, break off. It thinks in fragments just as reality is fragmented, and gains its unity only by moving through fissures, rather than by smoothing them over." Flouting the Cartesian precept to articulate continuously and exhaustively, moving from the simplest elements to the most complex, the essay dismisses the pretense that thought could achieve total comprehension of its objects. "Discontinuity is essential to the essay; its concern is always an arrested conflict" ("Essay" 161–64). But this "discontinuity" is relative. The essay makes up in aesthetic stringency what it forfeits in logical precision or discursive continuity. Instead of trying to present arguments in a foolproof deductive sequence, the essay's arguments "interweave as in a carpet" (160). In its rhetorical transitions, the essay, like music—Adorno regarded Schoenberg's serial method of composition as a model for philosophical form—"establishes internal cross-connections. . . . it co-ordinates elements, rather than subordinating them" (169–70). Defying the "scientific mentality" which bans rhetoric in favor of an allegedly neutral language, the essay thus "rescues a sophistic element" (168).

From Adorno's analogies, which emphasize the essay's aesthetic texture and transitions, one may infer that the rhetorical function of essaying is not merely to transmit the essayist's thoughts but to convey the feeling of their movement and thereby to induce an experience of thought in the reader. This notion would support Lukács's claim that the crucial thing about the essay's judgment is not the verdict but the process of judging. For Adorno (contrary to Nicol), the rhetorical-aesthetic dimension of presentation does not vitiate but rather enhances the essay's truth claims; it "obeys an epistemological motive" (164). This is true of Adorno's essayism. Without using the label, his theory tacitly identifies the essay with his agenda of "negative dialectics," or dialectics without synthesis or identity (Adorno, *Negative Dialectics*). Adorno's antinomian method is enacted rhetorically through paradox, irony, oxymoron, and chiasmus. In such expressions as "methodically unmethodical," "exact fantasy," and "arrested conflict," the dialectical play of opposites works against the illusion of stasis, identity, or totality, allowing the reader to feel the motion of transgressing epistemological taboos and boundaries. To read Adorno's essays is to be compelled to think dialectically. Their form is negative dialectics, crystallized.

As though in final reproach to the later Lukács for his obeisance to systems and "judgments," Adorno concludes by identifying the essay form with permanent revolt against orthodoxy of any kind: "The essay's innermost formal law is heresy" (171, trans. altered). The paradox of heresy as law marks Adorno's theory and practice of the essay. Constantly reenacting the obligatory heresy against perceived orthodoxy, his own writings come to resemble less an open-minded process of judging than a predetermined verdict. As he relentlessly inveighs against systems, his method finally becomes one itself (Wohlfarth 979). Instead of dissolving received standpoints, his method stakes out a position; it takes a stand.

In this respect, Adorno's practice of the essay is diametrically opposed to that of Montaigne. The individual is still the locus of experience, as in Montaigne's essays, but the function of subjectivity has changed considerably. In contrast to Montaigne's affirmation of the self in its richness and contingency, Adorno practices a self-restraint which is at once epistemologically and rhetorically motivated. The essay, for Adorno, tends toward "the liquidation of opinion or standpoint, including the one from which it begins" (166; trans. altered). So that the subject may experience the object without dominating it, the personality is kept in abeyance. It is true that Adorno's writings reveal an unmistakable persona, despite their forbidding philosophical style. But the speculative freedom and playfulness of Montaigne's essays, and their unabashed self-reference, are implicitly proscribed in Adorno's essays as breaches of philosophical protocol. The essay takes on the methodological role of "exact fantasy" in the service of negative dialectics. So it may be said that, in Adorno, the essay is subtly reinstrumentalized in its very critique of instrumentalization.

III

Central to the theories examined above is the historical conflict between fragmentary and totalizing modes of thought—between essay and system. The crisis of contemporary thought may be described in terms of this dilemma. On the one hand, in an era of totalitarianism, the inherent tendency of systems to closure, and their operational role in what has been called the "political economy of truth" (Foucault, "Truth" 131–33), continue to make the system suspect as an epistemological and discursive norm. On the other hand, the fragmentary-essayistic mode championed by some critics harmonizes with the accelerating compartmentalization of knowledge in academic institutions and in society at large. If critical thought does not aspire in principle to comprehend the entire sociocultural complex in which it operates but remains content with constructing allusive montages in a limited domain, it risks becoming uncritical and begins to reproduce rather than challenge the status quo. The response to this dilemma in the works of the French poststructuralists Jacques Derrida, Jean-François Lyotard, Roland Barthes, and Michel Foucault constitutes the most significant development in contemporary Continental essayism. These thinkers, no less than the Frankfurt School critical theorists, have felt the magnetic pull of philosophical systems—whether phenomenological, structuralist, Marxist, or psychoanalytical. And like the German theorists (the later Lukács being the obvious exception), the French poststructuralists have by and large resisted the systematic temptation by privileging fragmentation as an aesthetic and methodological principle. The two schools of theory diverge in their respective justifications of this principle. For the German theorists—still working, albeit critically, within a humanist-idealist paradigm—essayistic fragmentation serves two aims. First, it preserves freedom of imagination as a necessary moment of the essaying process; and second, it signals that the knowing subject in the process no longer plays the constitutive role reserved for it in idealist systems but defers instead to the object of cognition, following the "logic of its aporias." Contrariwise, the French theorists (the francophile Benjamin anticipates the poststructuralist view in this respect), extending the German post-Hegelian critiques of idealism and wishing to eliminate all vestiges of Cartesianism and humanism from their thinking, pronounce the Subject anachronistic and the Author dead. They are apt to justify discursive discontinuity with reference to the play of language or textuality operating autonomously, with no conscious subject in control (Barthes, "Work"), or to the libidinal vagaries and intensities which are found conspicuously at play even in critical or theoretical discourse (Lyotard, *Economie* 292–301). Lyotard exposes the lingering pieties and authoritarian power claims of theory conceived as metalanguage or master discourse, advocating instead a "paganized" discourse in which the search for truth becomes an "affair of style" ("Apathie" 9–10). If the Frankfurt School theorists regard consciousness as the locus of ideology and the scene of critical thought, the poststructuralists are preoccupied instead with language and discourse, looking less to epistemology than to avant-garde art and aesthetics for their discursive models. A utopian ideal in either case, the essay is for the German theorists a *cognitive* or *epistemic* utopia; for the French thinkers it would be, to use Roland Barthes's phrase, a "utopia of language" ("Lecture" 8).

This is not to suggest that the two schools have equal investments in the genre. The German thinkers ascribed to the essay the heroic role of defending critical and creative thought against the encroachments of instrumental reason, as embodied in systems. In contrast, the French thinkers have resisted identifying their projects with established genres, even questioning the very notion of genre (Derrida, *"Loi"*). They have at times distanced themselves from the essay in particular (Lyotard, *Economie* 303), mistrusting discourses of self-representation, whether the self appears in the foundational role of the Cartesian *cogito* or in the more congenial guise of Montaigne's essays. Despite such demurrers, the French theorists belong well within the tradition of philosophical essayism. It is telling that both Foucault and Barthes, systematic critics of bourgeois individualism in their early works, make the self in distinct ways a central concern of their late works, and each pays final homage to the essay as well. Citing the desire to "stray afield of oneself" as the motivation of his work, Foucault defines the essay as "the living substance of philosophy . . . , an 'ascesis,' *askesis,* an exercise of oneself in the activity of thought" (*Use* 8–9).

More significant in the present context than their differences is the fact that both schools respond, in overlapping historical phases, to the conditions of contemporary knowledge and research by producing essays as unmethodical method. Whatever their differences in terminology, both schools rebel against the primacy of systems and method. Both refuse demands for absolute objectivity—demands which usually mean bowing to another's construction of the object. These theorists propose not epistemological anarchy but rather the methodological recognition of contingency. In a passage on method in *Of Grammatology,* Derrida writes of deconstruction's (momentary) departure, along a "traced path," from the age of logocentrism: "The *departure* is radically empiricist. It proceeds like a wandering thought on the possibility of itinerary and of method. It is affected by nonknowledge as by its future and it *ventures out* deliberately. . . . We must begin *wherever we are*" (162). But neither school practices straightforward empiricism; both view thought as rhetorically and textually mediated. The essay's rhetorical method is not the traditional *inventio* based on manipulation of catalogued *topoi* or commonplaces: "Topological thinking . . . knows the place of every phenomenon, the essence of none" (Adorno, "Cultural Criticism" 33). Theorists of both schools refuse to separate the acts of thinking and writing, to regard writing as a mere instrument of thought. Faced with Nicol's option to serve the self or serve philosophy, they refuse the alternative. Unlike the systematic philosopher who rehearses his thoughts in private, deleting all traces of contingency from his discourse, the essayist, mindful that all thought is circumstantial, reflects on the circumstances of his own discourse, making them serve the thought at hand.

Revealing rather than concealing its rhetorical character, the essay carries on its Socratic mission: the critical discussion of culture in the public sphere. In practice, if not always in theory, both schools would agree with Adorno—who echoes Max Bense (420)—that the proper function of the essay is the critique of ideology ("Essay" 166). Its principal activity is the critical interpretation of texts. For this reason, theories of the essay necessarily have a hermeneutic dimension. The essay's mode of cognition is, in Wilhelm Dilthey's terms, "ideographic" rather than "nomothetic," concerned with understanding particular cases rather than with finding general laws. Max Bense's argument that the essay's method is "experimental" (417–18, 424) may be taken in a nonpositivistic sense: the essay makes heuristic and hermeneutical "probes" of phenomena, without utilitarian or universalizing intent. Of the hermeneutical principles common to the essayism of both (German and French) schools of theory, the most basic one is that there is no unconditioned standpoint. That is why the essayist must continually reflect on the context of discourse, and why in its very form the essay will bear traces of that contextuality. The interpretive practices of Adorno and Derrida shows striking parallels. In their approach to texts, both negative dialectics and deconstruction operate as *negative* or "heretical" hermeneutics; each approach has been likened to "negative theology" (Buck—Morss 90; Handelman 98—129). As readers, both Derrida and Adorno seek the anomaly, the exception which thwarts the rule. As critics, both play with binary oppositions to undermine traditional metaphysical hierarchies, showing not how to construct texts or systems of interpretation but how to undo canonical ones. And as theorists, both Adorno and Derrida are ultimately driven by philosophical systems in their very attempt to deconstruct these systems. Unfortunately, under the present conditions of knowledge and its dissemination, in which even the subtlest critical model is destined for commodification, the work of each theorist has tended to become mechanized, reified by its adherents, as though the price of its popularity were parodic exaggeration of the programmatic tendencies latent in each mode of essaying.

As these examples show, the essay's task is more difficult than ever, combining—to return to my initial example—the disciplinary functions of literary criticism with the broader one of ideology-critique. In the former, *intra*disciplinary capacity, the critical essayist must stay abreast of the considerable advances in techniques of analysis; he must be a specialist. In the broader capacity of counterideologist, however, he must relate cultural experience to the larger social complex—a complex in which the critic may, at certain junctures, find himself in strategic alliance with art against the imperial claims of theory. But it seems unlikely that justice can be done to both functions by a mode of criticism which plunges into the text or artwork on the work's own terms. The venerable plea for creative criticism, renewed by American deconstructors (for example, Hartman, *Criticism*), might be compatible with the claim that the essay practices unmethodical method: "unmethodical" insofar as it draws on the unregulated faculties and energies of art, the essay is "methodical" insofar as it bends to the more prosaic chores of humanistic knowledge—not only discovery but interpretation, commentary, synthesis. The dual function of criticism is not helped, however, by pretending that art and criticism are one. That art involves critical thinking, and that criticism may also create, as Wilde observed, does not justify abolishing the distinction. Criticism becomes uncritical when it thinks of itself as art, among other reasons because it thereby invites itself to be consumed as art, rather than as argument. Literary analysis of critical texts should attempt to illuminate the cognitive claims of the essay, not (necessarily) to undermine them—as though arguments could be answered merely by pointing accusingly at their rhetorical construction.

Precisely how paradigms of knowledge and their forms of presentation will change in response to cybernetic technology is an open question. Lyotard sees the essay as a form which will follow the pragmatics of postmodern science, practicing avant-garde experimentation in its search for new rules, new statements, and creative instabilities (*Postmodern* 81). Gregory L. Ulmer's *Applied Grammatology* tries to harness the new technology's progressive potential by codifying and adapting the method of Derrida's critical essays to electronic media, thus making it more accessible as a model both to academic essayists and to students in the classroom. But Derrida's method, though not immune to routinization, contains an unmethodical moment, the moment of imagination, which refuses to be programmed; attempts to program it anyway would generate more nonsense and dogma than insight. Ulmer's project not only downplays the friction between the epistemological dynamics of postmodern science and its current socioeconomic organization; it also assumes that a liberating force inheres in technical procedures rather than in their application in specific contexts, whether critical or artistic. No *esprit de finesse* attaches automatically to the essay, as any reader knows and as one sees in the instrumentalization of the form since Montaigne. The moment of freedom, of rebellion against *l'esprit géométrique,* is not a given of the genre; it must be reinvented each time an essayist sits down to write. Whether the form manifests a subtle mind or a square one depends very much on the essayist.

IV

The career of the essay is more than a matter of local interest for literary theory and criticism. Embodying as it does the perennial dialectic between the individual thinker and established thought systems, the genre invites reflection by philosophical anthropology as well. Like other cultural forms, the essay responds not only to changing external conditions but also to the stratum of the specifically human. This stratum does not evolve in isomorphic relation to society or technology. If it did, one could hardly begin to account for the chronic feelings of nostalgia, lost innocence, and crisis which have marked modern consciousness, motivating the major critiques of modernity at least since Rousseau. Insofar as artistic and critical form answer to this stratum, they continue to express residual needs which remain unfulfilled or repressed by civilization in its technical and societal modalities. As long as instrumental reason reigns, and as long as its injunctions prevail in society, the essay's aim will be to redress the imbalance through the critical interpretation of culture, as culture both registers and resists those injunctions. This does not mean that the essay clings to dated models of individuality, such as Montaigne's "honnête homme," but neither does it discard autonomy as an obsolete ideal. Nor does one promote the essay's aims by naively opposing the spontaneous, unmethodical moment of essaying to its critical or methodical moment. Only a commitment to maintain the tension between the two moments can keep the essay from getting mired in either faddism or dogmatism. The choice now is not between unbridled subjectivity and the absolute system; these are only ideal types, theoretical constructs. The situation of the modern essayist is better captured by Friedrich Schlegel's aphorism: "To have a system or not to have one—both are equally deadly for the mind. One has little choice but somehow to combine the two" (31; my trans.). In the current critical landscape, there are powerful temptations both in systems and in antisystems. Both are preemptive, colonizing modes of thought: wherever one finds oneself, the terrain has been mapped, the roads and lanes well laid out in advance. The contemporary situation calls for a less programmed, more venturesome mode of response, a kind of thought at once fragmentary and holistic, not governed by exclusive principles, whether systematic or unsystematic in nature. Perhaps the faculty most required of the modern critic is what Keats, admittedly to different purpose, once termed "Negative Capability, that is, when man is capable of being in uncertainties, Mysteries, doubts, without any irritable reaching after fact and reason" (350). For Keats, this faculty in a "great poet" meant that "the sense of Beauty overcomes every other consideration, or rather obliterates all consideration." Possession of this faculty would bring the essayist to a less extreme result, to an equipoise, restoring "all consideration" without eliminating the "sense of Beauty." It would lead, epistemologically speaking, to a qualified skepticism, allowing the essayist to entertain systems, to glean their energies and insights, without entirely succumbing to them. At the same time, it would enable him to resist the siren call of antisystems, with their reverse absolutism and methodological velleities. (Who, if not the essayist, will deconstruct the deconstructors?)

Toward the end of his career, Roland Barthes acknowledged that he had produced "only essays, an ambiguous genre in which analysis vies with writing" ("Lecture" 3). With its avowed antinomian character—its mosaic form, its unmethodical method—is the essay not inherently a pluralistic and interdisciplinary genre? At once "writing" and "analysis," literature and philosophy, imagination and reason, it remains the most propitious form for interdisciplinary inquiry in the human sciences. Its task is not to stay within the well-charted boundaries of the academic disciplines, nor to shuttle back and forth across those boundaries, but to reflect on them and challenge them. To accept the prevailing divisions and to stay dutifully within them would betray the essay's mission of disciplined digression. The essay's irregular path ("method" comes from the Greek *meta* and *hodos:* "along the way or path") registers the element of contingency which is common to all forms of genuine query. "Methodic groping is a kind of comradeship with chance—a conditional alliance," Justus Buchler has observed; "far from being, as some philosophers believe, the sign of weakness in a man or a method, [it] is the price that the finite creature is naturally obliged to pay in the process of search" (84–86). So perhaps it is truer to say that essaying is an *extra*disciplinary mode of thought. Entering the road laid down by tradition, the essayist is not content to pursue faithfully the prescribed itinerary. Instinctively, he (or she) swerves to explore the surrounding terrain, to track a stray detail or anomaly, even at the risk of wrong turns, dead ends, and charges of trespassing. From the standpoint of more "responsible" travelers, the resulting path will look skewed and arbitrary. But if the essayist keeps faith with chance, moving with unmethodical method through the thicket of contemporary experience, some will find the path worth following awhile.

Works Cited

Adorno, Theodor W. "The Actuality of Philosophy." *Telos,* 31 (Spring 1977):120–33.

_____. "Cultural Criticism and Society." In *Prisms,* trans. Samuel and Shierry Weber. London: Neville Spearman, 1967.

_____. "The Essay as Form." *New German Critique,* 32 (Spring 1984):151–71.

_____. *Negative Dialectics.* Trans. E. B. Ashton. New York: Seabury Press, 1973.

Auden, W. H. "G. K. Chesterton's Non-fictional Prose." In *Forewords and Afterwards.* New York: Random House, 1974.

Barfield, Owen. "The Rediscovery of Meaning." *The Rediscovery of Meaning and Other Essays.* Middletown, Conn.: Wesleyan University Press, 1985.

Barthes, Roland. "From Work to Text." In *Image-Music-Text,* ed. and trans. Stephen Heath. New York: Hill and Wang, 1977.

————. "Lecture in Inauguration of the Chair of Literary Semiology, Collège de France." *October,* 8 (Spring 1979):3–16.

Benjamin, Walter. *The Origin of German Tragic Drama.* Trans. John Osborne. London: New Left Books, 1977.

Bense, Max. "Über den Essay und seine Prosa." *Merkur* 3 (1947):414–24.

Buchler, Justus. *The Concept of Method.* New York: Columbia University Press, 1961.

Buck-Morss, Susan. *The Origin of Negative Dialectics.* New York: Free Press, 1977.

Derrida, Jacques. "La loi du genre/The Law of Genre." *Glyph,* 7 (1980):176–232.

————. *Of Grammatology.* Trans. Gayatri C. Spivak. Baltimore: Johns Hopkins University Press, 1976.

Foucault, Michel. "Truth and Power." In *Power/Knowledge: Selected Interviews and Other Writings, 1972–1977,* ed. Colin Gordon, trans. Colin Gordon et al. New York: Pantheon, 1980.

————. *The Use of Pleasure.* Trans. Robert Hurley. New York: Random House, 1986.

Friedrich, Hugo. *Montaigne.* Trans. Robert Rovini. Paris: Gallimard, 1968.

Gilbert, Neal W. *Renaissance Concepts of Method.* New York: Columbia University Press, 1960.

Handelman, Susan. "Jacques Derrida and the Heretic Hermeneutic." In *Displacement: Derrida and After,* ed. Mark Krupnick. Bloomington: Indiana University Press, 1983.

Hartman, Geoffrey. *Criticism in the Wilderness.* New Haven: Yale University Press, 1980.

Hunecker, James. "Concerning Critics." In *A Modern Book of Criticisms,* ed. Ludwig Lewisohn. New York: Boni and Liveright, 1919.

Janik, Allan, and Stephen Toulmin. *Wittgenstein's Vienna.* New York: Simon and Schuster, 1973.

Jay, Martin. *The Dialectical Imagination: A History of the Frankfurt School and the Institute of Social Research, 1923–1950.* Boston: Little, Brown, 1973.

Kazin, Alfred. "Introduction: The Essay as a Modern Form." In *The Open Form: Essays for Our Time,* ed. Alfred Kazin. New York: Harcourt Brace, 1961.

Keats, John. "Four Letters." In *Criticism: The Major Statements,* ed. Charles Kaplan. New York: St. Martin's, 1975.

Lacoue-Labarthe, Philippe, and Jean-Luc Nancy. *The Literary Absolute: The Theory of Literature in German Romanticism.* Trans. Philip Barnard and Cheryl Lester. Albany: State University of New York Press, 1988.

Luft, David S. *Robert Musil and the Crisis of European Culture, 1880–1942.* Berkeley: University of California Press, 1980.

Lukács, Georg. *History and Class Consciousness: Studies in Marxist Dialectics.* Trans. Rodney Livingstone. Cambridge, Mass.: MIT Press, 1971.

————. *Soul and Form.* Trans. Anna Bostock. Cambridge, Mass.: MIT Press, 1974.

Lyotard, Jean-François. "Apathie dans la théorie." *Rudiments païens.* Paris: Union Générales d'Editions, 1977.

————. *Economie libidinale.* Paris: Minuit, 1974.

————. *The Postmodern Condition: A Report on Knowledge.* Trans. Geoff Bennington and Brian Massumi. Minneapolis: University of Minnesota Press, 1984.

Montaigne, Michel. *The Complete Essays of Montaigne.* Trans. Donald M. Frame. 1965. Reprint. Stanford: Stanford University Press, 1981.

Nicol, Eduardo. *El problema de la filosofía hispánica.* Madrid: Tecnos, 1961.

Nietzsche, Friedrich. *The Portable Nietzsche.* Trans. and ed. Walter Kaufmann. New York: Viking, 1982.

Pater, Walter. *Plato and Platonism.* 1893. London: Macmillan, 1912.

Schlegel, Friedrich. *Kritische Schriften.* Munich: Hanser, 1964.

Ulmer, Gregory L. *Applied Grammatology: Poste-Pedagogy from Jacques Derrida to Joseph Beuys.* Baltimore: Johns Hopkins University Press, 1985.

Wilde, Oscar. "The Critic as Artist." In *Plays, Prose Writings, and Poems.* London: Dent and Sons, 1975.

Wohlfarth, Irving. "Hibernation: On the Tenth Anniversary of Adorno's Death." *MLN,* 94 (1979):756–87.

Woolf, Virginia. "The Modern Essay." In *The Common Reader.* 1st ser. 1925. 2d ser. 1932. New York: Harcourt Brace, 1948.

Itinerant Passages:
Recent American Essays

William Howarth

How to begin? A screen door opens, light and air spread into the room, a voice calls out. A man crossing a snow field suddenly halts in midstride, having glimpsed a fox. A lone car sweeps north, only its driver awake to see the dawn. These are opening moments from some of my own essays, and I am struck by how often they begin with motion, the setting forth on a journey.

Since the days of Herodotus, writers have sent readers traveling, but essays seem to have their own brand of itinerancy. As texts they open doors, take to the road, launch a stream of discourse. Their authors begin and move out, heading for uncertain destinations, carrying readers through a succession of events that pass like the flow of experience. Essays provide us with safe passage to ideas, arguments, stories with characters and dialogue—always unfolded as an ongoing process.

"Process" is a word now much in fashion, used by everyone from writing teachers to the makers of synthetic cheese. In its narrowest meaning a process is motion between two points, from here to there. The motion may be unique or recurring, and therein lies an important difference. A recurring process invokes order and certainty, the successions that establish traditional patterns—a line of monarchs, a rally in tennis. A unique process is eccentric and finite, coming to a definite end.

In American essays written after 1965, these two forms of motion often coexist in jostling opposition. During the tumultuous 1960s many writers turned instinctively to orthodox prose forms. Such counterculture classics as *Armies of the Night, Zen and the Art of Motorcycle Maintenance, Fear and Loathing in Las Vegas,* and *The Electric Kool-Aid Acid Test* all share the pattern of a cross-country journey, an epic quest that searches for personal and national identity. These songs of the open road reflect an old

American faith in westering, the hope that traversing the continent will bind us to its immense sprawl and expand our moral capacity.

Vietnam may have stirred this desire, for that land persistently eluded American possession. The war in Southeast Asia had no clear battlefront or enemy; its daily events presented no itinerary to Americans, only appalling chaos and stasis. Michael Herr best captures those qualities in *Dispatches,* six essays that vigorously resist causal integration and deny the usual mapping structures that link space or time. Reading a map of Vietnam, he writes, "was like trying to read the wind" (1). The same anomie affected civilian life, Michael Arlen observes in *Living-Room War,* a collection of essays on television, because that medium fractures continuity into a channel-flipping maze of unexplained events. For both writers Vietnam was a harrowing journey but definitely not America's traditional saga of exploration and settlement.

Something of the same pioneer story reappeared after 1975, in such works as *Pilgrim at Tinker Creek* and *Coming into the Country,* which celebrate back-to-the-soil lives and rugged American spaces. Yet neither Annie Dillard nor John McPhee follows a single itinerary; their books unfold as a series of essays, loosely related by different locales and seasons in Virginia and Alaska. This meditative structure enhances the authors' cool, unsentimental observations as they witness the food chain imposing its cheerless economy on all creatures, great and small. A far more strategic vision of competitive strife dominates *Of a Fire on the Moon* and *The Right Stuff,* two accounts of astronaut journeys built with strong novelistic designs.

The decade that began in 1985 will surely bring us new varieties of essay, but among them the itinerant motif will endure. McPhee has been composing a multivolume series, published in the *New Yorker* under the rubric "Annals of the Former World," which describes his journeys across America with professional geologists. Spanning all the books is Interstate 80, a national corridor that crosses the continent but also cuts deep into its surface. Pausing at frequent road cuts, McPhee reveals how geologists can imagine the history of continental evolution—events that vastly predate human imagination. Such journeying in time has grown increasingly complex in McPhee's writing, including briefer works. Here is a suggestive passage from his 1987 essay, "Atchafalaya."

> If you travel by canoe through the river-swamps of Louisiana, you may very well grow uneasy as the sun is going down. You look around for a site, a place to sleep, a place to cook. There is no terra firma. Nothing is solider than duckweed resting on the water like green burlap. Quietly you slide through the forest, breaking out now and again into acreage of open lake. You study

the dusk for some dark cap of uncovered ground. Seeing one at last, you occupy it, limited though it may be. Your tent site may be smaller than your tent. But in this amphibious new world, you have found yourself terrain. You have established yourself in much the same manner that the French established New Orleans. So what does it matter if your leg spends the night in the water?

This passage is about passage, the moving planes of space, time and thought. In a few hundred words, the journey of a lone canoeist evolves into a broad survey of regional history. By casting his lot with a tentative, second-person voice, "If you travel by canoe," McPhee aligns himself with readers, leading us toward a shared hypothesis: "So what does it matter if your leg spends the night in the water?" The journey ends as it began, in speculation, remaining an exploratory foray into an "amphibious new world." "Amphibious" means double-lived, in this case both fluid and solid, familiar and strange. Through these dualities McPhee effectively enacts the experience of discovery, the human "establishment" in unknown realms.

That theme takes its shape from an itinerary. As the canoe glides through forest and water, these passing images propel a smooth flow of motion toward "a dark cap of ground," a point of pause and rest. Once reached, this island becomes a ground for larger inquiry, the vision of founding New Orleans. The campsite provides a stable, central locus—positioned at the center of this passage, which itself stands near the essay's midpoint. That formal congruency presents an imaginative process, while the intimacy of "you" helps us to enact its procedures. In a conditional, amphibious world, McPhee has located terrain—and established us upon it.

Recognizing the itinerancy of a text also means accepting its serial conventions. Texts are progressive, moving within and along a linear matrix. The glyphs become words, phrases and sentences flow, and soon great volumes of prose are sliding along. Text is a chain, a road, a voyage. We scan the lines from side to side and top to bottom, turning pages as we go, and these sequences immerse us in the stream of language. Texts *are* journeys; as Aristotle noted, their language represents a series of related actions that form a plot, a continuous line of events from beginning to end.

But ever since Montaigne introduced the principle of casual, rumpled discourse, essays do not march smartly forward. To the linear models we could add that text is also a web, a maze, a dark and tangled forest. In that essay on Louisiana, McPhee often breaks apart his line of narration, jumping away from the abecedarian chain of history, ignoring an obvious beginning to settle in a later, more original point of insertion. His early piece on Atlantic City, "The Search for Marvin Gardens," presents a scattershot narrative, as mixed and kaleidoscopic in temporal sequence as Faulkner's deconstructions of storytelling.

For many recent essayists, chaos and turbulence have become staple themes, reflecting anxieties about the breakdown of orderly cultural structures. Ironically, this apocalyptic urgency has arrived on the wings of high technology. Satellite transmission now links the global village but cannot deliver it from greed, suspicion, and ignorance. We recall Thoreau's response to the magnetic telegraph, "But Maine and Texas, it may be, have nothing important to communicate" (52), or Henry Adams's warning that velocity destroys a culture's unity. In this age of Artificial Intelligence, the current joke runs, nothing is more powerful than Real Stupidity. Amid pervasive fears of collapse, the contemporary essay would not seem to offer much security.

For essays are not usually broad, comprehensive projects but "pieces" wrought on assignment and published diversely—in magazines, newspapers, even literary quarterlies. Much later, after the original occasions have faded, writers may gather these scatterlings into collections—never a bestselling genre with the public. The etymology of "essay" suggests *trial* or *experiment,* work not fully or finally formed. Collecting such material naturally arouses their author's expectations: how did these pieces emerge? do they form a body of work? The process of review often yields a metaphor that arranges and defines part of a career. Often as not, the metaphor describes a journey.

In her thirty-ninth year Alice Walker sifted through nearly two decades of lectures, reviews, and articles for a collection, *In Search of Our Mothers' Gardens.* The book's structure is not chronological but thematic, arranged in four parts under a title Walker first used in 1974, for an essay in *Ms.* about Southern black women. Her phrase "our mothers' gardens" descends from Virginia Woolf's "a room of one's own," but Walker has taken it outdoors, transforming a solitary, closed image of femininity into expansive, fertile spaces.

Walker's book unfolds as a searching journey for those imagined gardens, many Edens to reclaim. Her title phrase is deliberately inclusive, she explains, since the search for mothers is "a personal account that is yet shared, in its theme and its meaning, by all of us" (238). That pluralism also invokes her subtitle, "Womanist Prose," meaning feminist writing that is strong and inclusive, "Committed to the survival and wholeness of entire people, male *and* female" (xi). As her search reveals, one life has many mothers, in all guises and colors.

One of Walker's maternal figures is the novelist and folklorist Zora

Neale Hurston (1901–60), who was largely forgotten until Walker edited *The Zora Neale Hurston Reader*. In "Looking for Zora," Walker dramatizes this history of neglect by retelling her journey to Fort Pierce, Florida, to find Hurston's grave. After much searching she finally locates the unmarked site in an abandoned cemetery, full of weeds and imagined snakes. Walker buys a tombstone, inscribes it with Jean Toomer's phrase "A Genius of the South," and then gathers stories about Zora from townspeople. To gain their confidence, she pretends to be Zora's niece: "Besides, as far as I'm concerned, she *is* my aunt—and that of all black people as well" (102).

Walker's searching invariably leads back to the sources of her life as a writer. In "Beyond the Peacock: The Reconstruction of Flannery O'Connor," she goes with her mother to Milledgeville, Georgia, to visit two homes, her own and Flannery O'Connor's. The essay begins in a mood of resentment, posing herself and O'Connor as racial and cultural opposites, but eventually she comes to acknowledge their shared values. This turning begins with a conversation between the mother and daughter, held over lunch in a once-segregated restaurant. In that setting, the "reconstruction" of a famous white artist unfolds.

Both women ask why O'Connor kept peacocks in her garden. As the mother observes, "Those things will sure eat up your flowers." Walker raises the ante slightly, saying, "They're a lot prettier than they'd be if somebody human had made them." Although she is a religious skeptic, this response casts a metaphysical light upon the peacock's owner. Says the mother: "She must have been a Christian person, then," to which Walker assents: "She believed in everything, including things she couldn't see." Coming to this accord completes the reconstruction of O'Connor. Her mother asks, "Is that why you like her?" And, with a trace of surprise, Walker realizes: "I like her because she could *write*" (46).

This passage has the force of revelation, like "the shock of recognition" that Melville felt on first reading Hawthorne. Walker's epiphany arises from a generational dialogue, the searching reexamination of old prejudices. To understand the peacocks, she learns to see "beyond" them to the transcendent values they incarnate. That act of imagination grasps what all three women share, a will to believe in the unseen. Both mother and daughter, Christian and writer, can thus accept O'Connor as a figure who shares and reconciles their attributes. And by including this essay in her collection, Walker continues to journey beyond the peacocks, asking her original ideas to open and expand.

Collections induce recollection, seeing how works have shaped a career. This principle shapes McPhee's 1972 essay, "Pieces of the Frame," where stories about the Loch Ness monster assemble, within an enclosing frame, the image of human cruelty and monstrosity. A similar progression arranges Oliver Sacks's book *Awakenings,* a series of case histories about patients emerging from long Parkinsonian comas. Dr. Sacks wrote half of his stories for medical or literary journals, the rest for publication as a book. In creating a single volume he discovered entirely new ways of seeing the patients' response to drug therapy. The book thus recounts his own awakening, as he comes to see his role in the healing process: "Diseases have a character of their own, but they also partake of our own character" (206).

In most volumes of essays, the title metaphor yields entitlement, an author's self-definition. By gathering a series of essays under the title *Teaching a Stone to Talk,* Annie Dillard declares her pervasive interest in language: "We are here to witness. There is nothing else to do with those mute materials we do not need" (72). The world's mystifying silence raises a necessary question for her—why bother with words? Teaching stones to talk is a Zen-like riddle, she finds; one must shed language and accept silence, learn to hear what a wordless, stony existence has to say. Of course, she must use words to convey this very thought, but in her essays the itinerant mood is always contradictory and intuitive.

Frequently essays are presented to novice writers as models of the logical process. Mainly they chart the mind's motion, slipping from principle to example and through a series of examples to another principle. In teaching writing today we stress sequence and coherence, but too often the students remain mute as Dillard's stones, unable to speak. In the present clamor for cultural literacy, we may not be properly hearing this silence. Core curricula and rote learning will achieve results, but they are not conclusively the best modes of instruction for developing minds.

Joan Didion often voices her despair about the survival of thought in a brutal, irrational world. Yet paradoxically her essays portray nervous breakdown and self-annihilation in a cool, elegantly sculptured prose. The title of her first essay collection, *Slouching Towards Bethlehem,* alludes to Yeats's "The Second Coming," a poem that for her predicted "the evidence of atomization, the proof that things fall apart" that characterized the 1960s. In that decade the world she knew collapsed into shards, robbing her of both voice and audience. As a writer she came to suspect the worst, "that nobody out there is listening" (xi–xii).

Didion's second essay collection, *The White Album,* appropriates 1960s pop culture less despairingly, by replacing Yeats with the icons of rock musicians. Her title alludes to the Beatles' last album, actually called *The Beatles* but universally identified by its blank white cover. A largely noncollaborative set of songs, this album forecast the coming end of both the group and their era. While Didion's voice fears such closures, her essays cathartically purge the dread. In one cinematic "flash cut" (14) she enters a clinical report on her neurological condition: depression and catatonia, exacerbated by chronic episodes of migraine. Writing about this collapse becomes reconstructive, the act of self-healing.

By naming her disorders she subordinates and sequences them into text, where she maintains an authority. Narration is the traditional basis of healing, as patients describe symptoms and doctors interpret their stories. Hence Didion no longer fears that no one is listening: *she* hears these tales and they justify her purpose. Writing becomes not futile but heroic, shaping significance out of life's inchoate experiences. Thus she begins *The White Album*, "We tell ourselves stories in order to live. . . . We live entirely, especially if we are writers, by the imposition of a narrative line upon disparate images. . . . Or at least we do for a while" (11–12).

To write such a beginning anticipates the end of *The White Album*, that Didion survived her fears by writing them down. This victory is not merely personal but an offer of reassurance to the culture at large. Her tales of survival recall *The Crack-Up*, a book Edmund Wilson assembled from Scott Fitzgerald's uncollected essays of the 1930s. That, too, was a shattered decade, the national economic crisis mirrored in Fitzgerald's own spiritual collapse. In the pages of *Esquire* he cast aside his celebrated Jazz Age image and confessed to breakdown—yet the essays describing this process were taut, polished pieces of writing that renewed his confidence. After them he went on to finish *Tender Is the Night* and begin *The Last Tycoon*, flawed books but distinguished by their considerable ambition.

Coming through her own soul's dark night, Didion closes *The White Album* with a section titled "On the Morning After the Sixties." There she writes of lifeguards and orchidists, pastoral figures who protect and nurture life, surviving even in the face of California's high seas and brush fires. She recounts their stories of disaster and survival, moving beyond apocalypse to a morning dawn. At the end, she reports: "The fire had come to within 125 feet of the property, then stopped or turned or been beaten back, it was hard to tell. In any case it was no longer our house" (221). Her first line, about telling stories to live, still echoes, for here "it was hard to tell" is both a composing of experience—and an admission that it ultimately resists composition.

Didion's work reminds us that essays fulfill but also surprise our expectations, because they are both designed and improvised. After all the preliminary study and thought, the writing process still takes unexpected turns, reveals unforeseen connections. Asked if he planned his writing, E.

M. Forster replied, "How do I know what I think until I see what I say?" (Winokur, 16). The itinerancy of writing, its own being in motion, generates and arranges thoughts, and they take form from their movement, not their mass. Writers think less *about* writing than *through* it, they watch it unfold and grasp its meaning as it emerges. "If I know what I'm doing," Didion once wrote, "I can't do it" (Winokur, 18).

The "process writing" movement that now dominates college composition courses recognizes that writing is motion, a journey through constantly recurring cycles. The circuit spins repeatedly, through steps that involve gathering material, compiling and arranging it, then synthesizing a draft. Successive revisions follow, a learning process that reveals what to say and how to find a form—often a form that rehearses the writing journey. This faith in continuity values loose and imprecise forms, devoted to an ecological web of relationships rather than to strict hierarchies. Whitman envisioned such a cosmology in his poetic catalogues, linking the soprano in the loft with the carpenter cutting his beam. In contemporary American essays, high and low cultures often fuse; Yeats and the Beatles bear witness to the same general truths.

Process writing recognizes the itinerancy of text; it sees composition as ongoing, constantly in motion. Robert Frost's definition of poetry held that texts can make "a momentary stay against confusion." That balanced phrase suggests that art is a refuge but only for a moment. Joan Didion assembles such moments into a collage that she calls an album. Albums gather scraps of experience along a line of narration, offering a momentarily coherent account of fragmented times.

Writers such as Didion have also journeyed through the world of publishing, learning the procedures that put texts before a public. Working with the staffs of *Vogue* and *Life,* she saw that magazine editors have strong notions about "the book" and had to find her own way, following but also subverting the house standards to maintain her own. The personal essays she writes, with their curious divisions of anxiety and confidence, measure the ambiguity of this training.

In years to come we may see how other external factors affect essayists, such as writing on computers. That machine renders text as a rolling scroll, in motion on a seamless journey. Concerns about this new medium have mounted with its popularity. Writing in the *New Republic,* Edward Mendelson warns: "The computer eases the mechanical task of composition while quietly undermining coherence and truth." What no medium can alter is the fundamental linearity of text—and its attendant qualities of motion. Through their itinerancy, essays will continue to take us on passages—to bits of land where we may pass a night, sleeping with one leg in the water.

Works Cited

Arlen, Michael. *Living-Room War*. New York: Penguin, 1982.

Didion, Joan. *Slouching Towards Bethlehem*. New York: Dell, 1968.

———. *The White Album*. New York: Pocket Books, 1979.

Dillard, Annie. *Pilgrim at Tinker Creek*. New York: Harper's Magazine Press, 1974.

———. *Teaching a Stone to Talk*. New York: Harper and Row, 1982.

Fitzgerald, F. Scott. *The Crack-Up*. New York: New Directions, 1956.

Herr, Michael. *Dispatches*. New York: Avon, 1978.

McPhee, John. "Atchafalaya." *New Yorker*, February 12, 1987.

———. *Basin and Range*. New York: Farrar, Straus and Giroux, 1981.

———. *Coming into the Country*. New York: Farrar, Straus and Giroux, 1977.

———. *In Suspect Terrain*. New York: Farrar, Straus and Giroux, 1983.

———. *Pieces of the Frame*. New York: Farrar, Straus and Giroux, 1975.

———. *Rising from the Plains*. New York: Farrar, Straus and Giroux, 1986.

Mailer, Norman. *Armies of the Night*. New York: New American Library, 1968.

———. *Of a Fire on the Moon*. New York: New American Library, 1970.

Mendelson, Edward. "The Corrupt Computer." *New Republic*, February 22, 1988.

Pirzig, Robert. *Zen and the Art of Motorcycle Maintenance*. New York: Bantam, 1970.

Sacks, Oliver. *Awakenings*. New York: Dutton, 1983.

Thompson, Hunter. *Fear and Loathing in Las Vegas*. New York: Warner Books, 1971.

Thoreau, Henry D. *Walden*. Princeton: Princeton University Press, 1971.

Walker, Alice. *In Search of Our Mothers' Gardens*. Orlando: Harcourt Brace Jovanovich, 1984.

Winokur, John. *Writers on Writing*. Philadelphia: Running Press, 1986.

Wolfe, Tom. *The Electric Kool-Aid Acid Test*. New York: Farrar, Straus and Giroux, 1968.

———. *The Right Stuff*. New York: Farrar, Straus and Giroux, 1979.

Part Five

Pedagogy

A Common Ground: The Essay in the Academy

Kurt Spellmeyer

> The objectivity of dialectical cognition needs not less subjectivity,
> but more.
>
> —T. W. A DORNO, *Negative Dialectics*

I n his essay "Of the Education of Children," Montaigne recalls an encounter with two scholars who, on the road to Orleans, were followed closely by a third traveler, La Rochefoucauld: "One of my men inquired of the first of these teachers who was the gentleman that came behind him. He, not having seen the retinue that was following him, and thinking that my man was talking about his companion, replied comically: 'He is not a gentleman; he is a grammarian, and I am a logician'" (125). If the essay as a distinct genre begins with Montaigne, it also begins as an assault upon the scholasticism to which he alludes in this passage. Through his account of the two self-absorbed pedants, Montaigne makes light of the conception of knowledge that distinguishes so exactly between the grammarian and the logician, and he introduces, as an alternative to such distinctions, the example of La Rochefoucauld, the "gentleman," by which he means not a member of the ruling class but instead the questioner whose pursuit of understanding has carried him beyond the limitations of the customary. The new system of education proposed by Montaigne in his essay is designed to repair precisely that fragmentation of knowledge—into grammar, logic, theology, rhetoric, and so forth—which characterized scholastic discourse and which arose from still another fragmentation, between the "high" language of court and college and the "low" language of the street and the home. Unlike Montaigne's two erudite travelers, a person of genuine sophistication, a person like La Rochefoucauld, surmounts these divisions because he measures them against a unity exceeding the scope of any single discipline. Indeed, Montaigne repeatedly warns that the conventional branches of learning, because they are by nature specialized and mutually exclusive, obscure not only the complexity of real life but also the coherence. As an antidote to the tautological circularity which is a danger for all discourse, he commends the test of personal experience. "Let" the student "be asked for an account not merely of the words of his lesson, but of its sense and substance, and let him judge the profit he has made by the testimony not of his memory, but of his life" (110).

In contrast to Bacon, who reacted to the fragmentation of scholastic learning with the call for a unifying system, his "Great Instauration," Montaigne's real concern is not knowledge proper, but the relationship between individuals and the conventions by which their experience is defined and contained. To philosophers in the Middle Ages, the "world of experience" was simply an inferior copy of a purely intellectual reality, a reality mirrored more clearly in language than in sensation. Thus, in the *Monologion,* Anselm of Canterbury affirms that the Word "is not the likeness of created things" but their "true Existence" (45). As a demonstration of the process by which language, rather than determining the shape of experience, is shaped through the interaction of self and world, Montaigne's new genre, the essay, breaks irreparably the connection between words and "true Existence." The essay serves to dramatize the situation of the writer who moves beyond the familiar to bring language into closer accord with life. Against the systematic impersonality of scholastic tradition, Montaigne defends the central position of the author-as-speaker, at once subject and object in discourse. And yet the final purpose of the author's new and central role is not narcissistic introspection but the very opposite; Montaigne's entire program for the reform of education is intended to encourage a "personal worldliness" or "personal outwardness" that his learned contemporaries, the logician and the grammarian, would certainly have dismissed as a contradiction, an impossibility. For them, the rigor of scholarly discourse owed to an exclusionary purity—to a precision sustained by an impeccable logic. For Montaigne, convention was literally con-vention, a "coming together" of dissonant perspectives in order to restore the lived world, at the risk of imprecision and incongruity. If other, later essayists were not always as willing to endure this risk, or to acknowledge so frankly its importance to their success, the form of the essay nonetheless demands a self-conscious formlessness, a con-vention through contravention.

Although it has persisted from Montaigne's day until our own, and in spite of its continued popularity outside the university, the exploratory, contravening essay has become increasingly peripheral. At Rutgers, for instance, we offer classes in film studies, detective fiction, and the literature of fantasy, but no course apart from freshman English is devoted exclusively to the reading and writing of essays. Even in this setting, the essay's usefulness has been questioned by those who argue that the traditional "composition," with its intrusive authorial presence and its tolerance of indirection, fails to prepare students for the writing they must do when they leave our classes and go on to psychology, or political science, or philosophy, fields in which, it is commonly alleged, they cannot write from their own experience. Despite Bacon, Addison and Steele, Lamb, Hazlitt, Newman, and Carlyle—the list is already long enough, I think, to make my point—anthologists and scholars tend to see the universe of literary discourse as a triumvirate composed of poetry, drama, and "prose," either fiction or "nonfiction." The universe of academic discourse includes virtually every form of institutionalized writing taught outside freshman English, from lab reports to ethnographies. In the context of literary prose, the essay is too specialized; in comparison with writing in the disciplines, it is not specialized enough.

I suspect, however, that this neglect of the essay as an object of study in its own right reflects an unstated distrust of the form among professors of literature, and more recently, among teachers of writing, because it departs so radically in its rhetorical strategies and epistemological assumptions from its more prestigious, authoritative counterparts. The essay stands apart from both poetry and prose fiction, as well as from other forms of academic writing, in its emphasis upon the actual situation of the writer, and thus upon the personal nature, the "situatedness," of all writing. Consider these two passages, the first from an essay by Zora Neale Hurston. "I am colored but I offer nothing in the way of extenuating circumstances except the fact that I am the only Negro in the United States whose grandfather on the mother's side was *not* an Indian chief. I remember the very day that I became colored. Up to my thirteenth year I lived in the little Negro town of Eatonville, Florida. It is exclusively a colored town. The only white people I knew passed through the town going to or coming from Orlando" (152). The second passage comes from a work of literary criticism:

> Dickens is, then, opposed to any change in the political and economic structure of society, and places his hopes for amelioration in a change of heart, mind and soul in those who possess power, who will then disseminate the fruits of change over the lower echelons of society. Dicken's ideal State would be one of "benevolent and genial anarchy."

255

This is an insecure basis from which to launch a critique of society, and its insecurity becomes all the more obvious when we look outside *Hard Times* to Dicken's journalism of the same period. [Lodge 147]

From its inception with Montaigne, the essay purports to disclose the reflections of an actual person in response to actual events or to the reflections and beliefs of other people. Zora Hurston's essay, in which she examines the influence of race and history upon self-definition, begins with a radical personalization of the problem, not with "being colored," but with "I am colored." In his discussion of *Hard Times*, David Lodge employs the opposite rhetorical strategy, a strategy of ostensible detachment from his own situation as a writer. Speaking from—or rather for—the institution of literary study, Lodge's critique possesses an authority that Hurston's essay cannot claim, despite its aggressive promotion of private insight over public commonplace. And yet, however faithfully Lodge may hold to the method of his discipline, his assessment of Dickens remains no less a "rationalization," in Kenneth Burke's terms, than Hurston's "I am colored"; no less, that is, a "set of motives belonging to a specific orientation" (23).

By disguising authorial fallibility and bias, as well as the uncertainty of discourse itself, more "serious" forms of writing typically perpetuate an unequal relationship between the writer and the audience, and between the writer and the subject under scrutiny—Lodge in judgment of Dickens's politics, for example. The literary critic, the philosopher, the political scientist, and to some degree even the novelist, tender versions of experience in which their own ordeal of uncertainty, the ordeal that every writer endures, and from which no one ever escapes, has already unfolded beforehand, behind the scenes. Before such apparently effortless mastery, the reader must wait patiently to be instructed. In contrast, the essay foregrounds the speaker's movement from presentation to representation, from experience as "fact" to experience invested more fully with personal, and with social, meaning. Disallowing the pose of objectivity through which experts maintain their privileged status as "knowers," the essay dramatizes a process of appropriation concealed by other genres, a process never wholly methodical or disinterested. An essayist, such as Zora Hurston in the passage above, does not speak for Reason, History, or the Heav'nly Muse. Rather, she speaks as an individual in the uncertainty typified by Montaigne's own motto, "Que sais-je?" Even when the essayist has reached a tentative decision and begins to write with an intention to persuade, the obligation to persuade reaffirms her equality with the audience and sharply marks the limits of her reliability.

Because the essay, of all the genres in Western letters, acknowledges most openly the tentative, recursive, and conversational nature of discourse, its loss of prestige among teachers of writing is a predictable, though unnecessary, consequence of their legitimate dissatisfaction with writer-based, process-centered modes of instruction. As critics of the process model have persuasively argued, a purely psychological account of writing—of what happens to writers while they compose—ignores the methodological contexts that distinguish one form of discourse from another. By dutifully following the stages of a supposedly universal "writing process," our students may produce prose acceptable to the teacher in English 101, but these same dutiful students will meet with less success in history or philosophy unless they are taught to recognize the conventions of each discipline. Indeed, students trained to look within themselves when they compose may be less alert to discourse conventions than those who have received no training at all and may be less prepared to comply with the expectations of a real academic audience.

And yet, while teachers committed to a heuristics of process misconstrued the writer's situatedness by denying the historicity of language and audience, I believe that many teachers today have misconstrued this situatedness in the very opposite way, by insisting that the right to speak must be learned—or perhaps more accurately earned—through what is essentially the effacement of subjectivity. Ironically, this suspicion of personal writing may have originated in the efforts of theorists such as Ann Berthoff to reassert the sovereignty of the writer. As she contends in *The Making of Meaning,* "despite the talk of process and the active choices of an engaged composer, the new rhetorics, like the old rhetorics they claim to supplant, conceive of a world 'out there' that is to be manipulated by the writer" (102). Breaking with the notion of a fixed world "out there"—breaking with what is, in effect, a naive material determinism—Berthoff contends that the constitutive powers of language and the imagination allow the writer to create meaning rather than simply to discover it. But this critique of material determinism, if pushed to an extreme that Berthoff herself never intended, can also be used to defend an equally naive and constricting linguistic determinism: the view that people who do not share the same words cannot share the same world.

Supporters of this position maintain that the study of discourse conventions, the structure of an argument in philosophy or the uses of evidence in political science, furnishes the beginner with a content as well as a context, both defined by the "rules" of the discipline. In "Cognition, Convention, and Certainty," for example, Patricia Bizzell claims, "We cannot look at reality in an unfiltered way—'reality' only makes sense when organized by the interpretive conventions of a discourse community. Students often complain that they have nothing to say, whereas 'real-world' writers almost never do, precisely because real-world writers are writing for discourse communities" (232). Berthoff suggests that the conventions of a community or tradition retain their significance only when they are perpetually reinterpreted by individuals struggling with the complexity of experience, but Bizzell explicitly condemns "debilitating individualism" as the primary obstacle to effective writing because she assumes the language determines, in advance of experience, the meaning of "real-world" events. Whereas Berthoff advocates critical thinking, through a conjunction of disparate perspectives—convention with experience, the past with the present—Bizzell insists upon the primacy of systematic thinking, from within the boundaries of a single community. Although she advocates a program of instruction that will make the student's presuppositions "more clearly a matter of conscious commitment, instead of unconscious conformity," her conception of meaning as discipline-specific prevents her from valorizing a comparable reassessment of our own, institutional presuppositions (238–39). In this sense, Bizzell's most recent article, "Arguing about Literacy," must be seen as a significant departure from her earlier work, a departure arising from growing misgivings about the tacit demand for "submission" in the pedagogy of interpretive communities ("Arguing" 150).

While I agree that meaning can never be detached from its social context, I suspect that the prevailing tradition of discipline-specific writing instruction encourages both conformity and submission by failing to recognize in discourse what Bakhtin calls "heteroglossia." If, as he argues, every language without exception "represents the co-existence of socio-ideological contradictions between the present and the past" and "between different socio-ideological groups in the present"—if, in other words, discourse communities are not the monolithic unities that Bizzell suggests but "heteroglot from top to bottom"—then student writers cannot become more accomplished by ignoring their situatedness. Because languages "intersect" one another on many levels at the same time, entry into a community of discourse must begin, not with a renunciation of the "home language" or "home culture," but with those points of commonality that expose the alien within the familiar and the familiar within the alien (Bakhtin 291). By characterizing each discourse as essentially monological, the pedagogy of community conventions prevents novice writers from discovering, in their own commitments, the areas of concern they already share with us.

On the assumption that instruction in writing must start with the inculcation of a properly systematic way of thinking, one widely used text-book, *The Informed Writer,* opens with this observation:

> Will Rogers's famous quip, "All I know is what I read in the newspapers," has great truth. Most of what we learn about the world—events in the distant past or in distant countries, the collisions of subatomic particles or of corporate finance, the secrets of the beginnings of the world or of another person's mind—is filtered through written communication. Even when we learn things directly, we perceive and interpret that experience through attitudes influenced by the words of others. [3]

The author of the passage, Charles Bazerman, later characterizes writing as a conversation between the student and the writers who have preceded him, but the student's actual role in the conversation is negligible: "The first two parts of this book have treated you as consumers of knowledge—active, thoughtful, evaluative, selective consumers, but consumers nonetheless. You have learned to take knowledge in, understand it, and respond to it. You have learned how to discover the personal meaning and importance in texts. You have learned to evaluate and think about texts. And you have learned to make original statements using your reading" (329). Inexperienced writers become more experienced by "consuming," or internalizing, a discourse; only after it has been thoroughly consumed, and I presume "digested" through formal analysis, is the writer entitled to make "original statements." But originality has no place in Bazerman's pedagogy. During a student's "conversation" with the assigned readings, his or her private responses are largely irrelevant because the merit of any statement will be decided solely by the standards of public knowledge. Not only does Bazerman contrast personal values with "the way the world actually is," he also urges the student writer to "go beyond . . . feelings or internal conviction to develop the kind of argument and evidence others will accept" (329). While most teachers would agree that understanding and originality require a familiarity with discourse conventions, the admonition to suppress feelings and beliefs for the sake of public approval encourages an attitude of calculating alienation, the antithesis of Herbert Marcuse's notion of "praxis in the 'realm of freedom,'" praxis that does not require submission to "an 'alien' objectivity" (31).

The proponents of discourse-specific writing typically invoke the ethos of "empowerment"—of breaking down long-standing distinctions between student writers and "real" writers—but their sense of the term is often synonymous with pragmatic accommodation. Among textbooks which encourage accommodation as a preliminary to empowerment, the reductio ad absurdum may well be *Asking the Right Questions,* by M. Neil Browne and Stuart M. Keeley: "We think you would rather *choose* for yourself what to absorb and what to ignore. To make this choice you must read with a special attitude—a question-asking attitude. Such a thinking style requires *active* input from *you*" (2). "Active input," however, should not be confused with personal input. In responding to what they read, students have only two choices, "absorbing" the text or "ignoring" it, but neither approach allows them the liberty of reading and speaking from their own perspectives about the perspectives of others. Neither allows them to initiate a Bakhtinian dialogue, at once "double-voiced" and "internally persuasive" (325, 342). Like Bazerman and Bizzell, Browne and Keeley adopt the filter as an analogue for the interposition of discourse between the writer and his experience, and their remarks to student readers demonstrate the fundamental circularity of the language-as-filter model: "The inadequacies in what someone says will not 'leap out' at you. You must be an *active* searcher. You do this by *asking questions.* The best search strategy is a critical-questioning strategy. Throughout this book we will be giving you the critical questions to ask. A powerful advantage of these questions is that they permit you to ask revealing questions even when you know very little about the topic being discussed" (5). If the topic cannot be understood on its own terms without the "revealing questions" of an intervening filter, then the questions themselves are immune to the test of experience because they decisively control the nature of experience. Strictly speaking, Browne and Keeley's "active searcher" investigates the filter rather than the topic, in the best tradition of scholastic tautology. Rather than preceding the writer's encounter with an issue, authentically critical questioning should arise from this encounter in such a manner that the status of both the writer and the issue will be redefined. No matter how often they may urge students to ask questions in a dialogical manner, Browne and Keeley's model of inquiry is antidialogical because it severs language, not only from the contexts that give an issue its importance, but also from the intentionality described by Bakhtin as a "living impulse toward the object" (292).

By emphasizing the institutional rigidity of discourse while ignoring the ability of language to transcend the boundaries of one particular community or another, these new formalists have returned us to Montaigne's encounter at Orleans. A writer can think like a psychologist, or like an economist, but is there really no more inclusive or expansive way of thinking "from the outside"—the dialogical thinking which Montaigne enacts in his characteristic shifts of perspective, from Dante to Plato to Xenophon, from the sayings of Cicero to "Paluel or Pompey, those fine dancers of my time?" (112). As Adorno observes in "The Essay as Form," Montaigne succeeded in discrediting the "delusion that the *ordo idearum* (order of ideas) should be the *ordo rerum* (order of things)." Through a discourse that transgresses the propriety of discrete communities and challenges "the unconditional priority of method" itself, Montaigne points to a greater experiential and linguistic commonality (158). And if he is correct in his belief that such a commonality cannot be recovered except through transgression, then the rejection of individualism—and with it, the essay—as an obstacle to both discourse and community eliminates the only common ground which remains to the university.

Responding to his contemporaries within the academy, Montaigne opposed the assertion that any particular language, community or worldview could define absolutely the boundaries of human experience. "In comparison with most men," he affirms, "few things touch me, or, to put it better, hold me; for it is right that things should touch us, provided they do not possess us. I take great care to augment by study and reasoning this privilege of insensibility, which is naturally well advanced in me. . . . One must moderate oneself between hatred of pain and love of pleasure" (766–67). Without an ability to resist the coercive power of authoritative language by cultivating a sociable insensibility to what is known, presupposed, and accepted, our students will never be able to make the "conscious commitments" that the discourse-community theorists applaud. Montaigne may describe his writing as a process of self-questioning, but this self-questioning presumes that the refinement of knowledge begins with his own perspectives and presuppositions, not with their "disciplined" suppression. Instead of abandoning the practice of writing from the outside, teachers should recognize that English 101, with its tolerance for essayistic introspection and digression, is probably the last opportunity most students will ever have to discover the relationship of mutual implication, a relationship fundamental to all writing, between the self and the cultural heritage within which selfhood has meaning. To put it in the simplest terms, we do not deny the socially constituted nature of either learning or identity when we ask our students to write from their own situations, but I believe that it is both dishonest and disabling to pretend that writing, no matter how formal or abstract, is not created by persons, from within the contexts—historical, social, intellectual, institutional— of their lived experience. Whatever may have been the case in freshman classes fifteen years ago, writing from experience is not limited to summer vacations, first dates, or greatest embarrassments: the discussion of issues, events, and texts is also, inescapably, personal writing. It seems to me that the discourse-community theorists have mistaken the pose of objectivity, the approved dissimulation exemplified by David Lodge's assessment of Dickens, for an absence of personal commitment in the creation of a text. From the appearance of impersonality in the final product of writing, they have inferred that the process itself is impersonal.

Whatever sense of community we may associate with "higher education," our students inhabit a universe of discourse so fragmented that the allure of an impersonal knowledge, an automatic knowledge, becomes nearly irresistible. In response to this fragmentation, teachers may decide, with Elaine Maimon, to "deemphasize the informal essay and adopt a more sophisticated, multi-disciplinary approach," an approach that will familiarize beginners with the "modes of behavior" characteristic of "successful practitioners" in particular fields (2–3). But however "sophisticated" this approach may be, it cannot make the universe of academic discourse any less divided, nor will it guarantee any greater consistency between the world our students inhabit and the world of the academy, since learning a mode of behavior does not ensure an understanding of the values implicit within it. Still less does Maimon's approach invite a reasoned critique of such implicit values. By reifying the prevailing configuration of knowledge, by accepting this configuration as a fait accompli and supporting the narrow vocationalism which has created it, proponents of discipline-specific writing may spare themselves the recalcitrance of "science majors who were," in Maimon's words, "force-fed James Joyce," but they also discourage these same science majors from thinking that might culminate in necessary social change. Because the choice of a discipline is for most students a reflection of presuppositions which discipline-specific instruction leaves virtually unchallenged, I suggest that we teach freshman writing, not by attempting to simulate the lab report or the ethnography, but by calling attention to the writer's situatedness, a situatedness the essay takes as its central concern—not, perhaps, the freshman essay in its often-degraded variants, but the essay as literary tradition represents it, and as we should teach it in our classes. Whereas the defenders of a process-based pedagogy have failed to account for the differences between styles, the proponents of discipline-specific writing have overlooked what is in fact universal to all discourse. Although it may be true in an abstract sense that tradition determines what we write, from the perspective of the writer moved by Bakhtin's "living impulse," there is no way to allow conventions of discourse to guide the hand that holds the pen—who would not welcome such a guiding hand, when composing is so difficult and precarious? No matter how adept a writer becomes, the activity of writing always entails a radical loss of certainty. Not only have the discourse theorists confused product with process, but they have conflated writing as a demonstration of understanding—after a writer has worked through his or her uncertainty—with writing as a means of achieving understanding, an achievement that demands the willingness to surrender instrumental control. As Hans-Georg Gadamer observes, understanding in the encounter with a text begins as an effort to reconstruct the experience of questioning from which the text has arisen (333–34). Asked to write on a new and difficult reading, such as Walker Percy's essay "The Loss of the Creature," many freshmen will probably follow only a portion of his argument; perhaps they will miss his point altogether on the first try. But for the ones who succeed in entering Percy's world, the effort to understand will assume the form of a search for equivalents: to reconstruct the motives behind Percy's text, these students must start by rereading the "text" of their own experience from the standpoint of the question that Percy has posed, even while the question itself remains to some degree unclear.

Like Montaigne, Gadamer believes that the learner's presuppositions are the ground from which he or she views the world, and therefore the achievement of understanding requires, not the suspension of these presuppositions in some pretended neutrality, but a reaffirmation of the self, at first against the question and then within it. Balancing the past against the present, dialogical language allows us to "rise above the pressure of what comes to meet us in the world"—the pressure of racism, for example, in Zora Hurston's essay—and to declare our participation in the making of that world (402). When we ask our students to respond to an assigned text, we should not be too surprised, therefore, if they misread the text in order to make its question more fully a part of their own concerns. In Gadamer's situational hermeneutics, this misreading is not evidence of inattentiveness or lack of discipline but an indispensable preliminary to a more coherent interpretation. Only after the first misreading, when a disjunction has emerged—between the world as our students thought it to be and the world as others have represented it—will they be able to initiate the dialogue through which a new selfhood can be fashioned in response to the text, a text that will also be refashioned after each transformation of the self.

Initially, the strangeness of an unfamiliar point of view compels readers to look back at the events of their own lives, but once their understanding of these events has begun to change as a result of surveying them from a new perspective, they find that the text has opened up commensurately. Gadamer concludes from this dialogical process that understanding is never objective but always a disclosure of "the conversation that we ourselves are" (340). And if the dialogue continues long enough, it will move

263

toward what he terms a "fusion of horizons," a fusion of worlds, public and private. I believe this progression from disjunction to dialogue and fusion—like Montaigne's progression from insensibility to considered engagement—can be realized most completely within the transgressive form of the essay, and I am convinced the students who learn to use writing as a way of thinking dialogically achieve in the process a heightened awareness of their situation, an awareness which allows them to overcome past misunderstandings without at the same time disowning the past.

Although the discourse theorists imply that student writers today have become too independent, too ready to contravene the traditional, I find the very opposite to be true. Trained in the high schools to filter, absorb, and digest, they typically lack any sense of inquiry as a conversation. The following excerpt, from a paper submitted in an entry-level sociology course, is typical in this respect:

> The modern world in which we live is a complex and fast-moving one. Modern societies are plagued by reoccurring, extensive social problems. Although there exist many serious problems, the one which demands immediate examination and resolution is that of suicide among youths. Children are taking their own lives with an alarming frequency. Whatever the reasons may be for these tragedies, an emphasis must be placed upon preventing them rather than analyzing them after they have occurred.
>
> In this work, *Suicide: A Study in Sociology,* Emile Durkheim studies the various causes associated with suicide. He categorizes the different types of suicide into four basic groups: egoistic, anomic, altruistic, and fatalistic. All four of these classifications can be applied to the growing problem of youth suicide in society. . . .
>
> The classification of egoistic suicide can be applied to the problem of child suicide. It is not uncommon for children, particularly adolescents, to feel "left out." A child may become so hopelessly depressed, that he feels as if he has no worth.

Superficially, this passage is the work of an advanced student writer, insofar as it closely approximates the ideal of systematic, impersonal, "academic" discourse. And yet, despite this apparent sophistication, the discussion strikes me as ultimately unsuccessful because its impersonality is not simply a rhetorical posture but evidence of a pervasive absence of commitment. While he works hard to enter the discourse community, to comply with its rules and fulfill its expectations, the author has nothing of his own to say. A young man who must have felt "left out" more than once in his life, and who may even have contemplated suicide at some point, he obscures his situatedness from the beginning, by treating "youths" in the first paragraph as a synonym for "children." He has read the assigned material and has learned some of the conventions most typical of Durkheim's own prose, but whenever there is an opportunity to make a real discovery, to venture beyond the assigned reading into the realm of implication, through assent, disagreement, or the consideration of examples, he retreats again into summary.

This retreat is most obvious in the final paragraphs of the essay when, having ended a lengthy, three-page recapitulation of Durkheim, the writer proceeds to offer a number of terse suggestions—suggestions that his teacher intended to be the focus of the assignment—for addressing the problem of teenage suicides:

> There are many ways in which society could help to reduce the number of suicides among youths. For example, the answer may lie in the home. Parents and other family members must stick together in order to give one another support and encouragement. This would make a child feel as if he has worth as a brother, sister, or child as the case may be. . . . Another way for children to feel needed or wanted is to become a member of some sort of team, group or club. This could be done in or out of school. . . .
>
> Children can find a sense of worth through religion. A lack of religious values is one of the main reasons for the high suicide rates in modern countries. Religion gives people a purpose and direction, and it gives children reasons for suffering and hardship in the world.
>
> It would also be beneficial to develop various rap sessions and big brother and sister programs in the community. Often children do not feel they can talk to their parents, and these would provide other outlets.
>
> The previous suggestions are ways in which the tragedies of suicide among youths can be prevented and perhaps stopped completely one day.

With each paragraph shorter than the preceding one, the writer attempts to slip, as unobtrusively as possible, out of his text, and out of his own situation, before he has revealed too much of himself, as though any revelation of personality would violate the decorum of academic writing. Virtually all of the putative examples that he offers—a team, a group, a club—are not examples in any real sense, but disembodied types, often allusions to more detailed illustrations from Durkheim. Even in his discussion of family relationships, the writer presents us with a perfectly generic family, in which the members can be counted on to "stick together" and to offer one another the appropriate support in every situation. Rather than exploring solutions, as the assignment requires, he abandons the problem. And by attempting to exclude subjectivity from his discussion, he also forestalls any consideration of Durkheim's personality and motives, although the reconstruction of Durkheim's situation might have started him on the way to a more engaged reading.

KURT SPELLMEYER

In *Suicide* Durkheim makes any number of assertions which readily invite dispute, but the text dominates the student writer so completely that his response could not be more deferential or more perfunctory. His passivity is especially remarkable in view of the paper's first paragraph, where he announces, "Whatever the reasons may be for these tragedies, an emphasis must be placed upon preventing them rather than analyzing them after they have occurred." Following this initial resolution to appropriate the issue for his own purposes, he devotes three pages out of four to exactly the kind of analysis he eschews. Despite his respectfulness toward Durkheim, or perhaps because of it, he has also failed to understand the rhetorical implications of *Suicide,* which is intended to be, as the subtitle indicates, a "Study of Sociology," a demonstration of sociological method. In contrast to the student's disembodied examples, Durkheim's prose is densely furnished with supporting illustrations, which allow him to examine related forms of behavior in order to identify the cultural institutions that promote these forms: such is the method of "study" he intends his work to demonstrate. Fittingly enough, the student's proposals to reduce suicide are directed toward institutions also—the home, the group or club, the church, the community. But he cannot decide what to say about these institutions. To say something more, he could need to ask why they currently fail to discourage suicide. And to ask that question, he would need to adopt a critical attitude toward his own family, group, church, and community. They are, after all, the only institutions that he knows in detail, and the only ones against which he could test Durkheim's argument and method. His unwillingness to allow personal experience to intrude upon what he perceives as the objectivity of academic discourse finally prevents him from coming to understand such discourse.

In contrast, the student writer whose work I have excerpted in the passage below has submitted an essay which, although far less conventional in its organization, goes beyond summary to an active interpretation of the assigned reading, Sartre's "What is Existentialism"—interpretation in its root sense, as a "going between" two distinct positions—and to a use of Sartre's text as a way of reseeing her own values and assumptions. For purposes of comparison with the first student, I have chosen a writer who stands still further outside the circle of expertise, to whom an essay on Sartre might seem at first an impossible task:

> I have kept a pet rat for the past two and a half years. Not wanting to be separated from my friend Mickey (the name gave him [sic]), I decided to bring him to school to live with me. He remained his usual happy and healthy self for about three months. However, he suddenly became ill and deteriorated rapidly before my eyes. His sunken eyes and overall crippled state worried me

266

to the point of a panic-like state. Quickly I consulted several people about what I could do to help my pet. Sadly, each one confirmed my fear that it was too late for Mickey to be saved.

First, I called our family vet whose opinion I respected highly; he told me that Mickey would probably not regain his former good health, but that I could bring him in to be examined if I liked. My second call was to the pet store where I had gotten my rat in the first place. . . . Unfortunately, the man I talked with responded in a rather ignorant way, telling me that rats usually lived to be about 2 or 3 years old. . . .

Discarding this man's advice as worthless, I called my friend Chris figuring that he would offer me the most accurate guidance about Mickey. Chris has been raising rats for more than ten years, and has witnessed every aspect of their lives in captivity just about. After questioning me about the details of the symptoms, Chris told me that my pet was dying because of a cancerous tumor and could not be saved. Once I was able to locate the actual tumor under Chris's tutelage, I realized that Mick had a tangible, real disease and that it was up to me alone to end his pain. . . .

Jean-Paul Sartre tells us in his essay "Existentialism" that making a decision when faced with a moral issue is not so easy or personal as we may think it is: "To choose to be this or that is to affirm at the same time the value of what we choose." Furthermore, according to Sartre, any choice we make involving morals will affect not only ourselves directly but also all of humanity in general. When we are facing such an ethical decision, no matter how trivial it may seem to us, "we always choose the good, and nothing can be good for us without being good for all." One would not admire an image of Man as a cruel, inhumane beast. Ironically, it would be more humane and kind to kill Mickey to end his suffering. . . . Mickey was not born asking to be raised in a cage as a pet. He was not responsible for his taming nor for his fatal affliction. I had taken him and put him into a cage, and now I had to decide if he should be left alone to suffer just so that I could cling to the hope that he may get better and I could avoid having to mourn the loss of my pet.

Surely one of the most obvious features of this paper—aside from the juxtaposition of Sartre's sophisticated analysis against a narrative so thoroughly naive—is the omission of any reference to Sartre himself until the second page. Instead of beginning with a summary of Sartre's position, the writer holds him in abeyance (Gadamer would say that she rises above the pressure of Sartre's world) in order to consider the text of her own experience in a new light. As she explores this text, her text, she begins to notice ways in which her decisions about Mickey the rat correspond to Sartre's existential ethics. Retrospectively she realizes that her own behavior could be explained in existential terms, and in arriving at this recognition she offers two mutually sustaining interpretations: an interpretation of her text in terms of Sartre's, and an interpretation of Sartre's text in terms of an ethical crisis in her own life. As Gadamer suggests, it is impossible to achieve one without the other, even if conventions sometimes require a writer to conceal the personal engagement. Meaning itself presupposes such engagement: meaning is always meaning for someone, from within a specific context (esp. 340–41).

The bathetic quality of the account of Mickey's death would probably be conspicuous to a student more familiar with academic discourse, but this bathos is simply a measure of the writer's distance from our world, a distance that will not diminish—will not diminish in fact although it might in appearance—if she learns to imitate the language of the academy without gaining an ability to use that language on her own behalf. In spite of her initial situation of disadvantage, the form of the essay enables her to appropriate a territory which has become unmistakably Sartre's, the territory of "existence and essence," of "good faith" and "bad faith," of "condemnation to freedom." Whereas suicide and sociology, in the first student essay, belong exclusively to Durkheim, the writer of this second paper has begun to perceive that the area of meaning defined by Sartre is not strictly Sartre's, or strictly her own, but a common ground. However unsophisticated her account may seem to us, she employs narrative incident just as Sartre does, to furnish practical illustrations of philosophic principles: to a significant degree she has recognized, beyond the particulars of Sartre's argument, the way his argument operates rhetorically. If she continues to use writing in this fashion, as the means of discovering an enlarging horizon that every discourse can open to her view, she will gradually enter the community of "knowers" while retaining her own voice in the process. But if we demand from the start a demonstration of conventional proficiency, without the moments of naivete and indirection that are essential to any legitimate conversation, our students will remain outsiders, unempowered in our world and unaware of the forces which have created theirs. Although I recognize that the second writer is not ready to leave freshman English behind, I consider her essay to be a significant achievement, an essential first step in her progress toward work that is more complex intellectually and more self-conscious stylistically.

The essay on Durkheim, however, requires extensive revision, which I would initiate by urging its author to bring himself into the conversation, possibly in a preliminary "working paper" on the destructive forces in his life and the lives of his friends. Once he has completed this working paper, I might ask him to discuss what he supposes to be the most likely causes of teenage suicide and to make a case either for or against its inevitability. Only after he has placed himself within the context of Durkheim's question will he be prepared to understand the significance of Durkheim's analysis. To the degree that this writer still imagines that there is an anonymous, expert language which can protect him from uncertainty, he remains, for all his formal proficiency, a beginner. Like Foucault's persona at the opening of the *Discourse on Language,* he "would have preferred to be enveloped in words," a "happy wreck" carried along by the flow of language, instead of recovering a voice, and a self, through struggle in the "risky world of discourse" (215–16). Precisely because discourse is risky in the manner that Foucault describes, the writers we most admire, "academic" writers by any standard, are typically those who have learned to reinstate their voices within the language of a discipline—or rather, they have learned to enter a discipline by finding their own voices. Durkheim and Sartre are both examples; Burke is another, Gadamer another, and certainly also Foucault.

For Montaigne, the various traditions of learning are no more than compartments within a larger intersubjectivity. Not in any one of these compartments, nor in all of them together, can we "recognize ourselves from the proper angle," but only in the irreducible complexity of the "great world" (116). Insisting upon a meaning fully resident in the text, teachers in the period of New Criticism tyrannized student readers by concealing, albeit inadvertently, the sources of their classroom authority, which arose not from greater attention to words on a page but from a formidable knowledge of literature, of history, of philosophy, of "life." By reifying discourse communities as teachers reified texts a generation ago, we disempower our students in yet another way: whereas before they were expected only to look to an author's language, their task now is more complicated and more intimidating, to speak about such language in terms of extratextual conventions with which they are almost always unfamiliar. And poststructuralist teachers, with a knowledge of these invisible conventions, wield an authority that would probably have embarrassed their New Critical predecessors. The alternative, I believe, is to permit our students to bring their extratextual knowledge to bear upon every text we give them and to provide them with strategies for using this knowledge to undertake a conversation which belongs to us all.

Works Cited

Adorno, T. W. "The Essay as Form." Trans. Bob Hullot-Kentor and Frederic Will. *New German Critique,* 32 (1984):151–71.
Anselm of Canterbury. *Monologion.* In *Anselm of Canterbury,* ed. and trans. Jasper Hopkins and Herbert Richardson, vol. 1. Toronto: Mellen, 1974.
Bakhtin, M. M. *The Dialogic Imagination.* Trans. Caryl Emerson and Michael Holquist. Ed. Michael Holquist. Austin: University of Texas Press, 1981.

Bazerman, Charles. *The Informed Writer: Using Sources in the Disciplines.* 2d ed. Boston: Houghton Mifflin, 1985.

Berthoff, Ann. *The Making of Meaning: Metaphors, Models, and Maxims for Writing Teachers.* Upper Montclair: Boynton, 1981.

Bizzell, Patricia. "Arguing about Literacy." *College English,* 50 (1988):141–53.

――――. "Cognition, Convention, and Certainty: What We Need to Know about Writing." *Pre/Text,* 3 (1982):213–43.

Browne, M. Neil, and Stuart M. Keeley. *Asking the Right Questions.* Englewood Cliffs: Prentice-Hall, 1981.

Burke, Kenneth. *Permanence and Change: An Anatomy of Purpose.* 2d ed. Berkeley: University of California Press, 1954.

Foucault, Michel. *The Archaeology of Knowledge and the Discourse on Language.* Trans. A. M. Sheridan Smith. New York: Pantheon, 1972.

Gadamer, Hans-Georg. *Truth and Method.* 1975. Reprint. New York: Crossroad, 1986.

Hurston, Zora Neale. *I Love Myself When I Am Laughing.* New York: Feminist Press, 1979.

Lodge, David. *Language of Fiction: Essays in Criticism and Verbal Analysis of the English Novel.* New York: Columbia University Press, 1966.

Maimon, Elaine P., et al. *Instructors Manual: Writing in the Arts and Sciences.* Cambridge, Mass.: Winthrop, 1981.

Marcuse, Herbert. "On the Philosophical Foundation of the Concept of Labor in Economics." *Telos,* 16 (1973):9–37.

Montaigne, Michel. *The Complete Works of Montaigne.* Ed. and trans. Donald M. Frame. Stanford: Stanford University Press, 1958.

A Dialogic Approach to the Essay

Thomas E. Recchio

> In most books, the "I," or first person, is omitted; in this it will be retained; that in respect to egotism, is the main difference. We commonly do not remember that it is, after all, always the first person that is speaking. I should not talk about myself if there were any body else whom I know as well. Unfortunately, I am confined to this theme by the narrowness of my experience.
>
> —Thoreau

In my epigraph, Thoreau registers a series of assumptions about writing that continue to cause no end of trouble to writers of all sorts: that books (or any printed writing) should be impersonal or objective; that such impersonality conflicts inherently with the actual situation of a writer; that somehow authority in writing is confirmed in the surface objectivity of a text; and that if a writer acknowledges the limitations of the writer as simply a person writing, there is cause for doubt and trepidation. However, in registering such views in the passage above, Thoreau asserts his authority as a writer. The humility on one level is real, an expression of self-doubt that is always there for any writer, but on another level it is a gesture, a rhetorical strategy to claim his sovereignty over the territory (and the validity of that territory) which he is about to explore in his writing. The passage from Thoreau reveals, then, Thoreau's awareness of the prescriptive pressure exerted by his sense of the way he imagines others think he should write. And in the passage a moment surfaces of generative tension between that awareness and his own impulse to write from a basis of his own authority in his own voice. The passage helps us see one way in which a writer struggles to locate himself and to find his own voice within a discourse, to enter a dialogue that discourse itself preconditions and that he tries to control. (The presence lurking here is Mikhail Bakhtin. He will surface more openly later in this text.) By embracing his own subjectivity in retreating to Walden Pond and by reestablishing his connections to the community in writing *Walden*, Thoreau enacts, through the text and the circumstances surrounding its composition, the internal dynamics of most writers (professional or student) as they strive to control a language not of their own making.

As Thoreau's words so strongly imply ("It is, after all, always the first person that is speaking"), all writing begins in subjectivity. We can all recall, from our earliest attempts at penmanship in elementary school to our more recent attempts to produce polished prose for publication, the moment of blankness when we are confronted with the pages we must fill. The uncertainty of the moment never changes. We may develop great fluency in our written language, we may devise numerous strategies of invention, organization, argumentation, stylistic variation, and the like, but always our own hand moves the pen or taps the letters on the keyboard. Whether one accepts the notion that our language is constituted by the discourse community within which we write or the notion that we all write in our own idiolect, the existential moment when we feel trapped in our own subjectivity, the moment between the impulse (or requirement) to write and the actual writing, always feels the same. All writing, from the perspective of the writer, is problematic; it begins in the uncertainty inherent in the writer's situation. We can frame that situation in the romantic self/other, I/thou paradigm. There is the subjective consciousness of the writer, and there is everything "out there," a seemingly objective world. The act of writing fills the gap between self and other through language. Writing is, within this paradigm, essentially affirmative; it implies the possibility of transcending one's own subjectivity, of escaping the solipsism of self through language. Such an enterprise must be filled with doubt, and here the essay finds its strongest appeal. For the essay exploits the uncertainty of the writer's situation, transforming uncertainty into a fundamental quality of the essay form.

It is, however, a mistake to claim that the essay has a clearly definable form. As O. B. Hardison has observed in the keynote to this collection, the essay is protean. But consider, for a moment, the full phrase he used: Binding Proteus. For Hardison the essay can take any number of forms, the essayist's task being to find a way to bind the protean essayistic impulse. But if we refocus the terms "binding" and "Proteus" to consider the protean quality of the essay not as something to be bound but, paradoxically, as something that binds, something that connects, we have, then, a fruitful contradiction: a sense of tightness and connectedness in the word "binding" and a sense of fluidity, change, unpredictability in the name "Proteus." To address that contradiction, let me quote from an essay by Phillip Lopate that appeared in the *New York Times Book Review* on November 18, 1984, entitled "The Essay Lives—in Disguise." "Reading [Montaigne], . . . we are reminded of the original, pristine meaning and intention of the word, from the French verb *essayer:* to attempt, to try, to make an experimental leap into the unknown. Montaigne understood that, in an essay, the track of a person's thoughts struggling to achieve some understanding of a problem *is* the plot, is the adventure" (47). The protean quality of the essay emerges in the essay's lack of predictable, formal structural characteristics. "Binding" can be taken in two senses: on the level of style, "binding" can refer to the unifying quality of the writer's voice in the essay. But when we consider the writer's situation, "binding" suggests the effort of the writer to connect self to other through language, to enter a discourse shared by other writers, to enact the struggle that all writers experience.

The implication here is that a formalist approach to teaching the essay is misdirected because it ignores the dialogic quality of the essay. It ossifies a fluid form, turning it into a series of types: the narrative essay, the descriptive essay, the argumentative essay, and so forth. In fact, early in its history, the essay became a victim to formalist analyses which divided it into two basic and broad categories. In a brief historical account of the essay, Lopate claims that after Montaigne "came an inevitable specialization, which included the very un-Montaignean split between formal and informal essays. . . . the formal essay derived from Francis Bacon and is (to quote the *New Columbia Encyclopedia*) 'dogmatic, impersonal, systematic and expository' and written in a 'stately' language, while the informal essay is 'personal, intimate, relaxed, conversational, and frequently humorous' " (48). Such a fragmentation is misleading, the buried assumption being that the essay is univocal, but as Lopate also reminds us, "elements of one [type] often turn up in the other." As a way to define emphases, classification has its uses; however, once institutionalized, classifications tend to become rigid, inflexible either/or categories. In the hands of teachers, classifications become tools to simplify the complex, and such simplification ultimately becomes a source of confusion. Consider, for example, the admonition so many students take to heart in writing "formal" essays, that they should never use "I." Can we be surprised at their confusion when they see "I" liberally sprinkled in the pages of, for example, George Orwell's "Politics and the English Language"? In this formalist fragmentation academic discourse is dehumanized at one extreme and the expressive self excessively privileged, detached from the context of discourse, on the other. In the former case, the writer's task is to disappear, to subordinate self to discourse, trying merely to allow language somehow to appear objectively on the page. There is context but no voice. In the latter case, there is voice but no context. Such an extreme polarity has so distorted the strength of the essay in the curriculum that, rather than being the main mode of written discourse, inviting and encouraging students to gain control of their own language and of the world they are asked to explore through language, the essay has, in effect, been abandoned. Between the ubiquitous "organized transfer of information/argumentative" model of the research paper in undergraduate disciplines and the formalist or expressionist models used in expository writing programs, students have been forced to abandon any genuine search for meaning or even to conceive that a search for meaning is the animating force behind "real" writing.

Consider the following two passages from the papers of freshman students at Rutgers University. The first comes from a Sociology 101 course in which the students were asked to discuss whether they find any patterns of behavior toward deviants today that conform to Kai Erikson's analysis (in *The Wayward Puritans*) of Puritan behavior toward deviants. The second comes from an expository writing class (English 101, the standard course in which essays are putatively taught). Students were asked to explore their own sense of ethics in the context of the ethical positions in Erik Erikson's "The Golden Rule in the Light of New Insight," Edward Hoagland's "The Problem with the Golden Rule," and Jean-Paul Sartre's "Existentialism." First, the sociology passage:

> Deviance, which as Erikson explains, is any type of behavior which causes the people of a community to feel threatened, in turn causes the members of the community to enforce strict rules against it. He also states that a certain amount of deviance is always not only evident, but expected in a society, and that this amount is governed by the ways the community has or uses to handle them. He states on p. 25, that "Punishment varies with the circumstances of the crime." This implies that certain types of crime are more readily acceptable in a society than others. This is obviously true in our society. Vandalism, theft, even arson are to a great extent tolerated. However, the punishment for murder, rape, and drunken driving have become increasingly strict. The manner in which deviance is responded to depends greatly upon the attitude of the society observing it. This holds true in any of today's societies. The United States happens to be very lenient in regard to certain types of crime, whereas several countries in Europe handle it very strictly.

The writer's strategy here is infected with the objective impulse of the "formal" essay, the passage saturated with Erikson's ideas in paraphrase and quotation. There is no effort to test the validity of Erikson's discussion; rather, the writer hides behind Erikson's text, seeking only to validate Erikson's position. Having banished the "I" from the essay, the student writer has no way to bring her authority as an observer of her own world into any direct relation with Erikson's text. The objective style, in this light, reveals a closing off of possibility: the student writer has no perspective through which to approach Erikson. As a Sociology 101 student, she is not a sociologist, so she cannot borrow authority from her discipline as it were, but since she thinks that she must write a "formal" essay, she has surrendered the only authority she has, the authority of the first person. The misreading of "punishment varies with the circumstances of the crime" (note how the student alludes to different crimes instead of discussing the different circumstances of various versions of the same crime) is not, I think, a function of sloppy reading. It is an indication of fear. Fearful of her authority as a human being to look at anything real outside the text, uncertain of her ability to analyze the world around her and bring that analysis to bear on the authority of the assigned classroom text, the writer relies on a general list of types of deviant behavior in order to confirm the authority of the text. The misreading is a function of attitude toward text, an attitude that is reflected in the writer's strategy of disappearing somewhere inside the conventions of sociological discourse as practiced by Erikson. But as is so evident from the unevenness of style, such a disappearing act does not work. The writer is, after all, a person writing. Consequently, we can feel the clash between the suppressed voice of the writer, a voice struggling not to be, and a discourse that she neither understands nor controls.

Unlike the writer of the sociology passage, who reveals such distrust of self and full acceptance of the point of view of another, the writer of the English 101 passage on ethics reveals a voice simplistically accepting of the authority of her own experience.

In late July of this past summer, my best friend, Wendy, came to me for advice. She was facing a very serious dilemma, a dilemma that could change the rest of her life. She was pregnant. . . .

All through my life I was brought up to believe that abortion was murder, but when I reached high school I began to feel differently. Every year in high school, there were at least five new girls who were pregnant, ranging in ages from fourteen to nineteen. Most of these girls kept their babies and raised them themselves. These girls were still kids themselves. They were usually poor girls from broken homes. What kind of life was their baby going to have? It was in high school when I began to feel that in some cases abortion would be the most moral solution. . . .

> The next day when I saw Wendy, I told her about my conclusion and she agreed also. In Wendy's situation, I felt that an abortion was the only logical solution. It is now December and Wendy and I have both gone our separate ways. She had the abortion and everything turned out okay. Her life is now back in order and we now realize that she really did make the right decision, the right moral choice.

Although I spliced that passage together, omitting a number of details that hint at complexity, the narrative outline stands out with equal clarity in the original paper and the extracted passage. A person is confronted with a problem that forces a crisis of conscience; that crisis is worked out on a matter-of-fact, commonsense basis; a decision is made and acted upon, and everything turns out for the best. On the face of it, the personal narrative is controlled, focused, and concise, all qualities that teachers in our "culture of efficiency" applaud, but when we bear in mind that the writing problem was to explore one's personal ethics in the context of three readings—three other points of view, three other voices—on ethics, we can see that the personal narrative is an evasion. Confronted with an unfamiliar discourse, or intimidated by the authority of the written text, the student retreated into an exclusively personal narrative so predictable in form as to absorb and nullify any sense of struggle to achieve understanding.

The writing strategy revealed in both passages springs from a fear of uncertainty. Both writers avoided the questioning, the searching, the analysis that each assignment should have stimulated; they approached the problems not as problems to be explored, texts, observations, and experiences to be probed, but as formal exercises in composition. Each offered a conventional type of student paper: the objective report and the personal experience narrative. When asked to bring into dialogic relation the text of someone else's discourse and the text of one's own observation and experience, each writer avoided the dialogue. The first, hiding behind a mask of objectivity and totally skeptical about the authority of self, uncritically deferred to the authority of the discourse. The second, reducing the complex to an anecdote and either fearful of or skeptical about the authority of others' discourse, privileged the authority of experience. In effect, the writers resisted confronting the uncertainty of their situation as writers. Relying on certain formal conventions loosely associated with versions of the essay, neither writer was able to accept the anxiety and authority that the essay encourages. The univocal quality of both passages, the resistance against the complex, is symptomatic of the impoverished, formalist approach to the essay that currently dominates the teaching of writing in high schools, colleges, and universities.

In arguing for a dialogic understanding of the reading, writing, and teaching of the essay, I do not mean to dismiss the formal qualities of academic prose, nor do I intend to denigrate personal writing; rather, these polarities need to be fused. Let me return to Thoreau for a moment, who would seem to be a case study in the strength of personal writing, and quote the few lines that precede the passage with which this essay began.

> I should not intrude my affairs so much on the notice of my readers if very particular inquiries had not been made by my townsmen concerning my mode of life, . . . Some have asked what I got to eat; if I did not feel lonesome; if I was not afraid, and the like. Others have been curious to learn what portion of my income I devoted to charitable purposes; and some, who have large families, how many poor children I maintained. I will therefore ask those of my readers who feel no particular interest in me to pardon me if I undertake to answer some of these questions in this book. [704–705]

Immediately before Thoreau's eloquently simple claims about the primacy of experience ("I should not talk so much about myself if there were anybody else whom I knew as well"), he presents an unambiguously dialogic context for his writing. Even the reclusive Thoreau registers with clarity that he can claim meaning for his experience only insofar as it relates to the experience, perceptions, and language of others, that writing, while it may be saturated with subjectivity, depends for its context on other voices.

Mikhail Bakhtin in his "Discourse in the Novel" places this contingency in the context of discourse: "In all areas of life . . . our speech is filled to overflowing with other people's words, which are transmitted with highly varied degrees of accuracy and impartiality" (337). For Bakhtin, the world of discourse is heteroglot; each time we strive to make an utterance, we compete with the way others have used and use the words we choose. Assuming a kind of Hobbesian verbal universe, Bakhtin presents an image of multitudinous speakers struggling to gain control of a common stock of words. The implication here is that all uses of language, spoken or written, share similar characteristics; one way into an understanding of how written language works is to examine the processes and the verbal resources that speakers bring to spoken discourse.

As a new graduate student, I had come into the course "Introduction to Graduate Literary Studies" with a vague feeling that reading literature was like cracking an enemy communications code in a time of war. Consequently, I would read for the course with a great feeling of urgency and unreality. Early in the term, Robert Frost's "Home Burial" was under discussion. Reading as I was reading (and I am sure I was not alone in my approach), I had difficulty gaining access to the poem. The problem, of course, was not the poem; it lay in my inability to exploit my own intimate knowledge of the way discourse works in my daily use of language outside the classroom. To make me (and others in the class) recognize the expertise that I did not know I already had, the professor began to describe conversation between two people at the dinner table who were irritated about some insignificant detail, say, the fact that a salt shaker was empty. Such arguments typically seem out of proportion to the putative object of the argument because, in fact, such arguments are rarely about the immediate cause; rather some insignificant object, in this hypothetical case the empty salt shaker, becomes the focus for other dissatisfactions. (This seems a rather homey version of T. S. Eliot's notion of the "objective correlative.") In short, many daily conversations, argumentative or not, involve talking about one thing in terms of something else. There is a subtext, a deep structure of sorts, that we interpret and to which we respond in the context of what we know about the person with whom we are talking and what we know about her/his characteristic use of language. Such an insight is simple enough, but in providing me with that insight, in helping me to see that my knowledge of language was much deeper than I had ever imagined, that I could bring to reading poems, novels, plays, and essays the same verbal sensitivity that I employ when trying to read people, the professor empowered me as a reader, and later as a writer, in new and very productive ways.

In our everyday discourse, then, we continually interpret language, weighing such things as earlier conversations, things others have told us, past actions, and things expected to be but not said. Such continual acts of interpretation are, in large part, an aspect of discourse itself, for we cannot use language without explicitly or implicitly interpreting it and, in the act of interpretation, struggling to make language our own. Again Bakhtin:

> We can go so far as to say that in real life people talk most of all about what others talk about—they transmit, recall, weigh and pass judgment on other people's words, opinions, assertions, information; people are upset by others' words, or agree with them, refer to them and so forth. . . . At every step one meets a "quotation" or a "reference" to something that a particular person said, a reference to "people say" or "everyone says," to the words of the person one is talking with, or to one's own previous words, to a newspaper, an official decree, a document, a book and so forth. . . . Thus talk goes on about speaking people and their words everywhere. [338–39]

The amplitude of style in that passage neatly demonstrates the point that we talk about words as much as, if not more than, we do about people and things. And we find our own voice through and in the context of the voices that surround us.

Bakhtin's "Discourse in the Novel" richly suggests how discourse works outside the novel, in other forms of writing and in speech. Like my graduate school professor, Bakhtin makes explicit our daily linguistic processes, processes that feel intuitive because of continual repetition in constantly changing, active contexts. In clarifying the situation of speakers and of writers, Bakhtin's work connects the processes of speaking and writing, containing them within the concept of discourse. Discourse, for Bakhtin, by its very nature is contextual, multivoiced, and communal. The success of the struggle to make (or discover) meaning through language depends on the context within which language is used; the act of participating in discourse places individual speakers and writers in a dialogic relation with other speakers and writers in any possible number of discourse communities, the boundaries of discourse communities being, of course, blurred as the protean self, like the protean essay, moves among them. (It is worth noting at this point that in its root sense discourse means a moving back and forth.) As a result, each speaker or writer engages in a two-sided struggle. On the one hand, he struggles to transcend the subjectivity of the isolated self through language, to locate the self in a discourse and, on the other hand, to assert his own voice in an attempt to attain verbal authority and autonomy, that is, to salvage the defining subjectivity of self. According to Bakhtin,

> the importance of struggling with another's discourse, its influence in the individual's coming to ideological consciousness, is enormous. One's own discourse and one's own voice, although born of another or dynamically stimulated by another, will sooner or later begin to liberate themselves from the authority of the other's discourse. This process is made more complex by the fact that a variety of alien voices enter into the struggle for influence within an individual's consciousness (just as they struggle with one another in surrounding social reality). [348]

Whenever we speak or write, we are in a continual process of becoming through language. To wrench Goethe a bit out of context, our language (and ourselves) "immer wird, nie ist" (is always becoming, never is). An exclusively formalist approach to the essay falsifies the way language works by emphasizing rigid structures that deny the fluidity of discourse. Expressionistic, personal writing, in contrast, in avoiding a dialogue with other voices, falsifies the communal quality of language. The essay in its "pristine," Montaignean sense, however, is intensely dialogic, acutely sensitive to the pressures of other voices and to the imperatives of the subjective self. In considering the place of the essay in the college curriculum, it would be useful to clear away the excessive baggage that has accumulated around the categorizing of the essay as a form and to define the essay as a kind of writing that reflects most openly the struggle of individual writers to harmonize the conflicting demands of the self, language, and experience. Rather than considering the essay in terms of a series of model modes taught as ends in themselves, it would be more empowering to students were we to engage them through the essay in the dialogue of discourse, teaching the essay as a means, an approach to interacting with written texts, the texts of the students' own language and the texts of their experience. Montaigne's essays, published in 1580, provide a powerful stimulus for understanding the essay as dialogic.

"There is no desire more natural than the desire for knowledge," begins Montaigne in "Of Experience."

> We try all the ways that can lead us to it. When reason fails us, we use experience—
>
> Experience, by example led,
> By varied trials art has bred
> MANILIUS
>
> —which is a weaker and less dignified means. But truth is so great a thing that we must not disdain any medium that will lead us to it. Reason has so many shapes that we know not which to lay hold of; experience has no fewer. The inference that we try to draw from the resemblance of events is uncertain, because they are always dissimilar: there is no quality so universal in this aspect of things as diversity and variety. [106]

What is immediately striking about the opening of this passage is its refusal to simplify; reason, experience, and by implication the ability of any single mind to make sense of the world are all problematic; the organizing consciousness of the passage seems at the mercy of a Heraclitan universe, but the tone of the passage is oddly assured, the sentences direct and declarative. The counterpressure of uncertainty, however, suggests that Montaigne does not trust his voice completely; hence he quotes Manilius, another voice, to buttress his own. We can see a balance between Montaigne's personal vision and the authority of a discourse tradition. Such a balance, a continual navigating among various voices from the Roman, Greek, and Christian traditions in the pursuit of personal knowledge of the world, characterizes "Of Experience" as a whole. Toward the end of the essay, for example, Montaigne quotes Saint Augustine, Seneca, and Aesop in the space of four paragraphs. This juxtaposition of multiple voices is both exhilarating and unsettling.

> He who praises the nature of the soul as the sovereign good and condemns the nature of the flesh as evil, truly both carnally desires the soul and carnally shuns the flesh; for his feeling is inspired by human vanity, not by divine truth. [Saint Augustine; 134]
>
> Who would not say that it is the essence of folly to do lazily and re-belliously what has to be done, to impel the body one way and the soul another, to be split between the most conflicting motions?" [Seneca; 134]
>
> Aesop, that great man, saw his master pissing as he walked. "What next?" he said. "Shall we have to shit as we run?" [135]

We may add to these passages something of Montaigne: "Come on now, just to see, some day get some man to tell you the absorbing thoughts and fancies that he takes into his head, and for the sake of which he turns his mind from a good meal and laments the time he spends on feeding him-self . . . , and you will find that his ideas and aspirations are not worth your stew" (134). The effect of such an orchestration of voices in Mon-taigne's process of asserting his own voice is dazzling. The boundaries of the various discourse communities represented in the quotations blur as Montaigne's language moves through the discourse of the religionist, the moralist, and the fabulist; what Montaigne offers is an exploration of his experience of language as much as an explanation of his experience of the world and his shifting sense of self as it is created and transformed through writing. Montaigne's "personal" essay into experience is poly-phonic, since he refuses to separate the flux and variety of experience from the various modes of discourse that represent it. As Edward W. Said has argued about what he calls one of the "three special conditions" for the "seminal beginning conception of narrative fiction," "there [is] a strong sense of doubt that the authority of any single voice, or group of voices, is sufficient unto itself" (88). (It would be interesting to study the parallel development and complex relations between the two open genres, narrative fiction [that is, the novel] and the essay.) For Montaigne, such a doubt is not debilitating; it is leveling and liberating, so that Montaigne's voice becomes equal to the authoritative voices that he continually evokes. Such an equalizing uncertainty opens up the space wherein the individual voice can function. Montaigne's interaction with the written texts of his cultural tradition, a tradition shared by his readers, may sim-ply be a way in which he established common ground with his readers.

But equally it is a way for him to locate himself within and against that tradition. Montaigne's strategy of acceptance and questioning, of evoking authoritative texts for affirmation and denial, of juxtaposing texts that confirm, complicate, and contradict each other in substance and style, extends to his skeptical sense of language and of self.

Soon after expressing some doubt as to whether everyone will accept his manner of writing about himself, Montaigne writes the following about disputes. "Our disputes are purely verbal. I ask what is 'nature,' 'pleasure,' 'circle,' 'substitution.' The question is one of words, and is answered in the same way. 'A stone is a body?' But if you pressed on: 'And what is a body?'—'Substance.'—'And what is substance?' and so on, you would finally drive the respondent to the end of his lexicon. We exchange one word for another word, often more unknown" (112). If one were to substitute discourse for disputes, the passage would approximate in a Bakhtinian sense discourse as words generated in response to words, because the relation of words to things is difficult to establish and approachable only through more words. Viewed pessimistically, such an idea of discourse could be paralyzing: if words are only about other words, if language is a closed system that functions only in relation to itself, then what is the point? Viewed optimistically, however, the disjunction between language and things does not mean that things depend on language; things do exist and language is a way in which we struggle to place ourselves in relation to things, to locate ourselves in the world. So language registers the way we perceive things, not the things themselves. In this context, discourse opens up possibilities; tenuous as discourse may be in explaining the world of objects and events, seeing discourse as multivoiced and multiperspectived ensures the authority of every participant to engage in the struggle to make meaning through language. And since discourse depends on more than one voice, it is a powerful means of connecting human beings in community.

Some participants in any mode of discourse are more powerful users of language than others, so the center of authority in any discourse changes. Such considerations militate against the "my opinion is just as good as yours" fallacy behind which so many student writers hide in their desire to avoid the necessary work of forming meaning through language. The terms of any discourse, then, and the assumptions that one brings to any moment of discourse, are under constant pressure for revision. Here is Montaigne's version: "He who remembers having been mistaken so many, many times in his own judgment, is he not a fool if he does not distrust it forever after? When I find myself convicted of a false opinion by another man's reasoning, I do not so much learn what new thing he has

told me and this particular bit of ignorance—that would be small gain—
as I learn my weakness in general, and the treachery of my understanding;
whence I derive the reformation of the whole man" (115). In describing
the effect of his being convinced (one assumes in an exchange of language,
a moment of discourse) that a conviction he had held was no longer tena-
ble, Montaigne shows how his skepticism about the stability of language
applies to his sense of self. The moment Montaigne describes can be
taken as an example of the shifting center of authority that accompanies
any discourse. It is a moment when the authority of a preconceived position is surrendered to another which causes a reevaluation of the self, "the
reformation of the whole man." The freedom that discourse allows in this
regard is very unsettling in that it is a freedom that we are nearly forced to
take: the freedom to change, to recreate ourselves in the play of language.
Such freedom is enacted throughout the essays of Montaigne: it is suggested by the polyphonic voices that conflict, blend, and modify each
other in "Of Experience"; it is suggested by the presentation of language
as slippery, reflective of language itself, of points of view rather than of
things; and it is suggested in Montaigne's self-presentation that must feel
the pressure to change in the midst of the many voices that the self engages
in discourse.

My Bakhtinian reading of Montaigne, with its revision of the standard
institutional view of Montaigne's work as a record of a confident self
coolly examining the texts of a stable tradition, is consonant with the
practice of such poststructuralist interdisciplinary ethnographers as
Clifford Geertz and James Clifford. The work of both writers grows out of
an acute hermeneutical awareness, an awareness that understanding does
not develop linearly but is fundamentally transactional, reciprocal, and
dialogic. In *Local Knowledge*, for example, Geertz raises the following
question about his attempts to account for the "senses of selfhood" that
can be inferred through an analysis of the cultural "texts" of Java, Bali,
and Morocco. "What do we mean when we claim that we understand the
semiotic means by which . . . persons are defined to one another? That
we know words or that we know minds?" Geertz explains: "In answering
this question it is necessary, I think, first to notice the characteristic intellectual movement, the inward conceptual rhythm, in each of these analyses, and indeed in all similar analyses, . . . namely, a continuous dialectical tacking between the most local of local detail and the most global of
global structure in such a way as to bring them into simultaneous view"
(69). Geertz understands this "dialectical tacking" as a kind of reciproc-
ity, linking the particular instance of a symbolic moment to the context
that both generates and contains it. "Hopping back and forth between the

whole conceived through the parts that actualize it and the parts conceived through the whole that motivates them, we seek to turn them, by a sort of intellectual perpetual motion, into explications of one another" (69). Understanding for Geertz, then, is dynamic, not simply a recording, processing, and organizing but a generating of meaning through discourse (the movement of "hopping back and forth").

The position toward which Geertz is moving Clifford articulates more fully in his *The Predicament of Culture: Twentieth Century Ethnography, Literature, and Art.* While Geertz's practice is generative, registering the dialogue of symbolic forms of cultural practice and language, Geertz does not account adequately for the subjectivity of the self that is engaged in observing and finding language to make meaning of what is observed. In the opening section of his "Notes on the Balinese Cockfight," Geertz seems still to cling naively to the myth of rapport, that somehow the fact of a Western anthropologist's otherness can be put aside in a non-Western culture. In contrast, when he discusses a "discursive model of ethnographic practice," Clifford emphasizes the "intersubjectivity of all speech" (41). "Interpretive anthropology," he writes,

> by viewing cultures as assemblages of texts, loosely and sometimes contradictorally united, and by highlighting the inventive poesis at work in all collective representations, has contributed significantly to the defamiliarization of ethnographic authority. In its mainstream realist strands, however, it does not escape the general strictures of those critics of "colonial" representation who, since 1950, have rejected discourses that portray the cultural realities of other people without placing their own reality in jeopardy. [41]

Two features of Clifford's claims about interpretive anthropology seem consonant with Montaigne's essayistic practices: the "defamiliarization of ethnographic authority" effectively casts doubt on the adequacy of the notion of objective observation in the human sciences: observation is invention, is interpretation, and as a result, the authority of the observer is limited even as the range of what can be observed is extended. With the decentering of authority comes freedom. But such freedom is precarious; the "reality" of the observer is in "jeopardy," under pressure to be modified by the thing observed, probed, and engaged and leading potentially, in Montaigne's terms, to "the reformation of the whole man," to a transformation of the self.

Clifford's claims about the practice of anthropology, then, can be understood in terms of the practice of the essay. The self is deeply implicated in the practice of both, since an "inventive poesis" is at work in both; the subjective starting point of the anthropological observer and the essay writer is unavoidable, and the particular shaped patterns of language in the expression of both are conditioned by the context of those subjectivities. So if we grant that the essay records the track of an individual mind exploring and possibly resolving a problem, and if we grant that the capacities of individual minds are contingent upon their circumstances of experience and historicity, the essay must be open to a multiplicity of voices in order to become a means of attaining understanding. Such understanding can never be objective, closed off, immune to critique. As Clifford further claims,

> neither the experience nor the interpretive activity of the scientific researcher can be considered innocent. It becomes necessary to conceive of ethnography [and the writing of essays] not as the experience and interpretation of a circumscribed "other" reality, but rather as a constructive negotiation involving at least two, and usually more, conscious, politically significant subjects. Paradigms of experience and interpretation are yielding to discursive paradigms of dialogue and polyphony. [41]

This "yielding to discursive paradigms" in the context of the essay tradition is as much a return as a development; it is a movement toward reestablishing the authority of the self in discourse even as that authority, paradoxically enough, is called into question. (For a fully realized example of a paradigm "of dialogue and polyphony," see "Identity in Mashpee" in Clifford's *The Predicament of Culture*, 277–346.)

When our students begin to recognize the essay as fundamentally dialogic, they can then begin to see that the authority of texts that they read in their classes is never in any sense absolute; textual authority should always be under pressure, for it is provisional, limited, bound by the contexts that condition it. Once students begin to question the authority of a written text, their authority as interpreters of texts increases. Consider the following passage from a paper written in my English 101 class in the fall of 1987, which discusses the adequacy of the conclusion of Richard Rodriguez's "The Achievement of Desire."

> For instance, observe Rodriguez's imitative characteristic. This negative quality, which he associates with education, is still present within him. While assessing his life, he contradicts himself by recalling Hoggart's writing. Hoggart says, "[The scholarship boy] tends to make a father figure of his form master" (p. 434). Rodriguez goes on to say:
>
>> Hoggart's calm prose only makes me recall the urgency with which I came to idolize my grammar school teachers. I began imitating their accents, using their diction, trusting their every direction. The very first facts they dispensed, I grasped with awe (p. 434).

Though Rodriguez is consenting to have been an imitator in the above quotation, one cannot take his admission seriously because his words tend to
imitate the idea Hoggart formed in his analysis. This leaves us doubtful about
Rodriguez's ability to understand himself and formulate ideas or conceptions
without being influenced. Hoggart seems to be the "idolized" teacher and
Rodriguez still the "eager student grasping facts with awe." The door to the
room of confusion, conflicts, and fears which have haunted Rodriguez for so
long has remained temporarily closed by Hoggart's words. But another teacher or book will reopen the door once again to let out the suspicions, fears (of
desire) and confusion. Rodriguez must realize that his imitative quality, a
product of his education, is not extinguishable upon the end of education. He
must become conscious of his existing characteristic. And to do this he must
acknowledge it as a part of his personality.

One quality conspicuously lacking in this passage is fear. While there are
moments of vagueness in diction and syntax—and an unfortunate mis-
quoting in the phrase "eager student grasping facts with awe"—these moments result from the student's conceptual ambition, his feeling that he
can recognize and judge qualities in Rodriguez's writing that Rodriguez
himself did not see. In his probing of Rodriguez's text, the student is beginning to develop a critical sensitivity to the presence of other texts embedded in the one at hand and is detecting a Bakhtinian "interanimation"
of voices (although he does see that interanimation as discrediting
Rodriguez's claims). It is an open question whether reading Hoggart provided Rodriguez with a way of seeing his own experience more clearly or
whether reading Hoggart became merely another occasion for Rodriguez
to defer to an authority, but such "open" questions, questions that resist
definitive resolutions, are the basis upon which essays, genuine "attempts" at understanding, can be built. The voice in the passage by the
student has aspects of the two voices from the student passages quoted
earlier: there is an uneasy effort to convey a sense of objective authority
through the use of the third person, but at the same time there is a confidence of assertion that belies the third person, conveying a sense of individual voice. The passage by the student does not reflect a fully achieved
authority; such an achievement, however, can never truly be possible for
any writer, since the ground of authority in any discourse is unstable,
under pressure from a temporal reality that continually invites re-vision.
But as I noted earlier, this shifting ground of authority opens up spaces
within which writers can find the freedom to participate in discourse, to
move back and forth between a historically determined self and a language that both comes before and continues after the particular working
through of any particular essay. We should not leave this freedom "to

essay" solely in the possession of "great" writers (both past and present), relegating our students to the insipid and repetitive practice of the "five paragraph essay" and shielding them in the process from, to borrow a phrase from Richard Poirier, "the work of knowing." We should offer this freedom to our students and work hard to see that they take it.

"Essays," claims Phillip Lopate, "are usually taught all wrong: instead of being celebrated for their delights as literature, they are harnessed to rhetoric and composition, in a two-birds-with-one-stone approach designed to sharpen the students' skills in argumentative persuasion" (1). While I agree that essays are, in fact, "usually taught all wrong," to teach them as mere "delights" and to disassociate them from the teaching of writing would be equally wrong. It would be wiser to consider the strengths of the essay as an approach to writing that reflects most overtly and sensitively the situation of writers engaged in the endlessly shifting demands of discourse. Essays should not be taught as manifestations of the skills involved in writing as a craft, reduced to a catalogue of modes of expository writing in a formalist tradition. Such an approach reduces writing to an act of imitation, a kind of fill-in-the-blanks of this or that form as an end in itself. There are formal qualities in any piece of writing, but those formal qualities are determined by the purposes of individual writers working in different contexts, and these purposes and contexts may dictate an amalgam of forms in combinations that may bear little resemblance to the models offered in a textbook.

Too often the motive to write simply does not exist for students, since they see their assignments for the most part as exercises that must be completed for a grade. Their only stake in writing, then, is the grade, the stamp of approval from the teacher who functions as a mediator between the student and written discourse. For students, the problem is one of authority: how can their written work measure up to the standard of the experts? How can they compete with Orwell and E. B. White? For the teacher, the problem is more ambiguous: holding up Orwell and White as models, and never expecting the students to approach the sophistication, skill, and engagement of such writers, the teacher can only send conflicting signals. "Here is a standard that you will not attain, but write with good faith and do your best anyway" seems to be the message. Teaching the essay as an approach to the discourse of written language, as an attempt to engage in the dialogue of discourse, however, would shift the focus of the teaching of writing from empty, abstract forms that student writers must find some way to fill, to the student writers' role as participants in discourse, constant practitioners of spoken discourse whose expertise can be exploited as a means of effective writing to the end of making students participants in and shapers of the terms of written discourse.

Such a dialogic approach to teaching the essay would not exclude a consideration of traditional rhetorical modes, nor would it exclude or privilege personal, expressionistic writing. Instead it would encourage student writers to test the nature and assumptions upon which their personal voices and visions depend, first by uncovering the sources of their assumptions and then by placing their own voices and visions against the voices and visions of others. Placing "authoritative" texts in the context of discourse and inviting students to enter that discourse would decenter the authority within the discourse, opening up the space within which student writers can find their own voices, working toward a fusion of private and public experience and language. What is essential here is not to close off possibilities but to open them out, to exploit the strengths of the essay as a means of locating the self in discourse and discourse in the world. Of course, the precision of such locations is never absolute. As Montaigne says, "It is only personal weakness that makes us content with what others or we ourselves have found out in the hunt for knowledge. An abler man will not rest content with it. There is always room for a successor, yes, and for ourselves, and a road in another direction" (110).

Works Cited

Bakhtin, Mikhail Mikhailovich. *The Dialogic Imagination: Four Essays.* Austin: University of Texas Press, 1981.

Clifford, James. *The Predicament of Culture: Twentieth Century Ethnography, Literature, and Art.* Cambridge, Mass.: Harvard University Press, 1988.

Frame, Donald M., ed. *Montaigne: Selections from the Essays.* Arlington Heights, Ill.: AHM Publishing, 1973.

Geertz, Clifford. *Local Knowledge: Further Essays in Interpretive Anthropology.* New York: Basic Books, 1983.

Lopate, Phillip. "The Essay Lives—in Disguise." *New York Times Book Review,* November 18, 1984, pp. 1, 47–49.

Rodriguez, Richard. "The Achievement of Desire." In *Ways of Reading,* ed. David Bartholomae and Anthony Petrovsky. New York: St. Martin's, 1987.

Said, Edward W. *Beginnings: Intention and Method.* New York: Basic Books, 1975.

Thoreau, Henry David. *Walden.* In *The American Tradition in Literature,* 5th ed., ed. Sculley Bradley et al. New York: Random House, 1981.

Essay Form
and Auskomponierung

Douglas Hesse

Let me put it briefly: were one to compare the forms of literature
with sunlight refracted in a prism, the writings of the essayists
would be the ultra-violet rays.

—György Lukács

At a time when the writing-across-the-curriculum movement has encouraged disciplines to teach discipline-
specific forms, it is curious to watch English avoid the personal essay.
(In the best sense, of course, personal essays do not "belong" to English,
yet English has long claimed aesthetic language.) To a large measure this
avoidance is undoubtedly due to the essay's relegation to composition
programs. Here an entrenched service ethic scorns any writing that has
apparently little direct or indirect ("It will help you do better in your
major") financial return. However, this skittishness is likely due also to
perceptions of the seemingly ethereal form of the essay. Samuel Johnson's
definition—"Loose sally of the mind; irregular undigested piece; not a
regular and orderly composition"—early and most caustically articulated
the essay's apparent formlessness; and the essay has been branded with a
"lack of rigor" ever since.

Even though much current literary theorizing has largely dismissed formal approaches as politically naive, the genres that English has tradi-
tionally admitted for discussion have been subjected to formal analysis. I
argue that, until there exist at least serious preliminary attempts to account for form in personal essays, the status of these works as a genre—
and their place in the English curriculum—will be open to question. I
propose an approach to the formal analysis of a subclass of personal essays, those that contain stories. Essays that *are* stories (Orwell's "A Hanging," for example) appear to solve the problem of form. We recognize

stories *as* form whether or not we can say why, and at least stories can be put through the narratology of the late 1970s and early 1980s. But essays that merely *contain* stories raise different formal questions: how does the story fit in the essay? How does the larger form, the essay, assimilate another one, the story, and what does that assimilation suggest about essay form?

Beyond such questions lies another one that is even more fundamental. Descriptions of any genre attempt to explain characteristic ways in which works that represent the genre unify their characteristic elements. Yet can anything sensibly be said? It is possible to maintain that analysis yields statements that are ultimately not about the work at all. The whole approach is governed by a verbal Heisenberg Uncertainty Principle. As Susanne Langer put it, "A work of art is a unit originally, not by synthesis of independent factors. Analysis reveals elements in it, and can go on indefinitely, yielding more and more understanding, but it will never yield a recipe" (*Feeling* 105). The most comprehensive statement of form consists of analogy: "This is like that." Such propositions may offer the highest truth, but they withstand the least analysis. To say anything, then, one must discuss form as the relationship between elements, however disruptive the fragmenting may be. After all, the physicists' knowledge of Heisenberg has not kept them from doing physics. For the purpose of analysis, then, I propose crudely dividing essays-with-stories into two elements: story and not-story. This distinction will facilitate an explanation of essay form as the combination in various ways and proportions of two forming principles, one horizontal or diachronic, the other vertical or synchronic.

Two cautions are immediately necessary. The first is against hard and fast alignments of "story" with "horizontal" and "not-story" with "vertical." Stories in essays may be "locally" horizontal, forming by time-ordered succession, but globally vertical, functioning less to move the reader onward than to consolidate a position that the reader has already been asked to take. Likewise not-story elements may very well be horizontal. The second caution is against thinking that distinctions between story and not-story are easily made. Elsewhere I have argued that they are nearly impossible to preserve. I make the division here primarily for heuristic reasons.

Parts, Wholes, Reference, Order

In "On the Nature and Form of the Essay," written as a letter to Leo Popper, György Lukács affirmed Popper's view of form: "It was you who once formulated the great demand which everything that has been given form must satisfy, the only absolutely universal demand, perhaps, but one that is inexorable and allows of no exception: the demand that everything in a work must be fashioned from the same material, that each of its parts must be visibly ordered from a single point" (Lukács 6).

The two-part "great demand" raises two problems. The first is rooted in the necessity that everything in a work be fashioned from the same material. When an essay contains both story and nonstory, we perceive both elements to be of the same material, even beyond the fact that both consist of words. Our willingness and ability to do so extends even to extremely disjunctive texts as long as they bear the published-through-an-editor seal of approval. On a more sophisticated level, one can meet Lukács's condition by viewing "the same material" as some kind of common "deep structure" for an essay's story and nonstory material. This would explain the "fit" in an essay that consists entirely of story and a thesis that states its "point." Their surface structures (a one-sentence proposition versus a many-sentenced story) are merely vastly different. Yet composition textbooks notwithstanding, virtually no published essays are so simple.

Lukács's second demand, that each of the parts must be visibly ordered from a single point, is more problematic. The traditional reference point in an essay, at least in the parlance of the composition class, is its thesis. By tracing a piece's movements to and from thesis we might seem to represent its form. Suppose, following this tack, that we demanded some precise and "objective" depiction of the trace, perhaps in order to generalize about genre. One might attempt to do so mathematically, for example, by rendering form as the sum of all the vectors of an essay. Those vectors could be determined by partitioning the work into a number of cross sections, ascertaining in each partition the readers' distance from the "point," the speed with which they are traveling, and the direction in which they are heading: to or from or at a tangent. With such a metaphor, the form of an essay would be described by a calculus vector function:

$$f(t) = f_1(t)i + f_2(t)j + f_3(t)k \quad \text{[Salas 657]}$$

in which i, j, and k are vectors emanating from the origin and lying along the positive axes (x, y, and z) of a Cartesian coordinate system (Salas 613) and the functions f_1, f_2, and f_3 each describe distance, speed, and direction. Note that "distance from the point" of an essay may have to do both with levels of abstraction (in Francis Christensen's generative rhetoric, for example, a second-level modifier is "closer" to the top level than is a third) and with the nature of a particular piece of discourse. A near paraphrase of the point might be "closer" than a story that suggests the point.

I doubt that the calculus of essay form is possible. I know it would not be worth the time. Like G. D. Birkhoff's attempts at a mathematical approach to aesthetic measure, it would finally prove to be nearly comic. Better to consider "visibly ordered" in much looser terms; best, in fact, to remember that "visibly ordered" does not mean "specifiable by explicit coordinates."

What even constitutes Lukács's "single" reference point is troublesome. Let me state the issue metaphorically. The ordering point of a circle is its center, which is not part of the line that composes the geometric figure. The center of some essays, as thesis, is like the center of a circle and visible in the same way. The center of other essays defies easy location, the reader having to shift the work like a lump of clay on a potter's wheel until he finds the center. That phrase would strike a potter as odd, for the potter *centers* the clay, *does* something to it. Likewise, the reader invests the piece with coherence, with hints, perhaps, from titles. But though they tell us something about the content, titles say little about the form of their essays. One can always interpret "point" spatially rather than logically and refer everything in the essay back to the beginning: first, and then, and then. . . . Since the result so closely resembles the original text, this alternative hardly satisfies as analysis; its value, however minimal, is that of Pierre Menard's retelling of *Don Quixote* in Borges's story.

The issue of parts, wholes, and order in essays with stories, then, is but a manifestation of the broader problem of establishing a referent. Edward Hoagland's observation that the essay "contains a point which is its real center, even if the point couldn't be expressed in fewer words than the essayist has employed" (45), calls into question the very possibility of describing form by referring parts to a point *in* the essay. In some essays, rather, we do better to describe relations among elements as they simultaneously create a field of reference and derive a sense of formedness from that field. Such a practice underlies Langer's observation that "meaning is not a quality, but a function of a term. A function is a pattern viewed with reference to one special term round which it centers" (*New Key* 55). She offers the example of a musical chord (a function) and its root (the "one special term").

Auskomponierung

Lukács dated his letter to Popper October 1910, a year before Arnold Schoenberg published *Harmonielehre* (*Theory of Harmony*), in which he first mused theoretically about the chromatic scale as a basis for tonality (384–87). Schoenberg's twelve-tone compositions seriously challenge the "absolutely universal demand" for order from a single point. An understanding of that challenge and the relationship between tonality and form provides one way of understanding the form of narrative essays.

One possible strategy for coherence available to any composer involves making his composition tonal. We recognize certain musical compositions as unified, at least on one level, because of the hierarchy of pitch relationships they support. The tonal principle specifies that "all the events in a musical group (usually a complete work) should be co-ordinated by, and experienced in relation to, a central point of reference" (Samson, 2). One result of tonality is the listener's ability to assign notes a content value by relating them to these fundamental pitches and relationships. Composers have exploited this consequence for structural purposes, especially in the sonata form (Samson 167).

Graham George argues that the ability to comprehend a structure in large-scale works is mainly due to tonality. Either a piece is closed, in which case it begins and ends in the same key, or it is interlocking, in which case two closed structures overlap so that the piece ends in a key different from the one in which it started (29). What is crucial is the way structural tonality allows a listener to perform a "unifying mental act," gathering a series of elements into a "meaningful unit" (16).

Interpretation of form merely as tonality would lead to fairly unsatisfying analyses of individual works. Surely more can be said about form in Beethoven's and Mahler's first symphonies than that one is in this key, the other in that. The important thing is not tonality itself but the potential for a type of form that it makes possible. How is clearest in the theories of Heinrich Schenker, one of the most prominent—and controversial—music theorists of the twentieth century.

Equally troubled by excessive theoretical emphases on chords in isolation and by linear composition as a reaction to that emphasis, Schenker instead proposed that the essence of music is "compositional unfolding" (*Auskomponierung*), by which chords are made to extend in time through various means of "prolongation," which results in horizontalization (Jonas ix–xv). As Felix Salzer, one of Schenker's apostles, put it, "music *is* motion" (51). The problem is from where to where. Schenker postulated that each work has an *Urlinie*, a "primordial line," made possible by its tonality. As a result "points separated in time could be heard and understood as belonging together, because they constituted the initial and concluding points of an interval, rooted in nature and grasped as a unity" (Jonas xix). Behind this view of music as Auskomponierung, the horizontalizing of the vertical, if you will, is the concept of the *Ursatz,* the "primordial composition" that consists of a single chord (Jonas xx–xxi). The parallel with an essay's thesis, I think, is obvious.

It is helpful likewise to think of every essay as unfolding in two dimensions, one horizontal and the other vertical. On the crudest level the horizontal is obvious: words come one after the other on the page in a linear fashion, as melodies do. The parallel with the vertical is less clear. Music reveals its vertical dimension through chords and polyphonies. Verticalization in music would reach its limit in a work consisting entirely of a single chord comprising every possible pitch. Such a piece would "hold" the content of all possible compositions as an unabridged dictionary "holds" the content of all possible writings. However, prose comes in sentences, not in staves.

The sources of horizontal and vertical form in narrative essays become clear if one considers how the concept of "theme" differs in music and in writing. The theme of a musical composition is its principal melodic *passage,* a phrase (as opposed to a single note) that is longer than an "idea" or "motif." Compare this concept with theme in an essay: the rewards of studies, the delight of going on a journey, the mystery of death. Here "theme" has closer affinities with "subject" than with "thesis"; it has the form "the *x*-ness of *y.*" Although "subject" is used as a synonym for "theme" in music (Dunsby 1817), clearly the term refers to something qualitatively different from the subject of an essay—if not in terms of function, since both furnish the material the rest of the composition "works on," then in terms of status and the implications for form.

More closely corresponding to musical theme is story. After hearing the first half of a melody, we can sensibly predict the range of possibilities for the next few notes. We may not guess perfectly unless the work is highly conventionalized, for example, a rock song or the blues, whose chord and melodic progressions are well established. If we do not hear at all what we expect, we may be delighted by the surprise or even momentarily confused. Likewise, a highly conventional short story sets the limits of its future. We may not fully expect Della to cut her hair to buy Jim's watch fob, but we expect "Della to do something"; a jump shift to a surgeon scattering the remains of a cremated friend would seem very odd. Of course, if the story, like a popular song, is highly conventionalized, we may guess exactly what will happen, which self-parodic elements delighted the Russian formalists.

Kenneth Burke described four main kinds of form: progressive, consisting of two subvarieties, syllogistic and qualitative; repetitive (for example, twelve-tone music); conventional (for example, sonnet and sonata); and minor or incidental (various tropes, for example) (124–27). Themes and stories employ mainly progressive form, "turning the arrows of our desire," to use Burke's phrase, in one direction, then following them step by step, each successive quality putting us in a state of mind to receive another. Already composed of several elements, musical themes and stories continually unfold their forms, not just as far as the next note or event but beyond. While thesis controls our expectations of an essay's contents and allows us to gather them around a central reference, it does not control our sense of "what next?" Consider the difference between being given several random notes all in the same key, then being asked to compose the work from which they come, and being given some of those notes arranged in a melodic line. This is the difference between perceiving an essay's form by relating its parts to thesis and perceiving an essay's form by relating its parts to story.

Although I have arrived at the terms "vertical" and "horizontal" through music, their referential equivalents exist in structuralist theory and linguistics. An event in a story can be viewed either synchronically or diachronically. Suzanne Hunter Brown has reviewed this concept and aligned its synonyms—synchronic, paradigmatic, spatial, vertical, configurational, and achronological versus diachronic, syntagmatic, linear, horizontal, successive, and chronological (79). The most cogent expression of the two principles is Paul Ricoeur's observation that "every narrative combines two dimensions in various proportions, one chronological and the other nonchronological. The first may be called the episodic dimension, which characterizes the story as made out of events. The second is the configurational dimension, according to which the plot construes significant wholes out of scattered events. . . . To tell and to follow a story is already to reflect upon events in order to encompass them in successive wholes" (178). Personal essays are well formed when they invite and reward their readers' performance of this configurative act. They differ from articles and "logical" essays or from "pure" narratives in the way they create and combine the horizontal and vertical dimensions that Ricoeur describes. Following are discussions of example essays that tend toward vertical or horizontal form. In each pairing, I have selected one essay that is a "purer" example and another that is more hybridized.

Vertical Form

Essays that appear either to be hierarchically ordered from a thesis, stated or statable, or to expand an early established generalization tend to display vertical form. They might be characterized by the reader's inclination to read the parts of the essay as answers to the question "How do these relate to the subject or thesis?" In many ways this is the "normal" state of essays, whose purpose we conceive as explaining an idea or proving a point. Narrative in such essays is a means to those ends and serves an illustrative or explanatory function. The brevity of narration; certain positions of it, especially at the beginning and in the middle, when it does not deflect the essay; its status as anecdote rather than full-fledged story; its high degree of closure; and the presence of multiple narratives all characterize vertical form.

Earlier I mentioned the role that title plays in suggesting form. Consider the difference between "The Death of the Moth," which I discuss later, and any of the "Of" or "On" essays—Hazlitt's "On the Fear of Death," for example. Woolf's title makes two promises. One is that a single action will be described in the ensuing essay. This is not "The Dead Moth" or "The Moth," and we would have to strain to read "the moth" as "the race of moths." The second, since this is an essay, is that some pronouncements on the death of the moth will follow, an expectation that would be accented by a title such as "On the Death of the Moth." Permute it once more, pressing closer to a theme title, "On the Power of Death," and the fit between text and title slips. This last title is customarily reserved for essays that explore at a higher level of abstraction, in which narrative simply introduces or illustrates points. (Joan Didion, however, plays around with this convention in "On the Morning after the Sixties." "On" here possesses a double status, announcing both that this is a commentary on the morning after the 1960s and that this is what happened on the morning after the 1960s.)

Example 1: William Hazlitt, "On Will-Making"

With the exception of "The Indian Jugglers" and, possibly, "On Coffee-House Politicians," none of the essays in Hazlitt's *Table Talk* is occasioned by a specific event. "On Will-Making" is typical rather than exceptional. The mere presence of six anecdotes (seven if one counts a footnote) in an essay of this length is one evidence of vertical form. It flows and ebbs from generalization to illustration, each new generalization developing the theme stated in the first sentence: "Few things show the human character in a more ridiculous light than the circumstance of will-making" (113). Even then, the major parts of this essay are arranged in a generally chronological order. The earlier ones discuss how people resist making wills, the later the strange bequests made once a will has been written. Yet nothing links these parts causally one to the other.

Nor do any of the anecdotes connect directly with Hazlitt. All flicker with the vagueness of the preacher's stock illustrations drawn from a commonplace book. "I have heard of an instance of one person" begins the first (113). The second centers around "an elderly gentleman," the third "a celebrated beauty of the middle of the last century" (114), the fourth "one of the Thellusons some time back" (116), the fifth "a person who was addicted to a habit of lying" (117), and the last "a sir Thomas Dyot" (120). That they are not from Hazlitt's immediate experience partly accounts for the brevity of each anecdote; the first and second are but a sentence long. Here is the first: "I have heard of an instance of one person who having a feeling of this kind on his mind, and being teazed into making his will by those about him, actually fell ill with pure apprehension, and thought he was going to die in good earnest, but having executed the deed overnight, awoke, to his great surprise, the next morning, and found himself as well as ever he was" (113). Now, there's nothing inherently brief about this story. If we grant Hazlitt's claim of actually having heard it, we might attribute his unwillingness to develop the incident into a full-fledged story (Who was the person? How was he teased and why? What was the scene when he awoke? What happened then?) to a belief that one does not claim more than one knows. A more pertinent answer for this discussion is that a developed story would be discordant to the form Hazlitt has chosen, points followed by evidence, with utilitarian anecdotes coming not as proof but as slightly less abstract illustrations. Longer stories draw attention to themselves as stories, not as disposable containers of points.

The extent to which Hazlitt renders the stories transparent is clear in the style and length of the preamble to each. At one point Hazlitt observes that property is bequeathed "in such portions as can be of the least service" (115). He develops this idea with several aphoristic sentences, then shifts his point of view to the minds of those who struggle to preserve fortunes in a lump sum: "But to think of frittering it down, of sinking it in charity, of throwing it away on the idle claims of humanity, where it would no longer peer in monumental pomp over their heads; and that too when on the point of death themselves, *in articulo mortis,* oh! it would be madness, waste, extravagance, impiety" (116). Only having reached this distance from his own point of view does he refer to Thelluson's desire to preserve his estate intact. The careful modulation by summary limits the

297

spread of theme and story, and almost immediately Hazlitt returns to the style of commentary and pronouncement with which he began the section.

Two of the stories—the beauty's and the liar's—are longer. Both come in the middle, braking the reader after the quick opening anecdotes and before the equally brief closing ones accelerate him out of the essay. If Hazlitt had told the beauty's story immediately on the heels of the second anecdote, that story would have instilled a more significant horizontal element in the essay, its length relative to the others accomplishing a change in pace. But Hazlitt makes that shift in the discursive sentences interposed between the second and third anecdotes, and the story merely confirms the pace he has established.

"On Will-Making" never moves far from its thesis. Pared down to their thematically relevant information, each story is only slightly less abstract than the surrounding text. The sonata form employed by classical composers began by introducing a theme for development. Similarly, each of the anecdotes in "On Will-Making" develops the theme ever so slightly, never letting it pass completely out of hearing.

Example 2: Richard Selzer, "Bone"

The very title of Richard Selzer's essay "Bone," a thing rather than an action, hints at vertical form, and the presence of one relatively long story (about a third the length of the whole essay) does not counter that tendency. The essay presents a number of facts about bone—its strength, formation, regeneration, and degeneration—but these facts are transformed by a speaker entranced by the significance of bone, his voice at once casual, allusive, punning, and mock heroic:

> Bones. Two hundred and eight of them. A whole glory turned and tooled. Lo the timbered femur all hung and strapped with beef. . . . Out of this pelvis, endlessly rocking, drops man. [51]

> It is the trauma itself, the fact of fracture, that triggers the restoration. It is a cellular call to arms, a furious mobilization, an act of drive and instinct. It is the wisdom of Bone. [53]

> Upon the wall of some quiet library ensconce my skull. Place oil and a wick in my brainpan. And there let me light with endless affection the pages of books for men to read. [59]

As much as the bone to which everything here converges, this declaiming voice enamored of itself commonly denominates the parts of the essay. At one point Selzer quotes a passage of trochaic tetrameter from Longfellow and observes, "One now understands why he wrote this way. Once you start you can't stop!" (56). Nor can Selzer. Although nothing formally prepares us for the story that Selzer tells two-thirds of the way through the piece, something tonally does, namely the intrusive narrative presence, the essay resembling a Broadway musical, in which we think it not at all strange for music to break out. And just like violins stirring beneath the last lines of a dialogue bending toward song, Selzer's essay sounds two story chords immediately before his story, both cued by the first appearance in the essay of an actor and action: "A savage queen contrives from the skull of her young lover a wine bowl" (55). He quotes Longfellow's description of the Ottawa Indians' recovery of Marquette's skeleton. Then a warning: "I myself have confronted the hard fact of bone and have been changed by it. Listen" (56).

A friend, Barney, dies in a fall after asking Selzer to scatter his ashes in the forest. Unnerved by the sight of diamond-sized chunks of white bone mixed in the ashes, Selzer dumps the remains quickly, then retreats to a nearby park. Barney had warned him to do the job cheerfully; now a mysterious rattling from a trash can tells Selzer that he has failed. Finally, he kicks off the lid and an emaciated raccoon jumps out. The oddest quality of the story is its flippancy. A surgeon hardened by death may be bothered little by the death of a friend or, on the other hand, may react with the nervous, cheerfully excessive affectation that everything can be laughed off. But the story takes on the tone of the essay in which it is submerged. The extent to which that tone *is* appropriate derives from the fact that the essay has adopted it.

The story in "Bone," as the most "personal" of the essay's parts, does help explain the I who thrusts these words on us, but one hardly has the sense that the essay is ordered *from* the story or *as* a story. Immediately after the raccoon account, Selzer breaks away, not referring to it again, making clear that it is no more thematically important than any of the other parts of the essay. The final section begins "Most commonly, bone is afflicted with that ubiquitous degeneration that is known as ostearthritis, wherein the wear and tear of usage is expressed as the grinding down of the disks of cartilage that cap the ends of the bones like icing and that facilitate the movement of the joints" (59). A more precise "objective" voice emerges, the narrator sobered perhaps by the preceding story. Yet the chattily whimsical voice returns, ending the essay with a jibe at the human hubris of standing in defiance of gravity and the power of bone.

The main formal problem of "Bone" is that of progression. Coherent due to the voice that infuses it and the repeated tonic, "bone," the essay nonetheless creates little sense of forward progression among its parts even though Selzer mentions birth early and death late. This feature poses one major problem: how to end. Any significant break from the norm of an essay, whether that norm is exposition or narration, draws our attention. Probably the most significant effect of the story in "Bone" is that it creates "local" horizontal motion and, in turn, the promise of closure. Given the looseness of the essay, Selzer seems able to spin out countless perspectives on bone. But his interjection of a story figures the end of the essay, cadencing a return to the essay's first mode.

Horizontal Form

Essays that primarily give rise to the question "As a result of what has already happened, what will happen next?" tend toward horizontal form. Such essays, the reader can easily feel, exist because of a story. The discursive elements of such pieces function to develop their stories more than the stories function to clarify some point. The parts of the essay are ordered to enhance this telling, and in some essays, the story "storifies" even the discursive elements, especially in essays where reflection and commentary become part of the story; in them the "point" is not in addition to the story but part of it. Horizontal form is most obvious in essays that are virtually all story or that distribute a single story throughout their entire length.

Example 1: Virginia Woolf, "The Death of the Moth"

"The Death of the Moth" by Virginia Woolf is explicitly horizontal throughout, although the vertical dimension is plain; the essay lies squarely in the middle of the essay corpus. Its theme—the essence that is life and its inconsequentiality against the magnitude of death—manifests itself even in the form of the essay, which lives as long as words come one after the other on the page. The energetic early sentences, the rooks soaring into the air like a cast net, the moth itself zigging pure energy, dwindle to the quieter sentences of the last paragraphs. The movement to stasis is inexorable even on a stylistic level. The story's events make this progression even clearer.

Whether the account of the moth's death traces the actual development of Woolf's thoughts is unknowable; the idea could have come first, the story of the moth as a vehicle for expression later. The account, after all, is in the past tense. In fact, we cannot really know that Virginia Woolf did not invent the whole incident, nor does it matter. But presenting this theme through a story in the surface structure of the essay that we read, and in this particular manner, does. Many authors launch essays from story occasions to which they never look back. Woolf could have done the same here, reporting only action first, then reflecting on it. Or just the reverse: the analysis, then the event. However, Woolf fixes her thoughts on a temporal line as events within the story: "But, as I stretched out a pencil, meaning to help him to right himself, it came over me that the failure and awkwardness were the approach of death" (1:360). The extent to which everything is ordered by the moth incident counters the abstractness of this essay's theme. The first paragraph consists primarily of scene-setting exposition: here was the world beyond my window that mid-September morning. Yet the first three sentences tell about day moths, narrowing in the third to "the present specimen" (359). Such attention, followed by exposition, followed after the further signal of a paragraph by a return to that moth, lays out a range of possibilities for the future movement of the essay. Ideas will develop as the story of this insect unfolds, as long as Woolf keeps the story open. Were that story merely preamble to a twenty-page discourse on life and death, readers would perceive the forming principle changing within a few pages after the story.

In narrating the actions of the moth, Woolf also narrates the process of her discovery, leading readers to some final realizations that she ostensibly does not have when she first sees the moth and that readers do not have at the outset of the essay. The essay differs from those which merely position their theses at the end. Even though by the time Woolf published the essay's final draft she knew exactly what she had discovered and had carefully written the opening to fit, she retained the sense of developing rather than ever-present significance. The narration of discovery creates a type of horizontal motion even in essays devoid of narration, as William Zeiger has noted in his discussion of the exploratory essay. But exploratory motion has a different quality from story motion. In the former, one thought leads to another, this quality opening the way to that; the chain need not be logical or exclusive. In stories, order may seem more circumstantial than causal, but as "past experience selected" rather than "present experience created," it has fewer available options.

Example 2: E. B. White, "The Wave of the Future"

A little narrative properly handled can go a long way to establish horizontal form. This is the case in E. B. White's dissection of Anne Lindbergh's plea for tolerance of fascism in "The Wave of the Future." On a casual reading the essay appears to display vertical form because it emphasizes analysis. Having driven eighty miles to see a doctor about his nose, White "read[s] and re-read[s] *The Wave of the Future,* parked at the curb of a town of the present, watching the flow of life in a New England community on a winter's afternoon" (165). Then he walks into the doctor, still troubled by the book, learns that he has a highly allergic system, and leaves with an appointment for further testing: "I'm to go back Tuesday to be skin tested, to see what foods and pollens and bits of fluff disturb me, but none of them disturbs me so much as Mrs. Lindbergh's confession. These systemic disturbances are more mysterious than even doctors know; and these days he would have to scratch me with substances more subtle than rabbit's hair and duck's feathers to find my misery" (169). The rationale for setting the book review in the context of a day's business for a saltwater farmer lies partly in the circumstances of White's publishing it in "One Man's Meat," his column in *Harper's.* Yet submerging it in narrative is formally strategic.

The opening two paragraphs, the diarylike reports of boat building, have no bearing on the review, but they do on the reader's sense of the reviewer. Their clipped first sentences are those of a man content and relaxed, independent and casual: "Thursday. This morning made preparations for building a boat—the first boat I ever prepared to build. . . . Sunday. All morning at work boat-building" (164). The third paragraph begins with the same tone: "Tuesday. Arose at six on a cold morning and by truck alone to Waterville" (164). But although White sustains the same style into the next paragraph, the weight of his subject matter pushes him into fuller, if not more formal, sentences. The transformation of apparently trivial afflictions at the beginning of the essay into "systemic disturbances" at the end reveals how "The Wave of the Future" is the story of the book's effect and how White's grounds for criticism are personal as well as intellectual.

The essay displays horizontal form on two levels. The simplest is that of White having located his observations in time: "first I thought this, then I thought that," and so on. At one point White notes, "It seemed odd, sitting with my feverish nose and being told by Anne Lindbergh that fascism was the wave of the future" (166). The cheap justification for bringing up the nose: to pun on his reference to the stench of fascism in the next paragraph and his belief, in the subsequent paragraph, that the "new order" is basically destructive of "universal health." More important, though, mention of his nose regrounds the remarks in the situation he establishes at the outset. The references in the body of the review to the circumstances of his reading the book create an insistent progression of events. We know that he cannot sit in the truck forever; the essay, with White, must go somewhere.

Yet, this accounts little for the other of his attacks. The second, subtler, manifestation of horizontal form is White's emplotment of his response, giving successive ones the force of causality, not merely the accident of succession. His last—and harshest—attack is on Lindbergh's failings as a writer. In questioning her glib assertion that "the things one loves, lives, and dies for are not . . . completely expressible in words" (168), White diagnoses the most personally disturbing aspect of her work.

Conclusions

Between the vertical and horizontal poles range essays best read as the vertical horizontalized—Loren Eiseley's "The Judgement of the Birds," for example. At its outset, Eiseley announces his subject: the source of visions in lonely wilderness encounters. He then deploys five stories, four turning on birds, the fifth on an urban spider, with intervening passages that fairly scream "transition." The essay appears merely to be cast as theme and variations, a vertical work such as Hazlitt's "On Will-Making." And yet, beyond the local horizontal movement of each story is the larger horizontal form of the essay, each of its stories an event in the narrative that brings Eiseley (and his readers, I assume he hoped) to a realization that analysis sterilizes the visionary.

Other essays are best seen as the horizontal verticalized. For example, Annie Dillard's "An Expedition to the Pole" juxtaposes the narrative of her experience at a Catholic mass with accounts of various foolish polar expeditions. The disparate references finally coalesce into a fantastical scene on the ice. This wild succession is held together by the metaphor it builds: the folly with which people approach the holy is like that displayed in attempts to find the Northwest Passage on ships laden with china and sterling silver but empty of winter clothing. Whereas Eiseley's essay must create forward progression from story elements that are nearly too obviously similar, Dillard's must create some unstated proposition to give depth to what is otherwise mere reportage.

Readers' expectations that individual works should be clearly horizon-

303

tal or vertical probably account for the charges of formlessness that have been leveled at personal essays. It may well be that the personal essay appears formally unassailable because we have not yet been socialized into Auskomponierung as a forming principle. That "serious essays" should display vertical form, with the strata of propositions relating each part of the work logically and hierarchically to each other part, has been accepted—or, more important, has been *perceivable*—as a proper and reasonable state of writing since its prescription by classical rhetoricians. And stories? Anything narrative would obviously display horizontal form, "then and then and then" until closure. That narrative is natural and inevitable—a mode that is unavoidable because we live in time, even biologically encoded, as Frank Kermode suggested in *The Sense of an Ending*—is a venerable commonplace. Yet this truism has been steadily challenged at least since Roman Jakobson's argument that the realistic or natural is merely the conventional reified. We recognize stories as well formed because we have learned to do so. However, the personal essay as Auskomponierung creates form neither purely vertical nor horizontal in the manner that articles and stories do. In light of expectations, there seems to be no form at all. The relative youth of the personal essay, combined with a lack of scholarly attention, has left Austkomponierung "audible" as neither natural nor conventional but as quirky and idiosyncratic: loose and undigested.

The interplay of vertical and horizontal form is an issue hardly particular to essays. A good deal of recent theorizing about narrative has explored the ways in which works reconcile what Thomas Leitch has described as a teleological principle and a discursive principle. The teleological principle holds that meaning in stories derives from our expectation that they are leading somewhere and that closure will show us how everything that has happened has made sense. The discursive principle explains digression and accounts for those aspects of a story that delay closure. Certainly this aspect of narrative theory has important implications for the study of form in personal essays, which more than stories make explicit throughout the tension between being and becoming, idea and experience; in short, as I have argued here, between the vertical and the horizontal.

I doubt that discussions of form in personal essays will give these works enough critical weight to offset the onus against "impractical writing" in composition classes. Convincing proof will come through demonstrations of Auskomponierung in "extraliterary" discourse. Most immediately, however, arguments that essays do reward formal analysis will have the impact of aligning this genre with those that English studies seem willing to take seriously. I would wish more for the essay than its becoming grist for the theorist's mill, but I am willing to accept this fate for the essay as a means toward ultimately sanctioning the essay's place in the English curriculum.

Works Cited

Birkhoff, G. D. *Aesthetic Measure.* Cambridge, Mass.: Harvard University Press, 1933.

Brown, Suzanne H. "Dimension and Genre: Towards a Theory of the Short Story." Ph. D. dissertation. University of Pennsylvania, 1981.

Burke, Kenneth. *Counterstatement.* 2d ed. Los Altos, Calif.: Hermes, 1953.

Didion, Joan. "On the Morning after the Sixties." In *The White Album.* New York: Simon and Schuster, 1979.

Dillard, Annie. "An Expedition to the Pole." In *Teaching a Stone to Talk.* New York: Harper and Row, 1982.

Dunsby, Jonathan. "Theme." In *The New Oxford Companion to Music.* Oxford: Oxford University Press, 1983.

Eiseley, Loren. "The Judgement of the Birds." In *The Star Thrower.* San Diego: Harcourt Brace Jovanovich, 1978.

George, Graham. *Tonality and Musical Structure.* New York: Praeger, 1970.

Hazlitt, William. "On Will-Making." *Table-Talk; or, Original Essays.* Ed. P. P. Howe. Vol. 8 of *Complete Works.* London: J. M. Dent, 1931.

Hoagland, Edward. "What I Think, What I Am." In *On Essays,* ed. Paul Connolly. New York: Harper and Row, 1981.

Jakobson, Roman. "On Realism in Art." In *Readings in Russian Poetics,* ed. Ladislav Matejka and Krystyna Pomorska. Ann Arbor: Michigan, 1978.

Johnson, Samuel. *A Dictionary of the English Language, 1755.* Vol 1. New York: AMS Press, 1967.

Jonas, Oswald. "Introduction." In *Harmony.* By Heinrich Schenker. Chicago: University of Chicago Press, 1954.

Langer, Susanne K. *Feeling and Form.* New York: Charles Scribner's Sons, 1953.
_____. *Philosophy in a New Key.* Cambridge, Mass.: Harvard University Press, 1957.

Leitch, Thomas M. *What Stories Are: Narrative Theory and Interpretation.* University Park: Pennsylvania State University Press, 1986.

Lukács, Georg. "The Nature and Form of the Essay." In *Soul and Form,* trans. Anna Bostock. Cambridge, Mass.: MIT Press, 1978.

Ricoeur, Paul. "Narrative Time." *Critical Inquiry,* 7 (1980): 169–90.

Salas, S. L., and Einar Hille. *Calculus: One and Several Variables.* 4th ed. New York: John Wiley and Sons, 1982.

Salzer, Felix. *Structural Hearing: Tonal Coherence in Music.* New York: Dover, 1962.

Samson, Jim. *Music in Transition.* New York: W. W. Norton, 1977.

Schenker, Heinrich. *Harmony.* Ed. Oswald Jonas. Trans. Elisabeth Mann Borgese. Chicago: University of Chicago Press, 1954.

Schoenberg, Arnold. *Theory of Harmony.* Trans. Roy E. Carter. Berkeley: University of California Press, 1978.

Selzer, Richard. "Bone." In *Mortal Lessons.* New York: Simon and Schuster, 1976.

White, E. B. "The Wave of the Future." In *One Man's Meat.* New York: Harper and Row, 1983.

Woolf, Virginia. "The Death of the Moth." In *Collected Essays.* 5 vols. London: Hogarth, 1966.

Zeiger, William. "The Exploratory Essay: Enfranchising the Spirit of Inquiry in College Composition." *College English,* 47 (1985):454–66.

Contributors

Robert Atwan is the founder and series editor of the annual *Best American Essays*. He has published numerous college anthologies, including the *Harper American Literature* and *Popular Writing in America*. He has recently completed a book featuring the work of contemporary Soviet and American writers.

E. Fred Carlisle, provost and executive vice president for academic affairs at Miami University in Ohio, has published *Loren Eiseley: The Development of a Writer*.

George Core is editor of the *Sewanee Review* and adjunct professor of English at the University of the South. He has edited and coedited five books dealing with American literature, especially southern literature, and has written a book on New Criticism, which will be published soon.

James Cunningham is a black studies pioneer from St. Louis and an active poet, essayist, and educator whose scholarly interests range from rhetorical criticism and style theory to Afro-American literary thought.

Duane Edwards, associate professor at Fairleigh Dickinson University, has written scholarly studies of D. H. Lawrence and Thomas Hardy in addition to several short stories and poems. He has also compiled annotated bibliographies of Thomas Hardy and of D. H. Lawrence.

Nancy Enright has taught English composition and medieval literature at Rutgers University and has recently joined the Department of English at Seton Hall University, where she heads the computer-assisted writing program.

Rockwell Gray is chairman of the English program at the Kiskiminetas Springs School in Saltsburg, Pennsylvania. He is at work on a book of interviews with American writers and on a study of modern autobiography. His book *The Imperative of Modernity: An Intellectual Biography of José Ortega y Gasset* will be published soon.

Michael L. Hall is a member of the staff at the National Endowment for the Humanities. He has written and lectured on the Renaissance and on the essay.

O. B. Hardison, Jr., is university professor at Georgetown University in Washington, D.C. Formerly director of the Folger Shakespeare Library, he has written widely on culture, education, and technology as well as on medieval and Renaissance literature. His most recent book is *Prosody and Purpose in the English Renaissance*.

Douglas Hesse teaches at Illinois State University. He has published articles on composition and literacy and has led workshops on writing across the curriculum. He teaches a graduate course in composition theory to doctoral students at Illinois State University.

William Howarth teaches at Princeton University. He has edited Thoreau's journals and *The John McPhee Reader* and writes regularly for the *National Geographic* and the *New York Times*. He is studying the use of computers in writing.

Georgia Johnston is at present on leave from Rutgers University, where she has taught creative writing. She is preparing a study of Virginia Woolf's nonfiction.

R. Lane Kauffmann teaches in the Department of Spanish, Portuguese, and Classics at Rice University. He received an award for the most outstanding contribution during the second session of the Seton Hall Conference on the Essay. His book on the theory of the literary essay is in press.

Paul J. Korshin, professor of English at the University of Pennsylvania, has written and edited more than a dozen volumes dealing with eighteenth-century literature. He recently edited *Johnson after Two Hundred Years* and is the editor of the scholarly annual *The Age of Johnson*. He was appointed a Guggenheim fellow in 1987–88 for a study of Johnson's *Rambler*.

308

Barbara Mellix is assistant professor of English at the University of Pittsburgh and is fiction editor of the *Pennsylvania Review*. She has recently published the short story "The Captain's Lady." Some of her fiction and nonfiction will appear in two forthcoming anthologies.

Charles O'Neill teaches at New York University. He is working on a study of Yeats. In addition to poetry, he has published reviews in the *Irish Literary Supplement* and *Spirit* and conference reports for the New Jersey Council on the Arts.

Sherman Paul is professor of English at the University of Iowa. His most recent book of criticism is *In Search of the Primitive*.

Thomas Recchio has published articles in journals as varied as *Studies in English Literature* and the *Gestalt Society Journal* (Manchester, England). From 1982 to 1986 he worked in Japan as a consultant-editor for Japanese scholars in many fields who were publishing in English. He teaches at Rutgers University.

J. P. Riquelme, who teaches literature and humanities at Southern Methodist University, has written *Teller and Taylor in Joyce's Fiction*. A student of T. S. Eliot and literary modernism, he is writing a book on the modernist essay.

Scott Russell Sanders, director of the Creative Writing Program at the University of Indiana in Bloomington, is known for his fiction as well as for a successful collection of essays, *The Paradise of Bombs* (University of Georgia Press, 1987). His most recently published books of fiction appeared in fall 1988, the speculative novels *The Invisible Company* and *The Engineer of Beasts*.

Kurt Spellmeyer is director of the writing program at Rutgers University and is also acting dean of developmental education. He has written on seventeenth-century poetry and prose.